WITHDRAWN

A partnership between American Library Association
and FINRA Investor Education Foundation

American
Library
Association

Investor Education
FOUNDATION

FINRA is proud to support the American Library Association

# The Conscious Investor

# The Conscious Investor

## PROFITING FROM THE TIMELESS VALUE APPROACH

### John Price

**WILEY**

**John Wiley & Sons, Inc.**

Published by John Wiley & Sons, Inc., Hoboken, New Jersey.
Published simultaneously in Canada.

For general information on our other products and services or for technical support, please
contact our Customer Care Department within the United States at (800) 762-2974, outside
the United States at (317) 572-3993 or fax (317) 572-4002.

Wiley also publishes its books in a variety of electronic formats. Some content that appears in
print may not be available in electronic books. For more information about Wiley products,
visit our web site at www.wiley.com.

ISBN 978-0-470-60438-0 (hardback); ISBN 978-0-470-91097-9 (ebk);
ISBN 978-0-470-91098-6 (ebk); ISBN 978-0-470-91099-3 (ebk)

Printed in the United States of America.

10  9  8  7  6  5  4  3  2  1

*To my late father,*
*Ern Price,*
*who gave me my first shares when I was fourteen.*
*Thanks, Dad,*
*for your love and support.*

# Contents

# Acknowledgments

When I read the acknowledgments in other books I often think how fortunate the authors were to have had so many people help with their books. Now I find myself in the same privileged position. There have been many people who have played important roles at all stages of this book.

I am enormously grateful to Warren Buffett. Without his investing expertise coupled with the generous way that he answers questions at the annual meeting of Berkshire Hathaway and other times, this book would not even have gotten started. It is still clear in my mind the palpable excitement in the auditorium when my wife, Sandy, and I attended our first annual meeting of Berkshire Hathaway. Despite the fact that there were around 14,000 attendees, I had the feeling that he was talking to his family. His good humor, common sense, and integrity supported his wise words on investing in the stock market.

Next I am grateful to Roger Lowenstein, the author of *Buffett: The Making of an American Capitalist* (Random House, 1996). This excellent biography was life-changing for me. Lowenstein laid out Buffett's history with just enough information on his methods to whet my appetite for more. As an investor I was impressed by Buffett's stock market success. But as a mathematician and scientist I was even more impressed by the consistency of his results, outperforming the market almost every year for over four decades. This was far more than anything that could be expected by chance. I wanted to know how he did it. How did he achieve such success year after year over decades? I immediately put aside all my research and consulting on derivatives and risk management to focus on understanding Warren Buffett. At that moment I felt that my background as a research mathematician, computer programmer, educator, and writer came together. I read everything by Buffett and about him that I could get my hands on. He became my research project.

Approaching topics from a research perspective is natural for me since it forms the greater part of the two parts of my career, academic and business. Starting with the academic, I would like to thank Robert Edwards, my Ph.D. adviser. Robert generously read everything I wrote as I struggled toward understanding what was meant by research mathematics and to explain my ideas and results with more clarity and precision. Robert's guidance and encouragement went far beyond the usual role of a thesis adviser.

This was the start of my academic career, and I thank all of my colleagues at universities around the world where I have spent time in teaching or research positions. My happiest memories range from the solitude of my office, poring over books and manuscripts, to discussions in the common room, to time spent browsing through the dusty book and journal stacks in the libraries. Also I loved teaching the big first-year classes: They brought out the performer in me. In terms of research, I have been fortunate to work with leading people including (in alphabetical order) Gavin Brown, Michael Cowling, Tony Dooley, Alessandro (Sandro) Figà-Talamanca, Garth Gaudry, Ed Hewitt, Valery Kholodnyi, Henry Landau, John McMullen, Sid Morris, Larry Shepp, Alladi Sitaram, and Terry Speed. Apart from the publications we have written together in mathematics, physics, and finance, I have learned so much from these people. More generally, I am grateful to my colleagues at a range of universities including the Australian National University, Maharishi University of Management, University of Genoa, University of Maryland, University of Milan, University of New South Wales, University of Sheffield, and University of Washington (Seattle).

It is a pleasure to thank Ralph McKay, who in 1987 started an innovative company called Option Technology. It aimed at applying the newly developed methods of risk analysis using options to help importers and exporters manage their foreign exchange risk and developers manage their interest rate risk. I am grateful to Ralph for plucking me out of academia to join his company as head of research. Much of my time was spent working out pricing formulas for all sorts of exotic derivatives including barrier, compound, lookback, and many more. Some years later, part of this work grew into a research monograph written with Valery Kholodnyi called *Foreign Exchange Option Symmetry* (World Scientific, 1998).

After Option Technology it was a complete change of pace with a move to Maharishi University of Management in Fairfield, Iowa, as head of the Department of Mathematics. This is where I was handed the biography of Buffett by Lowenstein, mentioned earlier. It was the ideal place to dive into Buffett's methods: There were interested international faculty members to bounce ideas off, an intellectual and experiential framework provided by Maharishi to understand new approaches to knowledge, many enthusiastic investors to attend the workshops that I started to give, and a comfortable drive to Omaha, Nebraska, to attend annual meetings of Berkshire Hathaway.

What was needed now was some way of thoroughly testing the methods that I read about and those I was developing. This led to the development of Valuesoft, a collection of investing functions that operate within Excel. Once loaded, the functions become part of Excel and can be used and manipulated in the same way as the standard functions that come with the software. I am grateful to my son Matthew for helping me overcome a few programming hurdles in getting this up and running. Now I had a framework for testing functions with data for specific companies or with multiyear data from thousands of companies in commercial databases. I quickly began to add valuation functions to Valuesoft, a process that continues to the present time.

Next I would like to thank Ken Barrett. At the time Ken was an owner of Alliance Investment Services and he was the first financial professional to look at what I had developed. He said that it was what he had been looking for but had never found in the large number of presentations and workshops he had attended. It was his encouragement that spurred me to keep going. Later it was a pleasure to be associated with Alliance and to work with Ken, as well as with Brad Martyn, Scott Stanley, and Paul Begley.

From the United States I came back to the University of New South Wales. For five years I was head of a double degree program where students graduated in both finance and mathematics. This was a wonderful time since I had the opportunity to supervise the final theses of about 30 students. Topics ranged from trading methods through to some of the valuation methods described in this book. Around this time Andrew Bird formed Aspect Financial, which became Aspect Huntley and later Morningstar (Australia). I would like to thank Andrew for his support and the opportunity to consult for his company in its formative years.

I would also like to thank Margie Baldock. In 2000 Margie contacted me and said that she loved Valuesoft but wanted it automated and coupled with its own databases. With her creative background in marketing, the two of us, with my wife, Sandy, formed a company and this was the start of the Conscious Investor® investment software. We were fortunate in getting the programming expertise of Paul Shields, who took my code for key functions in Valuesoft and programmed them into a systematic, user-friendly setting which we called Conscious Investor. The package consists of three steps: scanning individual sectors or the whole market, reviewing companies in more depth, and finally calculating the likely profit. I also want to thank Bretton Day and especially Felipe Rodriquez for financial support that made the whole project viable. A few years later Felipe, Sandy, and I bought Margie's share of the business.

Since those early days, Conscious Investor has evolved with more features including an expert system to describe and interpret in plain English the main features and significance of key charts for individual companies, through to automatic margins of safety when calculating the likely profit from an investment. Other people I would like to thank for helping make Conscious Investor successful are Laura Courtney, Adam Dominik, Mary Huynh, Rajiv Jacob, Saurabh Shukla, and Kean Wong. I also want to thank Bill Clark for his marketing expertise and patience in working with me to clarify what I was trying to achieve. On the research side, I thank Clive Wong, Wayne Thong, and Xiao Xu, who were my research assistants at different times. I am grateful to Ed Kelly who, when he was at Trinity College in Dublin, carried out the first independent research on Conscious Investor. Over the years data for Conscious Investor has been supplied by Morningstar. In this area I have had a lot of help from a number of people at Morningstar including Elise Isaacson, Anna Nordseth, and Thu Pham (in the U.S.), as well as Andrew Doherty, Darryn Springett, and Jamie Wickham (in Australia). Thank you for your support and prompt replies to my questions.

At the start of 2009, Conscious Investor became part of Teaminvest. I particularly want to thank Teaminvest's Howard Coleman for recognizing the strengths of Conscious Investor and making it part of his vision for a truly unique package for serious investors. Howard's ability to analyze companies from a business perspective, to describe the factors that are crucial for their success, and to list their future risks was an eye-opener for me. It reminded me of what I had been told about the way Buffett could, in a short telephone call, give valuable insights to the managers of Berkshire's businesses.

In most cases, these were initially their own businesses that they had been running successfully for years. Also I want to thank Mark Moreland of Teaminvest for his marketing energy and drive.

Various people have read different versions and chapters of the manuscript. I thank you all for the time and care you have put into this. In many cases your suggestions have been the difference between a confused description and a readable explanation. In particular I thank Pauline Clemens, Charles Mizrahi, Ralph Rasmussen, Tom Rickenbacker, and Mark Riordan. Charles and I have had many conversations over the years which I have highly valued. His book *Getting Started in Value Investing* (John Wiley & Sons, 2007) is an excellent way to do just that, to get started in value investing. I also thank Charles for introducing me to Debra Englander, executive editor at Wiley. It has been a pleasure to work with Debby, as well as with Adrianna Johnson, Kelly O'Connor, and Claire Wesley, also at Wiley. Robert Miles is another person with whom I have had enjoyable "Buffett" conversations and dinners over the years. I particularly enjoyed his book *The Warren Buffett CEO* (John Wiley & Sons, 2003). I also thank Jim Brownlee for his support.

Finally, it is a huge pleasure to thank Sandy. Not only is she my wife, but she is also my best friend and confidant. She has always been completely supportive of everything that I have wanted to do and without her I have no doubt that I would not have gotten to the stage of writing a book. Even on the technical level her support for this book has been way beyond any marriage vows. For instance, with little background in investing and the stock market, she read every word that I wrote and made pertinent suggestions on content as well as style. Many times she pulled me up and prodded me to explain more clearly what I was talking about. Thank you, Sandy.

# Introduction

The stock market is an extraordinary outcome of human ingenuity. Buying shares on the stock market gives you ownership of parts of some of the world's greatest companies. For under a hundred dollars you can buy a piece of Microsoft or Intel, companies that have revolutionized the way we do business and, indeed, most parts of our lives. You can buy a piece of Wal-Mart or Costco, companies that have changed the way millions of people shop. Or, in a different direction, you can buy shares in new sustainable energy companies such as Suntech in solar energy or Vestas Wind Systems in wind energy, companies that are shifting how we see our relationship with our environment.

As a shareholder you have ownership rights such as voting for directors, receiving dividends, and sharing in the proceeds of a corporate liquidation. But as an investor the key goal is to choose stocks that will be profitable. This is the focus of this book: showing how to be a successful investor by determining the real value of stocks. This will be done through a careful analysis of quantitative methods of equity evaluation to determine whether an investment will make money or not. Putting it simply, we are going to examine what separates wealth winners from mere speculative hopefuls.

Successful investing depends on knowing what to buy and when to do it. Then it depends on knowing when to hold and when to sell. The problem is *how* to do this. We often talk about the stock market in terms of a human psyche with a mind of its own: euphoric highs, depressing lows, tedious doldrums. And it is hard not to think of it this way. For example, from 1975 to 1985, on average the U.S. stock market reflected around 50 percent of the value of the underlying assets, according to U.S. Treasury tables. This means that a very large investor, by buying all the stock of companies traded on U.S. markets, could get the lot for about half the price of what the overall market

1

was worth. Such an investor would be getting everything for 50 cents on the dollar. Then the market started climbing until in 2000 it was close to twice the value of the underlying assets. Next it crashed to undervalued levels in 2008 but has now crept up until it is slightly overvalued once again in early 2010.

Another example of the bipolar nature of the stock market is the price of Berkshire Hathaway, the company run by legendary investor Warren Buffett. Since he has been in charge of the company there have been four occasions when the price has dropped by around 50 percent. The first three times were in 1974, in 1987, and in 1998. Each time, like a punch-drunk fighter, it picked itself up off the canvas and headed for record highs. Consider the fact that Buffett bought his first shares in the business for $7.50 on Wednesday, December 12, 1962, and on Tuesday, December 11, 2007, almost exactly 45 years later, they reached $151,650, an all-time high. This is an average return of 24.65 percent per year. After that the price tumbled to a low of $70,050 on Thursday, March 5, 2009. Within six months it was back over $100,000, and by March 2010 it was over $125,000, so the chances are that the price will move to record highs once again. These massive price swings have little if anything to do with the underlying business. Every year the company, under the astute leadership of Buffett, continues to invest its capital in a wide range of quality businesses either via the stock market or through direct purchase of private companies. Except on two occasions, every year the equity of the business on a per-share basis has gone up, a remarkable record. However, if you only looked at the share price, you would conclude that the business was continually alternating between periods of wild success and dismal failure.

It is our job to look behind these manic-depressive swings of the overall market and individual companies where prices seem to oscillate between astronomical highs and pitiless lows. For example, what is it that drives the share price of Berkshire Hathaway upward over the years despite the short-term volatility? In a nutshell, it is the strength of the underlying business. For a start, when a company announces strong improvements in its sales and earnings, generally its price goes up. If it announces the opposite, generally its price goes down. More importantly, over a longer time frame, the prices of successful businesses tend to rise and the prices of poorly performing businesses tend to fall, the speed and sizes of these rises and falls depending on the degree of success or otherwise of the business.

Many years ago, Benjamin Graham, often referred to as the dean of Wall Street, said it clearly: "In the short term the market is a voting machine, in the long term it is a weighing machine."

What is it weighing? Value. And value and the valuation of equities are what this book is about. It is all about how to weigh or measure the value of stocks. If we can't measure value, then we cannot tell if any stock that we purchase is likely to be profitable. We are left to be kicked around by the market's whims and uncertainties. This is particularly true at the present time since, according to George Soros, we are experiencing the "the worst financial crisis since the 1930s." Yet history shows that it was during times of past turbulence and uncertainty that many astute investors made their greatest profits.

After making a purchase of shares in a company, it takes time to be sure that it was profitable and, hence, that it represented value. If the price goes up over our time frame we can look back and say that when we made the purchase the price we paid was good value. If the price goes down, we say the opposite. The problem facing every investor is to be able to determine at the time of the purchase whether the investment is likely to be profitable or not, and not wait until the price has actually gone up or down. This is done by measuring the real value of the equity when the purchase is being considered.

Like most important areas in life, this measurement of value is both a science and an art. It is both objective and subjective. As a science, measurement of value involves careful calculations using specific financial inputs based on approved and audited financial statements. The outcome is usually referred to as *intrinsic value*, which is taken as the true worth of the equity independent of investor and market opinions. The measurement of real value comes by comparing this intrinsic value with the actual price. If the intrinsic value is high compared to the price, then we are encouraged to go ahead with the purchase. Otherwise we would be wise to leave it alone.

At the same time, measurement of value is an art because there are actually dozens of ways of measuring intrinsic value, each with its own set of inputs. Often the outcomes for the same stock are hugely different so that which method to use and the levels of the inputs are judgments to be made. In this book each valuation method is followed by a clear list of its strengths and weaknesses so that you can make an informed choice if you wish to use that method. Just as importantly, you can be aware of what to watch out for when reading a report on a company that discusses its value using a particular valuation method.

The fundamental assumption of value is that over time, the price of a stock will move toward its true worth or intrinsic value. Just like a swarm of mosquitoes appear to be flying randomly, but overall unerringly move toward an uncovered arm, so the millions of investors drive the stock price, by a series of persistent up and down nudges, toward its value. The difference is that for mosquitoes the time frame is minutes, while for the stock market it can be months and even years.

In fact, this tendency of prices leads to a second assumption, namely that stocks that are more undervalued will initially rise in price more quickly than those that are less undervalued. In other words, they will have a higher rate of return. This means that we have two core questions when making investment decisions: How much is it really worth? And, if it is undervalued, is the market price substantially below the true worth? These questions, particularly the first one, are the focus of the methods covered in Chapters 6 to 10 and then again in Chapter 12.

The preceding discussion leads, however, to an even more fundamental question for investors, namely: What rate of return can I confidently expect to get? In the end, this is the all-important question for making investment decisions. Even if a stock is undervalued by 50 percent, it is no use as an investment if we do not have confidence at the outset about the growth of its price. For example, the fact that it is highly undervalued does not tell us when, or indeed if, the price will move upward in our time frame. The stock may continue to stay undervalued by 50 percent for years. As investors we want to know at the time of our purchase whether we are going to make money or not, and how much we are likely to make. In other words, what is our anticipated rate of return? This means that we don't even need to calculate intrinsic value provided we can calculate the expected rate of return. Methods are presented in Chapters 11 and 13 that go straight to such calculations.

The major stock markets around the world are maelstroms of activity. Every day, untold numbers of transactions are made by hundreds of thousands of people involving thousands of companies. With an online brokerage account and a basic home computer, it can be done with a few key strokes and mouse clicks. On one hand, are the parents at home with children on their knees, the office workers in their work cubicles, and the tradespeople on their Internet phones, all squeezing in a few transactions whenever they get the chance. On the other hand, there are the investment professionals sitting in front of banks of computer monitors, shifting millions of dollars, often in great spurts of activity. In every case, the goal is the same: to increase the net worth of their portfolios or the portfolios of their clients.

What does differ is the reasoning and strategy behind their decisions. These depend on many factors. The time element is one of them. For day traders, unless the price moves immediately in the way they want, they may well cut their losses and reverse the transaction. For savvy value investors it is the opposite: If the price of a stock goes down after they make a purchase, they are likely to buy even more. As an investor, rather than a trader, we want to find stocks that, compared to their market price, are undervalued according to clear criteria. In the opposite direction, if the price of a stock is substantially above its value, then it may be time to sell since it is likely that the price will drop.

There are two basic problems with the value approach, both related to the fact, stated previously, that there are many ways of calculating value. The first problem is that on an initial analysis all the methods can seem very plausible. In most cases, if the average investor and, I suspect, the majority of professionals were presented with any one of the methods with its accompanying rationale, they would accept it as the method to use. However, as stated earlier, the different approaches can give hugely varying results, in some cases differing by hundreds of percent. Even within some of the methods, just small changes in the way they are applied can result in impossibly large variations.

The second problem is that the methods all have different assumptions and requirements. Some methods apply in certain situations while other methods apply in quite different situations. To try to apply a single method in all situations invariably leads to misleading results. Unfortunately, investors and analysts are usually only familiar with a single method and keep applying it in every case. It may be a valuation method they were taught in a formal course, or it may be something they picked up from a book, web site, or software package. The point is, along with most areas of life, it is just not true that one size fits all. (Charlie Munger, Warren Buffett's longtime friend and vice-chairman of Berkshire Hathaway, is fond of saying that to a person with a hammer everything looks like a nail.)

Important as they are, these are still technical problems. There is an even bigger problem associated with valuation methods, what I call *mathematical intimidation*. There is a tendency for many people to accept as correct anything that comes from a mathematical formula. Normal common sense and discrimination seem to be put on hold at the sight of mathematical symbols placed in a formula. Even if the symbols and formulas are hidden in computer programs, there is still the tendency not to question the outcome. As we will see, this is particularly true for the discounted cash flow and dividend discount methods with their impractical use of infinite forecasts. These methods are not even scientific because their key assumptions cannot be tested.

## What Is This Book About?

With this in mind, the purpose of this book is to provide details of all the major equity valuation methods. Each method comes with a description of its motivation and justification, together with a list of its assumptions, so that it is clear which situations it can be applied to and which should be skipped over. Also, the strengths and weaknesses of each method are listed to make it easier to choose between competing methods. Which methods to use and how to apply them are not just theoretical problems. They impact decisions involving hundreds of millions of dollars for institutional investors. But for individual investors the stakes are often higher. Getting it right may mean the difference between a comfortable retirement and a struggle to make ends meet.

There is also an underlying theme in the book, which is really the path to the fundamental goal mentioned earlier of calculating the expected rate of return. This theme starts with the idea that intrinsic value or true worth on its own has no practical value for investors. It requires price to put it into action. And once you have included price, you are including, either directly or indirectly, price ratios such as price-to-earnings, price-to-free-cash-flow, or price-to-dividends ratios. (In fact, in the standard discount methods, you actually require forecasts of infinite strings of such ratios.) Now it becomes clear that you never had to actually calculate intrinsic value as a stand-alone dollar amount in the first place. This puts you in the fortunate position of recognizing that you can use one of a handful of key price ratios to calculate directly the actual rate of return that you can confidently expect.

In the introduction to the early editions of the best-seller *A Brief History of Time*, author Stephen Hawking wrote that he was told that every equation he put in the book would halve the sales. He resolved to have none but ended up with a single equation. The bad news is that I have sprinkled equations throughout the book, particularly the later chapters. After all, if we are going to talk about the intrinsic value of stocks, then we need a formula to work this out. This will enable those with a mathematical bent to have a clear and concise description of the methods. The good news is that you can hop over the equations as all the methods are also described in words. Moreover, most of the equations are consigned to appendixes. In addition, the methods are presented in such a way that the calculations are a natural consequence of the features and logic of the method. In other words, by understanding what is trying to be achieved with a certain method, we are led automatically to the calculations, rather than the calculations driving the method.

The first three chapters set up what we mean by *value*. The first chapter looks at the concept of intrinsic value, particularly in monetary terms as it applies to the stock market. What is intrinsic value? Does it really exist? What are the ways of measuring it? Chapter 2 covers the price-setting mechanisms and influences in the stock market. It also describes the difference between pure price theories and fundamental data theories. Briefly, pure price theories such as the efficient market hypothesis and technical analysis describe price movements with reference to the price itself. In contrast, fundamental data theories, the focus of this book, describe price movements as a longer-term response to the fundamental data of the underlying businesses or equities. Chapter 3 brings together Chapter 1 on intrinsic value and Chapter 2 on price, and introduces real value as a combination of intrinsic value and price. In broad terms, the greater the intrinsic value compared to price, the greater the real value.

Chapter 4 is an introduction to accounting and the roles of the four financial statements (balance sheet, income statement, cash flow statement, and equity statement) in providing the data for the valuation methods. I even include a brief discussion of off-balance-sheet obligations. Chapter 5 uses the data in the financial statements to describe the key financial ratios as part of the process of analyzing and filtering companies. The valuation methods themselves start in Chapter 6. For those who want to get straight into the actual methods, this is the place to start.

Most of the valuation methods are presented in three parts. The first part is a general description with minimal use of technical language. The descriptions list the type of data that is needed, including whether it can be taken straight from financial statements issued by the company or whether estimates are needed such as forecasts of the growth of earnings. As well, the type of output is clearly described. For example, in some cases the output is the direct statement of the intrinsic value of the stock. This needs to be compared with the current price to decide on what action, if any, should be taken. In other cases, rather than dollar value, the output indicates whether it is likely to be a profitable time to buy in terms of the expected return. A third case displays the outcome as the length of time that will be required for the earnings or dividends to cover the original outlay. The second part of the description of each method is more technical, giving either the specifics of the formula behind the method or, for the more complex methods, an outline of the formula. The final part of the description of each method is the list of strengths and weaknesses previously mentioned.

## Who Is This Book For?

The book is intended for all investors, from those just getting started in the stock market to experienced professionals. For experienced investors, I hope the book will provide a fresh look at any valuation methods that you are already using. Many of you may want to go straight to the chapters on the particular methods that you use. Hopefully they will also provide new variations of these methods, as well as encouraging you to consider including other methods in your approach. For other investors, as explained earlier, Chapters 1 to 5 provide an introduction to all the tools and ideas needed to understand, measure, and use the idea of value in the stock market. From Chapter 6 onward, the book will provide you with an overview of all the main methods so that, as you get started, you will have more confidence in what you are doing.

My father, who built hundreds of houses during his life, always told me to make sure that I had the right tools and materials before starting on a job. Don't just rush in. This is even truer in the stock market: Not knowing what you are doing could cost you a large proportion of your capital in a very short time.

Even if you do not think that you are actually going to do any of the value calculations described in this book, there are other reasons to have familiarity with the different methods. For example, perhaps you intend to have a financial planner or asset manager take care of your investments. The book will give you the ability to make more informed decisions regarding whom to choose. Often just a question or two will quickly separate someone who knows what they are doing from the mediocre crowd. Imagine the difference it would make to ask each potential manager what valuation methods they use, what assumptions they make when they use them, and their reasons for these choices. (If you don't get any answers, or the answers you get are not satisfactory, move on. For those who chose to invest with Bernard Madoff, this step alone would have saved them billions of dollars in total.)

Another reason to look at the different methods is that as you do so, you will be gaining valuable knowledge about important areas of company analysis. For example, when looking at the methods of Benjamin Graham, you would be learning how to identify risks by looking at the balance sheet. Or, when looking at dividend discount methods, you would be learning about the pros and cons of different dividend levels in relation to other aspects of the business. For example, does the current level of the dividend payout ratio add value or subtract it?

Since the book covers over 20 different valuation methods, it could be used as a reference book to get a quick check on methods that you may have read about, or a more in-depth analysis of a method you may be considering using. Finally, the web site www.theconsciousinvestor.org provides free access to functions that will enable you to implement some of the key methods that I describe.

One of the exciting benefits of knowing how to calculate value is that the volatility of stock prices becomes your friend instead of a frightening enemy. Knowledge of the true value of a stock gives you added confidence to set a price at which to buy—or, if you own the stock, at which price to sell. There is less likelihood of being seduced by glowing reports or press releases with the thought, "Perhaps they know something that I don't?" Everything becomes simpler. Once you have calculated the price that makes sense, you either buy the stock if this price exceeds the current price or you wait. Either the market price drops to the price you have calculated as good value and you buy, or it does not, and you do nothing. Alternatively, if you already own the stock, by comparing intrinsic value with its current price, the decision to sell, to hold, or to buy more becomes clear.

The title of this book is *The Conscious Investor*. The biggest cost to investors is that they are not conscious of what they are doing, what I call unconscious investing, which means following the crowd and not asking the right questions. In the case of this book, I hope that through reading it you will not just follow the crowd and you will end by knowing methods and strategies that others don't. I hope you will learn that, despite all the hype and madness on the surface, underneath you are dealing with real businesses with real products and services, and that you can profitably invest in them using well-founded, timeless value methods. I hope you become a conscious investor and experience the stock market as a lot of fun, with the process of building wealth and financial security a pleasure instead of a stressful duty.

I also use the term *conscious investor* (which, by the way, was coined by my wife, Sandy) in another way: someone who invests in companies with products and services they believe in and perhaps even use. In this sense, another component to being a conscious investor is accepting the responsibility of recognizing that measuring value also includes *how* the money is made, and not just the amount that is made. Investing in this way provides not just quantity, but also an additional layer of quality. It is like making a small nudge toward your own version of a better society and a more caring world.

# CHAPTER 1

## What Is Intrinsic Value?

*Intrinsic value is an elusive concept.*

—Benjamin Graham[1]

*Intrinsic value is an all-important concept that offers the only logical approach to evaluating the relative attractiveness of investments and businesses.*

—Warren Buffett[2]

Valuation methods start with the goal of calculating intrinsic value, the *true* worth of a stock based on established financial information and clear forecasts about the business. Intrinsic value is, or should be, independent of market opinion and investor sentiment. The basic assumption is that over time the price of the stock will move toward its intrinsic value. This means that knowing the intrinsic value of a stock, if only approximately, provides a firm foundation for all investment decisions, whether to buy, to sell, or to do nothing. In this sense, value comes from putting together and comparing intrinsic value and price. However, as we will soon see, the idea and use of intrinsic value is not as straightforward as it first seems.

## Intrinsic Value

The general idea is that the intrinsic value of a unit of stock in a publicly traded company is its *true* worth, which may be quite different from its market price. Over 70 years ago Benjamin Graham, often referred to as the dean of Wall Street, gave the following description:

> [Intrinsic value] is understood to be that value which is justified by the facts, e.g., the assets, earnings, dividends, definite prospects, as distinct, let us say, from market quotations established by artificial manipulation or distorted by psychological excesses.[3]

Around the same time, John Burr Williams[4] wrote about the "real worth" of equities and emphasized that it could actually be calculated in a precise manner from data obtained from financial statements coupled with judicious forecasts. Williams' methods put particular emphasis on current dividends and forecasts of dividends. The result was the dividend discount method, which is described in Chapter 8.

### Intrinsic Value

The theory of intrinsic value is that it is the *true* worth of a stock based on established financial information and clear forecasts about the business.

When someone starts to look at intrinsic value, often the first characteristic they notice is that there are many ways of calculating it, giving a wide range of results. The second problem is that, even if there is agreement on the method chosen to calculate intrinsic value, there is unlikely to be agreement on the levels of the input parameters in the calculations. This often leads to even wider variations in the calculations. *Sensitivity* is the size of the variation of the outcome compared to variations in the input. Some methods are very sensitive with just a few percentage points change in the inputs leading to twofold and higher variations in the output. Other models are more stable, meaning that the results do not vary much with changes in the input levels.

Just the same, by having an improved understanding of the assumptions and the parameters that go into the various calculations, we are in a stronger position to make better investment decisions. Without this understanding, we are vulnerable to many of the claims and statements by market participants and investment advisers. The other good news is that all the methods for calculating intrinsic value have different strengths and weaknesses. For example, some may be suited for companies with consistent levels of dividends while others may be better suited to companies that do not pay dividends. Furthermore, all the methods have been developed to meet specific needs and applied to good effect at different times.

Whatever definition of intrinsic value of a company is used, the overall idea is that the financial data from the company's current and historical financial statements forms the basis of the calculations. In addition, the calculations usually include forecasts of this data as to what it will be in the future or how it will grow.

The basic assumption is that, over time, the price of a stock will move toward its intrinsic value. If the price is $20 and the intrinsic value is $30, then it would be a good time to buy since the price would be anticipated to rise toward $30. In the opposite direction, if the price is $30 and the intrinsic value is $20, then it is time to sell. Burton Malkiel refers to this as the firm-foundation theory of stock prices. He writes:

> The firm-foundation theory argues that each investment instrument, be it a common stock or a piece of real estate, has a firm anchor of something called "intrinsic value," which can be determined by careful analysis of present conditions and future prospects. When market prices fall below (rise above) this firm foundation of intrinsic value, a buying (selling) opportunity arises, because this fluctuation will eventually be corrected—or so the theory goes.[5]

Benjamin Graham was questioned about this tendency when he appeared before the Senate Banking Committee in 1955. When asked by J. William Fulbright, the committee chair, why stock prices move up to their intrinsic value, he replied, "That is one of the mysteries of our business, and it is a mystery to me as well as to everybody else. [But] we know from experience that the market catches up with value."[6] There is actually a second part to this assumption, namely that stocks that are more undervalued will initially rise in price more quickly than those that are less undervalued. In other words, they will have a higher rate of return. Importantly, the research on different valuation methods mentioned throughout the book generally supports the assumption of the firm-foundation theory.

## The Basic Assumption of Intrinsic Value

The basic assumption of intrinsic value is that, over time, the price of the stock will move toward its intrinsic value.

As we will see, it is not hard to develop and support calculations for the worth of a stock and to call the result intrinsic value . . . but is there really such a thing, whether in the stock market or anywhere else? Despite all the talk about intrinsic value, is it just a will-o'-the-wisp with no real substance and not worth trying to track down? Experts in many areas, not just theoretical finance, argue these questions with weighty articles and books.[7] To avoid being stuck in existential quicksand, we are going to take a pragmatic approach and skirt around the main philosophical problems.

The core argument against intrinsic value in the stock market is that if it existed and could be properly measured, then everyone would know what it is. Consequently, no one would sell anything for a price less than the per-share intrinsic value and no one would pay more than this amount. There would be either no transactions or very few on any of the stock exchanges. One weakness of this argument is that perhaps intrinsic value exists for equities but the method for calculating it is so complex or abstruse that only a very small number of people can determine what it is. Even among those who can determine it, many may not bother.

We will take a down-to-earth approach in this book and look at intrinsic value in an operational sense. As a starting point, we define *intrinsic value* as any of the outcomes of the application of calculations that arrive directly at a dollar amount for the worth of a stock, where the calculations are based on defensible rational logic using two sets of inputs. The first set of inputs comes directly from the financial statements of the company and may include items such as equity and earnings per share. The levels of these input numbers are well defined and usually have a high degree of mutual agreement on their actual values. (But not always—we will see examples where there can be disagreement over some of the input figures based on such considerations as whether certain items should be expensed or capitalized. In the first case, the cost of the item is fully reported as an expense in the profit and loss statement; in the second case, only the depreciation appears there.) The second set of inputs involves forecasts of key financial parameters such as dividends and earnings per share. Based on opinion, these are much more variable between individuals.

This is the *direct* approach to intrinsic value. The intrinsic value is obtained directly as a dollar amount. Examples are the book value or equity per share, described in Chapter 6; or the dividend discount method, described in Chapter 8, where the intrinsic value is the discounted value of the dividends generated by the business over its life.

There is a second approach to intrinsic value in which the intrinsic value is calculated indirectly. As an example, in Chapter 11, price ratio methods calculate the expected total average annual return of a stock from particular input financial parameters over specified investment periods. Suppose that, to compensate for the risks associated with a business, a reasonable return is 14 percent per year. The intrinsic value is the price of the stock needed to achieve this return. It is like a reverse engineering exercise. Different prices are tried in the calculation until a price is found that gives the required return. Bingo! This is the intrinsic value according to the price ratio method with the associated input parameters.

Another example is the PEG ratio, defined in Chapter 10 as the ratio of the price-to-earnings ratio divided by the expected growth rate. In this setting, the intrinsic value is the price of the stock that would give a satisfactory level for the index. Suppose you are interested in a company that currently has a PEG ratio of 1.2. However, you believe that the company is trading at a fair price when its PEG ratio is 1.0. You invert the formula to find the price that gives a PEG ratio of 1.0; this price is the intrinsic value according to the PEG ratio method. In this case, the price of the stock exceeds the intrinsic value and so, according to this method, it is not a time to buy.

More generally, suppose we have a method for calculating an index associated with each stock that measures its worth. This could be the expected total average annual return, as just described. Another example is described in Chapter 9: Intrinsic value is the number of years it would take the earnings of the stock to pay back its price. Or it could be a more abstract index such as the PEG ratio described in the previous paragraph. In each case we can calculate a dollar amount as the price of the stock that would give a satisfactory or fair level for the index. This dollar amount is called the intrinsic value of the stock. Comparison with the current price determines what action to take: whether to buy, to sell, or to do nothing. Admittedly, this may seem a little theoretical at this stage but later chapters contain many examples.

In fact, since we can always turn calculations involving measures such as return or other various indexes into an intrinsic value in terms of dollars, it makes sense to expand the definition of intrinsic value. Quite simply, we define *intrinsic value* as the result of any calculation that evaluates the worth of a stock. In other words, we will talk about measures such as the expected return, the expected payback period, or the PEG ratio as the intrinsic value. We are not going to keep stating that the results of these calculations can always be converted into an actual dollar amount. Of course, as stated earlier for the direct method, to be included as a genuine method we require each method to have a firm, logical foundation with clear assumptions.

## Types of Intrinsic Value

Our operational definition of intrinsic value contradicts much of the financial literature, which assumes there is really only one approach, and that is via the discounted cash flow method. Even Warren Buffet explains that "intrinsic value can be defined simply: It is the discounted value of the cash that can be taken out of a business."[8] (It is often inferred from this statement that this is the method used by Buffett, although this is not what he actually says. Indeed, at the end of Chapter 7 we will see that he probably does not use this method.) Not only is discounted cash flow not a unique method for calculating intrinsic value, but we will see in Chapter 7 that it has many variations, with still more interpretations of these variations, giving a wide range of results. Should we be using free cash flows to the firm or free cash flows to equity for the "cash" in Buffett's definition? Or perhaps it is better to use dividends? Does it make sense to use a one-stage model, a two-stage model, or perhaps even a three-stage model?

Suppose we manage to gain agreement at the level of which variation to use. We may still be faced with quite different opinions on the appropriate values of the input variables. Buffett makes this clear when he continues: "Two people looking at the same set of facts, moreover—and this would apply even to Charlie and me—will almost inevitably come up with at least slightly different intrinsic value figures." (The "Charlie" to whom Warren Buffett is referring here is

Charlie Munger, the vice-chairman of Berkshire and long-term friend of Buffett.) It is actually much worse than this. In Chapter 7 we see that it is uncomfortably easy to come up with widely divergent intrinsic value figures rather than the "slightly different" figures referred to by Buffett.

## Many Variations of Intrinsic Value

In practice, there are many ways of calculating intrinsic value, giving a wide range of results depending on the method and the input parameters.

On top of the variations of discount methods and the extreme range of possible results, there are actually many other approaches to intrinsic value. The following is an introduction to the main types.

### Balance Sheet Calculations of Intrinsic Value

As is explained in detail in Chapter 4, the balance sheet is a snapshot of the financial position of a company at the end of its reporting period and includes such items as cash, receivables and payables, inventory, and short-term and long-term debt. They are listed in two categories, assets and liabilities, which in turn are broken into *current* assets and liabilities and *other* (noncurrent) assets and liabilities. Assets minus liabilities gives the *equity* of a company. When the equity is divided by the number of shares outstanding, we have the *book value*, a type of intrinsic value of the company.

To get a more conservative measure, Benjamin Graham, who was the master of balance sheet methods, would reweight the different line items to recalculate the book value. As an example, for his net current asset method he completely disregarded all the noncurrent assets and calculated a new book value, which he compared with the price of the equity. Chapter 6 looks at a range of balance sheet methods, including Graham's methods.

### Discount Methods of Intrinsic Value

Assume that a business intends to pay dividends over its entire life. We might be tempted to value the business as the sum of these dividends. This raises the problem, however, that if the business goes for an indefinite period, the sum of the dividends could grow to infinity. The problem is resolved by recognizing that payments in the future need discounting. The rate of the discount makes up for the lost revenue that could have been earned from an investment of equal risk during the period covered by the delay in payment. With this in mind, the dividend discount method declares that the intrinsic value is the sum of the discounted dividends over the life of the business.

This method has the severe difficulty of requiring forecasts of dividends over an infinite or unlimited period. Typically, this is done by making statements such that for 10 years the dividends are expected to grow by 8 percent per year and after that they are expected to grow by 3 percent per year. This method also requires forecasts of the discount rate over an unlimited period. It is these forecasts over an unlimited number of years that cause the most problems with the dividend discount method. This method and two variations using return on equity and residual income are covered in Chapter 8. Another variation called *abnormal earnings growth* is described in Chapter 12.

The partner to the dividend discount method is the discounted cash flow method. Instead of dividends, it uses free cash flow. As stated earlier, this is the standard method associated with the concept of intrinsic value. It is covered in Chapter 7.

## Payback Methods of Intrinsic Value

We all like at least to get our money back when we make an investment. It does not matter whether it is a used car, an investment property, or blue-chip stocks. If it is a used car or vacant block of land, we have the opportunity of getting our money back when we sell. If it is a rental property, we could think in terms of how long it will take for the accumulated rent to equal our purchase price. It is similar in the stock market. We could ask how long it will take for the sum of the dividends to reach the price paid for the stock—the shorter the time, the better. Or if the company does not pay dividends, we could use free cash flow or earnings. Finally, as for the discount methods, we could apply a discount rate to compensate for the lost revenue and the risk of not receiving the payments. The payback method measures the time taken for the discounted payments to equal or pay back the cost of the original investment. The method is explained in Chapter 9.

## Index Methods of Intrinsic Value

The methods just described provide results in terms that are immediately relevant to buying and selling decisions. They are in terms of either dollars and cents, expected return, or expected payback period. It is easy for investors to interpret their significance.

By contrast, index methods provide an index or ratio that gives a type of valuation score. It is necessary to look at a range of examples to be able to transfer the index level into an understanding of whether the equity is undervalued or overvalued. The most common index method is the PEG ratio, the ratio of the price-to-earnings (P/E) ratio of the company divided by a forecast of the growth rate of earnings expressed as a percentage. The PEG ratio method and several variations are covered in Chapter 10.

## Expected Return or Price Ratio Methods of Intrinsic Value

In equity markets, value is the combination of intrinsic value and price. It is generally approached by going from intrinsic value, to price, and then to value. In contrast, price ratio methods put intrinsic value, price, and value together right from the start. For example, by making estimates of the growth of earnings and dividends, and including the ratio of price and earnings per share (the P/E ratio), it is possible to determine what is the expected return over, say, the next five years. In this sense, value is measured by the percentage return that can be expected rather than whether the equity is selling at a price that is above or below a particular measure of a price-independent intrinsic value. Instead of answering the question: "How much is the stock really worth?" the primary question now becomes: "What rate of return can I confidently expect?" If you want an actual intrinsic value in dollar terms, it can be extracted as the price of the equity necessary to achieve a particular return.

Expected return or price ratio methods are more practical since they do not require the extreme forecasts used in discount methods. They are also distinct from the other methods in that they do not rely on the firm-foundation assumption that price moves toward some price-independent intrinsic value. Expected return methods are covered in Chapter 11.

### Miscellaneous Methods of Intrinsic Value

There are also various miscellaneous methods for calculating intrinsic value. For example, Benjamin Graham developed two simple formulas for calculating intrinsic value in terms of current earnings per share and forecasts of its growth. His second formula also included the yield on corporate bonds. Other methods do not provide a direct valuation but rely on choosing stocks through analyzing a range of factors such as return on equity and the P/E ratio. Options can also be used to value companies. These methods are gathered together in Chapter 12.

Figure 1.1 illustrates the different groupings of valuation methods. Some of the methods are applicable in certain situations, while others are more effective in quite different circumstances. However, they have all been applied to good effect at different times. For example, in the case of a company struggling to pay its debts, the best calculation of intrinsic value may be one of the balance sheet methods

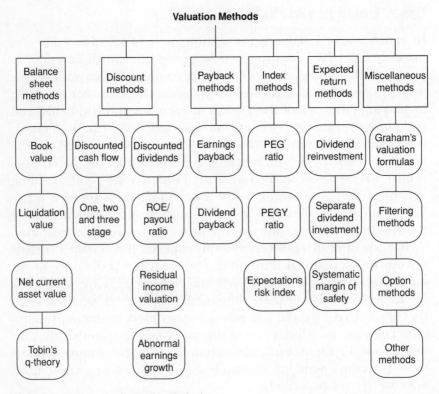

**Figure 1.1**    Taxonomy of Valuation Methods

described in Chapter 6. For a stable company with consistent growth in sales and earnings, discounted cash flow methods described in Chapters 7 and 8 or ratio methods described in Chapter 10 may be the most appropriate. If a quick rule-of-thumb check of value is needed, the PEG ratio may be the method of choice. Sometimes, measuring how long it will take for dividends to compensate for the outlay in buying stocks in a company may be critical. In this case, the best choice would be one of the payback methods of Chapter 9. When the company is a start-up with only a brief history, it may not be the actual method that is critical but rather that a generous margin of safety be used. These ideas are discussed in Chapter 13. To make it easier to choose the best methods in different circumstances, the strengths and weaknesses of each method are listed in detail after the description of the method.

 **Warning: Many Believe That Intrinsic Value Is Not Necessary**

It is important to state right at the outset that many stock market participants do not believe that the calculation of intrinsic value is either necessary or useful. They jump straight from price to value without considering intrinsic value. Some believe that levels and movements of share prices have patterns and regularities and that, properly understood, these patterns and regularities forecast whether prices are likely to go up, stay the same, or go down. The opposite view is that share prices are random, or sufficiently close to random, so that no profitable trading strategies are possible based solely on price movements. A third view is that price levels are due to the collective mood of investors. We briefly examine the evidence for these viewpoints in the next chapter. However, we take the view that the calculation of intrinsic value by a method or methods that you understand and are comfortable with is the essential first step in being a successful investor.

## The Bottom Line

1. Even though intrinsic value is often thought of as the true worth of an equity, in practice there are dozens of different definitions and methods with a wide variety of outcomes depending on the inputs. As shorthand, we

*(continued)*

will use intrinsic value to mean the result of any calculation that evaluates the worth of a stock according to a specific method with specific inputs.

2. The basic assumption is that over time price moves toward intrinsic value. The secondary assumption is that stocks that are more undervalued will initially rise in price more quickly than those that are less undervalued.

3. It is the relationship between intrinsic value and price that determines value. It is up to each individual investor to compare intrinsic value with market prices to make the most profitable transactions.

# Price Is What You Pay. . .

*The investor with a portfolio of sound stocks should expect their prices to fluctuate and should neither be concerned by sizable declines nor become excited by sizable advances.*

—Benjamin Graham[1]

*Price is what you pay. Value is what you get.*

—Warren Buffett[2]

There is a tendency to think that there is nothing much to understand about prices: All we need to know is that through the various stock markets, we have the opportunity to buy or sell shares at the prevailing prices. However, by probing more deeply into the mechanics of prices in terms of levels, movements, and theories, we increase the chance of market success.

The starting point of this analysis is that transactions in the stock market take place at the price available at the time of the transaction. Period. There are no negotiations or side deals. It is through the prices in the stock market that we interact with other investors. Furthermore, no matter what assumptions or calculations we make, once a bid is accepted most of any potential profit has been decided. The future movement of the price is out of our hands. In the opposite direction, once we sell, then the amount of our profit or loss is determined. For these reasons it is important to understand some of the major features of how prices are set and what information can be gained from market prices and their movements.

The focus of the book is on the measurement of the intrinsic value of businesses using fundamental data, and how this intrinsic value interacts with and drives the prices of the businesses in the stock market. Even so, there are other theories of prices that completely ignore all information about the underlying businesses. These are pure price theories that describe price levels and movements solely with reference to the price itself and perhaps the prices of other equities and indexes. As well, these theories may include the history of daily volumes of transactions. (In the language of mathematics, all these theories are part of what is called *signal analysis*. The movements of prices and groups of prices can be seen as signals over time, which are then analyzed using a range of mathematical techniques.)

There are two major pure price theories and it is useful to have at least a general idea of how they work. At one end we have the efficient market hypothesis, which states roughly that the prices at any time fully reflect all available information. At the other end is technical analysis, which states that future price movement can be predicted by a study of past patterns in prices and perhaps trading volumes. In the first case the history of prices leading up to the current price is completely irrelevant. In the second case, knowing the history of the prices is essential. These two approaches are like matter and anti-matter: They can only exist at the same time when kept well separated.

## From the Buttonwood Agreement to Mr. Market

Traditionally a *market* or *marketplace* is where people come to buy and sell goods. Today the terms also refer to virtual marketplaces on the Internet. Stock markets, also called stock exchanges and sometimes bourses, are more specialized. They focus on equities and other financial contracts. The first stock exchanges were informal gatherings established in Europe in the thirteenth century. In the United States, the New York Stock Exchange traces its origins to 1792 when 24 stockbrokers and merchants signed a trade agreement outside of 68 Wall Street in New York. They signed it under a buttonwood tree, giving rise to the name the Buttonwood Agreement.

Until recently, traders used a method called *open outcry* to carry out transactions in stock exchanges. Within the exchanges, they indicated the prices at which they were willing to buy or sell individual securities by calling out or using specific hand signals. At times there were waves of frenzied activity and noise as the traders did their best to fill their transaction orders. These days most trading is done via a network of computers. Brokerage firms lodge orders for purchases or sales of specific securities on behalf of their clients. Just as in markets for, say, farm produce, it is an auction environment, with the amounts that sellers are asking and that buyers are willing to pay openly available to the participants. The lowest selling price at any time is called the *ask* (or ask price or best ask) and the highest price anyone is willing to pay is called the *bid* (or bid price or best bid). The *bid-ask spread* is the difference between the two prices. When an equity is actively traded, the average bid-ask spread is small, often just a cent or two. In other cases the average bid-ask spread can represent 10 percent of the price or more, with transactions only taking place infrequently.

When the bid and ask prices match, a sale is triggered. If there are multiple bidders or sellers at a given price, then the sales are processed based on the time that the orders were lodged. In some cases a seller is willing to accept any price or a buyer is willing to pay any price. These are called *market* or *at market* orders and take place immediately after they are lodged. The computer program for computer-based exchanges automatically ensures that the highest price is obtained for sellers and the lowest price is obtained for buyers. In contrast, in an open outcry system this outcome is brought about by the actions of the traders and is enforced by the exchange and outside regulators. In both cases, sophisticated tracking programs monitor all the trading information and highlight any unusual price or volume movements. These are evaluated by the exchange regulatory staff to ensure that there was no fraudulent behavior or attempt at price manipulation.

Owning shares in a company is sometimes referred to as having a *long position* or *going long*. If an investor believes that the price will rise, then the usual action is to establish a long position (if no shares are already held) or add to any existing long positions. (There are also a whole range of so-called derivative contracts to take advantage of anticipated price rises, but this area is outside the scope of this book.) If an investor believes the price will fall, however, the choices are a little more complicated. There are two possible actions depending upon whether the shares in the company are already owned. If they are, then the usual action would be to sell them. But even if this is not the case, it is possible to profit directly from a drop in share price through what is called taking a *short position* or *short-selling* (*shorting*) the stock. This is done by borrowing stock in the company (usually

from a broker) and selling it with the requirement of buying the
same quantity back at a later date to return to the lender. The goal of
the short-seller is to choose stocks that will decline in price. This will
allow the stocks to be bought back at a lower price: The profit comes
because the price paid for them is less than the price at which they are
sold. The difference between this and a regular pair of transactions
is that for short-selling, the selling takes place before the purchase
instead of after it. If the price of the equity rises, the short-seller has
to buy back the equities at a higher price and so will incur a loss.

Now that most trading is done via computers, a huge amount
of information about prices and transactions is available to the ordinary investor, information that in the past was accessible only to the
brokerage houses and certain professionals. This makes it easier for
average investors to make informed decisions about what prices they
are willing to ask or to bid. There are different levels of information
supplied by online brokers. The basic level, called Level I, displays
the best bid and the best offer for a particular stock. This is the level
that you see on most web sites displaying stock market data. It is also
generally what you receive when you open a regular trading account
with an online broker. Often sites offer more detail to supplement
this basic information. Figure 2.1 is an example of a detailed quote

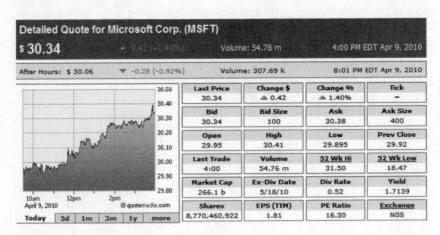

**Figure 2.1**    Detailed Price or Quote Data for Microsoft

The detailed quote shows a range of data including the price of the last trade, the highest bid price, the
lowest asking price, time of the last trade, basic financial data about the company such as the number of
shares outstanding, and other relevant information.

*Source:* Quotemedia (supplied with permission).

containing extra information such as basic financial data about the company, high and low prices over the previous 52 weeks, and dividend yield. It also displays information about volume, which is the number of shares that change hands over a period of time, typically a single day.

For those who want even more information, it is possible to open accounts that display what is referred to as *market depth*. This consists of lists of current bids and current asks including their prices and sizes. The bids from potential buyers are arranged in descending order with the highest bid at the top. Similarly, the asks from potential sellers are arranged in ascending order with the lowest asking price at the top. The display will also usually include the company representing the buyer or seller. As soon as there is match for the highest bid and the lowest ask, the exchange computers execute the transaction. By comparing the entries in these two lists, it may be possible to estimate the effect of future trades on the price. For example, if the highest offers are all close together and large in size, as trades take place there is less likely to be any downward price movement since the transactions will be taken up by these offers. This type of account is usually called a Level II account. These accounts will also typically include a list of all the recent transactions with their times and dates, transaction sizes, and the name of the exchange handling the transaction.

It is important to recognize that we have no control over the prices quoted on the stock exchange. Even though they are continually changing, prices are objective in the sense that they are set by the market and not by us. Our role is to decide whether to accept them and take action, or to wait. Benjamin Graham described prices as being set by a mythical character called Mr. Market. Each day for every stock, Mr. Market appears and offers you prices at which he will sell his share or buy your share of the company. On some days he sees the world through rose-colored glasses and is reluctant to sell unless he gets a very high price. He wants to be as confident as possible that he has squeezed every dollar out of his ownership of the stock before selling. On other days he is gloom and doom, naming a low price for the stock because he is worried it could go even lower.

Mr. Market has two important characteristics. The first is that he is present throughout every day, continually stating his prices. They might start low in the morning and rise as the day progresses, or they might do the complete opposite. Everything is possible. The second important characteristic is that he will continue this activity whether or not anyone takes up any of his offers. He is both persistent and tireless in his price setting, yet unperturbed whether they are acted upon or not. In other words, no one makes you buy or sell at any particular time. New prices are always being offered to you.

### Benjamin Graham and Mr. Market

Benjamin Graham's Mr. Market is both persistent and tireless in offering prices to buy or sell, and yet he is unperturbed whether they are acted upon or not.

## Charting and Technical Analysis

As stated in the introduction to this chapter, many participants in the stock market believe all that is necessary to be successful is a careful study of price levels and price movements. They believe it is possible to detect regularities and patterns in the movements of the offers by Mr. Market and transactions with him, sometimes accompanied by changes in trading volumes, which can then be used to make profitable forecasts about his future prices. This practice started with *charting*, making large-scale graphs of the levels of prices. Sometimes the charts displayed prices on a day-to-day basis but often they included intraday prices. Practitioners, called *chartists*, would pore over rolls of paper on which they graphed the prices, looking for various features using rulers, protractors, and compasses.

A basic feature sought by chartists was a series of price highs lying on a straight line and a corresponding series of price lows on a separate line. If these could be found, a line would be ruled connecting the highs and a separate line joining the lows. When these lines are parallel or close to it, they define a *channel* with the slope of the lines indicating the overall trend. If the price moves out of this channel it is called a *breakout*. The theory is that a breakout in the upward direction indicates that the price will continue to rise, a *buy signal*. A breakout in the downward direction is a *sell signal*. However, if the price is in the top area of the channel, it may be considered as a time to short the stock or to sell because the top of the channel is acting as a *resistance level*. If it is in the lower area of a channel, it may be considered as a time to buy or go long.

The next level of complexity concerns *reversals*, when the trend of a channel changes direction. These are associated with patterns with descriptive names such as *double bottoms* or *head and shoulders*. As its name indicates, a double bottom is a pattern made up of two consecutive troughs that are roughly equal with a moderate peak in between. The usual interpretation is that a double bottom signals the end of an intermediate or long-term downward trend. A head and shoulders pattern consists of three peaks with the center peak higher than the outside peaks. When there has been an upward trend followed by a head and shoulders pattern it is usually interpreted as the start of a new downward trend.

This is just a brief introduction to the type of features that chartists would look for when studying graphs of prices. With the advent of computers, particularly personal computers, the methods of charting quickly became widely available as comprehensive computer packages. Along with market data provided by various suppliers, which could easily be downloaded from central databases over the Internet, charting switched from being something for a few dedicated practitioners to a mainstream activity. Everyone from investment professionals in their Wall Street offices to parents working at home could now study price movements. In this new computer-based setting, charting is referred to as *technical analysis*.[3]

The main question is whether it is possible to make consistent profits by simply studying historical price levels and movements. What is the evidence that this can be done? Because of the importance of this question, we are going to spend some time setting it up and analyzing it.

### Price Movement and the Game of Rock Paper Scissors

Instead of looking at specific trading strategies, we are going to go back a step by looking for evidence that there are short-term patterns in price movements. To make the search more concrete, we are going to compare the search for particular patterns with competing in a game of Rock Paper Scissors, where your opponent is the stock market. In the game, players guess whether the opponent is going to display the hand signal for rock, paper, or scissors, and plays accordingly. In the stock market, the investor guesses whether the share price is going to decrease, stay the same, or increase, and trades accordingly. In Rock Paper Scissors, the strategy is to try to detect whether your opponent has some sort of bias and, if so, to take advantage of it. One strategy of the game is to detect whether your opponent is unconsciously using one of rock, paper, or scissors more than the other two possibilities.[4] Another strategy is to watch for any patterns in your opponent's throws, such as after two rocks they are unlikely to throw rock and are more likely to throw paper or scissors.[5]

In the stock market, the corresponding action is to look for strategies to increase the chances of correctly guessing whether the price of a particular stock is going to go down, stay the same, or go up. In this analysis we will keep it quite simple and not consider how far the price moves. We will only consider the direction of the move or whether it does not move at all. In this way, since we only consider three options, the study is closer to the game of Rock Paper Scissors in order to use it as a concrete reference point. In practice, price movements are much more complex than just these three possible outcomes. For example, as just noted, we pay no attention to the size of the daily price moves. In addition, within each day and over the days, the price of shares moves through all types of dips and peaks. Just the same, by first looking at this simplified question we can get a better understanding of the methods and requirements involved in studying price movements.

With this study we aim to answer two questions: Do patterns exist when we look at these three possible share price movements? And if they do, can we develop a trading strategy that exploits these patterns as is done in Rock Paper Scissors? In this case it would mean a profitable strategy.

To answer the first question we need a more formal setup. Consider the prices for shares in Microsoft. Each trading day, the price can go up, it can go down, or it can stay the same. Since it would be unusual for the price to stay exactly the same, we would not expect these three possibilities to occur with approximately equal frequencies. To overcome this we added a small zone or buffer around the price and only count a change as an upward or downward movement if the price moved outside this zone in the required direction. This is akin to saying that a trade is only profitable if the price moves by a certain minimum amount to allow for transaction costs and other fees.

We studied the closing prices of Microsoft for each trading day from January 2003 until the end of 2008, a period of six years. In this study we used $0.10 as the required movement price buffer. Since the price of Microsoft over the period of the study was usually in the range $20 to $30, it meant that we required a shift of approximately 0.4 percent in price before it counted as a price increase or decrease. The idea was to consider the movement in price from the closing price on one day to the closing price on the next trading day. There are three possibilities:

1. The price drops by more than $0.10; denote this case by $d$.
2. The price does not move in either direction by more than $0.10$; denote this case by $n$.
3. The price increases by more than $0.10$; denote this case by $u$.

Just as in Rock Paper Scissors, if the outcomes $d$, $n$, and $u$ appear randomly, it is not possible to devise a winning strategy, which in this case would mean a profitable trading strategy. In contrast, suppose we can discern a pattern in the outcomes. It need not be a deterministic pattern such as $d$ always follows $u$. Even the most inexperienced investor would not expect that. Rather, suppose a pattern occurs where certain combinations occur more frequently than would be expected by chance. For example, suppose that after two consecutive days when the price increases by more than $0.10$, it is more likely to drop by more than $0.10$ over the next day. In symbols, we write that $d$, rather than $u$ or $n$, is more likely to follow $uu$. Putting it another way, the triple $uud$ occurs with higher frequency than the triples $uun$ or $uuu$.

We will call these *probabilistic* patterns in price movements. In either case, whether we uncover a deterministic or probabilistic pattern, we would expect to be able to develop a strategy that would be profitable. To see whether there are any patterns in the levels of the prices, this study looked at prices over one-day, two-day, three-day, and four-day periods.

**One-Day Price Movements**  Over the six years of the study, the down movement $d$ occurred with a frequency of 35.63 percent, the neutral movement $n$ with a frequency of 30.63 percent, and the up movement $u$ with a frequency of 33.75 percent. From a statistical point of view, there was no significant difference between these frequencies and so we cannot conclude that any of the alternatives occurred significantly more often than the others.

**Two-Day Price Movements**   Over two days, there are nine alternatives: *dd, dn, du, nd, nn, nu, ud, un, uu*. If these were to appear
with equal frequency, the frequency would be 11.11 percent. The
actual outcomes were very close to this level; the lowest was *un* with
a frequency of 9.94 percent and the highest was *ud* with a frequency
of 13.62 percent. Once again, there was no significant difference
between the different frequencies.

**Three-Day Price Movements**   When the time period is three days,
there are 27 possible combinations of *d, n* and *u*. Instead of looking
at them as a total group, it seemed to be more informative to look
at some special cases, which amounted to analyzing whether prices
tended to trend in the same direction or tended to reverse. Traders
who believe that once prices start in one direction, they will continue
in the same direction, are referred to as *momentum traders*. Those who
believe that it is more likely that a direction, once established, will
reverse itself are called *contrarian traders*.

The first step in the study was to look at the occurrences of *dd* and
then see which was more likely after the third day, *ddd, ddn*, or *ddu*.
This was repeated with the possibilities *nnd, nnn* and *nnu*, followed
by the possibilities *uud, uun* and *uuu*. It turned out that in each case
the probabilities were, once again, approximately equal. There are
two important conclusions. The first is that if the price goes down
two days in a row, then on the third day it is equally likely to go down,
stay the same, or increase. The second conclusion is similar: If the
price goes up two days in a row, on the third day the price is equally
likely to go down, stay the same, or increase.

**Four-Day Price Movements**   Now the possibilities are more complicated since over four days there are 81 combinations of *d, n*, and *u*.
In parallel to the previous case, we will only consider what happens
after three days where either *ddd, nnn*, or *uuu* occurred. In each
case, we evaluate what happens on the fourth day. Is it *d, n*, or *u*? Figure 2.2 displays the results. Once again, the results were well within
what would be expected by chance based on the assumption that *d,
n*, or *u* would be expected to appear with equal probabilities.

These analyses of one, two, three, and four days did not uncover
any evidence that the days when the price went down, days when
the price stayed the same, and days when the price went up were
anything but random. Of course, this does not rule out other types

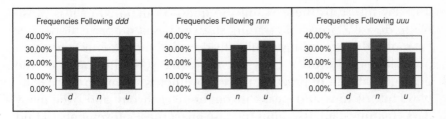

**Figure 2.2**   Frequencies of Price Movements

The three charts show the frequencies of *d* (a down movement), *n* (no change), or *u* (an up movement) following three days of all down, no change, or up movements. Even though there are variations of frequencies in each of the charts, the ranges are well within what could be expected as part of normal variations based on *d*, *n*, and *u* appearing with equal probabilities.

of patterns. For example, perhaps on every fifth trading day the price went up. This would need another type of test. Nevertheless, the evidence is strong that for Microsoft over the period of the study, the occurrence of days when the price went down, stayed the same, or went up is random in that they appear with equal probabilities and are independent of previous occurrences of these price movements. (Over the period of time for this study, there was a negligible overall downward trend in the price of Microsoft. If this was not the case and there was a significant trend in either direction, then it is likely that there would be probabilistic patterns in the occurrence of *d*, *n*, and *u*. For example, if there was a significant upward trend in prices, *u* would be more likely to occur than *d*. However, this is a result of an overall long-term trend and not of true short-term trading patterns.)

As a final comment, the idea of decomposing price movements into discrete possibilities is not as unusual as it may appear at first. For example, a standard approach to valuing option is to approximate price movement into two components, an up movement or a down movement. It is called the *binomial model*. It is used in place of the Black-Scholes method described later in the chapter, particularly when the options are very complex with many side conditions. The basic assumption of the binomial model is that the up movements and down movements are of a fixed proportion and occur randomly.

## Trading Strategies

Despite the preceding results showing that we could not find anything beyond what could be explained by random occurrences over four-day intervals, there is still the question of whether it is possible to devise a profitable trading strategy based on price alone. For example, the preceding results divide price movements into three possibilities: The price goes up, the price stays the same, or the price goes down. In practice, price movements are much more complex, full of dips and peaks throughout each day and over many days. Technical analysis aims to tease apart these movements to find patterns and regularities in order to make forecasts of price movements. These forecasts need to be sufficiently accurate to use as a basis for transactions that are overall profitable. Unfortunately, there is scant evidence showing that consistent profits can be made from trading, with a huge amount of evidence showing the opposite, namely that it is not possible.

A comprehensive study was carried out by David Aronson,[6] looking for profitable trading rules that withstood the tests of careful statistical methods. He back-tested and evaluated 6,402 rules using the S&P 500 Index over the period from November 1, 1980, to July 1, 2005, a period of over 24 years. When you are dealing with as many trading rules as this, even if none of them has any predictive power, just by chance some of them are likely to outperform the market by a significant margin. This problem is called *data mining*. It can lead to the adoption of rules that look as if they should outperform in the future based on past performance. However, the superior past performance is simply the result of chance because of the large numbers of trading rules that were examined. This problem is common with most trading software packages. Inexperienced users search through large databases of historical data to find trading methods that were profitable in the past. If enough rules are examined, they will eventually be found. However, they might not be profitable in the future. (Numerous authors have had fun with this idea of looking at large data sets and talked about the results of having a very large group of monkeys writing on typewriters. Eventually one will come up with a masterpiece.[7]) Fortunately, there are methods that help to test for the bias due to data mining. Aronson uses two of these in his study.[8] Aronson's conclusion is that none of the methods showed a profit above what could be explained by chance. In other words, anyone who employs any of the methods analyzed by Aronson is on very shaky ground if they expect to outperform the market.

**Warning: Claims for Trading Methods**

Be wary of claims regarding trading methods. There is little valid evidence showing that it is possible to get consistent profits from trading and a large amount of evidence showing that it is impossible.

The arithmetical concepts of calculating frequencies and averages and the geometrical concepts of lines and angles form the basis of the great majority of trading software packages. They use computers to perform large numbers of calculations, displaying the results in colorful lists, tables, and charts, but at their core they are only using elementary arithmetical and geometrical concepts. The methods trace back to charting techniques and, despite the attractive computer displays of the results, do not add anything that is fundamentally new.

There are technical analysis methods, however, that do use genuinely advanced mathematics and require large amounts of computer power. These are second-generation methods such as genetic algorithms and neural networks and represent a jump from the ideas just described. Broadly speaking, these methods examine the histories of prices and other data in search of complex patterns and correlations which are then used to make forecasts. These patterns are far beyond anything that can be picked up by scanning the data by eye or by applying the elementary search techniques of standard technical analysis computer programs. Neural networks can arrive at complex relationships between inputs and outputs by undergoing a training or learning period. The input data may be raw data consisting of prices, transaction volumes, and market indexes. As well, it may include derived data such as technical indicators including moving averages, fundamental indicators such as intrinsic value, and economic indicators such as levels of GDP. It is possible to include hundreds of data series when building these models. There is some indication showing that profits can be made using such methods.

In an analysis of 95 modern studies on technical analysis including genetic algorithms and chart patterns, Cheol-Ho Park and Scott H. Irwin found that 56 studies had positive results, 20 studies had negative results, and 19 studies indicated mixed results.[9] Despite the positive evidence on the profitability of some technical trading strategies, the authors assert that most of the empirical studies suffer from various problems in their testing procedures. One problem they mention is *data snooping*, a particular form of data mining. If a researcher tests 100 different trading strategies, even if individually none is expected to yield a positive result, by chance we could expect a handful of strategies to provide a significant outcome. There is now a temptation to publish the positive strategies as examples of profitable trading methods and ignore the failing tests. However, they are merely artifacts produced by chance.

---

### Benjamin Graham Talking about Price Fluctuations

Basically, price fluctuations have only one significant meaning for the true investor. They provide him with an opportunity to buy wisely when prices fall sharply and to sell wisely when they advance a great deal. At other times he will do better if he forgets about the stock market and pays attention to his dividend returns and to the operating results of his companies.

The most realistic distinction between the investor and the speculator is found in their attitude toward stock-market movements. The speculator's primary purpose lies in anticipating and profiting from market fluctuations. The investor's primary purpose lies in acquiring and holding suitable securities at suitable prices.

—*The Intelligent Investor*, p. 205

---

Faulty conclusions due to data snooping can also occur when different researchers independently test the same trading strategy. Suppose 100 different researchers examine a particular trading strategy. Suppose also that the expected performance of the strategy is neutral, meaning that over the long term no money is expected to be gained or lost. As before, just by chance some of the tests will yield significantly positive results. Suppose that there are five positive tests. The researchers responsible for these results are excited and publish their studies. In contrast, the 95 remaining researchers conclude that the trading strategy has no value and move on to other projects. The outcome is that there are five papers describing a particular trading strategy as passing statistical tests, showing that it is profitable. Yet if all the data was collected together and analyzed, the results would be seen as merely chance occurrences. Overall, anyone who thinks they can buy a software trading package off the shelf, perhaps study a few DVDs, and immediately start making money should be very careful.

### Stock Splits and Price Movement

When a company issues two or more shares for every share that is outstanding, it is called a *stock split*. For example, in a two-for-one split, all shareholder receives two shares in place of each single share that they hold. If a company had 20 million shares outstanding before the split, it would have 40 million outstanding after a two-for-one split. Whether and when a stock split is to occur is a decision made by the board of the company.

Strictly speaking, stock splits are only cosmetic since they amount to slicing the same pie into smaller pieces but do not change the proportion of the company owned by the investor nor the proportion of votes available to the investor. The usual reason expressed by the management is that it adds extra liquidity and puts the price in a range that is more accessible and easier to trade. Kent Baker, Aaron Phillips, and Gray Powell state in a survey article on stock splits that "managers report that the main motive for issuing stock splits is to move the stock price into a better trading range...the preferred trading range for these managers is from $20 to $35."[10] For example, if the price was $60 before a two-for-one split, to maintain the market capitalization of the business, the price should be $30 after the split.

To a large extent only the expected change in price takes place after a split: After a two-for-one split the price drops by one-half, after a three-for-one split it drops by two-thirds, and so on. Nevertheless, many see stock splits as more than simply moving the price into a favorable trading range. Based on the assumption that the board knows more about the value of the company than do analysts and shareholders, these investors interpret a stock split as a signal from the board that there is extra value in the company which is not reflected in the price of the stock.

Whatever the reason, academic studies show that when a stock split is announced, after the initial drop, prices rise more than would be expected by chance. For example, Jia Ye proposed and examined a trading rule that was to form a portfolio by buying equal dollar amounts of stocks that announced a two-for-one or three-for-one split. Once in the portfolio, the stocks were only sold after two years provided there were no further splits of the required type. He concluded that a portfolio following this rule outperformed the S&P 500 index by 5.29 percentage points per year over the 18-year period from the start of 1979 to the end of 1996.[11]

The downside of this study for individual investors is common to many academic studies involving trading rules, namely that they are based on holding very large portfolios. Because stocks are chosen using trading rules rather than intrinsic value calculations, their prices tend to be more volatile and their individual trends more dispersed. It requires a large number of stocks to average out the volatility and to achieve consistent results for the final portfolio. This means that the methods, even if they achieve statistically significant results, are usually not suitable for individual investors. For example, Ye's study required an average holding of 228 companies, which is outside the resources of most investors. Another difficulty is that the trading rules examined in academic studies frequently require high levels of trading.

In some cases, companies that have a history of stock splits institute a split in which the price drops below the price of the previous split. After such splits, Robert Conroy and Robert Harris showed that there was an even higher outperformance. They explained it as the board signaling that the prevailing market price was markedly undervaluing the company.[12]

Warren Buffett uses stock splits (or, more accurately, the lack of stock splits) to send a completely different signal to the investor public. As much as possible he deliberately avoids stock splits with Berkshire Hathaway (Berkshire) in order to keep the share price away from favorable trading levels. He wants to discourage trading in the stock and to encourage shareholders who are most likely to hold the shares for the long term. See the box "Warren Buffett, Berkshire Hathaway, and Stock Splits" for more details. Over the past few years, the price of A shares in Berkshire has exceeded $150,000. At these prices, it is not surprising that turnover in A shares is minimal.

Buffett, however, doesn't completely avoid stock splits in the shares of Berkshire. In 1994 he introduced a second class of Berkshire stock called Class B Common Stock with the original stock designated as Class A. Basically each share of the B stock has the rights of 1/30 of an A share and trades at approximately 1/30 of the price. So it was a stock split over a portion of the shares in Berkshire. Later, on November 3, 2009, the company announced that its board had approved a 50-for-1 split of its Class B stock. It was explained that this was necessary as part of Berkshire's purchase of the remaining stock in Burlington Northern Santa Fe Corporation (BNSF). Prior to this Berkshire owned 22.6 percent of the railroad company. Through the split it was able to accommodate holders of smaller amounts of BSNF shares who preferred a share exchange rather than a cash payment.

In rare cases, companies may perform a reverse split such as a one-for-two or a one-for-three split. Generally they occur when there has been a major drop in price and the reverse split is decreed in order, as for normal splits, to bring the price into a more favorable trading range, this time in an upward direction rather than a downward direction. Not surprisingly, the market views reverse splits as a desperate move by the company. A recent study looked at around 1,600 companies that did reverse splits. Allowing for volatility, the authors found that on average the stocks underperformed the market by approximately 50 percent over the three-year period after the split.[13] The reasons for a company proposing a reverse split have to be quite serious. One reason for reverse splits is to lift the share price because many institutional investors and mutual funds have rules against purchasing a stock whose price is below some minimum level. Also, there is a price requirement to be listed on any major exchange, such as $41.00 for the New York Stock Exchange. If a listed company drops below the requirement for an exchange it may be delisted. However, these are not rigid rules. For example, the financial difficulties during 2008 and 2009 caused some exchanges to lower their listing requirements.

The possibility of being delisted was part of the reason why AIG, the insurance and financial services company, announced on May 21, 2009 that they would do a reverse 1-for-20 split on July 1, 2009. According to the announcement by the company, "The primary purpose of the reverse stock split is to increase the per-share trading price of AIG Common Stock. AIG believes a reverse stock split will increase the price of AIG Common Stock, and thus allow a broader range of institutional investors to invest in AIG Common Stock, increase other investor interest in AIG Common Stock, and help ensure the continued listing of AIG Common Stock on the NYSE."

## Warren Buffett, Berkshire Hathaway, and Stock Splits

In the 1983 annual report of Berkshire Hathaway, Warren Buffett talked about stock splits, which at the time had never been enacted by the company.

We often are asked why Berkshire does not split its stock. The assumption behind this question usually appears to be that a split would be a pro-shareholder action. We disagree. Let me tell you why.

One of our goals is to have Berkshire Hathaway stock sell at a price rationally related to its intrinsic business value.... The key to a rational stock price is rational shareholders, both current and prospective....

In large part, however, we feel that high-quality ownership can be attracted and maintained if we consistently communicate our business and ownership philosophy—along with no other conflicting messages—and then let self-selection follow its course. For example, self-selection will draw a far different crowd to a musical event advertised as an opera than one advertised as a rock concert even though anyone can buy a ticket to either....

Through our policies and communications—our "advertisements"—we try to attract investors who will understand our operations, attitudes and expectations.... We want those who think of themselves as business owners and invest in companies with the intention of staying a long time. And, we want those who keep their eyes focused on business results, not market prices....

Were we to split the stock or take other actions focusing on stock price rather than business value, we would attract an entering class of buyers inferior to the exiting class of sellers....

We will try to avoid policies that attract buyers with a short-term focus on our stock price and try to follow policies that attract informed long-term investors focusing on business values. Just as you purchased your Berkshire shares in a market populated by rational informed investors, you deserve a chance to sell—should you ever want to—in the same kind of market. We will work to keep it in existence.

One of the ironies of the stock market is the emphasis on activity. Brokers, using terms such as "marketability" and "liquidity," sing the praises of companies with high share turnover.... But investors should understand that what is good for the croupier is not good for the customer. A hyperactive stock market is the pickpocket of enterprise....

> Splitting the stock would increase [transaction costs] cost, downgrade the quality of our shareholder population, and encourage a market price less consistently related to intrinsic business value. We see no offsetting advantages.

## Efficient Market Hypothesis

Two investors are walking along the street when one says that there is a $10 note lying at the side of the road. When the second investor just keeps walking, she is asked why. "If it was really there," she replies, "someone else would have already picked it up."

This is a fanciful illustration of the efficient market hypothesis. Pure price theories can be thought of as lying on a spectrum with technical analysis on one end and the efficient market hypothesis on the other. As explained earlier, technical analysis proceeds on the hypothesis that a careful study of price movements, perhaps coupled with changes in trading volumes, can be used to make profitable forecasts of prices that consistently beat the market. The efficient market hypothesis is the complete opposite. It concludes that this is impossible because no amount of analysis of past prices or past volumes will allow anyone to consistently outperform the market. This is because the core of the efficient market hypothesis is that the stock market is so efficient that all available information is factored into prices so fast that no one can take advantage of new information or new methods of analysis.[14]

### Efficient Market Hypothesis and Technical Analysis

The efficient market hypothesis states that all information is already factored into the share price and that the price responds immediately to reflect new information. Hence, knowledge of the history of the share price is irrelevant. This is the complete opposite of technical analysis, which states that future movement can often be deduced by knowing the history of the share price.

There may be profitable trading methods. However, the efficiency of the marketplace through the large numbers of people scouring the markets for profits means that a casual search for profitable technical analysis trading rules is unlikely to succeed. Suppose a trader observes that whenever the price of Microsoft goes up on the days Monday through Thursday, then it goes up on Friday. Next suppose that this trader notices on a particular Friday morning that the price has gone up on the previous four days. The natural strategy is to buy on that Friday morning and sell as late as possible during the afternoon. But if one trader notices this, then it is likely that thousands of others will also have seen it. This will mean that it becomes increasingly difficult to buy at a price on Friday morning that will ensure a profit over the day because the price will have been quickly pushed up by the higher number of buyers. Some particularly active traders might start to buy on Thursday afternoon. Others will notice this and buy on Thursday morning. And so it goes on until any advantage of tracking this pattern has been lost. Roughly what is taking place is that as soon as a pattern is observed, sufficient numbers of traders will see it and try to take advantage of it, and so the pattern will be lost. It is as if price patterns with the potential for persistence are consistently destroyed while they are still in an incipient stage.

Even more surprising is the conclusion that analyses of company fundamentals will not help you, according to the efficient market hypothesis, to consistently outperform the market. Suppose an analyst for a brokerage firm carefully studies the financial statements and public announcements of Suntech, a manufacturer of solar panels. The analyst looks at the contracts for sales as well as the contracts it has to maintain its supply of silicon and other essential raw materials. Putting it all together, the analyst reasons that Suntech is undervalued and recommends to the firm's clients that they buy the stock. The problem is that other analysts and investors will also have noticed this. All the information about Suntech is being continuously priced into the stock so rapidly that neither the analysts nor the clients can take advantage of it.

It is the same regarding business and economic forecasts. Prices adapt so quickly to all new information—including, for instance, company insiders buying or selling their stock, and forecasts about the business such as the likelihood of a takeover—that at any moment the prices must be *right* in the sense that they are the best possible estimate of future performance.

At one stage, support for the efficient market hypothesis was so strong that the financial economist Michael Jensen was prompted to write that he believed there to be "no other proposition in economics which has more solid empirical evidence supporting it."[15] Few would take such a view these days, and there are many documented weaknesses to the theory such as the existence of economic bubbles and sudden market crashes. Consider Black Monday (October 19, 1987) when the Dow Jones Industrial Average dropped by 508 points to 1,739, a drop of 22.6 percent. It is not possible under the efficient market hypothesis to suppose that the market "fully reflects all available information" before and after a drop of almost a quarter of its value in a few hours. At different times, it may be that the asset prices are correct or *efficient* compared to other asset prices. The problem is that they could all be wrong. For example, equity prices may have been correct relative to each other before Black Monday. But they were all over valued.

Another example is the pricing of collateralized debt obligations (CDOs) on subprime mortgage bonds before the onset of the global financial crisis in 2008. Relative to each other, they were probably fairly priced. Yet they were all overpriced with the credit ratings agencies failing to properly account for risks such as a nationwide collapse of housing values. Just the same, many studies show that the market is still very efficient.

In the setting of this high efficiency, the role of the investor is to look for corners of inefficiency for individual equities that are overlooked by the market. Warren Buffett summed this up when he wrote, "Observing correctly that the market was frequently efficient, [academics and many investment professionals and corporate managers] went on to conclude incorrectly that it was always efficient. The difference between these propositions is night and day."[16] At a later time, Buffett declared that he would be "a bum on the street with a tin cup if the markets were always efficient."[17]

### Risk and Return

There are a number of significant consequences of the efficient market hypothesis. The first is that the movement of prices of equities can be described by a widely accepted model that has only two interacting components: the general trend of prices (called *return*) and short-term random movements compared to the overall market (called *risk*). (The term *risk* also has a strict statistical definition which we describe later, related to movements of prices. It does not mean the risk of poor business performance of the underlying companies.) Suppose for the moment that the price of Microsoft has no day-to-day randomness. Also suppose that it does not pay any dividends, that there is always a buyer if I wish to sell the stock, and that the business is secure with no risk of collapsing. According to the efficient market hypothesis, its price growth would have to give me the same return as an investment in a secure bond. (If the growth exceeded the return of the bond, buyers would outnumber sellers in order to get the higher return and the price of Microsoft would rise. This would have the effect of lowering the future growth. Conversely, if the growth was lower than that of a bond, investors would sell, or short, Microsoft in order to purchase bonds, causing the price of Microsoft to drop. This would increase the future growth of the stock.)

Next, suppose that the price of Microsoft actually does have random fluctuations. Apart from any overall trend, the greater the fluctuations relative to the market, the riskier the investment since the outcome of any purchase becomes more uncertain. Putting all this together, we arrive at the conclusion that the best we can say about price movement is that every stock has the same basic rate of growth plus an extra rate of growth based on the randomness of the price compared to the randomness of the overall market. In other words, investors look to be compensated by an expected higher rate of return for any extra risk that they are willing to take. This is a qualitative introduction to the famous risk-reward relationship referred to as the capital asset pricing model (CAPM).

The actual risk-return relationship expressed by CAPM has a precise quantitative formulation, which we will outline. First we introduce the concept of the *beta* ($\beta$) of a stock. Suppose that for each small movement of the market the price of Microsoft on average moves by the same amount. Then Microsoft is said to have a beta of 1.0. If the price tends to move twice as much as market movements it is said to have a beta of 2.0. If it only moves by half as much, then it has a beta of 0.5. At the end of 2009 Microsoft had a beta of 0.96 calculated over the previous year. The beta of Wal-Mart was even lower: 0.24. In rare cases it is possible to have a beta that is negative. For example, at the end of 2008 Wal-Mart had a beta of –0.12. This means that on average, when the market went up the price of Wal-Mart tended to go down, and vice versa. In the risk-return relationship, beta is a measure of the risk. Technically, it is the sensitivity of the equity returns to the market returns.

The next two inputs in the CAPM are the risk-free interest rate and a general risk premium. In the United States the risk-free rate is typically the Treasury bill rate. In other countries, it is usually some sort of government rate, interbank rate, or rate derived from complex financial instruments. Let us suppose that the risk-free rate is 2 percent. The general risk premium is the market return that is expected on average over and above the risk-free rate. Let us suppose that the risk premium is 7 percent, meaning that on average investors in the stock market expect their performance to exceed the risk-free rate of 2 percent by 7 percent. We can now state the key conclusion of the capital asset pricing model: The expected return of an equity is the risk-free rate plus beta times the risk premium. Using the preceding numbers, this means that the expected annual return of an investment in Microsoft is $2 + (0.96 \times 7)$, which is 8.72 percent. For Wal-Mart, the expected annual return is $2 + (0.24 \times 7)$, which is 3.68 percent. This is not the place to go into a lengthy analysis of the pros and cons of CAPM. Basically, it is an extreme simplification of the world of investing. It is an example of building a mathematical model of expected equity performance based solely on a statistical analysis of price movements.[18]

## Historical Volatility and Option Pricing

A second consequence of the efficient market hypothesis was the development of a remarkable formula to calculate the fair price of options. Options come in two basic types, call options and put options, both of which can be bought or sold. A *call option* is a contract that gives the right but not the obligation to buy an equity (or any other financial asset or contract) at a specified price at a specified time or period in the future. For example, it could be anytime in the next 12 months, or anytime in the next 24 months but after the first 6 months. Its partner, a *put option*, is identical except that the right to buy is replaced with the right to sell.

Options are a means of transferring risk from one party to another. For example, suppose I purchase shares in Intel for $14.50 but I am worried that the price could drop below $14.00. For a small price, I can purchase a put option that gives me the right to sell for $14 at a time or period in the future. Now I have no risk on the downside since, if the price drops below $14.00, I can ask the counterparty to buy the stock from me for $14.00. At the same time, I can still benefit from any rises in the price of Intel. For a fee, the downside risk has been passed from me over to the purchaser of the put option. Call options and put options are the simplest examples of what are referred to as *derivative contracts* or simply *derivatives*. These are contracts that are *derived* from the value of underlying assets rather than contracts to buy or sell the assets themselves. According to the Options Clearing Corporation, in January 2010 there were almost 210 million open equity option positions on U.S. stock exchanges with approximately 16 million new equity option contracts each day.

Derivatives are used even more in foreign exchange markets. Importers and exporters use them to protect or hedge the risk of exchange rates moving against them for payments that they have to make or receive at specified times in the future. Primary producers and resource companies also use derivatives to hedge against adverse price movements of their products. Asset managers use them to hedge against adverse movements of stock prices. On the other side of the derivative contracts are those individuals or companies who are willing to take on extra risk for a price, just as an insurance company does. Or it may be those who have an opposite risk: an exporter in the United States selling goods in Germany against an importer in Germany buying them. The export side wants to protect against receiving less for the goods because of adverse exchange rate movements, while the import side wants to protect against having to pay more.

The extensive use of options stems from the work of Fischer Black, Robert Merton, and Myron Scholes in developing a formula for calculating their fair value. (In 1997 Merton and Scholes were awarded the Nobel Prize in economics for this work; Black had died a few years earlier and so was not eligible.) The formula is commonly called the Black-Scholes option pricing formula or the Black-Scholes-Merton formula. Even though there is a certain amount of controversy around the formula, it is still indispensable in analysis and modeling of options, at least as a starting point.[19]

Although not as common a practice as it used to be, options also can form a part of the remuneration or bonus packages awarded to management and employees of publicly traded companies. The rationale for this is that there is no cash outlay by the business, so it is more frequently used by newer companies that are holding less cash. Stock options awarded for this purpose are usually priced according to the Black-Scholes formula. In the notes to a company's annual report you will often see a comment such as, "We use the Black-Scholes option pricing model to estimate the fair value of the share-based option awards consistent with the provisions of SFAS No. 123(R)."[20]

A key assumption of the Black-Scholes formula is that the ratio of the prices of shares over any fixed time period is random. As we saw earlier, this is a direct consequence of the efficient market hypothesis. It does not matter whether the time period is hours, days, weeks, or longer, the assumption remains the same: The ratio of prices over each fixed time period is random. This does not prove that these ratios are *actually* random. However, given the reliance on the formula throughout the world's financial institutions and the amount of testing that is carried out, it suggests strongly that they are random—or very close to it. With this starting point, any claims that prices are not random and that it is possible to develop profitable trading methods need to be examined even more closely.

The size of the randomness that is assumed for the Black-Scholes formula is called *volatility*. For the great majority of investors, the key measurement of prices is whether they are trending upward, staying at approximately the same levels, or trending downward. What differs is the time frame of these movements. For day traders, what counts is the nature of the movement during each day; for those looking for long-term value, it could be years or even decades. For many traders, watching price levels is not enough—they also watch the volatility of prices. On some exchanges it is even possible to speculate on changes in volatility of prices rather than merely their direction. As stated earlier, a key assumption in the Black-Scholes formula is that price returns over different time periods are random. More specifically, the assumption is that the returns follow a type of randomness called a *normal distribution*, known in everyday language as a *bell curve* because of its bell-like shape. The width or standard deviation of this distribution on an annualized basis is the formal definition of *volatility* or *historical volatility*.[21]

But watch out! In practice, it generally happens that the distribution of returns has fatter tails and is more peaked than would be observed if they were normally distributed. (This does not mean that daily returns are not random, just that the type of randomness cannot be described using a normal distribution.) The most important consequence is that larger price movements, both up and down, appear (slightly) more frequently than would be expected if the distribution were normal. Generally this is interpreted as price movements being more risky than would appear from a simple analysis because of the higher-than-expected rate of large price movements. You can think of it as prices drifting along without much change when quite suddenly there are large unexpected movements, a genuine sting in the tail. This causes mispricing of options using the Black-Scholes formula.

As an example of these characteristics of equity returns, we analyze the price data for Microsoft. First let's look at some background. Suppose that on two consecutive days the closing prices of Microsoft are $34.62 and $35.03. Dividing the difference between these two prices by the first price shows that the return for the day is 1.18 percent. When this calculation is done day after day, the resulting returns are dispersed over a range of values. When it is calculated on an annualized basis, the standard deviation or average spread of this dispersion is the volatility of the prices.[22] Figure 2.3 shows the result of carrying this out for Microsoft and compares the distribution of daily price returns for Microsoft (the bars) to a normal distribution with the same mean and standard deviation (the curved line).

As foreshadowed, the distribution of returns differs from the normal distribution in two ways: It is weighted more toward very small returns and toward very large returns. In simple terms, compared to the normal distribution, less price movement happens on a day-to-day basis and then, unexpectedly, there are large changes.[23]

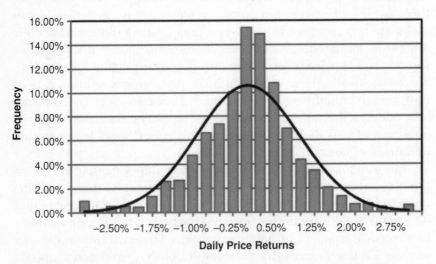

**Figure 2.3**   Frequencies of Daily Price Movements Compared to a Normal Distribution

The bars represent the frequency of daily price returns or percentage movements for Microsoft from January 2003 to December 2008. The smooth line represents the frequencies if the movements were to follow a normal distribution with the same mean and standard deviation. The main features are that the actual frequencies compared to the normal distribution are higher for very low returns and very high returns in both directions. In other words, the distribution of actual returns is more peaked and has fatter tails than the corresponding normal distribution. These features are common to almost all financial data.

Specifically, in terms of the normal distribution in Figure 2.3, daily movement larger than three standard deviations should only happen approximately every 400 days on average, yet it happened for Microsoft every 60 days on average. The pervasiveness of the occurrence of fat tails throughout a large range of phenomena, and not just for financial markets, has recently been explored in great detail by Nassim Nicholas Taleb.[24] It can be a major problem for reinsurers when they are working out their rates. Often they do not have to make a payout for lengthy periods, so there can be a tendency for them to lower their premiums. But then they are suddenly faced with multiple large claims that can damage, even cripple, the company.

Even though in practice the returns are generally not quite normally distributed, they are still almost always very close to it. No mathematical model can be perfect, but the assumption that returns are normal is sufficiently accurate for most situations. When this assumption used in the Black-Scholes formula it creates a slight distortion of the fair value of the options. But the distortion is only minor compared to other assumptions used in the formula such as that volatility must remain constant.

The larger price swings occurring more often than generally expected may be unsettling for the average investor, but in reality they often provide opportunities to buy quality stocks at unexpectedly low prices and to sell at generously high prices. For savvy investors volatility provides the opportunities for higher profits due to buying when stocks are heavily undervalued and selling when they are substantially overvalued. For option traders, volatility is a crucial element that they have to watch closely. The reason for this is that, as just indicated, volatility needs to be incorporated into any pricing models of options.

There is another approach to modeling price movement called the binomial model. The Black-Scholes formula models price movement by assuming that returns over any time period are random and follow a normal distribution. As we saw in Figure 2.3, this is quite an accurate description of what actually takes place. Instead of the normal distribution, the fundamental assumption of the binomial model is that returns can only take one of two values, commonly called an up return and a down return. This means that the movement of prices is approximated by a series of random choices between two possible movements. It is as if a coin is tossed to see whether the price moves up or moves down. Once that is done, the coin is tossed again to decide on the next movement. Repeating this over small time intervals provides an accurate description of price movement. (The flexibility enters by first deciding on the sizes of the price movements and their probabilities.)

This approach is an alternative to the Black-Scholes model for calculating the fair value of options and is used by many public companies. For example, the 10-K report of the kitchen-equipment company Middleby Corporation states, "The fair value of restricted share grant awards for which vesting is subject to market conditions have been estimated using binomial option-pricing models." The binomial approach is particularly useful for complex options with a wide range of side conditions involving such things as vesting periods, dividend strategies, and performance hurdles. From our perspective as investors looking for a rational approach to finding value, the important point about these models is that there is a huge amount of theoretical and empirical evidence showing that, in the short term, equity prices are random.

 **Warning: Randomness of Prices**

There is a huge amount of theoretical and empirical evidence showing that, in the short term, equity prices are random. It takes time for the strengths or weaknesses of a company to replace this randomness as the primary component of the share price. It is this time factor that allows us to benefit from undervalued stocks.

**Slippage, Gaps, and Liquidity**   Even if you are confident that you have found a profitable trading method, there are the dangers of not actually being able to make a trade at the price you specified or planned for. These problems are related to slippage, gaps, and liquidity. *Slippage* refers to the situation where a purchase is executed at a price higher than planned or a sale is executed at a price lower than planned. Slippage can occur in a fast-moving market when only a few trades are made at each price before trading moves to the next price. It can also occur through what is called *gapping*, when a stock trades in a certain range of prices and then the price suddenly jumps to a new range that does not overlap the first one. Consider Microsoft. On Friday, October 3, 2008, it traded in the range $26.24 to

$27.47, closing at $26.32. On Monday, October 6, Microsoft opened below the range of the previous trading day at $25.63 and traded in the range $24.14 to $25.99 throughout the day. Since there was no overlap between these two ranges, gapping occurred.

Less frequently, prices can gap in an upward direction. For example, on July 16, 2008, Bank of America (BAC) traded in the range $19.04 to $22.92 and closed at $22.67. The next day BAC opened at $23.95 and traded in the range $23.80 to $26.50. This is an example of upward gapping since the range on the second day was above the range on the first day with no overlap. On the first day BAC closed at $22.67 and on the second day it closed at $26.50, a gain of 16.9 percent.

One way that can help to avoid losses due to slippage is to use one of the various types of conditional orders. For example, if the current ask price is $24.00 and you place an order to buy, it could be that by the time the order is received the price has moved to $24.25. However, if you place a limit order at $24.00, then the broker is required to fill the order only if a price of $24.00 or less can be achieved. It is even possible to place a limit order at, say, $23.75. In this case, the order will be filled only if the price drops to $23.75. In general terms, a *conditional order* is an order placed with a broker that can only be filled when certain conditions are met. Conditional orders free you from having to constantly monitor the market.

Related to these problems is the occurrence of *low liquidity*, signified by low trading volumes on a day-to-day basis relative to the size of the transaction that you would like to make. This may have the effect of causing a large difference between the price at which you can buy an equity and the price at which you can sell the same equity. This difference is called the *bid-ask spread*. When the equity is traded, it may also have an impact on the price by pushing up the price when buying the equity or pushing it down when it is being sold. Of course, this is only likely to happen when the size of the transaction is large compared to the daily volume.

The problems of slippage, gaps, and liquidity are mostly associated with a short-term market perspective accompanied by high trading activity. The small dollar losses that may be involved in these problems can turn into a significant proportion of overall profits. However, since these losses occur at the times of the transactions, the longer the holding period, the less important are these transactional issues.

**Earnings Surprises**    Slippage and gapping of prices can be created by earnings surprises. All the large companies are followed by 10 or more analysts who regularly provide forecasts of earnings. The forecasts can be for the next few quarters or for one or two years. Analysts may also make forecasts for the average annual growth rate over the next five years. Different financial firms and web sites average these forecasts and create what are referred to as *consensus estimates*. For example, in February 2010, the MoneyCentral web site showed that earnings estimates for Wal-Mart Stores for the current quarter were provided by 23 analysts. Their estimates ranged from a low of $1.05 to a high of $1.16 with an average of $1.12. If the actual earnings exceed $1.12 it is called a *positive earnings surprise*. If they are below $1.12, it is called a *negative earnings surprise*. Often a positive earnings surprise is accompanied by a sudden rise in price, and a negative earnings surprise by a sudden drop in price. One study of more than 22,000 forecasts showed that this is particularly true when there is high agreement among the forecasts provided by the analysts.[25]

## The Bottom Line

1. Prices are continually supplied to us via quotes on stock markets. It is important to see these prices as an opportunity to buy equities that we have already decided we want to buy at prices we want to pay, rather than to rely on price movements to make this decision.
2. Technical analysis methods and the efficient market hypothesis are pure price theories with enthusiastic adherents. Most research, however, suggests that they are a distraction from rational, well-founded methods for investment success.

# CHAPTER 3

## . . . Value Is What You Get

*What is a cynic? A man who knows the price of everything and the value of nothing.*

—Oscar Wilde[1]

*We have received far more than a dollar of market value gain for every dollar of earnings retained.*

—Warren Buffett[2]

When we buy something, we want value. Whether it is a loaf of bread, a used car, a beachside house, or a Lear jet, we want value for every dollar we spend. In some cases, the measurement of this value is personal, such as whether to enroll at an art course at a local community college. In other cases it is more objective: buying a new refrigerator for $100 less than it costs at the store around the corner. Sometimes the value is immediate: buying a sandwich when you are hungry. Other times it may take years or decades for the value to be evident, such as buying land at the edge of a city.

In broad terms, the essence of value is the margin by which our needs are met by an exchange. That margin defines the degree of value. Our concern in the following chapters is more limited than a general investigation of value. It is limited to the measurement of the *monetary* value associated with stock market transactions. The value derives from the spread between our purchase and sales prices combined with the dividends we may have received along the way. This may be within a restricted time frame or it may be open-ended.

In the previous chapter we viewed price as objective—at each moment the market specifies the price and we choose whether to buy or sell, or do nothing. In contrast, even though intrinsic value is defined as the true value of a unit of stock, in practice it is highly subjective with many competing definitions and calculations that result in a wide variety of outcomes. These outcomes become even more diverse depending on the inputs into the calculations. In this chapter I bring these two components together and present real value as a combination of the price of the stock and its intrinsic value, a combination of objective and subjective factors.

## Value and Stock Market Transactions

Value is a slippery concept. It is the fact that we all have different ideas of what represents value that causes transactions actually to take place. For example, if I walk into a store and buy a loaf of bread, at that moment I value the loaf of bread more than or equal to the money that I pay. If this were not the case, then I would not make the purchase. From the other side, the store owner values the money more than or equal to the bread; otherwise, once again, the transaction would not take place.

It is the same in any stock market. Transactions take place because the seller decides that the money to be gained from the sale is at least as valuable as owning the parcel of shares. At the same time, the buyer believes the opposite is true: Owning the parcel of shares has more value than the money needed to complete the transaction. You can actually think of the stock market as buying and selling based on one's assessment of value. If you believe the price of a stock represents sufficiently good value, you may decide to buy. Of course, the person selling to you thinks that the cash from such a transaction represents better value than owning the stock. The irony is that both sides see the other person as giving up value and passing it over to them. The nub of the problem is that everyone has their own ideas of what represents value. In the context of this book and the later chapters on the different ways of measuring intrinsic value, we start by defining value as a relationship between intrinsic value and price. We describe this now and follow it up later with a broader discussion of value. (For simplicity, we will continue to talk about the intrinsic value of an equity, but what is really meant is the intrinsic value of an equity calculated according to a particular method with specified inputs and assumptions.)

Clearly, intrinsic value on its own tells us nothing about the attractiveness of a possible investment. As an example, if the intrinsic values of two equities are $100 and $50, we cannot tell which is likely to be the more profitable investment. We also need their prices or market values. Once we know the intrinsic value of an equity *and* its price, their ratio provides us a measure of value: The higher the intrinsic value over the price, the greater the value; and, conversely, the lower the intrinsic value beneath the price, the less the value. The reason we can say this follows from the assumptions of the firm-foundation theory described in Chapter 1. The basic assumption is that over time, price moves toward intrinsic value. The secondary assumption is that stocks that are more undervalued will initially rise in price more quickly than those that are less undervalued.

To formalize the relationship between price and intrinsic value, we introduce the *value ratio* as the ratio of intrinsic value to price. By the very definition of intrinsic value, a value ratio of 1.0 provides the dividing line between a purchase that adds value and one that subtracts value: The higher the value ratio is above 1.0, the greater the value, and the lower the value ratio is below 1.0, the less the value. In symbols, we say that the value ratio (VR) is $V/P$, where $V$ is the intrinsic value and $P$ is the price.

Before going further, it is worth pointing out that *value* is a very overworked word with many different meanings. When I use the word *value* on its own, I mean it in the sense of "the worth of something compared to its price" (*Concise Oxford English Dictionary*, 2004). In the setting of the stock market, this means the intrinsic value of a stock compared to its market value or price. If it is necessary to place emphasis on this meaning of value, I will use the term *real value*.

### Real Value = Intrinsic Value + Price

Real value comes from combining intrinsic value and price: The greater the intrinsic value compared to the price, the greater the real value. The value ratio is defined as the ratio of intrinsic value divided by price.

In the previous example of two equities with intrinsic value $100 and $50, suppose their prices are $80 and $75, respectively. In the first case the value ratio is $100/80 = 1.25$, and in the second case it is $50/75 = 0.67$. Hence the first equity represents more value as a

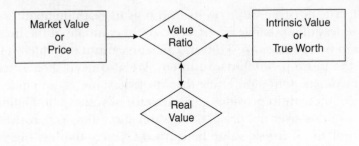

**Figure 3.1**     The Components of Value

possible investment rather than the second one. Figure 3.1 illustrates the relationship between intrinsic value or true worth, market value or price, and the value ratio.

Figure 3.1 also links the value ratio with real value. This relationship, however, is more personal. Table 3.1 gives an indication of an association between the two. For example, allowing for uncertainties in the inputs and calculations, we could say that a stock with a value ratio above two represents excellent value. Other circumstances that may affect the required levels of the value ratio are the risks of the company in areas such as its market capitalization, debt levels, track record of sales and earnings, and product strength and differentiation.

### Value and Value Investing

The standard definition of *value investing* is focusing on stocks that have low price/earnings ratios or low price/book ratios. The other end of the scale is *growth investing* in which the focus is on stocks that have high price/earnings ratios or high price/book ratios. The rationale for growth investors to pay these higher prices for each

**Table 3.1**     Value in Terms of the Value Ratio

| Value Ratio | Value |
| --- | --- |
| Above 2.0 | Excellent |
| Between 1.25 and 2.0 | Good |
| Between 1.00 and 1.25 | Above average |
| Between 0.75 and 1.00 | Below average |
| Below 0.75 | Poor |

dollar of earnings is the anticipation that the earnings will grow at a faster rate than the average for all companies. Warren Buffett and others have criticized this distinction as artificial. In the 1991 annual report of Berkshire Hathaway, Buffett explained that in his view it is a result of "fuzzy thinking." He continued:

> In our opinion, the two approaches are joined at the hip: Growth is *always* a component in the calculation of value, constituting a variable whose importance can range from negligible to enormous and whose impact can be negative as well as positive. In addition, we think the very term "value investing" is redundant. What is "investing" if it is not the act of seeking value at least sufficient to justify the amount paid? Consciously paying more for a stock than its calculated value—in the hope that it can soon be sold for a still-higher price—should be labeled speculation (which is neither illegal, immoral nor—in our view—financially fattening).[3]

Whether you search for value in low-growth stocks or high-growth stocks, the goal is the same: to find value.

When searching for value in the context of intrinsic value, the fundamental assumption of the firm-foundation theory that price tends to move toward intrinsic value implies that, over time, the value ratio will tend toward 1.0. Early in his career, Warren Buffett had the opportunity to ask Benjamin Graham about this tendency. During 1954–1956, Buffett worked for Graham at Graham-Newman in New York and before that he studied under him at Columbia. While working for Graham, he asked how we can be sure that a stock that is undervalued by the market will eventually rise. In a 1974 interview in *Forbes*, Buffett said that Graham "just shrugged and replied that the market always eventually does. He was right—in the short run, it's a voting machine, in the long run, it's a weighing machine." Buffett continued, "Today on Wall Street they say, 'Yes, it's cheap, but it's not going to go up.' That's silly. People have been successful investors because they've stuck with successful companies. Sooner or later the market mirrors the business."[4]

Of course, if the movement of the price toward the intrinsic value is too slow, then the return may be modest. There is a big difference between a stock doubling in price in a few years compared to its taking a decade or more. In addition, if the time lag is too great, other factors may arise and change the assumptions in the initial calculations of the equity's intrinsic value. For this reason, even once a purchase is made, it is important to continue to monitor the ratio between intrinsic value and price. Suppose a stock is purchased because the price is markedly lower than the intrinsic value. If later factors lower the calculation of intrinsic value relative to price, the equity may no longer be attractive to hold. Selling the equity at this point may be the rational choice. The factors could be a decline in earnings, dividends, or other inputs into calculation, resulting in lower intrinsic value calculations. Conversely, the price may have risen so high relative to the intrinsic value that, once again, selling is a sound choice.

The vulnerability of the intrinsic value to changing factors is higher when the calculation of the intrinsic value involves longer-term forecasts. We will come back to this topic when discussing the various methods used to calculate intrinsic value. In particular, it will be crucial to address how far into the future we are required to make forecasts of input variables for our calculations. We will also need to assess the vulnerability of the results of the calculations to changes in these input variables.

**Value Ratio: The Chicken *and* the Egg**     There is no need to calculate intrinsic value as an actual stand-alone amount in order to determine whether the equity is likely to represent value. As we have just seen, what is needed is the value ratio (VR), which is the ratio of intrinsic value to price; both intrinsic value *and* price are combined in the value ratio. This means that it is not necessary to start with a specific calculation of intrinsic value $V$; quite the opposite. In many cases the calculation of the VR is simpler, with the process giving more insight, if price is incorporated right at the start, as opposed to first calculating intrinsic value and later comparing it with price $P$. This may seem like a small point. But given a general vulnerability to behavioral biases described later in this chapter, if a new or changed viewpoint has a more intuitive basis, the benefits can be significant.

Consider the dividend discount method described later in Chapter 8. This method states that intrinsic value is the discounted value of all the dividends paid out by a company over its life. However, dividends on their own tell us little about the attractiveness of an investment. The attractiveness, or otherwise, depends on the financial outlay required to receive these dividends. For example, two stocks may both pay an annual dividend of $1.00. But there is a big difference if one stock is available for $100 and the other for $10. In other words, what is more important than the actual dividends is the ratio of dividends to price, the *dividend yield*. With this in mind, when we use the dividend discount method and head straight for the VR as a whole instead of going via a calculation of intrinsic value *V*, we see that the value ratio is the discounted value of all the forward dividend yields of a company over its life. The primary focus shifts to dividend yields and their contribution to the value ratio and away from merely the sizes of the dividends.

The same shift of focus occurs with the other discount methods. For example, in the discounted cash flow method described in Chapter 7, the ratios of free cash flow to price become central, rather than the free cash flows themselves. It is not a question of whether the chicken (the price) or the egg (the intrinsic value) comes first or which one is more important, but rather that they are both needed in the final result. This understanding will be particularly important in the ratio payback methods in Chapter 9 and the price ratio methods in Chapter 11, which deliberately include price right from the start.

## Hindsight Value

Returning to general issues regarding value, to know whether a purchase actually represents good value requires the passing of time. No matter what sort of bargain you think it is, it is only after a certain amount of time that you can be certain of this. Andrew Smithers refers to this as *hindsight value*.[5]

Suppose you purchase a used car for a price that you consider is an absolute steal. It is only after owning it, and most likely using it, for a period of time that you can know whether this is true. In rare circumstances the period of ownership may only be minutes. For instance, as soon as you have signed the papers, someone comes along and offers you a price that is so much higher that you accept it on the spot. This would be akin to the price of a stock rising so significantly as soon as you have made your purchase that you decide to sell it immediately.

A second and more likely scenario is that you own the car for a number of years, after which you resell it or scrap it. After you have done this, you can decide whether your original purchase provided value or not. You would do this by taking into account the service the car has provided, the running costs, and the sale price (which would be zero in the case of scrapping the car). This is similar to purchasing a stock and holding it for a period of time. When you sell, taking into account the dividends that you have received and the final selling price, you can say whether the original purchase represented value.

There is a third ownership scenario that lets you know whether you made a good choice before selling or scrapping the car. It is the case where the service that you receive from the car grows to a level greater than what you originally paid for the vehicle. In this case you know that you have received value even if you neither sell the car nor scrap it. In the stock market this would be similar to the case where the dividends received are such that they have covered the original purchase price irrespective of any changes in the stock price. The over-arching point is that no matter how confident you are at the time of the transaction, value is always uncertain. It is only with hindsight that this uncertainty can be reduced or even eliminated.

## Behavioral Biases

A major obstacle to performing a rational calculation of intrinsic value, whether on its own or combined with price, is that we all have unconscious biases. Some of the ways these biases may influence us include:

- We may have different biases about the most suitable method to calculate value.
- Even if there is agreement on the method, we may have different biases on the values of the inputs.
- Even if there is agreement on the methods and the inputs, we may have different biases on how to interpret the results and what course of action should be taken.

Biases in the market place come under the general title of behavioral investing, an active and lively area of research. The biases can be grouped under the areas of (1) heuristic simplification, covering the ways we introduce various rules of thumb in decision making; (2) frame dependence, covering the ways in which decisions depend on the form or setting of the problem; and (3) social biases, covering the ways we are influenced by others. There is a large literature on behavioral biases; we will just give a few examples from each of these three areas.

> ### The Effect of Behavioral Biases
>
> Behavioral biases often prevent us from performing a rational calculation of intrinsic value or a rational analysis of intrinsic value and price.

In their key 1974 paper,[6] Amos Tversky and Nobel laureate Daniel Kahneman described an experiment where people were asked questions such as the percentage of African nations in the United Nations. Before they answered, a wheel of fortune with the numbers 1 to 100 was spun in front of them. The wheel was rigged to give only the results 10 or 65 on each spin. The median response to the preceding question for those who saw the wheel display the number 10 was 25, and the median response for those that saw 65 was 45. Even though the participants knew that the data was irrelevant and believed that it was random, it still influenced their answers. This effect is known as *anchoring*, and is an example of heuristic simplification.

In the stock market, investors frequently anchor their decisions on information that they are familiar with, even though there may be little or no evidence that it has any bearing on the outcome. For example, Werner de Bondt[7] looked at over 21,000 predictions by investors over the period 1987 to 1992. He found that their predictions for movements in the Dow Jones Industrial Index for the following six months were influenced by the movement of the index during the week prior to the survey. A rise in the index significantly increased the percentage of bullish investors, and a fall in the index significantly increased the percentage of bearish investors. The conclusion was that investors, observing short-term trends, anchored their opinions on these trends by assuming that they would continue over longer periods in the future.

Even the professionals in the area seem to be caught in the anchoring trap, particularly in areas where very long-term forecasts need to be made. In the discount models covered in Chapters 7 and 8, one of the key inputs is the *discount rate*. This is the percentage rate that is required by investors (creditors, owners, and other providers of capital) to compensate for the risks associated with the company. In the discount methods, forecasts for this rate have to be made for an infinite number of years. Hence it would seem that the forecasts for this rate would vary considerably between companies. Yet this is not the case. There are actually only slight differences, 1 or 2 percent, between analyst forecasts for large international icon companies with massive cash reserves and for small national businesses in highly competitive industries. Another key variable in discount methods is the forecast of the long-term growth rate. Again, this seems to vary little between companies, even when they are widely divergent in size, sector, and capital structure. This suggests that forecasts and estimates in valuation formulas are vulnerable to the bias of anchoring, with this vulnerability highest in the area of key inputs in discount valuation methods.

Turning to frame dependence, in the stock market this potential bias shows up through the attitudes people have toward gains and losses. It is common for people to make one decision if a problem is framed in terms of gains and a very different decision if it is framed in terms of losses. The following is an experiment that I regularly carry out in my investment workshops. This experiment (with different numbers) was first conducted by Kahneman and Tversky. Consider two scenarios involving a simple choice between two alternatives:

> **Scenario 1.** In addition to whatever you own, you have been given $1,000. Which of the following two alternatives would you choose?
>
> **A1:** A sure gain of a further $500.
>
> **B1:** A 50 percent chance of gaining a further $1,000 and a 50 percent chance of gaining nothing.

After asking this question of the workshop participants, I ask them to put it out of their minds as best they can and consider a second scenario, again involving a simple choice between another two alternatives.

> **Scenario 2.** In addition to whatever you own, you have been given $2,000. Which of the following two alternatives would you choose?
>
> **A2:** A sure loss of $500.
>
> **B2:** A 50 percent chance of losing $1,000 and a 50 percent chance of losing nothing.

In scenario 1, regularly 80 to 90 percent of the participants choose option A1 with the remainder choosing option B1. The sure gain of

$500 is more appealing for most than a 50-50 chance of $1,000 or nothing. When it comes to the second scenario, the responses are usually the complete opposite: Roughly 80 to 90 percent choose option B2 with the remainder choosing option A2. This time most of the participants find that the 50-50 gamble is more appealing. The surprise is that on closer inspection, the first options in both scenarios have exactly the same outcomes as do the second options in both scenarios. In both scenarios, the first option results in walking away with $1,500 and the second option results in a 50-50 chance of walking away with $1,000 or $2,000.

Despite the equivalence of the scenarios, most people switch from the first option in scenario 1 to the second option in scenario 2 because of the way the choices are framed. The evidence from the results of the first scenario is that generally people do not want to gamble if the expected return is the same as the guaranteed profit. In contrast, in the second scenario where it was framed so that one of the options was a sure loss (even though they received an extra $1,000 at the start), they were willing to gamble to avoid this occurring. In simple terms, the pain of loss is stronger than the joy of success.

One of the most pervasive examples of a social bias, the third group of behavioral biases in the stock market, is *herding*. This is the tendency to take particular actions because most others are doing it. Herding is considered one of the prime causes of market bubbles and market crashes. Robert Olsen explains that another example of herding behavior can be seen in the results of earnings forecasts by analysts. He observes that experts' earnings forecasts exhibit a positive bias and a disappointing level of accuracy. After conducting a study of 4,000 corporate earnings estimates by company analysts, Olsen concludes that an explanation for this is that the human desire for consensus leads to herding behavior among earnings forecasters. The forecasters appear to be concerned about being in line with consensus forecasts rather than relying on independent analysis.[8]

## The Selling Dilemma

Many investors feel comfortable making choices about when to buy equities based on value but are much less confident when it comes to selling. Evidence for this statement is the range of contradictory adages that are commonly stated to guide—or justify—selling decisions. If the price of a purchase goes down, we commonly hear, "Don't sell until it comes back to the price you paid for it" as well as the conflicting, "Always use stop-loss orders to sell automatically if the price drops by 10 percent." In the opposite direction, if the price goes up, two common sayings are "Always lock in your profit" and "You can't go wrong taking a profit." These are in direct disagreement with another saying: "Let your profits run."

The first thing to realize is that these adages are based on price movements and not on estimates of the value of the equities being considered. In other words, they are trading rules from charting or technical analysis and are not principles based on value measurements. Once we analyze the dilemma from the perspective of value, everything falls into place. The truth is that at each point in time, no matter what happened in the past, the decision for each equity in a portfolio is always how to maximize the value in the future. Putting aside issues such as capital gains taxes and transaction costs, it is irrelevant whether the current price is above or below the purchase price. The general rule is that the time to sell is when we are very confident that we will get significantly more value for our money elsewhere.

### The Value Rule for Selling

The value rule for selling is to monitor your portfolio and sell only when you are very confident you will get significantly more value for your money elsewhere.

Two phrases in the preceding sentence need to be emphasized: *very confident* and *significantly more value*. Such a sell-buy transaction pair only makes sense if all the signs indicate that the new investment will perform significantly better than the old one. We do not start dancing in and out of stocks because we believe one is going to outperform another by only a few percent. As stated, this is only a general rule to decide whether to sell or not. For example, you may sell because you need the cash. But, of course, if this is the case, at that point the cash has more value for you than any of the anticipated benefits of owning the equities. Other reasons to sell could be to move to riskier or less risky investments, to realize tax losses, or to rebalance your portfolio. Also, you need to take into account the amount of confidence and understanding you may have built up with the original company versus the proposed new company.

Moving from a familiar company to an unfamiliar one adds a certain amount of risk.

A corollary of the preceding selling rule is do not sell until you know what you are going to do with the money. Research by Brad Barber and Terrance Odean[9] shows that when people sell, on average the stocks they buy underperform the ones they sell, the complete opposite of what is intended. The authors identify one of the reasons for this outcome as the tendency for investors to be overconfident about their ability to interpret information. (Overconfidence about our abilities is another behavioral bias.) It may also be that after selling, especially if they have made a profit, they are in a rush to get back into the market and do not spend sufficient time evaluating their new investments before purchasing.

It is interesting to note that the selling rule described earlier can have a wider application if we take an expanded view of the concept of value. For example, it may be that the price of an equity in your portfolio has gone up so much that more value would be obtained by selling the stock and putting the money in an interest-bearing bank account rather than another equity. If this intention is clear before the sale, then there is likely to be more comfort in having the money in the bank with less anxiety about having to get back into the market as quickly as possible. There may be more chance of avoiding the phenomenon observed by Barber and Odean just described, namely buying stocks that underperform the ones that were sold. An even broader interpretation of the rule would be allowing yourself to decide whether you would get more value by selling a particular stock and taking your family or friends on a holiday to Cancún.

### What about Buy-and-Hold?

The buy-and-hold strategy is that whenever you buy equities in a company, you are going to hold them forever, or at least for a very long time, without regard to their price. This makes little sense. For example, if the price has run up so much that they are now highly overvalued and that there are clear opportunities to get a significantly better return elsewhere, what would be the point in continuing to hold? Just the same, a quick search on the Internet shows that many people argue for such a strategy. Let us have a brief look at some of these arguments (including the opinion of many that this is what Warren Buffett does) with the aim of improving our own investing knowledge and strategies.

**Value Investing**   Some seem to equate buy-and-hold with value investing. However, they are not the same. Value investing simply means looking for investments that represent real value. As explained earlier, once purchased, they are held so long as no other investments would allow you to get significantly higher value with confidence. Generally this means a long-term view without being influenced by short-term market and price fluctuations. However, it does not mean holding regardless of the price.

**Efficient Market Hypothesis**   In Chapter 2 we briefly introduced the efficient market hypothesis that all equities trade at their fair value. If this is the case, then it does not matter what and when we buy (apart from risk associated with beta). So buy-and-hold makes the most sense since it minimizes transaction and taxation costs. However, this hinges on accepting the efficient market hypothesis, which, as we explained, has few followers these days.

**Is Buffett a Buy-and-Hold Investor?**   Many people argue that Warren Buffett is a buy-and-hold investor and therefore it makes sense for us do the same. But there is much evidence that this is not the case, starting with a comment by Alice Schroeder, who had extensive access to Buffett when she was writing *The Snowball: Warren Buffett and the Business of Life*. She thinks that "the biggest misconception about him is that he is a 'buy and hold forever investor.' " According to Schroeder, "He has never said that, but people take little snippets and slices of things that he said, and they turn them into mantras or slogans."[10]

Even a casual analysis of his records shows that he regularly buys equities but does not hold them indefinitely regardless of price. As a specific example, during 2002 and 2003, Berkshire bought 1.3 percent of PetroChina Company Limited for $488 million, a price that valued the entire business at about $37 billion. In the 2007 annual report, Buffett wrote that at the time, "Charlie and I then felt that the company was worth about $100 billion." By 2007, its price had dramatically increased to a level, according to Buffett, that was comparable to "other giant oil companies." Buffett sold the holding for about $4 billion. This is just one example. For around 10 years Berkshire has been required by the SEC to report its holding each quarter using a 13F form. These forms can be used to track all the transactions of the company.

Regarding the statements made by Buffett that some interpret as indicating that he is a buy-and-hold investor, they merely say that for a select few companies, he "expects" to hold them permanently. For example, in the 1986 annual report, he wrote: "We should note that we expect to keep permanently our three primary holdings, Capital Cities/ABC, Inc., GEICO Corporation, and the *Washington Post*. Even if these securities were to appear significantly overpriced, we would not anticipate selling them." Since that time, Capital Cities/ABC was bought by the Walt Disney Company. This gave Berkshire a large holding in Disney, which it has subsequently sold. GEICO is now a fully owned subsidiary of Berkshire and the holding in the *Washington Post* is unchanged.

Ten years later, in the 1996 annual report of Berkshire, Buffett introduced the idea of "The Inevitables" and said that Coca-Cola and Gillette could have this label. Since that time, Gillette has been bought by Procter & Gamble. Berkshire has sold some of the shares that it received as part of this sale but still has a very large holding. Apart from stock splits, Berkshire's holding in Coca-Cola is unchanged since 1994.

The upshot is that, with a few exceptions, Buffett regularly adds to and subtracts from the great majority of the Berkshire holdings in publicly traded companies. (However, as we will see later in the chapter, this is not the case for companies fully owned by Berkshire.)

As we move through the valuation methods in the later chapters, it makes most sense to take a long-term view when buying to allow time for the market to recognize the value and to ignore short-term business and market fluctuations. But this does not mean "buy and hold." Even though a long-term perspective is taken when buying, it is just as important to continue to monitor your portfolio and sell when you are confident that you can do significantly better elsewhere.

### Time, Risk, and Size

Even when we restrict ourselves to value in a financial setting and overcome—or at least recognize—our behavioral biases, there are still three difficulties: time, chance, and size. Any final assignment of value needs to incorporate and make allowance for these three attributes.

Consider time. Earlier we talked about the importance of time in being able to make a final evaluation of whether a strategy provided value or not. Time also enters when we have to compare events that occur in different periods. Suppose we are offered $100 now or a guaranteed $100 in one year. The rational choice would be to take the immediate payment. The reason for this is that the $100 could be invested in a guaranteed bank deposit in order to receive more than $100 in one year. Suppose, instead, that we are offered $100 now or a guaranteed $200 in one year. Except in a case of extreme immediate need, in most economies the rational choice would be to take the $200 in one year since it would be extremely unlikely that an immediate $100 could be converted to $200 in one year. This means that somewhere between $100 and $200 there is an equilibrium amount, such that we see it as equal value to accept the $100 now or the equilibrium amount in one year. In technical terms, what we are talking about is the time-value of money and how it has to be incorporated in any value calculations or judgments.

Next let us look at risk. Suppose that the payment in one year is not guaranteed. For example, suppose there is a 90 percent chance of receiving payment in full and a 10 percent chance of a complete default. We would increase the preceding equilibrium amount to compensate for the risk of not receiving anything. In the stock market, investors seek a higher return whenever the risks associated with a particular company are higher. (We saw how this requirement of a higher return to compensate for the risk is built into the capital asset pricing model outlined in the previous chapter, where risk is defined in terms of the beta of the stock.)

To see how size enters, suppose you are offered a choice with an equal chance of receiving $5 or paying $1. Most people would accept this choice, reasoning that losing $1 is not a major consequence compared to the chance of gaining $5. Instead, suppose the amounts were $500 and $100. Then fewer people would accept the choice since losing $100 is a more serious outcome than losing $1. As the amounts increase, say to $5,000 and $1,000 or to $50,000 and $10,000, the number of people accepting this choice would decline. In real-life situations, investors may happily adopt particular investment strategies for a certain proportion of their portfolios but would not apply them to their full portfolios.

In summary, suppose we are completely happy both with the method we intend to use to calculate intrinsic value and with the input variables. Whether the outcome has enough value when compared to the price to make a purchase also depends on the timing, the risks involved, and the size of the transaction.

## Ethical Issues and Value

Another issue is whether, for social, ethical, or personal reasons, we want to include other forms of value in the decision process. For example, Warren Buffett regularly writes in the annual report of Berkshire that he and Charlie Munger, the company's vice chairman, have an "attitude . . . that hurts our financial performance: Regardless of price, we have no interest at all in selling any good businesses that Berkshire owns. We are also very reluctant to sell sub-par businesses as long as we expect them to generate at least some cash and as long as we feel good about their managers and labor relations." This is a clear statement of the fact that Buffett and Munger attach significance to continuity of ownership and labor relations as part of their evaluation of investments.[11]

Other investors may consider ethical issues when they assess companies in areas such as the manufacture and sale of alcohol or tobacco products, the provision of gambling products or services, the development and use of genetically engineered foods, or revenues gained from the nuclear energy industry. There is also the area of labor relations just mentioned and fully respecting labor laws at home and abroad. Thinking through issues such as these while looking at the impact of the products and services of companies on society and the environment is part of being a conscious investor.

## The Bottom Line

1. In the stock market, the firm-foundation theory states that over time, price moves toward intrinsic value.
2. Assuming that price moves toward intrinsic value, a second aspect of value is how quickly this movement takes place. Hence, value comes from combining intrinsic value and price: The greater the intrinsic value compared to the price, the greater the value.
3. An awareness of behavioral biases, such as a strong aversion to losses leading to the retention in a portfolio of poorly performing businesses, is a key aspect of all value analyses involving intrinsic value and price.

CHAPTER 4

# Follow the Money

*Learn all the accounting that you can.*

—Warren Buffett[1]

*The purpose of financial reporting is to obtain cheap capital.*

—Martin Fridson and Fernando Alvarez[2]

**M**ost publicly held companies are extremely complex, receiving millions and often billions of dollars in revenue each year via a huge range of operations managed through a maze of cash transactions, sales contracts, and loan facilities. On top of this, those with overseas sales and operations will have sophisticated arrangements to handle the problems associated with sales being made in various currencies. Consider the U.S. companies in the Standard & Poor's 500 Index. Over the 12 months ending April 2010, they had average annual sales of $18.1 billion, net income of $1.1 billion, and long-term debt of $8.7 billion. This massive amount of financial information has to be compressed and summarized in such a way that it is possible for an individual to have a reasonable idea of the level of current financial health of a company, how it compares with previous years, and its strengths and weaknesses compared to other companies in its sector and the wider market. The financial statements and their associated notes aim to achieve this by presenting the data in standardized formats following what are referred to as generally accepted accounting principles (GAAP). Putting it simply, the financial statements allow you to "follow the money."

## A Basic Understanding of Accounting

There are two reasons why it is important to have at least a basic understanding of accounting principles and financial statements when using valuation formulas. The first reason is that the inputs of the formulas are made up of data taken directly or indirectly from the financial statements. Direct data includes items such as sales, net profit, assets, and liabilities. Indirect items that are often required can be calculated from entries in the financial statements and include ratios such as return on equity and dividend payout ratio. Hence it is important to know where to look for these items—which financial statements and their whereabouts in these statements. In many cases different companies will use different names for the same entity, so it is also important to have knowledge of these variations to ensure that you are not sidetracked before you have properly started. (Brief definitions of the most common specialized accounting terms are listed in the Glossary at the end of the book.)

The second reason that accounting knowledge is important is that it lets you apply levels of confidence to any forecast that you are required to make in the formulas. For example, suppose the income statements of two companies look essentially the same. Based on this, you may make similar forecasts for their earnings over the next year. Or, if you are going to use forecasts made by analysts, you may find that two analysts make similar forecasts. However, suppose a closer reading of the balance sheet shows that the first company has considerably more debt than the second one. This may cause you to have less confidence in the forecasts for the first company, leading you to require a higher safety margin.

### Role of Financial Statements

Financial statements give us a window into the operations of a company and provide the material for intrinsic value calculations.

Financial statements give us a window into the operations of a company. As outsiders we cannot really know the level of creativity and strategic thinking of management or how thoroughly they weigh their options before making decisions. We can know little of the management style or the morale within a company. Nevertheless, in the end what we are after is confidence in any measurements or forecasts that need to be made regarding the assets or profits of the company in order to perform intrinsic value calculations. An understanding of the key features of the financial statements is important for achieving this goal.

There are two opposing views of financial statements. The first is that they provide an unbiased presentation of the financial picture of the company. The bookkeepers, accountants, and financial officers employed by the company have followed the rules established through GAAP and have arrived at essentially the only possible set of numbers. Furthermore, if there is any doubt, we can be reassured that the financial statements have been scrutinized by an independent auditing firm which has given a final seal of approval.

We know that there are companies that have a criminal intent and as a consequence present a fraudulent set of accounts: the Enrons of the world. As individual investors we hope that these cases are rare and that the auditors and sharp-eyed independent analysts will pick up any problems before too much damage is done. Putting aside such extreme cases, the supporters of this benign view of accounting would likely agree with Howard Schilit:

> The primary goal of financial reporting is the dissemination of financial statements that accurately measure a company's profitability and financial condition.[3]

The opposing view of financial statements is that those preparing the statements have an underlying agenda, namely to present the company in the best possible light. The proponents of this view argue that there is sufficient flexibility in what is required to be included and in the way it is presented that a misleading impression of the profitability and success of the company may be evoked.

Martin Fridson and Fernando Alvarez write about the "adversarial nature of financial reporting."[4] From this perspective it is important to be vigilant and skeptical, much like lawyers in a court case. Both sides are required to be honest, but this does not stop them from doing all they can to play up the positive side of the results and downplay the negative side.

As an example, if a financial item is not considered to be *material*, it does not have to be included in the relevant financial statements.

However, there is some flexibility in just what is material and what is immaterial. Commenting on this, Arthur Levitt, a former chairman of the U.S. Securities and Exchange Commission (SEC), in a speech to the NYU Center for Law and Business declared:

> ... some companies misuse the concept of materiality. They intentionally record errors within a defined percentage ceiling. They then try to excuse that fib by arguing that the effect on the bottom line is too small to matter. If that's the case, why do they work so hard to create these errors? Maybe because the effect can matter, especially if it picks up that last penny of the consensus estimate.[5]

In other words, some companies may consistently exaggerate their strong points and play down their weak points but at such a low level that they slip under the radar of their auditors and the SEC. They do this while keeping an eye on the consensus estimates of analysts. For example, they may want to avoid any negative earnings surprises because often they cause a drop in price. Similarly, getting a positive earnings surprise of just a single cent can have a favorable effect on the share price. Microsoft was famous (or infamous) for having a positive earnings surprise for 12 quarters in a row.

### Principal Financial Statements

After some preparation, this chapter will look at the four principal financial statements prepared by publicly traded companies. They are:

1. *Balance sheet*. Also referred to as the statement of financial position or condition, it gives a snapshot of a company's assets, liabilities, and net equity at the end of the reporting period.
2. *Income statement*. Also referred to as the profit and loss statement (or P&L), it covers the revenues or sales and expenses over the reporting period.
3. *Cash flow statement*. Also referred to as the statement of cash flows, it covers the cash flows of a company in the areas of operating, investing, and financing activities.
4. *Equity statement*. Also referred to as the statement of changes in shareholders' (or stockholders') equity, it covers all the items that change the equity of a company over the reporting period.

**Warning: Accounting Requirements**

It is very easy to become weighed down by the amount of accounting knowledge that you may believe you need to have. For prudent investors it is important to have a reasonable understanding of accounting principles. However, there are thousands of books on accounting and it could become an overwhelming pursuit to achieve any sort of mastery of the subject. Our job as investors rather than professional accountants is to use the financial statements to aid our understanding of companies we are interested in—not to be able to do a full financial work-up on the business. Having two or three accounting books as references is useful, but more than that is a personal choice.[6]

## Follow the Money

Whether you just flip through them or read them in detail, it is easier to make sense of financial statements if you have a number of questions in your mind while you go through them. One set of questions relates to following the money. These questions fall into three categories:

1. How much money came in over the reporting period and where did it come from? What were its sources in terms of sectors of the business and national and international regions? How does it compare with previous periods?
2. What was it used for? How much money did the company spend or distribute? On what? How does it compare with previous periods?
3. How much money did the company manage to keep? What do they intend doing with it? What did they do with the money they kept from previous years?

Another set of questions relates to financial ratios. We look at these in Chapter 5.

**Sources of Information**   There is a large amount of information readily available on publicly listed companies. Some of this information is required by the SEC and has to be filed by each company within specified periods during and after the fiscal year. Other information is published in the form of newsletters, press releases, and general announcements.

SEC law requires that companies provide ongoing disclosure of key information. In other words, if material events take place within a company, they must be reported promptly. The business cannot wait until the next official quarterly report or annual report if this is outside the time requirement. This reporting is done through a publicly available Form 8-K. The following list will give you an idea of the sort of ongoing information that the SEC requires be disclosed by companies:

- Changes in control of a company.
- A company's acquisition or disposition of a significant amount of assets.
- A company's bankruptcy or receivership.
- Changes in a company's certifying accountant.
- Resignations of a company's directors and circumstances for the departure of a director.
- Change in a company's fiscal year and amendments to a company's articles of incorporation or bylaws.
- Termination or reduction of a significant business relationship.
- Creation of a direct or contingent financial obligation that is material to the company.
- A change in a rating agency decision, issuance of a credit watch, or change in a company outlook.
- Movement of the company's securities from one exchange or quotation system to another.
- Unregistered sales of equity securities by the company.
- Material modifications to rights of holders of the company's securities.
- Earnings releases.
- Changes in earnings guidance.

The SEC also has a full-disclosure regulation which requires that if a company intentionally discloses material nonpublic information to one person, it must simultaneously disclose that information to the public at large. This eliminates older procedures of giving special briefings to analysts who would then be able to provide inside reports to key clients. Warren Buffett has stated many times that when he buys shares in a public company, he uses the same information that is available to the general population. He does not contact the company to have an inside chat with the CEO or any of the senior management. He also does not visit the company.

Table 4.1 is a list of some of the main documents on publicly held companies. Except for the annual report, they are available through the SEC web site. Most companies have investor relations sections on their web sites where these reports plus other relevant information can be found. The most important report for investors is the 10-K, which is published each year. By law it is required to contain a section called "Management's Discussion and Analysis" or, more fully, "Management's Discussion and Analysis of Financial Condition and

**Table 4.1**  Main Documents for Public Companies

| | |
|---|---|
| Form 10-K | Every public company is required to submit a report using Form 10-K each year. It is a working document containing a comprehensive overview of the company's business and financial condition. It will frequently have a thorough discussion of such items as the risks associated with the business, its main competitors, and any seasonality issues. Depending on the size of the business, it must be submitted within 60 to 90 days after the end of the financial year. The 10-K report must be audited. |
| Annual Report | The annual report is the principal document used by most public companies to disclose corporate information to their shareholders. It usually contains an opening letter from the CEO or the chairman, financial data, results of continuing operations, and indications of future programs. Smaller companies may simply mail the 10-K form as their annual report. Larger companies often make the annual report a very colorful document with photos of the board and senior management, vistas of the company operations, and glowing interviews with senior management. |
| Form 10-Q | Publicly held companies file a report on a Form 10-Q for each of the first three quarters of the company's fiscal year. This provides a continuing view of the company's financial position during the year. |
| Form 8-K | As part of the ongoing disclosure of information, certain information must be reported on a Form 8-K rather than on the next 10-K or 10-Q report. |
| Proxy or Form DEF 14A | A proxy statement is mailed to shareholders to announce the annual meeting. It will contain information about matters to be voted on, including the election or reelection of board members. It will also contain important information on director and management compensation and stock holdings. |

Results of Operations." It is usually simply referred to as the MD&A. If time is limited, reading this section should be the highest priority. The standards for MD&A state that it should address:

- The entity's mission and organizational structure.
- The entity's performance goals and results.
- The entity's financial statements.
- The entity's systems, controls, and legal compliance.
- The possible future effects on the entity of existing, currently known demands, risks, uncertainties, events, conditions, and trends.

Whether you use the annual report or the MD&A section of the 10-K report, the aim is to answer the question whether management is honest, rational, and acting in the best interests of shareholders. If there are any doubts, it may be wise to move on to another company.

### Download Key Reports

It is useful to download key reports such as the 10-K to your computer from the SEC web site. Then you can search on terms such as *risk*, *competition*, *debt*, and *dividends* to get useful information without having to read the whole report. Downloading reports also makes it easier to compare earlier reports to verify whether the company actually achieved any goals stated in previous years. For example, if two years ago the company stated that it was aiming to increase revenue in a particular division, it can be revealing to check whether it succeeded. A company with a history of setting goals and not achieving them is probably not going to be a successful investment.

Another important report is the Proxy Statement, which is required to be filed before the annual meeting. Also called the Form Def 14A (Definitive Proxy Statement) it contains details of executive and director compensation covering areas such as base salaries, bonuses, non-equity compensation, stock awards, options, and deferred compensation. It is also required to contain a section called "Compensation Discussion and Analysis" in which management explains the objectives of the compensation program and what it is designed to reward. The first thing to consider is whether the presentation on compensation in the Proxy Statement is clear and easy to understand. The overall level of the compensation to management and directors relative to the size and performance of the business is important. However, it is equally important to understand if it is distributed in a way that is best aligned with our requirements as shareholders.

The remainder of the chapter describes and analyzes the key features of financial statements and indicates where to find them. The analysis is primarily based on the retailer Wal-Mart. Once the fundamental data has been established in this chapter for Wal-Mart, later chapters will build on it when it is time to look at the different valuation methods. There are a number of reasons I chose Wal-Mart. First, it is one of the most well-known companies in the world. Second, huge numbers of people have direct experience with the company. Third, the overall operations of the company are straightforward, selling consumer items through an extensive chain of large retail stores. Together these mean that it is more likely that readers will have a sense of what some of the data means in terms of their own experience or articles in the press. Fourth, the financial data and company performance is sufficiently generic that it is easy to describe and illustrate key analysis methods without getting caught up in anomalies and special cases. Nothing that is written should be taken as a recommendation to invest in Wal-Mart from any perspective. For example, as explained in Chapter 13, because of its size some see Wal-Mart as having excessive control over the prices it pays to its suppliers.

## Balance Sheet

The *balance sheet*, also called the *statement of financial position*, provides a summary of the equity of the company provided by its shareholders, what the company owns in terms of assets, and what it owes to its lenders as liabilities. The core relationship is:

$$\text{Assets} = \text{Liabilities} + \text{Shareholders Equity}$$

An *asset* is a resource that has the potential to generate future cash inflows or to reduce future cash outflows. The assets can be broken down into monetary assets, fixed assets, inventory, and intangible assets. Conversely, *liabilities* are expected to lead to a future cash outflow or the loss of a future cash inflow.

The balance sheet is an example of accrual accounting, which means that revenue and expenses are recognized in the periods in which they are earned or incurred, irrespective of whether any cash was involved. For example, if a sale is completed with payment to be made in 30 days, this is called a *receivable* and appears as an asset on the balance sheet. In the opposite direction, if an agreement is made to pay for an item in 30 days, this is called a *payable* and appears as a liability on the balance sheet. A typical arrangement is called end of month plus 30: If purchases are made within a particular month, they would be payable within 30 days from the end of that month.

### Balance Sheet

The balance sheet or statement of financial position gives a snapshot of the assets and liabilities of a business at a single point in time.

The first section of the balance sheet consists of the assets of a business. Those assets that would be turned into cash within 12 months under normal operating conditions are called *current assets*. They are listed from the most liquid to the least liquid, typically in the order of cash, cash equivalents, accounts receivable, inventory, the portion of prepaid accounts which will be used within a year, and short-term investments.

*Cash equivalents* are highly liquid short-term assets that can be readily turned into cash. *Accounts receivable* is the outstanding balance owed to the business on credit sales. This must be reported at its net realizable value, meaning the net amount owing less an allowance for doubtful accounts. This allowance is an estimate made by the company based on past experience of management, the company's collection policies, customer quality, and perhaps even the state of the economy. If a loss actually occurs, it must be written off and adjustments made to the level of allowances for doubtful accounts.

*Inventory* is a company's raw materials and finished and unfinished products which have not yet been sold. If the inventory will be sold within 12 months, it is included as part of the current assets. Otherwise it is included as noncurrent assets. *Short-term investments* are investments made by the company in such items as Treasury bills and various short-term debt instruments that have a maturity of less than 12 months. Typically they are used as a safe place to park money but are still reasonably accessible with minimum cost.

After the current assets come the noncurrent or *long-term assets*. Typically these are *fixed assets* such as plant, property and equipment, and long-term investments. They may also include inventory that is not likely to be sold within the next 12 months. Fixed assets are displayed as their actual cost less depreciation. Obviously some assets such as land can appreciate in value. However, the Financial Accounting Standards Board (FASB) in the United States does not allow upward revaluation. This is not the case in other countries such as the United Kingdom and Australia where revaluation is allowed to align value with market prices.

The next section of the balance sheet is concerned with the liabilities of a company. As with assets, it is in two halves; the first half lists the *current liabilities* while the second half lists the remaining liabilities. The current liabilities are listed from the most liquid to the least liquid with typical items being payables and short-term loans. *Payables* are money owing to suppliers and other creditors, typically for inventory or services. If the time frame is less than 12 months, they are included as current liabilities. The same applies for short-term loans—their period needs to be less than 12 months. The remaining liabilities are usually made up of long-term debt. They can also include deferred federal income tax liabilities and pension and lease obligations.

One of the most contentious issues for balance sheet entries is the treatment of *intangible assets*, the nonmonetary assets that cannot be seen, touched or physically measured. For example, if a business is started it may develop a strong brand name. This brand name has value for the business but it will not appear on the balance sheet of the original company. However, if the business was sold for an amount that exceeded its equity, the difference would appear on the balance sheet of the purchasing company as *goodwill*.

Some of the forms of intangible assets include trade secrets, copyrights, patents, trademarks, and goodwill. These are called *legal intangibles* since it is possible to have right of ownership over them; they can be sold to other companies and their ownership can be defended in court. There are also *competitive intangible assets* associated with the human capital of a business. As the name suggests, they help give a company a competitive advantage even though they cannot be bought or sold in the same way as legal intangibles. They are more difficult to define and usually arise through experience. Examples are general know-how and reputation. Some intangible assets such as trademarks and goodwill are taken to have an indefinite life. In such cases they have to be examined each year for any loss in value. If this occurs, the amount of the impairment will be entered in the income statement as a loss. Other intangible assets such as copyrights and patents are described as having a specified useful life and are amortized over this life by specified schedules.

The main balance sheet is prepared at the end of each financial year with three further balance sheets at the ends of the intervening quarters. Each is a snapshot of the company at those positions in time. In the annual report and 10-K report, the balance sheet always shows the company's position for the last day of the financial year as well as its position on the last day of the preceding financial year. It is important, when looking at a balance sheet, to get into the habit of also looking at the figures for the preceding year as a point of reference.

### Check the Notes to the Financial Statements

At the bottom of the financial statements there will be comments such as "See accompanying notes" or "See accompanying notes to the consolidated financial statements." These refer to specific items in the statements and expand on the relevant entries. They are an important source of extra information.

The final section in the balance sheet is called *stockholders' equity* or *shareholders' equity*. This is simply the assets minus the liabilities and represents the ownership of the company. The owners are the ones with the greatest risk should the company run into difficulties because they will be the last to be paid. Conversely, should the company be successful (and these are the type of companies we are looking for), then the owners or shareholders will benefit through an increased share price or higher dividends. Furthermore, these benefits to shareholders are open-ended whereas, in most cases, the company only has fixed-interest or fixed-amount obligations to the creditors listed earlier in the balance sheet. When equity is divided by the number of shares outstanding, it is called *book value*. It is examined in detail in Chapter 6 as a method for valuing companies.

The total shareholders' equity is typically broken into four parts: preferred stock, common stock, additional paid-in capital, and retained earnings. *Preferred stock* is a hybrid between common stock and a bond; for example, it typically pays a guaranteed dividend whereas dividends paid to holders of common stock are at the discretion of the board. *Common stock* is a theoretical value calculated by multiplying the par or stated value of the stock by the number of common stock shares outstanding. The par value is the minimum price that the shares can be initially sold for and has no relationship with the actual market price. *Additional paid-in capital* represents the amount by which the original sale of shares exceeded their par value. Combining the first two items gives the total amount of money received by the company by direct sale of its shares. Once the shares have been sold by the company, further transactions are between investors and are carried out independently of the company. Hence they do not appear in any of the financial statements. The fourth item, *retained earnings* (or *deficit*), is the total amount of earnings received by the company over its life minus payments to shareholders as dividends or cash. Also referred to as *accumulated earnings* (or *deficit*), it is money that the company has decided to reinvest in the business rather than pay out to its shareholders. It is not cash sitting in the business (although some of it may be).

There may be a fifth item in the section on total shareholders' equity called *treasury stock*. This item is related to a company buying back its own stock. When a company does this, there are two possibilities: Cancel the shares or hold on to them. When the shares are held by the company, they are called treasury stock. At first it may be thought that treasury stock should be listed as an asset in the same way that other stock purchases by the company would be included on the balance sheet. This is not done, however, since treasury stock has a number of distinguishing restrictions, such as not paying dividends and not giving the company as its owner any voting rights. It also does not give the company the right to receive any assets in the case of its liquidation. The result is that treasury stock is listed as an offset. For example, in the balance sheet for Burlington Northern Santa Fe Corporation (BNI) dated December 31, 2008, one line reads: "Treasury stock, at cost, 202,165 shares and 189,626 shares, respectively ($8,395)." This means that BNI has purchased its own stock, paying a total of $8,395 million, and has not cancelled it. It is listed as an offset or negative amount in the equity section of the balance sheet because it can be thought of as being paid out from the additional paid-in capital and so offsets the total amount received.

Treasury stock is essentially the same as unissued stock in the company, which is stock that has been authorized by the charter of the company but has not been issued. The effect of a company buying back its own stock is discussed in Chapter 5 in terms of the effect that it has on key financial ratios.

### Off-Balance-Sheet Items

Recently the issue of off-balance-sheet financial activities has become crucial in understanding the performance of companies. This is particularly true of banks. For example, writing for *Bloomberg*, on July 13, 2008, Bradley Keoun declared that there were an

> ... additional $1.1 trillion of assets that New York-based Citigroup keeps off its books: trusts to sell mortgage-backed securities, financing vehicles to issue short-term debt, and collateralized debt obligations, or CDOs, to repackage bonds. Now, as Citigroup prepares to announce second-quarter results July 18, those off-balance-sheet assets, used by U.S. banks to expand lending without tying up capital, are casting a shadow over earnings [with] more than $7 billion of losses.[7]

As the name implies, *off-balance-sheet* activities or arrangements are rights and obligations of a company which are sufficiently at arm's length that they are not included on the balance sheet as assets or liabilities. In particular, they occur when the company does not have direct control over the activities or arrangements but because of certain guarantees they may be a source of potential risk to the company even though they are not recorded as liabilities. Some of the names and acronyms used to describe them include structured investment vehicle (SIV), special purpose entity (SPE), and collateralized debt obligation (CDO). They are used to transfer the risk from the parent company and its shareholders to others who are willing to take on the risk. Nevertheless, the parent company is always left with some commitments or obligations even if there is only a remote chance that it will be called upon to meet them. Problems occur when extraordinary circumstances come about, triggering these commitments to be fulfilled, resulting in the items being brought onto the balance sheet of the parent company as was the case with Citigroup mentioned earlier.

Even countries can engage in off-balance sheet transactions. For example, in 2002 Goldman Sachs, the New York–based financial firm, helped Greece raise $1 billion of off-balance-sheet funding through complex derivative contracts. This enabled Greece to mask its growing deficit since the funding did not appear as a liability on its balance sheet. It was not until early 2010 that information on this arrangement was publicly available.[8]

Since the original Greek transactions, the European Union regulations now require the full disclosure of any similar off-balance-sheet arrangements. Regulations have also changed for U.S. publicly listed companies. Since 2003, as part of the Sarbanes-Oxley review, the SEC requires that companies provide an explanation of their off-balance-sheet arrangements within a subsection of the "Management's Discussion and Analysis" (MD&A) section in their disclosure documents. Even though there is considerable latitude in the amount of detail that is both required and given, this is another reason to read the company's MD&A, as recommended earlier. The box titled "Off-Balance-Sheet Arrangements for Wal-Mart" gives an explanation of the off-balance-sheet arrangements presented by Wal-Mart Stores, Inc. in its 10-K report for the year ending January 2010. The entries are required to be clearly itemized.

The main items in a balance sheet and a typical layout are shown in Figure 4.1. The first section is assets, starting with the current assets and followed by the remaining assets. After that, there are the current liabilities followed by the remaining liabilities. The last part of this section is the breakdown of shareholders' equity.

Consolidated balance sheets for Wal-Mart are shown in Table 4.2 for the fiscal years ending January 2009 and January 2010. Before looking at some of the key numbers, there are two points to note. First, the financial years end on January 31 of each year, in contrast with most other companies which have their financial years coinciding with calendar years. This setup is actually common for retail companies, because the period from November through January is usually their busiest and most profitable time of the year. The retailers want to get this information into the hands of their shareholders as quickly as possible. (To keep everything consistent, when we talk about, say, the financial year 2010, we mean the financial year ending January 31, 2010.)

## Off-Balance-Sheet Arrangements for Wal-Mart

In addition to the unrecorded contractual obligations discussed and presented above, the company has made certain guarantees as discussed below for which the timing of payment, if any, is unknown.

In connection with certain debt financing, we could be liable for early termination payments if certain unlikely events were to occur. At January 31, 2010, the aggregate termination payment would have been $109 million. The two arrangements pursuant to which these payments could be made will expire in fiscal 2011 and fiscal 2019.

In connection with the development of our grocery distribution network in the United States, we have agreements with third parties which would require us to purchase or assume the leases on certain unique equipment in the event the agreements are terminated. These agreements, which can be terminated by either party at will, cover up to a five-year period and obligate the company to pay up to approximately $41 million upon termination of some or all of these agreements.

The company has potential future lease commitments for land and buildings for approximately 348 future locations. These lease commitments have lease terms ranging from 1 to 40 years and provide for certain minimum rentals. If executed, payments under operating leases would increase by $59 million for fiscal 2011, based on current cost estimates.

*Source*: Wal-Mart 10-K report for January 2010.

The other point to note is that Wal-Mart does not have a line called "Total Liabilities." Some companies omit this calculation, making it just that much harder to spot any unfavorable results or trends. Another complication is that Wal-Mart has noncontrolling interests in various subsidiaries in South America. The company reports these separately in the equity section of its balance sheet. For example, the balance sheet distinguishes between shareholders' equity in Wal-Mart and total equity, which includes the equity from noncontrolling interests. Consolidated net income is also reduced by the amount attributable to the noncontrolling interest to arrive at net income attributable to Wal-Mart.

The key entries include current assets, which were $48,949 million at the end of the 2009 financial year, dropping to $48,331 million the following year, giving a slight decrease of around 1.3 percent.

Assets
  Current assets
    Cash and cash equivalents
    Accounts receivable
    Inventories
    Other current assets
  Total current assets
    Investments
    Plant, property and equipment (fixed assets)
    Intangible assets
  Total assets
Liabilities and Shareholders' Equity
  Current Liabilities
    Accounts payable
    Short-term borrowing
    Other current liabilities
  Total current liabilities
    Long-term debt
    Other long-term liabilities
  Total liabilities
  Shareholders' equity
    Preferred stock
    Common stock
    Additional paid-in capital
    Retained earnings
    Accumulated other comprehensive income

**Figure 4.1**   Typical Layout of a Balance Sheet

There was an increase in cash and cash equivalents of $632 million but this was more than offset by a decrease in inventory of $1,351 million. There was little change in the total assets: $163,429 million at the end of the 2009 financial year and $170,706 million at the end of the next financial year. Current liabilities increased slightly from $55,390 million to $55,561 million.

Since the Wal-Mart shareholders' equity was $70,749 million at the end of the 2010 financial year, subtracting this from the total assets results in total liabilities of $99,957 million. Another way to approach this result is by first calculating the noncurrent liabilities and adding it to the current liabilities. The noncurrent liabilities is the sum of five items: long-term debt ($33,231 million), long-term

**Table 4.2**   Consolidated Balance Sheets for Wal-Mart (Amounts in Millions)

|  | 2010 | 2009 |
|---|---|---|
| **ASSETS** | | |
| *Current assets* | | |
| Cash and cash equivalents | $7,907 | $7,275 |
| Receivables, net | 4,144 | 3,905 |
| Inventories | 33,160 | 34,511 |
| Prepaid expenses and other | 2,980 | 3,063 |
| Current assets of discontinued operations | 140 | 195 |
| Total current assets | 48,331 | 48,949 |
| *Property and equipment* | | |
| Land | 22,591 | 19,852 |
| Buildings and improvements | 77,452 | 73,810 |
| Fixtures and equipment | 35,450 | 29,851 |
| Transportation equipment | 2,355 | 2,307 |
| Property and equipment | 137,848 | 125,820 |
| Less accumulated depreciation | (38,304) | (32,264) |
| Property and equipment, net | 99,544 | 92,856 |
| *Property under capital leases:* | | |
| Property under capital leases | 5,669 | 5,341 |
| Less accumulated amortization | (2,906) | (2,544) |
| Property under capital leases, net | 2,763 | 2,797 |
| Goodwill | 16,126 | 15,260 |
| Other assets and deferred charges | 3,942 | 3,567 |
| **Total assets** | **$170,706** | **$163,429** |
| **LIABILITIES AND EQUITY** | | |
| *Current liabilities* | | |
| Short-term borrowings | 523 | 1,506 |
| Accounts payable | 30,451 | 28,849 |
| Accrued liabilities | 18,734 | 18,112 |
| Accrued income taxes | 1,365 | 677 |
| Long-term debt due within one year | 4,050 | 5,848 |
| Obligations under capital leases | 346 | 315 |
| Current liabilities (discontinued operations) | 92 | 83 |
| Total current liabilities | 55,561 | 55,390 |
| Long-term debt | 33,231 | 31,349 |
| Long-term obligations under capital leases | 3,170 | 3,200 |
| Deferred income taxes and other | 5,508 | 6,014 |
| Redeemable noncontrolling interest | 307 | 397 |

Table 4.2    (*Continued*)

|  | 2010 | 2009 |
|---|---|---|
| *Equity* | | |
| Common stock ($0.10 par value) | 378 | 393 |
| Capital in excess of par value | 3,803 | 3,920 |
| Retained earnings | 66,638 | 63,660 |
| Accumulated other comprehensive loss | (70) | (2,688) |
| Total Wal-Mart shareholders' equity | 70,749 | 65,285 |
| Noncontrolling interest | 2,180 | 1,794 |
| Total equity | 72,929 | 67,079 |
| **Total liabilities and equity** | $170,706 | $163,429 |

Fiscal years ended January 31.

obligations under capital leases ($3,170 million), deferred income taxes and other ($5,508 million), redeemable noncontrolling interest ($307 million), and the equity in the noncontrolling interest ($2,180 million). This comes to a total of $44,396 million for 2010. Adding to the current liabilities ($55,561 million) gives $99,957 million for the total liabilities, as just stated.

For most industrial companies, receivables are approximately equal to payables. In contrast, cash-based businesses such as Wal-Mart usually have very high payables compared to their receivables. For the financial year ending January 2009 the receivables for Wal-Mart were only $3,905 million compared to accounts payables of $28,849 million. People pay at the checkout in cash or use credit cards. In most cases the credit card payments are processed within 24 hours and so for the great majority of transactions the money is in the Wal-Mart bank account within a day. This means that they are not included in the receivables item of the balance sheet. This leaves the question as to what transactions actually appear as receivables. In its 2009 annual report Wal-Mart gives the answer:

> Accounts receivable consist primarily of receivables from insurance companies resulting from our pharmacy sales, receivables from suppliers for marketing or incentive programs, receivables from real estate transactions and receivables from property insurance claims. Additionally, amounts due from banks for customer credit card, debit card and EBT [electronic benefit transfer] transactions that take in excess of seven days to process are classified as accounts receivable.

**Warning: Revisions of Balance Sheet Items**

One of the biggest problems associated with the balance sheet is that assets can be subject to sudden and substantial revisions. Consider a company that purchases a piece of specialty machinery for $500,000. As soon as the equipment is installed there are issues of value, even before questions of depreciation rates arise. To the company the machinery is worth $500,000 since that is what was paid for it. However, if the company wished to take out a loan using the machinery as security, the lender is likely to put a much lower figure on it. Why? The lender, if he needs to foreclose on the loan, may find it difficult to find a buyer for the machinery.

In 2007 and 2008 many of the largest financial institutions had massive write-downs of their assets associated with subprime debt obligations. As an example, on January 15, 2008, Citigroup announced "write-downs of $17.4 billion on subprime-related direct exposures" for the fiscal year 2007. Then on April 18, 2008 it announced further "write-downs of $6.0 billion on subprime-related direct exposures" for the first quarter of 2008. For the second and third quarters it announced further write-downs.

Even with companies involved in actively traded commodities there can be major revisions of asset value—as when, for example, mineral or oil reserves prove to be less than the original estimate. In 2004 Shell cut its proven oil and gas reserves by 20 percent, resulting in a number of class actions by investors claiming that the company had misled them.

Another warning concerns changes in the current assets, particularly cash and cash equivalents. Businesses need a certain amount of cash to run their day-to-day operations. It is also helpful to have cash available for any emergencies. Just the same, if cash is increasing over the years faster than the general growth of the business, it may mean that the company does not have any opportunities to use it profitably; so it just sits on the balance sheet. Or this extra cash could be hidden in increased receivables by providing services or products that are not paid for. In either case, it may eventually mean slower growth. Table 4.2 shows that Wal-Mart had a small increase in cash and cash equivalents from $7,275 million to $7,907 million during the last financial year, which is roughly in line with the general growth of the business.

An item that may not be familiar to many people is the line "Accumulated other comprehensive loss." *Comprehensive income* relates to transactions that affect the equity outside of net income but are not shareholder transactions such as stock repurchases, stock offerings, or dividend payments. They are explained in more detail in the section on equity statements later in this chapter. For the moment, simply note that the accumulated other comprehensive loss has decreased from $2,688 million to $70 million, meaning a drop of $2,618 million during the financial year 2010.

## Income Statement

The *income statement* or *profit and loss statement* (P&L) gives rise to two commonly used terms: the top line and the bottom line. The *top line* of a business refers to the total sales or revenue coming into the business. This is usually from the sale of goods and services to customers. Companies may also receive revenue from interest, dividends, or royalties paid to them by other companies. In the income statement the revenue is placed on the first line, giving rise to it being referred to as the top line of a business. From this amount the company pays for the purchase of raw materials and for manufacturing finished products. This is referred to as the *cost of sales*.

The company also pays operating and selling expenses plus general and administrative expenses. Finally, the company pays interest on any loans it may have and makes provision for income taxes. After paying all the expenses and costs, what is left is called *net income* or *earnings*. Because of its position in the income statement, it is often referred to as the *bottom line*. (Note that it is usually not the true bottom line of the income statement. Most often it is followed by various per-share entries and calculations.)

### Income Statement

The income statement or profit and loss statement describes how the revenue or top line of a business is transformed into its net income or bottom line. It presents the data over a period of time, usually the financial year or one of its quarters.

As just explained, the typical income statement starts with revenues and makes adjustments for the cost of goods sold, including depreciation on the assets used to produce the revenues, and any selling, general, and administrative (SG&A) expenses. The result from this first set of calculations is called the operating profit, or simply earnings before interest and taxes (EBIT). The next step is to subtract interest expenses, giving the taxable income. Removing the taxes leads to the net income or earnings. Finally, this is adjusted for discontinued operations, extraordinary items, and changes caused by accounting changes.

The final figure is divided by the number of shares outstanding. Usually two figures are presented, corresponding to *basic shares outstanding* and *diluted shares outstanding*. When options are awarded to management and staff as bonuses, even though they are not yet publicly traded shares, they are included as part of the diluted shares outstanding. Also items such as the conversion of convertible bonds and preferred shares need to be included in this number. The final results are called *basic earnings per share* and *diluted earnings per share*. It is prudent to run your eye over the lines describing the share numbers to compare the differences between the basic and diluted numbers, and to see if there have been any trends in total numbers over the past financial years.

If the company pays dividends, there is another line called *dividends declared per common share*. The ratio of dividends to earnings is called the *payout ratio*. The remainder of the earnings are kept back in the company and used for expansion and investment purposes. The proportion that is retained is called the *earnings retention ratio*. Consider Wal-Mart. As shown in its income statement (Table 4.3), for the financial year ending January 31, 2010, the company reported sales of $405,046 million and net income of $14,335 million. (As indicated in the section on the balance sheet, the focus is on the results attributable to Wal-Mart excluding the amounts to the noncontrolling interests.) This means that customers spent approximately $405 billion in the stores during the year. After paying all expenses incurred in generating those sales, the company is left with around $14 billion. From the statement of cash flows (Table 4.4), the company paid $4.2 billion as dividends to its shareholders. From these two figures we can calculate the dividend payout ratio and the dividend retention ratio. The payout ratio is 4.2/14.3 or 29.4 percent, and the retention ratio its complement, namely 70.6 percent.

Sometimes a company has a business transaction that is very unusual or out of the ordinary. Such transactions are displayed separately in the income statement, generally under the heading of extraordinary items. To qualify they should be unusual and not likely to reoccur in the foreseeable future under normal conditions. For example, because of its rarity, losses due to a hailstorm in Hawaii may qualify as an extraordinary item for an orchard owner. But it would not qualify for the insurance company that covered the loss, since insuring unlikely events is part of an insurance company's normal operations.

Intangible assets are an increasingly significant economic component of companies. It used to be that goodwill and other intangible assets were amortized in a standardized manner over time. New regulations now talk about *impairment*, which must be measured at least annually and entered into the income statement. Consider the case of eBay Inc., the online auction company. In August 2005 eBay purchased the Internet-based telephone company Skype for $2.6 billion. However, in the 2007 10-K report of eBay, the company stated that the benefits were not what they anticipated and it lowered its projections of the value of Skype for future operations. As a result it included an impairment of goodwill of $1.4 billion as an operating expense in its income statement.

Figure 4.2 shows a typical layout for the income statement. As previously explained, it starts with revenues and moves down through the various costs and expenses.

The statement of income for Wal-Mart is shown in Table 4.3 for the three years ending January 2008, 2009, and 2010. Some of the key

Revenues
− Cost of goods sold
− Selling expenses
− Administration expenses
= Operating profit or EBIT
− Interest expenses
   = Earnings before taxes
   − Taxes
      = Net income before extraordinary items
      + Gains (losses) from discontinued operations
      + Extraordinary gains (losses)
      + Changes because of changes in accounting methods
        = Net income after extraordinary items
Basic net income per share
Diluted net income per share
Average shares outstanding
Diluted average shares outstanding
Dividends declared per common share

**Figure 4.2** Typical Layout of an Income Statement

**Table 4.3**   Consolidated Statements of Income for Wal-Mart (Amounts in Millions except Per-Share Data)

|  | 2010 | 2009 | 2008 |
|---|---|---|---|
| *Revenues* | | | |
| Net sales | $405,046 | $401,087 | $373,821 |
| Membership and other income | 3,168 | 3,287 | 3,202 |
|  | 408,214 | 404,374 | 377,023 |
| *Costs and expenses* | | | |
| Cost of sales | 304,657 | 304,056 | 284,137 |
| Operating, selling, general, and administrative expenses | 79,607 | 77,520 | 70,934 |
| Operating income | 23,950 | 22,798 | 21,952 |
| Interest: | | | |
| Debt | 1,787 | 1,896 | 1,863 |
| Capital leases | 278 | 288 | 240 |
| Interest income | (181) | (284) | (309) |
| Interest, net | 1,884 | 1,900 | 1,794 |
| Income from continuing operations before income taxes | 22,066 | 20,898 | 20,158 |
| *Provision for income taxes* | | | |
| Current | 7,643 | 6,564 | 6,897 |
| Deferred | (504) | 581 | (8) |
|  | 7,139 | 7,145 | 6,889 |
| Income from continuing operations | 14,927 | 13,753 | 13,269 |
| Income (loss) from discontinued operations, net of tax | (79) | 146 | (132) |
| Consolidated net income | 14,848 | 13,899 | 13,137 |
| Less consolidated net income attributable to noncontrolling interest | (513) | (499) | (406) |
| Consolidated net income attributable to Wal-Mart | $14,335 | $13,400 | $12,731 |
| *Basic net income per common share* | | | |
| Basic income per common share from continuing operation | $3.73 | $3.36 | $3.16 |
| Basic income (loss) per common share from discontinued operations | (0.02) | 0.04 | (0.03) |
| Basic net income per common share | $3.71 | $3.40 | $3.13 |
| *Diluted net income per common share* | | | |
| Diluted income per common share from continuing operations | $3.72 | 3.35 | 3.16 |
| Diluted income (loss) per common share from discontinued operations | (0.02) | 0.04 | (0.03) |
| Diluted net income per common share | $3.70 | $3.39 | $3.13 |
| *Weighted-average number of common shares* | | | |
| Basic | 3,866 | 3,939 | 4,066 |
| Diluted | 3,877 | 3,951 | 4,072 |
| Dividends declared per common share | $1.09 | $0.95 | $0.88 |

Financial years ended January 31.

entries are revenues increasing from $373,821 million to $405,046 million (top line), and net income from $12,731 million to $14,335 million (bottom line), from 2008 to 2010. On a per share basis, this is a growth in earnings from $3.13 to $3.70. In the past year, dividends were $1.09 per share, giving a dividend payout ratio of 1.09/3.70 or 29.4 percent, confirming an earlier calculation.

As mentioned earlier, checking any changes in the number of shares outstanding is important. In the case of Wal-Mart, the number of shares outstanding in the *basic* category had dropped from 4,066 million to 3,866 million over two years. In the *diluted* category the number dropped from 4,072 million to 3,877 million. In both cases, the drop is around 200 million shares or 5 percent.

 **Warning: Use EPS, Not Net Profit**

What is important for us as investors is changes in the company on a per-share basis. This means that, for example, we should focus on growth in earnings per share (EPS) and not net profit. In some cases the growth in net profit can be at a high level compared to the growth in EPS because the company has been issuing large numbers of shares. Consider the telecommunications giant AT&T Inc. Over the three years ending December 31, 2009, net profit grew by an average 19.44 percent per year, an attractive result. However, because the number of shares outstanding increased by over 50 percent during this time, EPS only grew by an average of 3.90 percent per year, not much different from the rate of inflation.

Although they are usually not mentioned directly in the income statement, there are also expenses related to share-based compensation. For example, in Wal-Mart's 10-K statement for the 2010 fiscal year, we read:

> As of January 31, 2010, the company has awarded share-based compensation to executives and other associates of the company through various share-based compensation plans. The compensation cost recognized for all plans was $335 million, $302 million, and $276 million for fiscal 2010, 2009, and 2008, respectively, and is included in operating, selling, general and administrative expenses in the accompanying Consolidated Statements of Income.

Some of this compensation is in terms of options which need to be valued. We described the standard methods for this in Chapter 2, and these are what Wal-Mart uses. The company explains that their fair value is estimated using the Black-Scholes-Merton option valuation model and that the expected volatility used in the formula is based on historical volatility.

On some financial web sites you might see a reference to *normalized earnings* or *normalized income*. These are the net income of a company, adjusted for nonrecurring or unusual items. They are an attempt to provide information that is more representative of the performance of the company rather than include items that are likely to be one-off. One difficulty is that since they are not GAAP quantities, there may be differences between different providers of the data due to different protocols for extracting them from the financial statements. Another less common use of the term *normalized earnings* refers to the earnings that have been smoothed to allow for the effect of economic cycles.

 **Warning: Revenue Recognition**

The two most egregious distortions of the income statement are recognizing revenues before their time and delaying the reporting of expenses. In 1998, Arthur Levitt, the former head of the SEC, described this problem of manipulating the recognition of revenue as like a premature opening of a bottle of wine. "You wouldn't pop the cork on that bottle before it was ready," he said. "But some companies are doing this with their revenue—recognizing it before a sale is complete, before the product is delivered to a customer, or at a time when the customer still has options to terminate, void, or delay the sale."[*]

In the same speech, Levitt talked about the opposite practice, overstating expenses in the good years with the intent of remedying this distortion in later years to smooth out earnings. He declared that an "illusion played by some companies is using unrealistic assumptions to estimate liabilities for such items as sales returns, loan losses, or warranty costs. In doing so, they stash accruals in cookie jars during the good times and reach into them when needed in the bad times." One way that companies can manipulate their overall profit is by treating transactions as revenues or expenses instead of as capital assets,

[*]Arthur Levitt, "The Numbers Game," speech to the NYU Center for Law and Business, New York, September 28, 1998.

or vice versa. This is called *capitalizing* the transactions. Consider a cost that is capitalized; only the depreciation or amortization is treated as an expense in the income statement instead of the whole amount. This means that most of the costs are shifted to later periods. The transaction will also appear as an asset on the balance sheet and a debit on the statement of cash flows.

A famous example is America Online Inc. (AOL). During its fiscal years ending June 30, 1995, and June 30, 1996, AOL rapidly expanded its customer base as an Internet service provider through extensive advertising efforts, principally through distributing millions of computer disks containing AOL startup software to potential subscribers. For fiscal years 1995 and 1996, AOL capitalized most of the costs of acquiring new subscribers using these methods as *deferred membership acquisition costs* (DMAC). This means that the costs were reported as an asset on its balance sheet, instead of expensing them as they were incurred. For fiscal years 1993, 1994, and 1995, all reported expenses regarding DMAC were amortization amounts. This made a massive difference to the income statement. Had these costs been properly expensed as incurred, AOL's 1995 reported pretax loss would have increased from $21 million to $98 million (including the write-off of DMAC that existed as of the end of fiscal year 1994), and AOL's 1996 reported pretax income of $62 million would have been decreased to a pretax loss of $175 million. The reason that AOL attempted to capitalize these DMAC costs was that it contended that it operated in a sufficiently stable business environment so that it was confident of recovering its outlay. The SEC disagreed and successfully sued the company.

## Read the First Note to the Financial Statements

In the first note to the financial statements, often called "Summary of Significant Accounting Policies and Related Matters," companies are required to state their policy on revenue recognition. Although not foolproof, reading this policy will help an investor avoid companies that are front-loading their revenue by declaring it earlier than warranted. It will also describe the basis for the company's estimates of sales returns.

## Statement of Cash Flows

The *statement of cash flows* is like a giant checkbook that summarizes all the cash transactions of the business for the period of the financial statements. The annual statement of cash flows summarizes the cash transactions for the previous financial year, while the quarterly statements of cash flows do the same for the quarters.

The key difference between the statement of cash flows and the previous two financial statements is that the statement of cash flows deals with cash while the other two use accrual accounting and contain noncash items such as receivables and payables (found in the balance sheet) and depreciation (found in the income statement). In this way the statement of cash flows completes the cycle of the financial statements by linking together the results in the balance sheet and the income statement by adjusting them for or netting out their noncash components.

There are many examples of companies of all different sizes and industry types that have healthy net profit but struggle to have the money to pay for day-to-day expenses such as employee wages and supplier bills. A careful analysis of the statement of cash flows could reveal this. Sometimes it is painfully clear. For example, excluding allowances for deferred taxes, the statement of cash flows for General Motors shows that the cash from operating activities had gone from a loss of $2.3 billion during 2003 to a loss of $27.9 billion during 2007. By mid-2009 the company said that it had $172.81 billion in debt with just $82.29 billion in assets. It filed for bankruptcy, making it the fourth-largest bankruptcy in U.S. history and the largest industrial company to do so.

The statement of cash flows is in three parts: operating activities, investing activities, and financing activities. The *operating activities* section mainly concerns that part of the business associated with the sale of goods or revenue for services and payments for inventories and operating expenses such as salaries. It represents the cash generated by the business internally.

The second two sections describe the cash generated by the business from external sources. The *investing activities* section focuses on transactions associated with assets such as property, plant, and equipment, and debt or equity securities (except those that are treated as cash equivalents). The third section, *financing activities*, includes:

- Transactions with creditors such as the proceeds from and repayments of borrowings.

- Proceeds from issuing the company's own shares and the repurchase of these shares.
- Payment of dividends.

## Cash Flow Statement

The cash flow statement or statement of cash flows is like a summary of the company's checkbook divided into three parts: operating, investing, and financing activities. It strips away the noncash items in the income statement and often vividly indicates when a company is having financial difficulties.

We will just look briefly at some of the items in the cash flow from operating activities and how they can be derived from the income statement and balance sheet. This procedure is called the indirect method. Starting with the bottom line of the income statement, the net profit is adjusted to arrive at the cash collected from customers. If there has been an increase in accounts receivable over the past year, then the amount of the increase is subtracted from the net profit since more profit was recognized than was received in cash. In the opposite direction, if there was a decrease in receivables, the amount of this decrease is added to the net profit.

Similarly, if there has been an increase in accounts payable over the past year, then the amount of the increase is added to the net profit since the company was able to increase the amount of deferred payments to its suppliers for the purchase of inventory or services. In the opposite direction, if there was a decrease in payables, the amount of this decrease is subtracted.

The next step is to adjust the cash position for any changes in inventory: If there is an increase in inventory, the difference is subtracted because more cash was required in the purchase of inventory than was included in the net profit. Explaining it differently, extra cash has been used to purchase inventory that has not yet been sold. In the opposite direction, if there was a decrease in inventory, the amount of the decrease is added to the net profit. The result of these adjustments is the cash paid to suppliers.

| |
|---|
| Net profit (loss) after tax |
|    Add: |
|        Depreciation expenses |
|        Amortization expense |
|        Loss on sale of plant and equipment |
|        Increase in interest payable |
|        Increase in prepaid expenses |
|        Increase in accounts payable |
|        Increase in taxes payable |
|    Subtract: |
|        Gain in sale of plant and equipment |
|        Increase in accounts receivable |
|        Increase in interest receivable |
|        Increase in inventories |
| Net cash provided by operating activities |

**Figure 4.3**  Typical Layout of Cash Flows from Operating Activities

Indirect method for cash flows: Adjustments are made to arrive at the net cash flows from operating activities from the net profit.

Figure 4.3 is a summary of the adjustments used in calculating the net cash flow from operating activities using the indirect method. As explained, it starts with the net profit (or loss) after taxes and then reconciles it with the noncash items to arrive at the net cash provided by operating activities.

Table 4.4 is the consolidated statement of cash flows for Wal-Mart. Many of the items are carried over or calculated from the balance sheet and income statement. For example, in the consolidated statements of income, the consolidated net income is $14,848 million for 2010. This becomes the first entry at the top of the cash flow statement. In the overall cash transactions for the financial year ending January 31, 2010, the net cash provided by operating activities is $26,249 million, which is offset by net cash used in investing activities of $11,620 million and $14,191 million used in financing activities. After allowing for the effect of exchange rates on cash of $194 million, this means a net increase in cash and cash equivalents of $632 million. The previous year, the increase in cash and cash equivalents was $1,706 million and the year before, a decrease of $2,198 million.

**Table 4.4**    Consolidated Statements of Cash Flows for Wal-Mart (Amounts in Millions)

|  | 2010 | 2009 | 2008 |
|---|---|---|---|
| *Cash flows from operating activities* | | | |
| Consolidated net income | $14,848 | $13,899 | $13,137 |
| Loss (income) from discontinued operations, net of tax | 79 | (146) | 132 |
| Income from continuing operations | 14,927 | 13,753 | 13,269 |
| *Adjustments to reconcile income from continuing operations to net cash provided by operating activities* | | | |
| Depreciation and amortization | 7,157 | 6,739 | 6,317 |
| Deferred income taxes | (504) | 581 | (8) |
| Other operating activities | 301 | 769 | 504 |
| *Changes in certain assets and liabilities, net of effects of acquisitions* | | | |
| Increase in accounts receivable | (297) | (101) | (564) |
| Decrease (increase) in inventories | 2,265 | (220) | (775) |
| Increase (decrease) in accounts payable | 1,052 | (410) | 865 |
| Increase in accrued liabilities | 1,348 | 2,036 | 1,034 |
| Net cash provided by operating activities | 26,249 | 23,147 | 20,642 |
| *Cash flows from investing activities* | | | |
| Payments for property and equipment | (12,184) | (11,499) | (14,937) |
| Proceeds from disposal of property and equipment | 1,002 | 714 | 957 |
| Proceeds from (payments for) disposal of certain international operations, net | — | 838 | (257) |
| Investment in international operations, net of cash acquired | — | (1,576) | (1,338) |
| Other investing activities | (438) | 781 | (95) |
| Net cash used in investing activities | (11,620) | (10,742) | (15,670) |
| *Cash flows from financing activities* | | | |
| Increase (decrease) in short-term borrowings, net | (1,033) | (3,745) | 2,376 |
| Proceeds from issuance of long-term debt | 5,546 | 6,566 | 11,167 |
| Payment of long-term debt | (6,033) | (5,387) | (8,723) |
| Dividends paid | (4,217) | (3,746) | (3,586) |
| Purchase of company stock | (7,276) | (3,521) | (7,691) |
| Purchase of redeemable noncontrolling interest | (436) | — | — |
| Payment of capital lease obligations | (346) | (352) | (343) |
| Other financing activities | (396) | 267 | (622) |
| Net cash used in financing activities | (14,191) | (9,918) | (7,422) |
| Effect of exchange rates on cash | 194 | (781) | 252 |
| Net increase (decrease) in cash | 632 | 1,706 | (2,198) |
| Cash and equivalents at beginning of year | 7,275 | 5,569 | 7,767 |
| Cash and equivalents at end of year | $7,907 | $7,275 | $5,569 |

Fiscal years ended January 31.

**Warning: Examine Net Cash Flow from Operating Activities**

A key warning sign from the statement of cash flows is that the net income substantially exceeds the net cash flow from operating activities. If this happens it may mean that the earnings of the company are of doubtful quality. This is even more serious if the net cash flow from operating activities is negative while the net profit is positive. In the case of Wal-Mart, for 2010 net cash flow from operating activities was $26,249 million and the net profit was $14,335 million, so these problems did not occur.

**Positive and Negative Cash Signs**

Two signs of a cash-healthy company that you can keep a lookout for in the statement of cash flows are:

1.  Cash provided by operations is positive and trending upwards. After all, this represents the core activities of the business. (This is the case for Wal-Mart.)
2.  Cash flows from operating activities are more than sufficient to cover cash used for investing. (Again, this is the case for Wal-Mart.)

In the opposite direction, a positive cash flow due to financing activities and not operations may mean trouble. It could be that the company is taking on a lot of debt. (There are three items relating to debt in the cash flow statements for Wal-Mart: short-term borrowings, issuance of long-term debt, and payment of long-term debt. Overall, the net proceeds from these items were $4,820 million in 2008, followed by net decreases of $2,566 million in 2009 and $1,520 million in 2010. So there is nothing to be concerned about in terms of size and direction. Note, however, this is the result of cash flows from changes in debt positions. It does not mean that the company may not already have unreasonably high levels of debt. This question is addressed in Chapter 5.)

## Equity Statement

The fourth financial statement is called the *statement of changes in stockholders'* (or *shareholders'*) *equity* or simply the *equity statement*. As the name suggests, it contains a breakdown of the items that change the equity over a financial year. Publicly traded companies have only been required to prepare this statement since 1998. The items in the statement are of two types: (1) shareholder transactions such as stock repurchases, stock offerings, or dividend payments, and (2) nonshareholder transactions. These latter transactions are referred to as *comprehensive income*.

The first item within the comprehensive income is net income, which can be entered from the income statement. The other items, which collectively are called *other comprehensive income*, are generally not so well known. They include foreign currency translation adjustments, minimum pension liability adjustments, unrealized appreciation of certain investments, and certain gains or losses on derivative contracts which affect equity but are not included in the income statement. Consider the item called foreign currency translation adjustments. If a U.S. company has an operation that is relatively self-contained and integrated within a foreign country, then translation adjustments that arise from consolidating that foreign operation do not impact cash flows and are not included in net income. However, it is required that these adjustments be included as part of comprehensive income in the equity statement. The general format of a shareholders' equity statement is shown in Figure 4.4.

Equity at start of period
  Comprehensive income
    Net earnings
    Other comprehensive income
      Foreign currency translation adjustments
      Minimum pension liability adjustments
      Unrealized appreciation of certain investments
      Certain gains or losses on derivative contracts
      Other items
  Total comprehensive income
  Dividends
  Other stockholder transactions
Equity at end of period

**Figure 4.4**  Typical Layout of the Equity Statement

### Equity Statement

The equity statement or the statement of changes in shareholders' equity describes the changes in a company's equity over the reporting period. An important component is comprehensive income, which includes all changes in equity during a period except those resulting from shareholder transactions such as investments by shareholders and distributions to shareholders.

Another way to understand the equity statement is in terms of what is called the *clean surplus relationship*. As a broad generalization, in each accounting period the equity at the end of the period is equal to equity at the start plus the income over the period less the dividends paid. On a per share basis, this is called the clean surplus relationship and is written as:

$$B' = B + e - d$$

where
  $B$ is the book value at the start of the period
  $B'$ is the book value at the end
  $e$ is the earnings per share over the period
  $d$ is the dividends paid over the same period

As we have just indicated, this is not the full story. The equity statement shows that, apart from net income and dividends, there may be extra shareholder transactions and extra entries in comprehensive income, which invalidates the relationship. Just the same, it is a "very reasonable approximation."[9] The clean surplus relationship plays a crucial role in a number of the valuation methods in later chapters, particularly the variations of the dividend discount method in Chapter 8.

Table 4.5 summarizes the equity statements for Wal-Mart over three years. At the start of the year is the total equity of the company, which can be read straight from the balance sheet (Table 4.2). For example, at the start of the 2010 financial year the equity was $65,285 million, which rises to $70,749 million at the end of the year. During the year the company received $14,335 million in net income (seen in the income statement, Table 4.3) and paid out $4,217 million in dividends (seen in the cash flow statement, Table 4.4).

**Table 4.5**   Consolidated Statements of Shareholders' Equity for Wal-Mart
(Amounts in Millions)

| | |
|---|---:|
| *Balance on February 1, 2007* | *$61,573* |
| Consolidated net income | 12,731 |
| Other comprehensive income | 1,356 |
| Cash dividends ($0.88 per share) | (3,586) |
| Purchase of company stock | (7,691) |
| Stock options exercised and other | 385 |
| Adoption of accounting for uncertainty in income taxes | (160) |
| *Balance on January 31, 2008* | *$64,608* |
| Consolidated net income | 13,400 |
| Other comprehensive income | (6,552) |
| Cash dividends ($0.95 per share) | (3,746) |
| Purchase of company stock | (3,416) |
| Stock options exercised and other | 991 |
| *Balance on January 31, 2009* | *$65,285* |
| Consolidated net income | 14,335 |
| Other comprehensive income | 2,618 |
| Cash dividends ($1.09 per share) | (4,217) |
| Purchase of company stock | (7,397) |
| Purchase of redeemable noncontrolling interest | (288) |
| Stock options exercised and other | 413 |
| *Balance on January 31, 2010* | *$70,749* |

In most cases the components of the other comprehensive income are shown in the equity statement. However, some companies
now report the breakdown of the comprehensive income in a separate table. Table 4.6 shows the components of comprehensive income
for Wal-Mart for the three most recent financial years. For example,
Table 4.5 shows that during the 2010 financial year the other comprehensive income was a profit of $2,618 million. In Table 4.6 this
is shown to be made up of profits of $2,854 million from foreign
currency translation and $94 million from net changes in fair value
of derivatives (this takes us back to the Black and Scholes formula
mentioned in Chapter 2), with losses of $220 million in minimum
pension liabilities and $110 million in net currency translation at-
tributable to the noncontrolling interests. Notice that the amount
$2,618 is precisely the increase in accumulated other comprehensive
income discussed in the earlier section on the balance sheet.

If the clean surplus relationship were to hold on a company-wide
basis, the equity at the end of the year should equal the equity at the
start of the year plus net profit less dividends. This means that the

**Table 4.6** Supplementary Statements of Shareholders' Equity for Wal-Mart (Amounts in Millions)

|  | 2010 | 2009 | 2008 |
| --- | --- | --- | --- |
| *Comprehensive Income* | | | |
| Consolidated net income | $14,848 | $13,899 | $13,137 |
| Other comprehensive income: | | | |
| Currency translation | 2,854 | (6,860) | 1,226 |
| Net change in fair values of derivatives | 94 | (17) | — |
| Minimum pension liability | (220) | (46) | 138 |
| Total comprehensive income | 17,576 | 6,976 | 14,501 |
| *Less amounts attributable to the noncontrolling interest* | | | |
| Net income | (513) | (499) | (406) |
| Currency translation | (110) | 371 | (8) |
| Amounts attributable to the noncontrolling interest | (623) | (128) | (414) |
| Comprehensive income attributable to Wal-Mart | $16,953 | $6,848 | $14,087 |

Fiscal years ended January 31.

equity on January 31, 2010, should be:

$$\$65,285 \text{ million} + \$14,335 \text{ million} - \$4,217 \text{ million}$$
$$= \$75,403 \text{ million}$$

However, it is only $70,749 million, a difference of $4,654 million. Where did this equity go? Apart from the comprehensive income just described, there are two other entries. The first is the purchase of company stock for $7,397 million. The purchase of company stock is money used by Wal-Mart to buy back its shares. (We knew that the company was buying back its shares since the number of shares outstanding was seen to be decreasing in the income statement.) Notice that the net foreign currency translation was a profit for the fiscal year ending January 2010 compared to a substantial deficit the previous year. The positive item of $413 million is a result of the exercise of options directly with the company by option holders. Usually these are employees and management who had been awarded options because of performance bonuses.

Table 4.7 shows the difference between the actual equity at the end of the year and the equity that would have resulted from the clean surplus relationship. The entries in the last column compare the discrepancy to what would be expected from the clean surplus relationship. Even though they affect the balance sheet, we cannot actually call the entries in the last column income or loss since they would then have to be included in the income statement. We had

**Table 4.7**  Clean Surplus Discrepancy for Wal-Mart

| (1) End of Financial Year | (2) Equity at Start of Year | (3) Earnings | (4) Dividends | (5) Equity at End of Year | (6) Clean Surplus Discrepancy |
|---|---|---|---|---|---|
| Jan. 31, 2008 | $61,573 | $12,731 | $3,586 | $64,608 | $6,110 |
| Jan. 31, 2009 | $64,608 | $13,400 | $3,746 | $65,285 | $8,977 |
| Jan. 31, 2010 | $65,285 | $14,335 | $4,217 | $70,749 | $4,654 |

Column (2) shows the equity at the start of the financial year in column (1). The earnings and dividends are shown in columns (3) and (4) while column (5) shows the equity at the end of the year. Column (6) is the difference between the *clean surplus equity* (defined as equity plus earnings net dividends) less the actual equity at the end of the year.

a similar problem with the balance sheet. Off-balance-sheet transactions were introduced earlier in the chapter as obligations or guarantees of the company which are not included in the balance sheet. The entries in the equity statement (apart from net income and dividends) have a similar relationship with the income statement. They are types of payments or receipts (or obligations to make these transactions) that are not included in the income statement but still affect the equity. In this sense one can think of them as off-income-statement transactions.

In some cases these off-income-statement transactions may have direct advantages such as when a company buys its own stock, listing it as the entry "purchase of common stock." This is commonly called a *buyback*. But beware: A company may be purchasing stock with one hand while handing it out just as fast, or faster, with the other. The usual reason for this is that the company is awarding a large amount of share-based compensation and bonus payments to employees and management.

## Look for Any Trends or Sudden Changes

Run your eye over the historical levels of comprehensive income in the annual report or 10-K report, looking for any trends or sudden changes. If you see any of these events, try to isolate and understand the transactions that are primarily responsible for them. Also compare the levels of the comprehensive income with the levels of the income of the company.

A further consideration is that if the stock is overvalued, then it does not make sense for anyone to buy the stock, including the company itself. If you own shares in a company, but don't think that it represents value to buy more, then welcoming actions of the company to buy back its own shares is not logical. The company is using its money (i.e., *your* money) to overpay for assets. In the case of Wal-Mart, the income statement (Table 4.3) showed that the company has been reducing the number of shares outstanding over the past two years.

 **Warning: Consistently Low Comprehensive Income**

If in most years the comprehensive income is consistently below the net income, then it would be sensible to lower any growth forecasts, particularly forecasts of earnings per share, that you may have made. The reason for this is that the company has been accumulating losses in comprehensive income aside from the regular income, which may indicate that the economic situation is worse than it would appear from an analysis of the income statement.

### The Bottom Line

1. It is important to have at least a basic understanding of accounting principles and financial statements to be able to understand, apply, and interpret valuation formulas.
2. There are four principal financial statements: the balance sheet, giving a snapshot of a company's assets, liabilities, and net equity at the end of the reporting period; the income statement, describing the revenues or sales and expenses over the reporting period; the cash flow statement, covering the cash flows of a company in the areas of operating, investing, and financing activities over the reporting period; and the equity statement, covering all the items that change the equity of a company over the reporting period.
3. Approach the financial statements as tools to allow you to follow the money. Where did it come from and how much was it? What was it used for? How much was left over?

# CHAPTER 5

# Everything Is Number and Ratio

*We are eager to hear from principals or their representatives about businesses . . . earning good returns on equity.*

—Warren Buffett[1]

*Combining numbers from different financial statements unleashes vast new analytical power.*

—Martin Fridson and Fernando Alvarez[2]

The Pythagoreans of ancient Greece pictured the world as being made up of number and ratio. We can think of the previous chapter on financial statements as describing companies in terms of number. In this chapter we look at the second part of the Pythagorean depiction by using financial ratios to assess companies. A financial ratio is not a valuation method in the sense that intrinsic value is. Just the same, such ratios are useful in helping to determine whether an investment is likely to be successful.

Consider a company that had a return on equity (ROE) of 20 percent for a number of years with all the signs indicating that this level will continue into the future. Assume that it pays no dividends. As a general approximation, its earnings per share (EPS) will grow by around 20 percent per year. If the price-to-earnings (P/E) ratio stayed fairly constant, this would represent an average annual return of 20 percent per year. This means that its price will double in less than four years and will triple in around six years. In 10 years the price will have grown by over 600 percent. Even if the P/E ratio halves over the next 10 years, it would still return around 12 percent per year, a profitable investment by most people's standards.[3] In contrast, if a company's return on equity is only 5 percent and seems likely to remain level in the future, it is unlikely to be a successful investment. Put another way, money cannot come from nowhere. Therefore, the ability of management—as measured by ratios such as return on equity—is a crucial indicator of whether to invest in a particular company.

Another role of financial ratios is to compare companies of different sizes. One company may have net profit of $10 billion, another only $10 million. It makes no sense to compare directly the financial statements of these two companies, whereas financial ratios provide useful comparisons. For example, the first company might have produced its profit using equity of $100 billion and the second company with $50 million. By dividing earnings by equity we see that the return on equity for the two companies is 10 percent and 20 percent. This provides us with a means of comparing the two companies: The second company is getting twice the return on equity of the first company, something to be welcomed by investors looking for value.

## Ratios Galore

The first issue to face is that there are virtually an unlimited number of financial ratios. No matter how big your list of ratios, it seems it is always possible to find one more. Also, most of the standard ratios have alternative definitions. To help overcome this difficulty, in this chapter I chose a core selection of financial ratios based on common use and my experience. They are in the areas of management performance, debt, and liquidity. For some of the ratios I will indicate what levels we should look for as pointers toward potentially valuable investments. And, to help clarify the definitions and how they are put together from entries in the financial statements, the ratios will be calculated for Wal-Mart using data from the previous chapter.

In evaluating a company for an investment portfolio, we can use financial ratios in three ways:

1. Examine the company's financial ratios as a guide to its strengths and weaknesses.
2. Compare the financial ratios in step 1 with the ratios of other companies and with the average ratios for the sector and the overall market.
3. Review the history of the financial ratios of the company for signs of favorable or unfavorable trends.

Financial ratios also act in a support role for the valuation methods described in later chapters. For example, healthy financial ratios such as a low debt-to-equity ratio make it more likely that the price of a seemingly undervalued company (that is, via some valuation method) will rise to the company's intrinsic value.

Apart from different web sites and financial institutions using variations of the same ratio, differences can even occur when they use the same definition. This is because the users often have different rules for extracting the data used in the ratios from the financial statements. When the ratios are published by the company itself, even further variations in the results can occur. Another variation can occur in the results depending on whether rounding is done before or after the calculation is performed. (An unpleasant consequence is that it can be enormously time consuming to try to duplicate any of the ratio results displayed on web sites or in financial reports without having access to the specific method they use and their data rules.)

We can protect ourselves from this problem by not looking for companies that just scrape through any prescribed ratio levels or thresholds that we may have set. Rather, we want to find companies that top required ratio levels by significant amounts. This makes it less likely that we will get tripped up by the variations of any individual ratio or by different rules for selecting data. If a company's ratio *strongly* passes one variation and one set of data, then it is almost certainly going to pass all the other variations with comparable data. Another advantage is that we have a safety buffer should things not quite go to plan. For example, suppose our valuation method requires that a company achieves a 15 percent return on equity over the next five years. By focusing our search on companies that had a 20 percent return on equity over recent years, we have the possibility of the type of investment we want while still allowing for a decline in business performance.

## Companies That Strongly Pass Thresholds

Look for companies that strongly pass any prescribed ratio levels or thresholds that we may have set and not those that just scrape through. This will establish a margin of safety and help avoid the problems of different variations of the same ratio and different methods of selecting the data used in the calculations.

## Management Performance Ratios

It is impossible for outsiders to know much about the abilities of management in running a business in areas such as style, clarity of analysis, creativity, and foresight. What we can do, though, is bypass these questions and go straight to the bottom line for management and ask how well management is using the resources it has available to it. We call these *management performance* (or simply *management*) *ratios* and look at four of them: return on equity (ROE), return on capital (ROC), return on assets (ROA), and net profit margin (NPM). They are displayed in Table 5.1.

Buffett and other analysts make it very clear that they consider return on equity and return on capital to be very important. For example, each year in the annual report of Berkshire Hathaway, Buffett writes that he is "eager to hear from principals or their representatives . . . about businesses earning good returns on equity while employing little or no debt."[4] (We will come to the issue of debt shortly.) Also, Buffett often talks about return on capital. For example, in the 2007 annual report, he declared that "a truly great business must have an enduring 'moat' that protects excellent returns on invested capital." Charles Mizrahi talks about return on equity as his "deserted island" indicator and writes, "If I could only have one piece of information about a company, I would want to know the ROE."[5] For Pat Dorsey, return on capital is "the best benchmark of a company's profitability."[6] A lot of the effectiveness of return on equity comes from the fact that it combines financial data from both the balance sheet and the income statement.

**Table 5.1**　Summary of Main Management Performance Financial Ratios

| Ratio | Method of Calculation | What It Measures |
|---|---|---|
| Return on equity (ROE) | Net profit / Total equity | Measures the profitability of the company from the perspective of equity. |
| Return on Capital (ROC) | Net profit / Total capital | Measures how well management is using the funds, equity plus long-term debt, that they have available to them. |
| Return on assets (ROA) | Net profit / Total assets | Measures the efficiency of the company in generating profits from its assets. |
| Net profit margin (NPM) | Net profit / Net sales | Measures how much the company keeps from each dollar of sales. |

Instead of net profit, the numerator can be replaced by operating income or pretax income.

The reason for the importance of ROE as an indicator of a successful investment can be seen in two steps. First, as explained later in this chapter, high ROE leads to high growth in earnings (assuming that the company can reinvest its earnings at the same rate). Second, Chapter 11 explains how high growth in earnings leads to high growth in the share price. Putting these two steps together gives the result that high ROE leads, over time, to high growth in price, what we all want as investors.

---

### Why High Return on Equity Is Desirable

High return on equity generally leads to high growth in earnings which, over time, leads to high growth in price.

---

*Return on equity* is defined as the net profit over a financial year divided by the common stock equity at the end of the period. It is a key measure of how well a company is performing for its shareholders. If return on equity is and has been low with little sign that it will improve in the future, then it is unlikely that it will be a satisfactory investment. Table 5.2 shows that Wal-Mart's return on equity for the 2010 financial year was 20.26 percent, an excellent level. Put another way, if we were regularly getting a return of around 20 percent on our equity, then I am sure we would be very happy investors.

As stated earlier, most of the main financial ratios have alternative definitions. Sometimes different financial institutions even use different data—or rather, they use different rules for extracting the required data from the financial statements. I won't keep discussing these variations. However, in the simple case of return on equity I will look at a few examples. These will give an indication of the range

**Table 5.2**  Return on Equity Calculations for Wal-Mart

| Entry | Financial Statement | Table | Amount |
|-------|---------------------|-------|--------|
| Net profit | Income statement | 4.3 | $14,335 |
| Equity | Balance sheet | 4.2 | $70,749 |
| Return on equity | | | 20.26% |

Data is in millions of dollars. Return on equity of 20.26 percent is calculated as $14,335 million divided by $70,749 million.

of variations that you might encounter, and reinforce the idea that it is pointless and time consuming to spend too much effort analyzing and comparing the different methods. It is more fruitful to choose a method and a reliable data source and use them consistently. But there is a disclaimer: If any of the ratios calculated from or supplied by different sources differ by significant amounts, it may be worthwhile to investigate the reason.

Morningstar averages the equity at the start and the end of the year. Since the equity at the start of the year ending January 31, 2010, was $65,285 million and at the end of the year it was $70,749 million, the average over the whole year was $68,017 million. Dividing the net profit of $14,335 million by this average gives 21.08 percent for return on equity.

A different approach is taken by Thomson Reuters and Standard & Poor's. They adjust the net profit by a loss of $79 million due to discontinued operations, giving $14,414 million for the new value. Dividing by $68,017 million (the average of the equity at the start and end of the year), gives 21.19 percent for return on equity. The data and analysis company Value Line uses different rules for selecting the data for net profit. They display net profit as $14,404 million. Dividing by $70,749, the equity at the end of January 2010, gives return on equity equal to 20.08 percent. Zack's Investment Research display return on equity on their website as 20.65 percent for the end of January 2010.

The second management ratio in the table is *return on capital*. It is a partner to return on equity and vitally important for measuring the effectiveness of management. Once again, turning to Buffett: "We believe a more appropriate measure of managerial economic performance to be return on equity capital [rather than simple growth in earnings]."[7] The basic idea is that it measures the profit of the business in terms of the capital employed to create that profit. Within this framework there are even more variations than there were for return on equity. For instance, the numerator can be net profit, net profit plus interest, or net operating profit. Value Line even uses net profit plus half the interest paid. The capital as the denominator starts with equity and adds various amounts related to debt. In some cases only long-term debt is used while in others current debt is also included.

The simplest definition of return on capital is the ratio of net income to the sum of total equity plus long-term debt and capital lease obligations. It may also include short-term debt and capital lease obligations. Using this definition (without the short-term entries), Table 5.3 shows that Wal-Mart's return on capital for the 2009 financial year was 13.38 percent. This is an acceptable level. A standard variation requires the interest paid on the debt and obligations under capital leases to be added to the net income in the numerator. This balances what was done in the denominator where the debt was added to the equity. In the case of Wal-Mart, Table 4.3 shows that the interest on the debt was $1,787 million and the interest on the capital leases was $278 million. When these amounts are added to the net profit of $14,335 million the new denominator becomes $16,400 million. Dividing by $107,150 million as described in Table 5.3 gives return on equity equal to 15.31 percent.

For some companies there is no difference between return on equity and return on capital because there is no debt. A difference between the two ratios as large as that for Wal-Mart means that the company has fairly high debt. We will see that this is, indeed, the case when we look at debt ratios. Note also that there are variations in the name of the ratio such as *return on invested capital* and *return on equity employed*.

*Return on assets* is similar to return on equity except that equity is replaced by assets. Since equity is assets minus liabilities, except in the case when the company has no liabilities, return on assets is less than return on equity. The calculations for Wal-Mart are shown in Table 5.4

There are variations of all the previous ratios. In some cases, for example, the equity, capital, or assets at the end of the period are replaced by the averages of their values at the start and the end of

**Table 5.3**   Return on Capital Calculations for Wal-Mart

| Entry | Financial Statement | Table | Amount |
|-------|--------------------|-------|--------|
| Net profit | Income statement | 4.3 | $14,335 |
| Equity | Balance sheet | 4.2 | $70,749 |
| Long-term debt | Balance sheet | 4.2 | $33,231 |
| Long-term obligations under capital leases | Balance sheet | 4.2 | $3,170 |
| | | Return on capital | 13.38% |

Data is in millions of dollars. The return on capital of 13.38 percent is calculated as $14,335 million divided by $107,150, which is the total of $70,749 million, $33,231 million, and $3,170 million.

**Table 5.4**    Return on Assets Calculations for Wal-Mart

| Entry | Financial Statement | Table | Amount |
|---|---|---|---|
| Net profit | Income statement | 4.3 | $14,335 |
| Assets | Balance sheet | 4.2 | $170,706 |
| | Return on assets | | 8.40% |

Data is in millions of dollars. Return on assets of 8.40 percent is calculated as $14,335 million divided by $170,706 million.

the period. Another variation is to calculate the ratios before or after extraordinary items. In the short term (that is, over time spans of a few years), recalculating ratios before extraordinary items makes sense since we want to see how management is performing with respect to normal operations. In the longer term, however, if a company continually has impairment costs and costs related to extraordinary items, then it may be better to include them in earnings calculations. This is because these losses (or gains) will impact the business over time just as much as the results from the regular operations of the business. For example, if an enterprise regularly pays out large sums for companies and then writes them down by substantial amounts after a few years, then these observations should not be dismissed because each individual item is considered extraordinary. It may be that the profits of this company are always going to be hurt by write-downs of poorly chosen acquisitions. What is important is to look for companies with ratios that are well inside any of the usual thresholds so as to give a wide margin of safety to allow for variations in definitions and accounting approaches.

## The Importance of Management Performance Ratios

Use management performance ratios such as return on equity and return on capital to measure the ability of management. Unless they are at reasonable levels, it will be hard for an investment to be successful.

*Net profit margin* is the ratio of earnings or net profit divided by sales or revenue. It measures the amount of money coming in from the activities that is actually kept after all the expenses. This ratio varies enormously between industries and is a key component

**Table 5.5**    Net Profit Margin Calculations for Wal-Mart

| Entry | Financial Statement | Table | Amount |
|---|---|---|---|
| Net profit | Income statement | 4.3 | $14,335 |
| Net sales | Income statement | 4.3 | $405,046 |
| | | Net profit margin | 3.54% |

Data is in millions of dollars. The net profit margin of 3.54 percent is calculated as $14,335 million divided by $405,046 million.

of the DuPont analysis of return on equity discussed later in this chapter. Table 5.5 shows that Wal-Mart's net profit margin for the 2010 financial year was 3.54 percent, a fairly typical level for high volume retailers.

## Look for Consistency

Look for levels of these management ratios that are high and consistent. During most years a satisfactory level for return on equity and return on capital is 10 percent, but more desirable is 15 percent or above. When Warren Buffett was interim chairman of Salomon Inc. during its time of problems in 1991, he indicated that 15 percent was the level he looked for. As part of an interview for *Forbes* he stated, "As long as we can make an annual 15 percent return on equity, I don't worry about one quarter's results."[8]

##  Warning: Contracting Equity

Return on equity can be high for two reasons: Either the earnings are high or the equity is low. Make sure return on equity has not been pumped up by a contracting equity through too many write-downs or devaluations. Another way that the equity can drop significantly is through share buybacks. The result is a sudden jump in return on equity. The effect of buybacks on ROE and other ratios will be examined later in the chapter.

## Debt or Leverage Ratios

The next set of ratios measure different aspects of debt in terms of leverage (the amount of debt compared to various measures of the

**Table 5.6**   Summary of Main Debt or Leverage Financial Ratios

| Ratio | Method of Calculation | What It Measures |
|---|---|---|
| Debt ratio | $\dfrac{\text{Total liabilities}}{\text{Total assets}}$ | Measures degree of financial leverage as the proportion of assets financed by liabilities. |
| Debt to equity | $\dfrac{\text{Total debt}}{\text{Equity}}$ | Measures the relationship of debt to equity. |
| Financial leverage multiplier | $\dfrac{\text{Total assets}}{\text{Total equity}}$ | Measures the degree to which the company is financed through debt. |
| Interest coverage ratio | $\dfrac{\text{Pretax income} + \text{Interest expense}}{\text{Interest expense}}$ | Measures how many times interest expense could be increased and still be covered by pretax income. |

These are the main debt or leverage ratios. Instead of total debt, other measures of debt such as long-term debt, interest-bearing debt, or total liabilities can be used.

assets of the company) and interest coverage (the ability of the company to meet its interest payments). We include four ratios: the debt ratio, debt to equity, financial leverage multiplier, and the interest coverage ratio. Each of these ratios measures a different aspect of debt and is shown in Table 5.6. Generally speaking, companies are best served if they take on some debt, assuming that they can use it at a higher rate than they pay for it. However, too much debt can make a company vulnerable to any increases in interest rates or claims by its creditors for early repayment of debt. It can also prevent the company from taking advantage of expansion opportunities that require extra capital.

The first ratio is the *debt ratio*, defined as total liabilities divided by total assets. Since we are talking about total assets, we are going beyond the normal use of the term *debt* in the sense of specific debt contracts. However, an alternative definition takes this into account and defines the debt ratio as interest-bearing debt divided by total assets. Notice that since the numerator (total liabilities) is included in the denominator (assets), the debt ratio can never exceed 100 percent. Table 5.7 shows the calculations of the debt ratio for Wal-Mart based on its balance sheet in Chapter 4. (Recall that Wal-Mart did not actually include total liabilities in its balance sheet. However, we carried out this straightforward calculation in the text.)

The next ratio, *debt to equity*, measures the ratio between the funds supplied by creditors, which is debt, and the funds supplied by investors, which is equity. In the event of bankruptcy, creditors must

**Table 5.7**   Debt Ratio Calculations for Wal-Mart

| Entry | Financial Statement | Table | Amount |
| --- | --- | --- | --- |
| Total liabilities | Balance sheet | 4.2 | $99,957 |
| Assets | Balance sheet | 4.2 | $170,706 |
| | | Debt ratio | 58.56% |

Data is in millions of dollars. The debt ratio of 58.56 percent is calculated as $99,957 million divided by $170,706 million

be paid before owners and so the debt-to-equity ratio is a measure of risk associated with the business. Usually the debt-to-equity ratio only includes long-term debt. However, because of the ease with which companies can roll over short-term debt, many companies use short-term financing to fund long-term projects. This just means that it pays to be alert when using any of these ratios. As a broad rule of thumb, be particularly careful with companies that have a ratio of debt to equity above 50 percent.

 **Warning: The Debt Ratio Can Be Misleading**

If a company has a lot of debt, sometimes it will tend to put more attention on the debt ratio in its reports than on the debt-to-equity ratio. This is because the debt ratio is always below 100 percent and so it looks more benign. The debt-to-equity ratio is a better indicator of the debt level of a company, so use it as a starting point when evaluating the debt position of a company.

Table 5.8 shows that Wal-Mart's debt-to-equity ratio for the financial year 2010 was 51.45 percent.

**Table 5.8**   Debt to Equity Calculations for Wal-Mart

| Entry | Financial Statement | Table | Amount |
| --- | --- | --- | --- |
| Long-term debt | Balance sheet | 4.2 | $33,231 |
| Long-term obligations | Balance sheet | 4.2 | $3,170 |
| Equity | Balance sheet | 4.2 | $70,749 |
| | | Debt to Equity | 51.45% |

Data is in millions of dollars. The debt to equity ratio of 51.45 percent is calculated as $36,401 million (which is the total of $33,231 million and $3,170 million) divided by $70,749 million.

## Warren Buffett Talking about Debt

Warren Buffett has a clear opinion about the dangers of high levels of debt for Berkshire Hathaway or when considering companies to invest in. Here are few examples taken from annual reports of Berkshire Hathaway.

"Good business or investment decisions will eventually produce quite satisfactory economic results, with no aid from leverage." (1986)

"A small chance of distress or disgrace [because of high debt] cannot, in our view, be offset by a large chance of extra returns." (1988)

"The roads of business are riddled with potholes [because of debt]; a plan that requires dodging them all is a plan for disaster." (1990)

"Debt is a four-letter word around Berkshire." (2001)

"We use debt sparingly and, when we do borrow, we attempt to structure our loans on a long-term fixed-rate basis. We will reject interesting opportunities rather than over-leverage our balance sheet.... The financial calculus that Charlie and I employ would never permit our trading a good night's sleep for a shot at a few extra percentage points of return." (2008)

The last debt ratio we consider is the *financial leverage multiplier*, defined as total assets divided by total equity. Since assets are equal to equity plus liabilities, the ratio of assets divided by equity equals 1.0 plus liabilities divided by equity. This means that if the financial leverage multiplier is 1.0, the company has no liabilities; the further it is above 1.0, the greater the liabilities compared to the equity. It is called a multiplier instead of a ratio since it measures the multiplying effect of extra liabilities. Table 5.9 shows that Wal-Mart's financial leverage multiplier for the financial year 2010 was 2.41.

The final ratio in this section is called the *interest coverage ratio*. It measures the ability of the company to pay its interest bill and is defined as earnings from continuing operations before interest and taxes over a financial year (commonly called EBIT) divided by the interest expense over the same period. The higher the ratio, the bigger the safety margin the company has in being able to pay the interest on its loans. It is also called *times interest earned*. Anything below 2.0 should be watched carefully, while below 1.0 means that

**Table 5.9**   Financial Leverage Multiplier Calculations for Wal-Mart

| Entry | Financial Statement | Table | Amount |
|---|---|---|---|
| Total assets | Balance sheet | 4.2 | $170,706 |
| Equity | Balance sheet | 4.2 | $70,749 |
| | | Financial leverage | 2.41 |

Data is in millions of dollars. The financial leverage multiplier of 2.41 is calculated as $170,706 million divided by $70,749 million.

the company is not earning enough to pay its interest bill. Table 5.10 shows that Wal-Mart's interest coverage ratio for the 2010 financial year was 11.44. All the entries are from the income statement shown as Table 4.3 in Chapter 4.

### Examine How the Debt Is Being Used

The level of debt is important, but perhaps more important is what the debt is being used for. Look for any spikes in the debt-to-equity ratio over past years. If there are any, try to ascertain what the extra debt is being used for. Buying companies that have little relationship with the core business is a warning sign. Alternatively, buying companies that augment the existing business may be a sign that management wants to be more active in growing the business and is not content with internal organic growth. Notice whether the business has taken on extra debt in the past but has managed to reduce it to reasonable levels over the next two or three years. This is a sign of the ability of management to make sensible acquisitions and then integrate them quickly into the overall business.

###  Warning: Zero Net Debt

Be alert when companies state that they have zero net debt. It does not mean that the company has no debt. *Net debt* means total debt less cash and other similar liquid assets, so zero net debt simply means that it could, in principle, pay all its debts. However, most companies need reserves in cash and cash equivalents to be able to operate, so it is not feasible to use all of them to pay off debt.

**Table 5.10**   Interest Coverage Ratio for Wal-Mart

| Entry | Amount |
|---|---|
| Income from continuing operations before income taxes and minority interest (1) | $22,066 |
| Minority interest loss (2) | ($513) |
| Debt income (3) | $1,787 |
| Capital leases income (4) | $278 |
| Earnings from continuing operations before interest and taxes (EBIT) (5) | $23,618 |
| Interest expense (6) | $2,065 |
| Interest coverage (7) | 11.44 |

Data is in millions of dollars. Line (5) is the sum of lines (1), (2), (3), and (4). Line (6) is the sum of lines (3) and (4). Line (7) is line (5) divided by line (6). Hence the interest coverage ratio 11.44 is calculated as $23,618 million divided by $2,065 million.

## Liquidity Ratios

The third group of ratios (shown in Table 5.11) describes the liquidity of the business in terms of its ability to meet its short-term debt and liability obligations. The *current ratio* is a measure of how well the company is able to withstand a sudden demand on its current liabilities. Would it be able to pay them relatively easily if they were suddenly all called in? If the current ratio is below 1.0, then the company may have difficulties meeting its short-term obligations. Conversely, if it is too high, then it may be that it is not using its current assets efficiently. The *quick ratio* is similar to the current ratio except that the numerator only consists of the assets that can be accessed quickly, namely cash plus receivables. A weakness of the current ratio is that

**Table 5.11**   Summary of Main Liquidity Financial Ratios

| Ratio | Method of Calculation | What It Measures |
|---|---|---|
| Current ratio | Current assets / Current liabilities | A basic measure of short-term liquidity. |
| Quick ratio | Cash + Receivables / Current liabilities | A variant of the current ratio that includes only those current assets that can be quickly converted into cash. |
| Total asset turnover | Revenue / Assets | A measure of the efficiency of the company's use of its assets. |

it includes inventory, which may be of doubtful value if the company is required to liquidate it quickly. Therefore, it is recommended that both ratios be considered since the quick ratio does not include inventory. (The quick ratio is also called the *acid test*.)

Currently, the average levels of the current ratio and quick ratio for the companies in the S&P 500 Index are approximately 2.1 and 1.6, respectively. Using these average levels as a guideline, broadly speaking, a current ratio or quick ratio that is high could mean that the company has a lazy balance sheet and is not making maximum use of its current assets. For example, it may be that inventory is building up because of slowing sales. So it is not necessarily true that the higher the current ratio and quick ratio, the better. In the opposite direction, if the ratios are low, the company could be in danger of defaulting on payables or loans.

### Current Ratio and Quick Ratio

As a broad rule of thumb, a high current ratio or quick ratio is not necessarily a positive sign, but if it is low or trending down it is generally a negative sign.

There are times when these simple comparisons with average levels can be misleading since acceptable levels of the current ratio and quick ratio vary considerably between industries and even between companies within an industry. For example, retail stores, particularly supermarkets, tend to have lower ratios. Most of their revenues are in cash, so they have low receivables and hence low current assets. At the same time, commonly their agreements with their suppliers give them 30 days or longer to pay, so they have high payables and hence high current liabilities. Tables 5.12 and 5.13 show that Wal-Mart's

**Table 5.12**   Current Ratio Calculations for Wal-Mart

| Entry | Financial Statement | Table | Amount |
|-------|---------------------|-------|--------|
| Current assets | Balance sheet | 4.2 | $48,331 |
| Current liabilities | Balance sheet | 4.2 | $55,561 |
| | | Current ratio | 0.87 |

Data is in millions of dollars. The current ratio of 0.87 is calculated as $48,331 million divided by $55,561 million.

**Table 5.13**   Quick Ratio Calculations for Wal-Mart

| Entry | Financial Statement | Table | Amount |
|---|---|---|---|
| Cash and equivalents | Balance sheet | 4.2 | $7,907 |
| Receivables | Balance sheet | 4.2 | $4,144 |
| Current liabilities | Balance sheet | 4.2 | $55,561 |
| | | Quick ratio | 0.22 |

Data is in millions of dollars. The quick ratio of 0.22 is calculated as the
total of $7,907 million plus $4,144 million (which is $12,051 million)
divided by $55,561 million.

current ratio and quick ratio for the financial year 2010 were 0.87
and 0.22, typical levels for high volume retailers.

### Examine Ratio Levels

As a general rule, a current ratio of 1.25 or above and a quick ratio of 0.75 or
above are satisfactory levels for industrial companies. But make allowances for
companies where the standard levels are much lower, such as supermarkets
or retail stores. Also, any adverse trends or sudden changes in the levels of
the current ratio and the quick ratio are just as important as the actual levels.
If the levels are trending downward, this could be a sign that the company is
having cash difficulties, forcing it to allow its payables to increase in relation
to its receivables.

Although not strictly a liquidity ratio, we also include *total asset
turnover* in this group. Defined as revenue divided by assets, it measures the efficiency of a company in using its assets to generate sales
or revenue—the higher the number the better. In general terms,
companies with a high total asset turnover have low profit margins,
and companies with a low total asset turnover have high profit margins. Examples of these associations are given in the description of
the DuPont analysis later in the chapter. Table 5.14 shows that Wal-
Mart's total asset turnover for the financial year 2010 was 2.39.

## Return on Equity

Earlier in the chapter we talked about the importance of return on
equity (ROE). Why is it important? Because in broad terms, high

**Table 5.14**   Total Asset Turnover Calculations for Wal-Mart

| Entry | Financial Statement | Table | Amount |
|-------|---------------------|-------|--------|
| Revenue | Income statement | 4.3 | $408,214 |
| Assets | Balance sheet | 4.2 | $170,706 |
| | Total asset turnover | | 2.39 |

Data is in millions of dollars. The total asset turnover of 2.39 is calculated as $408,214 million divided by $170,706 million.

ROE leads to high growth in earnings, and high growth in earnings leads to high growth in the share price. In this section we look at ROE more closely, first via the DuPont analysis which teases apart ROE into its key constituents related to markup, turnover, and debt. Then we look at the relationship between return on equity and the growth of earnings and dividends: why high ROE leads to high growth in earnings and possibly high growth in dividends.

### DuPont Analysis of Return on Equity

One retailer might have a low markup and high turnover. Another might have a high markup and low turnover. A third might have both low markup and low turnover, but employ more debt. The DuPont analysis shows how to quantify statements such as these, allowing performance of a company to be compared with previous years and with other companies. This is done by analyzing return on equity in terms of markup, turnover, and debt. By looking at these components separately as well as piecing them back together in the return-on-equity ratio, we are in a better position as investors to understand the strengths and weaknesses of a business. We are also in a better position to be aware of any actions or developments in a business that could lead to problems further down the track. For example, suppose a company has been maintaining its level of return on equity at a consistent level. Then it might be assumed that it is "business as usual." However, through a DuPont analysis it would be possible to see whether, for example, the asset turnover has been decreasing and the company has been maintaining its return on equity through increased financial leverage, something that is not sustainable.

The DuPont analysis of return on equity is generally credited to Donaldson Brown while he was working at E. I. Du Pont de Nemours and Company (DuPont) during the 1920s. It proceeds by decomposing return on equity (ROE) into three components describing markup, turnover, and debt. These components are:

1. Operating efficiency, measured by net profit margin (NPM).
2. Asset use efficiency, measured by total asset turnover (TAT).
3. Financial leverage, measured by the financial leverage multiplier (FLM).

Notice that NPM is net profit divided by total revenue, TAT is total revenue divided by total assets, and FLM is total assets divided by equity. Hence, when they are multiplied together the result is net profit divided by equity, which is return on equity. This means that we have the following formula:

$$ROE = NPM \times TAT \times FLM$$

which is referred to as the DuPont analysis of return on equity. As usual, all the ratios need to be studied from two perspectives:

1. Current levels and perhaps their levels relative to similar businesses.
2. Trends or sudden changes in the levels.

### DuPont Analysis of Return on Equity

The DuPont analysis analyzes return on equity as a product of markup (net profit margin), turnover (total asset turnover), and debt (financial leverage multiplier).

As a general point, companies from different sectors and industries may have similar returns on equity, but when scrutinized using the DuPont analysis it becomes clear that they may be obtained in quite different ways. For example, retail companies such as supermarket chains tend to have very low net profit margins and moderately low financial leverage. To obtain a satisfactory return on equity they need to have high asset turnover. For this reason, when analyzing a chain of retail stores it is prudent to look at growth of same-store sales rather than solely relying on the company continually opening new stores to obtain growth.

Wal-Mart is an example of a company that has low profit margins, around 3 to 4 percent, but achieves excellent return on equity through a high total asset turnover and judicious use of leverage. For example, Wal-Mart might spend $1,000 buying a shipment of cans of baked beans. Even though when they are sold, the store might only make a profit of $30, it can immediately spend the new amount of $1,030 to buy another shipment of the product. If this is repeated four times in a year, the company has made a profit of $120 on the original $1,000, a return on equity of 12 percent. Suppose that instead of using its own $1,000 to make the original purchase, it only uses $500 and borrows the rest, the return on equity is now 24 percent. (To keep the analysis simple, we are disregarding the effects of taxes, interest, and other expenses.) In this way the company uses high turnover and leverage to boost its low net profit margin.

Other industries, such as fashion and high-tech, with strong brand names and intellectual property, often have much higher profit margins. In this case, the ability to increase sales through an increase in prices becomes a crucial issue. An example of a high net profit margin company is Microsoft Corporation (Microsoft) with a net profit margin of around 25 percent. Another example is Coach Incorporated (Coach), the designer and marketer of handbags and other accessories, with a level of approximately 19 percent. These companies typically have much lower turnover of their assets and rely on a high net profit margin to attain satisfactory levels for their return on equity.

Finally, there are industries that achieve high return on equity through taking on substantial debt, giving them high financial leverage. Banks and financial institutions often fall into this category. Their levels would be considered unacceptably risky for most industrial companies. American Express, the global payments and travel company, is an example of a company with a very high level of financial leverage; it is over 8.

Table 5.15 lists a breakdown of the return on equity of Wal-Mart, Microsoft, Coach, and American Express using the DuPont analysis. The return on equity for these companies ranges from high to very high. Using the DuPont analysis it becomes clear that they generate this return in quite different ways.

**Table 5.15**   DuPont Analysis of Selected Companies

| Company | Ticker | Return on Equity | Net Profit Margin | Total Asset Turnover | Financial Leverage |
|---|---|---|---|---|---|
| Wal-Mart | WMT | 20.26% | 3.54% | 2.37 | 2.41 |
| Microsoft | MSFT | 36.83% | 24.93% | 0.75 | 1.97 |
| Coach | COH | 36.75% | 19.30% | 1.26 | 1.51 |
| American Express | AXP | 14.79% | 8.69% | 0.20 | 8.61 |

Return on equity is a product of return on equity, net profit margin, total asset turnover, and financial leverage.

As stated earlier, apart from being a deeper comparative analysis of different companies, the DuPont method can help track any key business trends that may not be apparent from a simple examination of the history of the return on equity. For example, the net profit margin may be decreasing but the decrease is being masked by an increase in financial leverage. Table 5.16 shows the history of return on equity and its components as presented in the DuPont analysis for Wal-Mart for the past six years. There has been a slight downward trend of the net profit margin until 2009, from 3.61 percent to 3.30 percent. In dollar terms, it means that instead of earning $3.61 on each $100 of sales, it is now only $3.30. Slight as it is in dollar terms, proportionally it represents a drop of close to 10 percent in profit for the same amount of sales. Expressed in this way, it becomes clearer how this was camouflaged in the actual return on equity by the slight increases in turnover and leverage. However, last year the net profit margin picked up again to 3.54 percent. Overall Wal-Mart has shown a remarkable level of consistency.

**Table 5.16**   DuPont Analysis of Wal-Mart

| Year (Jan 31) | Return on Equity | Net Profit Margin | Total Asset Turnover | Financial Leverage |
|---|---|---|---|---|
| 2005 | 20.79% | 3.61% | 2.37 | 2.43 |
| 2006 | 21.12% | 3.60% | 2.26 | 2.60 |
| 2007 | 18.33% | 3.24% | 2.30 | 2.46 |
| 2008 | 19.70% | 3.36% | 2.31 | 2.53 |
| 2009 | 20.53% | 3.30% | 2.48 | 2.50 |
| 2010 | 20.26% | 3.54% | 2.37 | 2.41 |

The table shows the return on equity, net profit margin, total asset turnover, and financial leverage for Wal-Mart over the past five financial years.

## Return on Equity and the Growth of Earnings and Dividends

Being able to estimate the growth of earnings or the growth of dividends is crucial for the successful application of many of the valuation methods in later chapters. The accuracy of these estimates is enhanced by understanding the relationship they have with return on equity. The basic relationship is that when the ROE is constant, the growth rate in earnings is approximately equal to the ROE times the earnings retention rate.

As an example, start with a company with initial book value of $10. Assume the company has earnings of $1.50 over the first year. Also assume that the earnings retention rate is 70 percent. This means that 30 percent of the EPS or $0.45 is paid out as a dividend. Assuming the clean surplus relationship, the book value at the end of the first year is $10 + 1.5 - 0.45 = \$11.05$. Hence book value has grown by 10.5 percent. Since ROE is assumed constant, the earnings must also grow by this rate. How does this compare with our assertion about the growth rate of earnings? Since ROE is calculated using equity at the end of the year, the return on equity is $1.50/11.05$ or 13.57 percent. Hence we expect that EPS will grow by $13.57 \times 0.7$ or 9.5 percent, which is close to the actual growth rate for earnings of 10.5 percent.

### Estimate of Earnings Growth Using Return on Equity

Assuming that the return on equity remains constant, the growth rate of earnings is approximately equal to return on equity times the earnings retention rate.

An important particular case is when there are no dividends. When this occurs, the growth rate of earnings is approximately equal to the return on equity. In the previous example, assume that no dividends are paid so that the retention rate is 100 percent. In this case the book value at the end of the year is $11.50, showing that it has grown by 15 percent and hence earnings are growing at 15 percent per year. Turning to return on equity, we see that it is $1.50/11.50$ or 13.04 percent. Hence, as asserted, the growth rate of earnings is approximately equal to the return on equity.

If we assume that the payout ratio for dividends also remains constant, a similar relationship holds for dividends, namely that the growth rate in dividends is approximately equal to ROE times the earnings retention rate.

### Estimate of Dividend Growth Using Return on Equity

Assuming that the return on equity and the payout ratio remain constant, the growth rate of dividends is approximately equal to ROE times the earnings retention rate.

Another variation of this relationship between return on equity, growth of earnings, and the payout ratio is based on the *forward return on equity*, defined as the earnings over a financial year divided by the equity at the start of the year. Think of it as a measure of the level of earnings that can be generated over a financial year using the equity at the start of the year. This time, assuming that the forward return on equity is constant, the growth rate of earnings is equal to the forward return on equity times the earnings retention rate.

 ### Warning: Is the Business Able to Use the Retained Earnings?

Apart from the accuracy of the clean surplus relationship, the other assumption in these formulas is that the return on equity remains constant. This requires that the extra equity, namely net profit after dividends, can be employed at the same rate as the existing equity. This is why it was suggested in Chapter 4 to keep an eye on whether cash and cash equivalents are growing faster than the general growth of the business. It may mean that the company is having difficulty finding a profitable use for the extra equity.

These formulas are derived in Appendix A. They are also used in Chapter 13 on margins of safety as part of the approach to estimating the growth rate of earnings. (As indicated by the examples earlier in the chapter, there is also a third variation of return on equity. It uses the average of the equity at the start and the end of the financial year. Obviously the result will be somewhere between the standard and forward versions of return on equity. For the types of companies that we are interested in with stable and high return on equity, the differences between the three definitions will not be significant. Generally we will only use the definition that uses equity at the end of the year as was done in Table 5.2 and occasionally make reference to forward ROE.)

**Dividend Policy**   At this point it is worth saying a few words about the way companies use their earnings to pay dividends. After all, understanding the dividend policy of management is a key part of trying to forecast the growth of a business. Even more importantly, it should be a key part of deciding whether to even consider the company in the first place.

In some cases a business should not pay dividends or, at least, should only pay a low level of dividends. This is when it has need for the capital and to pay out a higher level of dividends would make it difficult to maintain its economic strength. This could be the situation when it has a low return on assets ratio and inflation is high. Commenting on this situation, Warren Buffett[9] said that if such a company paid out earnings, it would likely lose ground in one or more of these areas:

- Its ability to maintain its unit volume of sales.
- Its long-term competitive position.
- Its financial strength.

Buffett continued, "No matter how conservative its payout ratio, a company that consistently distributes restricted earnings is destined for oblivion unless equity capital is otherwise infused."

Assuming that the company can pay earnings without jeopardizing its economic strength, the major criterion for a shareholder-oriented company is whether the action will add value to the shareholders. In principle this is quite simple. There are two cases:

1. The company has the opportunity to earn higher rates on retained earnings than could reasonably be expected to be earned by the shareholders for the same level of risk should they receive the money as dividends.
2. It is unlikely that the company will earn higher rates on retained earnings than could reasonably be expected to be earned by the shareholders should they receive the money as dividends.

In the first case, if you require a return of 15 percent per annum before investing in a company to compensate you for the associated risks and uncertainty, then an ROE of 10 percent is not going to cut it. This is particularly true if there is no good reason to expect that it will be higher in the foreseeable future. (We will see calculations showing the validity of this requirement in Chapter 8 on dividend discount methods.) Hence it makes economic sense for the business to retain its earnings and not pay dividends. In the second case, it would be better for the company to pay dividends.

The profitability of the retained earnings will depend on how management applies its earnings. For example, the company might have two divisions, one earning a higher rate on its equity than the other. Call them Hi Division and Lo Division. If they are roughly the same size then the stated return on equity for the total business would be the average of the two returns. But suppose Hi Division has no opportunity to use extra capital whereas Lo Division does. In this case, the company would only be able to invest any retained earnings at the lower rate. Conversely, suppose Hi Division has the opportunity to use any retained earnings whereas Lo Division does not. Then the company would be able to invest any retained earnings at a higher rate.

Of course, it is not easy to tell from the outside which divisions in a business generate high returns and which divisions generate low returns. It is not even easy to tell from the outside which divisions can actually use any retained earnings. What we can do as investors is look for companies with high and consistent return on equity and scrutinize the company reports to get as much information as possible regarding how they spend their net profits. When we have done this, then we are in a better position to judge whether the dividend policy is in alignment with the aims and actions of the company, and in alignment with our goals as investors.

Another point is that they do not have to be formal divisions within a company. For example, one "division" might be the cash in the company while the other "division" is the actual operations of the company. If the company is not able to use its net profits to expand the business, they may end up being left in the cash division. This would generally result in lower performance of the business over time.

In the case of Berkshire Hathaway, Warren Buffett has made it clear that he believes that he creates more value by not paying dividends so that he has maximum capital available to him to find and invest in large, profitable companies, which he refers to as elephants. "Our basic principle" he explained to shareholders of Berkshire Hathaway, "is that if you want to shoot rare, fast-moving elephants, you should always carry a loaded gun."[10]

## Price Ratios with Earnings and Dividends

Prices of equities and related ratios are not strictly part of this chapter since prices are not in the financial statements but are outcomes of market opinions and actions. Nevertheless, earnings and dividends are found in the financial statements, and since the ratio between prices and earnings and between prices and dividends are so important, we will briefly discuss them here. The price-earnings ratio (or price-to-earnings ratio, or P/E ratio) is the ratio of the price divided by earnings per share. Suppose that the price of an equity is $30.00 and the EPS is $2.00. Then the P/E ratio is 30/2, or 15. Since $2.00 added to itself 15 times is $30, another way of thinking about the P/E ratio is that it is the number of years (in this case, 15) it would take for the EPS ($2.00) to add up to the price of the equity ($30.00), assuming that the EPS stays constant each year. This makes it clear why sometimes the market is willing to buy equities with very high P/E ratios (say over 25); at the time there is a general consensus that the earnings of the company will grow strongly. Conversely, the belief that the earnings will not grow and may even decrease will result in the stock being traded at low P/E ratios, perhaps 10 or lower.

It is common to see different P/E ratios being simultaneously quoted on different web sites or by different analysts. There are two reasons for this. The first is that, even though EPS is quoted in the financial statements of publicly traded companies, different web sites and different stock analysis firms often have different protocols regarding what they include in the final determination of earnings and what they do not. For example, sometimes the company data is modified to remove unusual or nonrecurring events.

The second reason for the variations that can be seen in P/E ratios is that the EPS in the ratio may be calculated over different time frames and may even include consensus analyst forecasts. Table 5.17 shows the four main variations.

It is common in any list of current prices of publicly traded companies to state the P/E ratio. Generally this is the current price

**Table 5.17**  Variations of the Price-Earnings Ratio

| Name | Description of the EPS used in the P/E ratio | Comments |
|---|---|---|
| Trailing financial year P/E ratio | EPS over the most recent financial year. | This method is the easiest to calculate since all it needs is the current price and the EPS from the most recent annual report. The problem is that as time moves closer to the next release of annual data, there is an increasingly large time gap between the period of the EPS and the current price. |
| Trailing 12 months P/E ratio or current P/E ratio | EPS over the most recent 12 months. For quarterly data, this means that EPS is calculated as the sum of the four most recent quarters. | The advantages of this method are that it uses company data (no forecasts) and the gap between the period of the EPS and current time is a minimum. This is the most common method and if no extra description is given, it is most likely the method that has been used. |
| Forward P/E ratio | Consensus forecast of EPS over the next four quarters. (Some data providers and analysis companies will use their own EPS forecast.) | This method uses the consensus forecast of EPS over the next four quarters. If earnings are expected to grow, then the forward P/E ratio will be less than the current P/E ratio. Conversely, the forward P/E ratio will be higher than the current P/E if earnings are expected to decrease over the next 12 months. The disadvantage is that it relies heavily on analyst forecasts, which may not be reliable, instead of on data from the financial statements of the company. |
| Weighted or balanced P/E ratio | EPS as a combination of the EPS over the most recent two quarters and forecasts of the next two forecasts. | This method attempts to overcome the mismatch between EPS being calculated over 12 months and price being quoted at the current time. A weighted average is used to combine the EPS over the two most recent quarters and consensus forecasts over the next two quarters. If the current time is midway through a quarter, the four quarters in the calculation are given equal weight. Otherwise they are weighted according to the distance through the current quarter. |

divided by the EPS found over the four most recent quarters in the financial statements of the company. This is the second variation in Table 5.17 and is referred to as the *trailing 12 months* P/E ratio or sometimes simply the *current* P/E ratio. Unless stated otherwise, this will be the variation used in the remaining chapters.

Because of the widespread availability of the P/E ratio, it makes sense to be able to make maximum use of it by understanding its strengths and weaknesses as an investment tool. What meaning can we deduce from its different levels? We look at this question in detail in Chapters 11 and 13.

In the meantime, one way to get a sense of what is a reasonable level for the P/E ratio is via the *earnings yield*, the inverse of the P/E ratio. In other words,

$$\text{Earnings yield} = \text{Earnings per share}/\text{Share price}$$

If we think of EPS as the money generated by the company on your behalf for each share or unit of stock that you own in it, this terminology makes sense: Earnings yield is the return or yield in terms of earnings on the money outlaid to buy shares in the company. Looking at the earnings yield is a reminder that, unless there is a growth in earnings, the return on investment may be quite modest. For example, a P/E ratio of 20 represents an earnings yield of 5 percent since 1/20 is equal to 0.05 or 5 percent. A P/E ratio of 10 represents an earnings yield of 10 percent. Table 5.18 gives a range of P/E ratios and the corresponding earnings yields.

It is reasonable as a simple rule to think of EPS in this way, namely as money generated by the company on behalf of the owners of each share in the company. As a start, if the company pays out all its earnings as dividends (in other words, if the dividend payout ratio is 100 percent), then this is literally the case. There are even cases where

**Table 5.18**  Relationship between P/E Ratios and Earnings Yield

| P/E Ratio | Earnings Yield | P/E Ratio | Earnings Yield |
|-----------|----------------|-----------|----------------|
| 5         | 20.00%         | 15        | 6.67%          |
| 7.5       | 13.33%         | 20        | 5.00%          |
| 10        | 10.00%         | 25        | 4.00%          |
| 12.5      | 8.00%          | 30        | 3.33%          |

companies routinely have payout ratios above 100 percent. For example, a real estate investment trust (REIT) is required to distribute at least 90 percent of its taxable income to shareholders annually in the form of dividends. Because this distribution is calculated before tax, the actual proportion that is paid out as dividends may exceed the earnings, giving it a dividend payout ratio that exceeds 100 percent.

Even if the company pays no dividends, it could be using the money to expand the business or to buy back its shares. In both cases it is anticipated that the EPS will grow, in the first case because the total earnings has grown and in the second case because the number of shares has decreased, cutting the earnings pie into fewer slices. Hence, in both cases it is anticipated that the growth in EPS will contribute to the value of the holding.

The same type of ratio can be formed with dividends. *Dividend yield* is defined as the dividends per share over the recent four quarters (or over the most recent financial year) divided by the current price. In other words,

$$\text{Dividend yield} = \text{Dividends per share/Share price}$$

As a final comment, what is important about earnings per share and dividends per share is not their actual values, since this depends on the number of shares that are outstanding. Rather, the main importance is their values relative to the current share price, since this is the yield or return on the money required to buy shares in the company. At a deeper level, in Chapters 7 and 8, price yields, dividend yields, and other yield variations will be seen as important components of measuring the value of equities using discount valuation methods.

## Ratios and Share Buybacks

When companies buy back their own shares, it is reasonable to expect that some of their financial ratios will be affected. This section looks at some of the ways that this happens.

The ideal rationale for a share buyback has three requirements:

1. The company has spare cash.
2. It believes that its shares are selling at or below fair value.
3. It has no better investment opportunities.

Of course, as explained in Chapter 4, in practice there may be less rational reasons for performing buybacks, such as trying to hold down the number of shares outstanding because of the large numbers of bonus shares being awarded. In such cases, the company may be paying higher than fair value for its own shares.

The company may make its purchases through a normal stock exchange, in which case it is referred to as an *on-market buyback*. Alternatively, blocks of stock can sometimes be bought directly from shareholders, typically from large institutional investors. This is referred to as an *off-market buyback*. Once such a purchase is made, as explained in Chapter 4, there are two possibilities: Cancel the shares or hold them as treasury stock. (These two possibilities may be closely related. In some cases a company may be regularly buying back its shares on the open market. It will accumulate these as treasury stock until a sufficiently large parcel is held. Only then will it apply to cancel them.)

To see the effect of buybacks on different ratios, we will keep the analysis simple by assuming that the price the company is paying for the shares represents fair value and that there are no other actions of the company that would dilute the number of shares. Also, we deliberately choose the numbers so that the price-to-book (P/B) ratio is 3.0, which is near the average ratio of 3.45 for companies in the S&P 500 index.

Suppose that initially the company has 2,000 shares and that total equity is $66,667 so the book value is $33.33 per share. Assume that net profit is $10,000 so that earnings per share is $5.00. Finally, assume that net cash is $60,000, debt is $20,000, and assets are $200,000. This means that capital (equity plus debt) is $86,667. These figures are shown in the second column of Table 5.19. Assume also that the market price of the shares is $100 and that the company does not pay any dividends.

Now suppose that the company buys back 500 of its shares at market price. (In practice it is unlikely for a company to buy back 25 percent of its shares, particularly at one time. But we deliberately use this high proportion to exaggerate the effects in order to make them more apparent.) This will cost the company $50,000. We are going to consider two extreme scenarios. The first scenario assumes that the company borrows $50,000 to buy the shares. The second scenario takes the other extreme by assuming that the shares are bought out of the cash of the business with no extra borrowings.

**Table 5.19**   Changes in Financial Structure Due to a Buyback

| Financial Item | Pre-Buyback | Scenario 1 | Scenario 2 |
|---|---|---|---|
| Net profit | $10,000 | $10,000 | $10,000 |
| Cash | $60,000 | $60,000 | $10,000 |
| Debt | $20,000 | $70,000 | $20,000 |
| Total equity | $66,667 | $16,667 | $16,667 |
| Assets | $200,000 | $200,000 | $150,000 |
| Capital | $86,667 | $86,667 | $36,667 |
| Shares outstanding | 2,000 | 1,500 | 1,500 |
| Earnings per share | $5.00 | $6.67 | $6.67 |
| Book value | $33.33 | $11.11 | $11.11 |

The column titled "Pre-Buyback" is the financial position of the company before the buyback, assuming that the initial price was $100. The financial positions of the company after the buyback are shown as scenario 1 (the shares are bought from extra debt) and scenario 2 (the shares are bought from existing cash).

These two scenarios are shown in the third and fourth columns of Table 5.19.

Next we look at some of the key ratios that we considered earlier in the chapter. Table 5.20 shows what happens to them under the two scenarios. Return on equity jumps from 15 percent to a staggering 60 percent in both cases. Return on capital stays the same for the first scenario but more than doubles for the second scenario. Debt to equity and financial leverage also increase markedly.

How should we interpret the disquietingly large jump in return on equity shown in the table? Is it real or imagined? Is it something we can build on to help forecast growth in earnings or is it an artifact

**Table 5.20**   Changes in Financial Ratios Due to a Buyback

| Financial Ratio | Pre-Buyback | Scenario 1 | Scenario 2 |
|---|---|---|---|
| Return on equity | 15.00% | 60.00% | 60.00% |
| Return on capital | 11.54% | 11.54% | 27.27% |
| Debt to equity | 30.00% | 420.00% | 120.00% |
| Financial leverage | 3.00 | 9.00 | 9.00 |

The column titled "Pre-Buyback" is the financial position of the company before the buyback assuming that the initial price was $100. The financial positions of the company after the buyback are shown as scenario 1 (the shares are bought from extra debt) and scenario 2 (the shares are bought from existing cash).

of accounting methods? The answer is that it is a combination of both explanations. The best way to understand it is in terms of the discussion earlier in the chapter on companies with two divisions, Hi Division and Lo Division. Hi Division has a high return on equity and Lo Division has a low return on equity. As stated at the time, they do not have to be actual divisions. For example, Lo Division might consist of the nonessential cash in the business, and Hi Division the remainder or operating part of the business. Let's call them CD (cash division) and ND (noncash division). In general, CD will be earning a low ROE with most of the net profit coming from ND. For simplicity, assume that CD is not earning any profit. If the cash in CD is not essential for the viability of the business, it may make sense for the company to divest itself of this division.

For our buyback example, instead of selling CD, in a sense the company actually gives it away. We can see this because the equity of CD as a business was $50,000 and after the buyback the equity of the entire company dropped by $50,000. (In return for giving CD away, it reduces the number of shares outstanding.) Having gotten rid of a large low-return part of the business, it is natural to expect that the ROE would rise. In this particular example, the numbers are exaggerated to make the argument clearer. But the conclusion is valid, namely that after a share buyback, the ROE should increase. This gives background to why the ROE jumps from 15 percent before the buyback to 60 percent after this action.

This is the good news. Now for the bad news. Usually we can be reasonably confident that high return on equity means high growth in earnings (assuming that there are no dividends). However, in this buyback example, we do not have any security about the growth based on the high post-buyback return on equity. As explained earlier in the chapter, forecasts of growth based on return on equity depend on the company having opportunities to use the extra equity (which is the net profit) at the existing levels of the return on equity. In the current example, we need to ask if the company can continue to invest its yearly net profits at 60 percent. Not only is it not possible to answer this question, but with the data available we cannot even get any guidelines. The reason for this is we do not have the necessary history of the company or any reasonable forecasts of its future. For example, before the buyback was the net profit being invested in ND at the same ROE year after year? If so, growth based on the high ROE for the post-payback business is feasible. Or was most of the net profit each year simply accumulating in the cash account? In this case, there is not likely to be any increase in growth of the post-payback business.

In practice, future growth is likely to lie between the original ROE and the ROE after the buyback. One way to approach the problem is to take the equity used in the buyback and to add it back to the original equity. Now use this to recalculate return on equity and the other basic ratios and use these to examine the business. Of course, in this simple example, you will have a return of equity of 15 percent, the original level. This is like a worst-case scenario. In practice, the growth of earnings is likely to be higher than would be implied by this level of ROE.

The final step in the analysis of the impact of share buybacks on the finances of a company is to look at the effect on price and the P/E and P/B ratios. It is not possible to make precise statements, only an indication of what is likely to happen. Just like the outcome after stock splits described in Chapter 2, there can be a marked gulf between the rational outcome and what actually happens. The primary analysis hinges on what happens to the market capitalization since this is the best estimate of the fair value of the entire business. Before the buyback the market capitalization was $200,000 (2,000 shares at $100 each). After paying out $50,000, the new market capitalization should be $150,000. But now there are only 1,500 shares, so the share price should remain at $100. This means the P/E drops to 15 (calculated as $100 divided by $6.67) while the price-to-book jumps to 9.0 (calculated as $100 divided by $11.11). These results are shown in Table 5.21.

Because of the drop in the P/E ratio, even though Table 5.21 shows that the fair price of the shares was the same before and after the buyback, in practice the actual price after the buyback is higher. This is based on an understanding that the company has cleaned up

**Table 5.21**   Changes in Price Data Due to a Buyback

| Price Data | Pre-Buyback | Scenario 1 | Scenario 2 |
| --- | --- | --- | --- |
| Market capitalization | $200,000 | $150,000 | $150,000 |
| Share price | $100 | $100 | $100 |
| P/E ratio | 20 | 15 | 15 |
| P/B ratio | 3 | 9 | 9 |

a lazy balance sheet that was overshadowing the genuine growth of the operating part of the business. (Notice, though, that the price-to-book value has jumped from 3.0 to 9.0, which may put downward pressure on the price.)

The preceding discussion assumed that the company cancelled its shares after the buyback. The other alternative is for the company to hold the shares that it repurchased as treasury stock. However, exactly the same analysis holds since treasury stock is neither listed as equity nor counted in the number of shares outstanding.

Generally it is a good sign when a company buys back its shares. An extreme example is the purchase of Washington Post shares by Warren Buffett for Berkshire Hathaway. In mid-1973 Berkshire Hathaway made purchases of Washington Post, putting together a holding representing around 10 percent of outstanding shares. Over the years, Washington Post has actively repurchased its shares so that Buffett's original holding (with the redemption of a small number of shares in 1985) now represents 18.1 percent of the company. However, just as for any other purchase, if the shares of the company are overpriced, then it does not make business sense for anyone to purchase them, including the company itself. It is important to make your own assessment of their value. If they are undervalued, share buybacks by the company will enhance the value of your investment. Otherwise they will destroy value.

 **Warning: Examine the Reasons for Any Buybacks**

There may be other reasons for a company engaged in a share buyback that are more akin to a public relations activity than the creation of value. Often when a company makes a buyback, it actively promotes this action to the investment community as an example of its responsible attitude toward its shareholders. In many cases, however, a closer analysis shows that the same company has been issuing large numbers of shares and options to management and other personnel as performance rewards and incentives. When this happens it may be that the total number of shares outstanding actually increases despite the share buybacks. For this reason it is recommended that you keep an eye on any changes in the number of shares outstanding, no matter what statements are made by management.

## The Bottom Line

1. Financial ratios are important to get an idea of the current strength of a company and any favorable or unfavorable trends.
2. Key ratios such as return on equity and return on capital give a good indication of the ability of management and hence whether an investment is likely to be profitable.
3. Ratios provide a means of comparing a company with other companies and with the overall sector and market averages.

# CHAPTER 6

# Measuring Value by Taking Snapshots

*"How much is the business selling for?"... this should be the first question in considering a stock purchase.*
—Benjamin Graham and David Dodd[1]

*The balance sheet is a remarkable invention.*
—Martin Fridson and Fernando Alvarez[2]

In 1932 Benjamin Graham wrote a three-part series of articles for *Forbes*, titled "Is American Business Worth More Dead than Alive?" He argued that a careful analysis of the balance sheets of large numbers of companies showed that their cash and other liquid assets, after allowing for liabilities, were often higher than the prices paid for them on the stock exchange. This was a revolutionary idea, and the success of these articles gave Graham the impetus to write his famous book *Security Analysis*, a classic in investing literature. In this chapter we look at the main ways that balance sheets can be used to find undervalued stocks.

As we saw in Chapter 4, the balance sheet provides a snapshot of the value of certain aspects of a business in the two categories of assets and liabilities. A problem much more serious now than it was in Benjamin Graham's time relates to intangible assets such as intellectual property. These assets make up a significant portion of the wealth of modern businesses but are not included on the balance sheet. A second problem is that even when a tangible asset is included, the value assigned to it may differ substantially from its fair value. Just the same, by modifying the terms in the balance sheet, and in some cases by ignoring them altogether, there are times when it is at least possible to assess whether a company is worth investigating further. With this in mind, we will look at a range of valuation methods based on analyses of the balance sheet including book value, liquidation value, net current asset value, and replacement value.

Apart from whether or not the method is based on entries in the balance sheet, another important distinction between the methods in this chapter and those in the following chapters concerns the use of forecasts. In a strict sense, every investment involves forecasts in one way or another. For example, even if you purchase a certificate of deposit from a bank or invest in a municipal bond from a local government with specified interest rates, you are implicitly forecasting that you will receive the payments in full and on time as promised in the agreement with the issuer. It is the same with the items on the balance sheet. If a value is assigned to inventory, for example, there is a forecast that this is what would be received for them, apart from certain allowances, should they need to be sold.

The valuation methods in the later chapters require much more in the area of forecasts, including direct forecasts of the growth rates over extended periods of time, of financial quantities such as earnings, cash flow, or dividends. Because such forecasts tend to be difficult, they often result in large errors. In contrast, the methods in this chapter require only the mildest of forecasts of balance sheet items as just described. Therefore, the valuations provided by these methods have a high level of consensus among investors and analysts. Where there is less consensus is in the significance of these valuations as indicators of whether an investment is likely to be profitable. But the valuations may at least present a case for further research on a company.

## Book Value

The simplest valuation method using the balance sheet is *book value*, the value in the "books" or accounts on a per share basis. It is defined as shareholder equity divided by the number of shares outstanding. In this sense, book value is an accounting measure of value rather than an economic measure. If the values of the items on the balance sheet represented their true value, then book value would be obtained by taking all the assets, realizing their listed values, paying off the liabilities, and dividing what was left by the number of shares outstanding.

As mentioned earlier, intangible items—including patents, trademarks, licenses, brand names, mastheads, and copyrights—are not necessarily included on a company's balance sheet. Also, those items that are included may be listed with valuations that differ markedly from their market values. The smaller the role of intangible assets, the closer to book value a company's market price is likely to be. For this reason, companies in the "bricks and mortar" category tend to have prices closer to book value than, for example, high-tech companies. The *price-to-book ratio* or P/B ratio is often quoted, but we could calculate it on our own. As an example, let us start with the company that we have been studying the most, Wal-Mart. The balance sheet (Table 4.2 in Chapter 4) shows that its shareholder equity for the 2010 financial year was $70,749 million and the income statement (Table 4.3) shows that the number of shares outstanding (diluted) was 3,877 million. The book value is calculated as 70,749 divided by 3,877 which is $18.25. Since the price of Wal-Mart was around $55.00, the price-to-book ratio was 3.01.

Other companies have quite different P/B ratios. For example, in March 2010, the Internet search company Google had a book value of $133.30. Since its price at the time was $549.00, its P/B ratio was 4.12. A completely different type of company that had an even higher P/B ratio is the money transfer company Western Union. Its book value and current price were $0.51 and $17.06, respectively, so its P/B ratio was 33.45. In contrast, the book value and price of E*Trade Financial, an online broker, were $1.98 and $1.62, giving it a P/B ratio of 0.82.

Examples such as these show that the price-to-book ratio on its own is a poor indicator of value. The ratio may, however, be a useful guide to changes in value of a company when it is tracked over time. It may also assist in choosing promising investments from a sector by comparing the P/B ratios of all the companies in the sector and giving (slightly) more weight to those companies with lower P/B ratios. As indicated earlier, this would have to be done with care because of the reporting issues related to intangible assets and whether the assets were developed from within the company or purchased from the outside.

## Track Book Value over Time

Book value or equity per share is a poor indicator of value on its own, but it can be a useful guide to changes in value when tracked over time or compared with similar companies.

### Example: Berkshire Hathaway

Berkshire Hathaway (Berkshire) is the holding company run by Warren Buffett. It has market capitalization of approximately $180 billion consisting of a portfolio containing investments in over 100 publicly traded companies and ownership of around 80 other companies. According to the 2009 annual report of the company, the main investments in publicly traded companies are The Coca-Cola Company (with a holding valued at $11.4 billion) and Wells Fargo & Company ($9.2 billion). Some of the largest companies owned by Berkshire are Fruit of the Loom (approximately 24,500 employees) and Shaw Industries (approximately 30,000 employees).

Each year in its annual report, Berkshire uses book value to compare its growth with the growth of the S&P 500 index. (See the box titled "Warren Buffett, Berkshire Hathaway, and Book Value" for Buffett's explanation of why he does this.) As an example, at the end of 2006, the book value of Berkshire was $70,282.83 while at the end of 2007 it was $78,011.04, representing an increase of 11.0 percent.[3] Over the same period, the S&P 500 index grew from 1,418.30 to 1,468.36, an increase of 3.5 percent. It is stated in the 2009 annual report that over more than 40 years, the book value of Berkshire increased by an average of 20.3 percent per year compared to an average of 9.3 percent for the S&P 500 index.[4]

More interesting for investors looking for extra value is tracking the book value of Berkshire together with its price. Figure 6.1 compares the book value of Berkshire and the market price of its Class A shares at the end of each calendar year. It is clear that they have tracked each other fairly well for the years 1998 to 2007. For example, from 1999 until the end of 2007 the average annual return of the price of Class A shares was 8.1 percent and the average annual growth of its book value was 8.4 percent, so the two growth rates were almost exactly the same over this period.

## Warren Buffett, Berkshire Hathaway, and Book Value

In the 1997 annual report of Berkshire Hathaway, Warren Buffett wrote:

We regularly report our per-share book value, an easily calculable number, though one of limited use. The limitations do not arise from our holdings of marketable securities, which are carried on our books at their current prices. Rather the inadequacies of book value have to do with the companies we control, whose values as stated on our books may be far different from their intrinsic values.

The disparity can go in either direction. For example, in 1964 we could state with certitude that Berkshire's per-share book value was $19.46. However, that figure considerably overstated the company's intrinsic value, since all of the company's resources were tied up in a sub-profitable textile business. Our textile assets had neither going-concern nor liquidation values equal to their carrying values.

Today, however, Berkshire's situation is reversed: Now, our book value far understates Berkshire's intrinsic value, a point true because many of the businesses we control are worth much more than their carrying value.

Inadequate though they are in telling the story, we give you Berkshire's book-value figures because they today serve as a rough, albeit significantly understated, tracking measure for Berkshire's intrinsic value. In other words, the percentage change in book value in any given year is likely to be reasonably close to that year's change in intrinsic value.

However, there were also times, such as 1999 and 2005, when the price lagged behind the book value. Specifically, from 1999 to 2005 the average price-to-book ratio was 1.69 with the lowest being 1.48 in 1999 and 1.49 in 2005. Then in 2008, when the book value dropped, the price dropped by much more. The difference between book value and price was even larger at the end of 2009. Based on the assumption that over time the two figures should maintain a similar rate of growth, the lags in 1999, 2005, 2008, and 2009 would indicate that these would be preferred times to invest in Berkshire in order to get a higher return.

This conclusion is borne out for 1999 and 2005 by a closer examination of the numbers. The average annual return in the price of Berkshire for two years after 1999 was 16.1 percent. Even better was the 26.4 percent average annual return for the next two years after 2005.

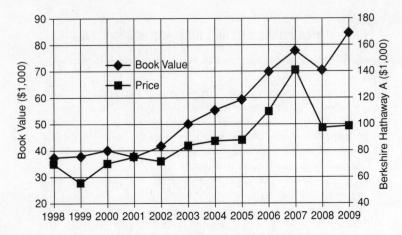

**Figure 6.1** Comparison of Book Value and Price for Berkshire Hathaway

The figure compares the movement of the book value and the price of Class A Berkshire Hathaway shares. (The axis on the left is for book value and the axis on the right is for the share price.) The data is for the end of each calendar year which corresponds to the financial year of the company. It is easy to see from the figure that the ratio of price to book value is at its lowest in 1999, 2005, 2008, and 2009, and at its highest in 2001.

What about the gains after 2008? During 2009 there was a big increase in book value but only a marginal increase in price. Hence, on book value alone, the expected higher returns did not eventuate during 2009 even though the book value grew strongly. In fact, the gap between book value and price got even wider.

The question for us as investors is, could we have selected the most profitable times to invest in Berkshire and avoided the other times? One way would be to wait for historically low levels of the price-to-book ratio. Up until 2007, for example, 1999 and 2005 were the only two years when the price-to-book-ratio was below 1.55. This means that buying when the PB ratio was below 1.55 would have given the higher returns just described. At the end of 2008, however, the ratio dropped even lower, to 1.37, and then lower again at the end of 2009, to 1.17. Interestingly, in the first two months of 2010 the price of Berkshire progressed by 20.8 percent. The price is now above $125,000, up from a low of $70,000 just 12 months earlier. It may be that the price and book value will continue to track each other, but the lag in the price's reflection of changes in book value is just a little longer than usual.

## What's in a Name?

Whether or not the intangible items are included in the calculation of book value, there are ways of getting an estimate of the value of certain components of intangible items. One of these is brand value. Each year Interbrand Corporation, a leading brand consultancy headquartered in New York, in conjunction with *Newsweek* publishes a list of the values of the best global brands. It also publishes the values of many national brands. The value is calculated using proprietary techniques based on estimates of the discounted value of the brand's expected earnings. Interbrand emphasizes that the brand value is calculated using publicly available information and that it builds a consensus estimate with data from a range of analysts' reports.

As an example of just how much a brand can be worth, in 2009 Interbrand determined that the most valuable international brand is Coca-Cola, valued at $68.73 billion. The next two brands on the list are IBM and Microsoft, valued at $60.21 billion and $56.65 billion, respectively. To give an idea of the size of these brand names and how little of their value is reflected on the balance sheet, consider Microsoft. All the property and equipment owned by this company and used to manage and produce its products is only valued at $49.28 billion, less than the estimated value of the brand.

For investing purposes it is useful to know what proportion of the stock price can be attributed to the value of the brand. This is even truer for the mega-brands such as Coca-Cola, IBM, and Microsoft, since generally they have been developed in-house and so will not appear on the balance sheet. Determining this proportion can be done by calculating the value of the brand on a per-share basis using public data published by Interbrand and comparing it with the stock price. As previously stated, Coca-Cola has a brand value of $68.73 billion. Since it has 2.32 billion shares outstanding, the brand value per share is $29.63. Given a stock price of $57.48, 51.54 percent of price may be attributed to the brand value.

This gives some idea why Coca-Cola spends so much money to maintain its brand strength. That strength is its largest asset, representing more than half of the market capitalization of the business. Put another way, without its brand name Coca-Cola would be just another company selling sugary water formed by the addition of flavored syrup. But with its brand, an average of 1.6 billion servings per day pour out of its cans and bottles around the world.

**Table 6.1**    Ratio of Brand Values and Book Values to Price

| (1)<br>Company | (2)<br>Ticker | (3)<br>Brand to Price | (4)<br>Book to Price | (5)<br>Total |
|---|---|---|---|---|
| Coca-Cola | KO | 51.54% | 18.01% | 69.55% |
| IBM | IBM | 36.48% | 11.03% | 47.51% |
| Microsoft | MSFT | 21.49% | 15.63% | 37.12% |
| GE | GE | 28.91% | 70.81% | 99.73% |
| Nokia | NOK | 70.68% | 36.46% | 107.14% |
| McDonald's | MCD | 46.72% | 19.10% | 65.83% |
| Google | GOOG | 17.53% | 18.67% | 36.20% |
| Toyota | TM | 25.44% | 93.06% | 118.50% |
| Intel | INTC | 28.95% | 36.75% | 65.70% |
| Disney | DIS | 50.43% | 61.81% | 112.24% |

The companies in the list have been chosen as typical examples from those with the highest brand values as calculated by Interbrand Corporation. Columns (1) and (2) are the names and tickers of the companies. Column (3) is the ratio of the brand value per share divided by the stock price, column (4) is the ratio of the book value divided by the stock price, and column (5) is the sum of columns (3) and (4).

Table 6.1 displays some of the companies with the highest global brand values calculated by Interbrand,[5] the values of these brands as a proportion of stock price, and the proportion of the stock price made of book value. (Usually the price-to-book ratio is the one that is calculated. In Table 6.1 the inverse of this ratio, namely the book-to-price ratio, is displayed to compare the proportion of the price composed of book value with the proportion of price composed of brand value.) The final column is the sum of the proportions from the book value and the brand value. In some cases this final proportion may be overstated because part of the brand value may be contained in the book value.

### Strengths and Weaknesses of Valuation Using Book Value

It has long been recognized that book value is of limited use for investors. Benjamin Graham, for example, wrote in 1934 that the value of assets as shown on the balance sheet "has lost practically all its significance."[6] Whatever significance it had back then is even lower today, with the advent of computers and the Internet leading to a higher proportion of assets not being recorded on the balance sheet. Just the same, book value can have a role to play. Its main benefit is not so much as a direct valuation of a company, but as a measure of trends in value and, less importantly, as a measure of relative value compared with similar companies. We start with the strengths of valuation using book value.

*Strength 1: Accessible data.* The data for calculating book value is easily accessible from the balance sheet. (The number of shares outstanding may need to be obtained from the income statement.)

*Strength 2: Simple calculation.* Book value is very simple to calculate and may even be stated directly in the reports prepared by the company.

*Strength 3: Mutual agreement.* There is a high level of agreement on the items required for the calculation and hence on the final value.

*Strength 4: Consistent comparisons.* Book value in the form of the price-to-book ratio provides a clear quantitative value for a stock. It can be tracked over time to see if there are any spikes or trends in its size. It can also be compared with the ratios of other companies and with sector and market averages. In this way book value can act as an indicator of whether a company is deserving of a more thorough analysis.

*Strength 5: Widely reported.* The price-to-book ratio is often reported by brokerage and other financial web sites for all publicly traded companies.

*Strength 6: No forecasts.* No forecasts of financial items such as earnings, free cash flow, or dividends are required for the calculation of book value.

The following is an outline of the main weaknesses of using book value.

*Weakness 1: Limited information.* Because book value is calculated solely from the balance sheet, it is an accounting method that reaches its value by using limited information about the company.

*Weakness 2: Too simple.* The actual calculation oversimplifies the notion of the value of a company.

*Weakness 3: Poor estimate.* Many key assets owned or controlled by a business, such as brand names, are often not included on the balance sheet or, if they are there, the value assigned to them does not represent fair market value. Hence, right at the outset, book value is a poor estimate of the value of a business.

## Liquidation Value

Sometimes you will see a notice in a store window or an advertisement stating that a store is having a liquidation sale. This means that the capital tied up in selected items in the store has to be made liquid by selling them to the public. The implications are that it must be done quickly and that the prices will be very low.

When the term *liquidation value* is applied to items or goods owned by a company, it does not necessarily mean that they are actually going to be sold. Rather, liquidation value is an estimate of the amount of money that would result if all the assets were sold and the liabilities paid with everything done in a reasonably orderly manner. In most cases in a normal, growing business, the liquidation value per share is significantly lower than the share price. In contrast, if a business is struggling with its sales and earnings, the liquidation value may exceed the share price. This usually indicates that the company should go out of business. In some cases the liquidation is forced on the company by its creditors because they no longer have confidence that they will be paid in a timely manner under the terms of their contracts. In other cases the decision to liquidate is based on an analysis by management, with the result that the process can be carried out in a more orderly fashion. In either case, it may result in a takeover by an outside company. Quite often the company orchestrating the takeover will break up the original company and sell off the components.

The value of inventory as recorded on the balance sheet can be substantially different from its liquidation value. Accounting regulations require companies to carry inventory at the estimated value that will be received for it, taking into account such factors as depreciation, changes in consumer preferences, and market supply. This is not hard to do for an operating business in a profitable industry. However, if the inventory is forced to be sold in a liquidation sale, then the business may only receive a fraction of this reported value.

Consider a chain of clothing stores. So long as the stores are selling the inventory at a reasonable rate, its value on the balance sheet will be a fair estimate of what the company can expect to receive for it. But the outcome will be completely different if the clothing needs to be liquidated since it is then likely to be sold to a wholesaler or remnant dealer. The same dichotomy applies to equipment and machinery. The value of the equipment and machinery as recorded on the balance sheet is usually substantially higher than its liquidation value, particularly if the business is in a distressed condition or in an industry that is suffering.

Consider Berkshire. When the Buffett Partnership, an investment partnership of which Warren Buffett was the general partner, bought control in 1959 it was a textile company. In early 1967, cash generated by the textile operation was used to fund the entry of Berkshire into insurance via the purchase of National Indemnity Company. Some of the money came from earnings and some from reduced investment in textile inventories, receivables, and fixed assets. From then on, Buffett increasingly diversified the holdings of Berkshire so that a smaller and smaller portion of the earnings of the company came from the textile part of the business.

Various attempts were made to increase the efficiency and viability of the textile business. In the end it seemed to Buffett and the board of the company that the only outcome was going to be an unending series of losses. At this stage, in 1980, with no prospective purchasers, the decision was made to liquidate the business. Unfortunately there was little demand for most of the equipment and machinery. As an example, looms bought for $5,000 each could not be sold for even $50 in early 1981. They were finally sold for scrap at $26 each.[7]

As investors, it would make sense to have at least a general idea of what the liquidation value of a company might be. In most cases, however, there are so many intangible assets and goodwill items that this is impossible to do with any degree of accuracy by simply looking at the items as they appear on the balance sheet and taking them at face value. What we can do, though, is get a figure that is an estimate of the liquidation value or perhaps even lower. The idea is that if the share price is less than this estimate on a per-share basis, it may represent a profitable investment.

### Graham Liquidation Value Strategy

Benjamin Graham recognized the usefulness of being able to estimate the liquidation value of a company as a means for locating

**Table 6.2**   Benjamin Graham's Estimates of Liquidation Values

| Type of Asset | Percent of Face Value | |
| --- | --- | --- |
|  | Normal Range | Rough Average |
| Cash assets | 100% | 100.0% |
| Receivables | 75–90% | 80.0% |
| Inventory | 50–75% | 66.7% |
| Fixed assets | 1–50% | 15.0% |

The column titled "Normal Range" is the range of the percentages of the face values suggested by Benjamin Graham, and the column titled "Rough Average" is an approximate average percentage for each of the classes.

potential investments. In his book *Security Analysis* he proposed a systematic approach based on the idea that liabilities are to be taken at their stated values but the assets are of "questionable value."[8] This means that the assets shown on the books must be reduced from their face amounts, with their new values varying according to the class that they are in. These classes are ranked according to an estimate of what percentage of their face value could be realized in the event that they were required to be quickly sold. The ranges of these percentages as determined by Graham are shown in Table 6.2 along with a rough guide to the average value for each of the classes. Once the assets were modified in this way, the liabilities were subtracted as usual. This was taken as an estimate of the liquidation value of a company.

Instead of using these broad classes, it is possible to gain more accuracy by looking at individual items on the balance sheet and giving them weights based on their particular characteristics. The following describes some of the ways that this could be done.

**Liquidity of the Asset**   Graham weights cash as 100 percent because it is completely liquid for obvious reasons. The same would apply to cash equivalents such as U.S. government Treasury bills and bank certificates of deposit, should they be included on the balance sheet. Other cash equivalents such as corporate and municipal bonds would depend on their ratings by agencies such as Moody's and Standard and Poor's.

**Specialization of the Asset**   If the asset is a straight commodity, then it would likely be properly valued on the balance sheet. After all, a barrel of oil or a bale of cotton is the same no matter who owns it. But if the cotton has been converted into pink leotards, then its weighting will depend on the need for this attire. If pink leotards are in fashion, they will need a completely different weighting than if they were a trend that has passed.

In the example of the textile component of Berkshire described earlier, because of their specialization, the liquidation price of the looms was approximately 0.5 percent of their purchase price. (It may not have been quite as bad as that since, because of depreciation, the looms would necessarily have been carried at a much lower value than their purchase price. Nevertheless, the message is clear. In the case of liquidation, the values of all the assets have to be reassessed with a view to substantially marking them down.)

**Health of the Sector**     The industry in which the company operates is also important. If the industry is booming, there may still be demand for the assets of the troubled business. But if the industry is struggling, it may be very hard to sell the inventory (the syndrome of buggy whip companies when the automobile came along).

Graham explained that this method was not meant to calculate an exact value for the liquidation value of a company, but rather to form a rough idea of this value to see whether the shares were selling at a price less than what might be gained if a liquidation sale were to take place. If this is the case, then it may be sensible to invest in the company.

### Graham Liquidation Value Strategy

Benjamin Graham proposed modifying the values of the assets listed on the balance sheet and recalculating book value with these new values to make it a better indicator of undervalued opportunities.

### Strengths and Weaknesses of Valuation Using Graham Liquidation Value

It is difficult to estimate the liquidation value of a company from the outside. Hence, liquidation value does not lend itself to being a workable valuation method that can be applied with consistency. However, using the rough averages in Table 6.2 it is possible to produce a systematic modification of book value as an estimate of liquidation value. We refer to this as the *Graham liquidation value of a company.* The following is a summary of the strengths and weaknesses of valuation using this measure of value, starting with the strengths.

> *Strength 1: Accessible data.* The data for the calculation of the Graham liquidation value is easily accessible from the balance sheet. (The number of shares outstanding may need to be obtained from the income statement.)
>
> *Strength 2: Simple calculation.* Graham liquidation value is simple to calculate.
>
> *Strength 3: Mutual agreement.* There is a high level of agreement on the items required for the calculation (but not, perhaps, on the weighting given to them as described in Table 6.2).
>
> *Strength 4: Consistent comparisons.* The Graham liquidation value can be tracked over time to see if there are any spikes or trends in its size. It can also be compared with the values of other companies and with sector and market averages. In this way it can act as an indicator of whether a company is deserving of a more thorough analysis.
>
> *Strength 5: No forecasts.* No forecasts of financial items such as earnings, free cash flow, or dividends are required for the calculation of the Graham liquidation value.

The following is an outline of the main weaknesses of using Graham's method.

> *Weakness 1: Limited information.* Because the Graham liquidation value is calculated solely from the balance sheet, it is an accounting method that reaches its value by using limited information about the company.
>
> *Weakness 2: Too simple.* The actual calculation oversimplifies the notion of the value of a company.
>
> *Weakness 3: Poor estimate.* Many key assets owned or controlled by a business, such as brand names, are often not included on the balance sheet or, if they are there, the value assigned to them does not represent fair market value. Hence, right at the outset, even though the values of the assets are modified, the Graham liquidation value is a poor estimate of the value of a business.

## Net Current Asset Value

Fifteen years after the publication of *Security Analysis*, Benjamin Graham wrote *The Intelligent Investor*.[9] The book was aimed at the general investing community and was, according to Warren Buffett, "by far the best book on investing ever written."[10] In this book Graham simplified the reduction method just described by discounting all the noncurrent assets to zero while leaving everything else fixed. In terms of the Graham liquidation value previously discussed, this means that the average percentages of face value in Table 6.2 are set at 100 percent for the first three items (cash assets, receivables, and inventory) and at 0 percent for the fixed assets. This new measure, obtained by subtracting all the liabilities from the current assets and calculated on a per share basis, is referred to as *net current asset value* (NCAV). Usually NCAV is negative. Occasionally it is positive. Even more occasionally it exceeds the share price. These are the companies that Graham was searching for when he wrote: "It always seemed, and still seems, ridiculously simple to say that if one can acquire a diversified group of common stocks [satisfying this condition], the results should be quite satisfactory."[11] In other words, Graham stated that if you could find a diversified group of companies with their prices below their NCAV levels, you could expect to do well.

We will say that a stock satisfies the NCAV criterion if its NCAV exceeds its share price. As just stated, these were the stocks sought by Benjamin Graham, particularly if the ratio of price to NCAV was even less than two-thirds. Graham would pay little attention to the quality of the companies, instead attempting to buy large numbers of them to gain protection from excessive volatility through diversification. In most years Graham's company would hold at least 100 of these companies. Much of their volatility was because they were hanging in a no-man's land between crashing into bankruptcy and oblivion on one side and pulling themselves together to reemerge as successful companies on the other. Warren Buffett called this the "cigar butt" approach to investing. (See the box titled "Warren Buffett and 'Cigar Butt' Stocks.")

Despite Buffett's hesitancy about this style of investing, careful studies have described excellent returns using this method. Reporting in the *Financial Analysts Journal* in 1986, Henry Oppenheimer carried out such a study over the period 1970 to 1983.[12] Each year a portfolio was formed consisting of companies that had a share price no more than two-thirds of its NCAV. After each 12 months the portfolios were liquidated and new ones formed.

### Warren Buffett and "Cigar Butt" Stocks

In the 1989 annual report of Berkshire Hathaway, Warrant Buffett wrote:

> If you buy a stock at a sufficiently low price, there will usually be some hiccup in the fortunes of the business that gives you a chance to unload at a decent profit, even though the long-term performance of the business may be terrible. I call this the "cigar butt" approach to investing. A cigar butt found on the street that has only one puff left in it may not offer much of a smoke, but the "bargain purchase" will make that puff all profit.
>
> Unless you are a liquidator, that kind of approach to buying businesses is foolish. First, the original "bargain" price probably will not turn out to be such a steal after all. In a difficult business, no sooner is one problem solved than another surfaces—never is there just one cockroach in the kitchen. Second, any initial advantage you secure will be quickly eroded by the low return that the business earns. For example, if you buy a business for $8 million that can be sold or liquidated for $10 million and promptly take either course, you can realize a high return. But the investment will disappoint if the business is sold for $10 million in ten years and in the interim has annually earned and distributed only a few percent on cost. Time is the friend of the wonderful business, the enemy of the mediocre.

The results were remarkable. If $10,000 was invested in the NCAV portfolio at the start of the study, by the end of 1983 it would have grown to $254,973. In contrast, if the same amount of money was invested in benchmark portfolios selected from the New York Stock Exchange and the American Exchange, it would have grown to $37,296. If invested in a small firm index, it would have grown to $101,992. In percentage terms, this represents annual growth rates of 28.3 percent for the general NCAV portfolio, 10.7 percent for the benchmark portfolio, and 19.6 percent for the small firm index. A parallel study with similar results was carried out by Joseph Vu using stocks from Value Line over the period 1977 to 1984.[13]

The type of companies that tend to be picked up using this method are those with a large inventory but which are having a tough period with depressed sales and little or no earnings. If the company pulls through, then there will be quite a boost in earnings and hence the share price. If it doesn't, it goes into bankruptcy and the inventory is sold off at bargain prices.

## Net Current Asset Value

Another balance sheet method of Benjamin Graham called net current asset value recalculates book value with all the noncurrent assets set to zero. When share price is less than net current asset value, often the stocks are close to bankruptcy. Nevertheless, studies have shown that portfolios of these stocks have strongly outperformed the market.

How easy are these stocks to find? Oppenheimer found about 50 each year during his study and not the hundreds referred to by Graham. In later years, quite often only one or two companies passed this criterion of having a price less than its net current asset value.[14] In 2007 and early 2008, because of the financial crisis, there were a number of companies in the residential housing sector that passed the NCAV criterion since they were holding considerable inventory in terms of land, houses in progress, and completed houses. But this inventory has either been written off or sold so that they no longer satisfied the criterion. For example, in 2006 Beazer Homes USA Inc. had inventory of $3.6 billion and three years later this had dropped to $1.3 billion.

### Strengths and Weaknesses of Valuation Using Net Current Asset Value

On a company-by-company basis, calculating value using net current asset value is really a simplified variation of the Graham liquidation value described earlier in this chapter. For this reason, the strengths and weaknesses are basically the same as the strengths and weaknesses of this earlier approach. For example, its strengths are that the data for the method is easily accessible, it is simple to calculate, there is a high level of agreement, it provides quantitative and consistent comparisons, and no forecasts are required. Its weaknesses are that it uses limited information, oversimplifies the notion of value, and is a poor estimate of value.

Rather than using the calculation to make decisions about individual companies, it seems that the method is most effective when applied as a screening process for large numbers of stocks. This is supported by the research by Oppenheimer and by Vu, previously outlined. It is also supported by Benjamin Graham himself; he wrote that the method of choosing stocks passing the NCAV criterion can work "*if* you can find enough of them to make a diversified group, and *if* you don't lose patience if they fail to advance soon after you buy them"[15] (italics in the original). The following is a summary of the particular strengths and weaknesses of the NCAV criterion for building a portfolio.

> *Strength 1: Extensive testing.* The NCAV method has been extensively back-tested with excellent results. At the time of the tests it was possible to find a reasonable number of companies satisfying the condition.

The following is an outline of the main weaknesses:

> *Weakness 1: Insufficient stocks.* The back-testing results were based on finding fairly large numbers of companies passing the NCAV criterion. This was also stated as a requirement by Benjamin Graham. However, it may not be possible at all times in the stock market. Without this diversification, it is likely that any portfolios formed using this criterion would be extremely volatile.

> *Weakness 2: Requires discipline.* Companies that satisfy the NCAV criterion are generally in a distressed state and are losing money while holding large amounts of inventory—"cigar butts," as Warren Buffett said. They are not like other companies with depressed prices for which it may be possible to find something about them that indicates that there could be a turnaround in their fortunes. Rather, from the outside they tend to have few redeeming features; otherwise they would not satisfy this extreme condition. Reports written about these companies tend to be very gloomy, so it needs firm discipline to buy and hold them for the specified period, generally 24 months.

## Other Balance Sheet Methods

Apart from the approaches via liquidation value and net current asset value just discussed, Benjamin Graham regularly referred to the balance sheet when evaluating possible investments. For example, in *The Intelligent Investor* he described a selection method for industrial companies for "defensive investors" with a list of seven criteria, several derived from the balance sheet.[16] They are:

1. Adequate size.
2. A sufficiently strong financial condition.
3. Continued dividends for at least 20 years.
4. No earnings deficits in the past 10 years.
5. Ten-year growth of at least one-third in per-share earnings.
6. Price of stock no more than $1\frac{1}{2}$ times net asset value.
7. Price no more than 15 times average earnings over the past three years.

Regarding the first item in Graham's list, he writes, "Our idea is to exclude small companies that may be subject to more than average vicissitudes especially in the industrial field. (There are often good possibilities in such enterprises but we do not consider them suited to the needs of the defensive investor.)"[17] His criterion was not less than $100 million in sales. Given that his book was written over 35 years ago and that average inflation over that time was approximately 4.5 percent per year, this would translate into sales of around $850 million today. This restricts the choice to approximately the largest 1,200 companies on the U.S. market.

It is the second item that is most relevant for us since it concerns the balance sheet. Graham's explanation of what is meant by a "sufficiently strong financial condition" has two parts. First, the current assets should be at least twice current liabilities. In the language of financial ratios, what Graham is saying here is that the current ratio must be at least 2.0. This is a difficult hurdle to achieve and would almost never be met by large retailers. as noted in Chapter 5 in the discussion on Wal-Mart. Second, Graham brings in a restriction on debt, this time through the idea of *working capital*, which is defined as current assets less current liabilities. He asks that long-term debt not exceed working capital. This is the same as asking that the current assets exceed current liabilities plus long-term debt.

Thus, the part of the criterion based on working capital and debt is very close to requiring that NCAV is positive except that long-term debt replaces all noncurrent liabilities in the definition of NCAV. For public utilities instead of industrial companies, Graham asks that the debt should not exceed twice the equity of the company, which is the same as asking that the debt-to-equity ratio should be limited to 50 percent.

The remaining five items in Graham's list are self-explanatory. It is worth noting that the requirement of earnings stability (item 4) and earnings growth (item 5) play a central role in the price ratio methods of Chapters 11 and 13.

## Replacement Value and Tobin's q-Theory

Suppose you own a 20-year-old Ford Taurus. Because of its age and mileage, you may not be able to sell it except for its scrap metal to a junk car dealer. The price that you would be paid is called its *liquidation value*. There is another type of value called *replacement value*, which is an estimate of how much it would cost to replace the car for your continued use. Suppose that the car still serves you well as an extra vehicle. If you needed to replace it, most likely you would need to pay considerably more than you would have received for it as scrap metal. This shows that generally replacement value is higher than liquidation value.

This idea of replacement cost or replacement value for a used car can be extended to companies. When this is done, one conclusion is that the fair value of a business needs to be close to its replacement cost. Consider a business that produces widgets. Suppose the market capitalization of this business greatly exceeds the establishment of a new widget business. Enterprising financiers will keep building widget companies and floating them on the market at a substantial profit until the world has a glut of widgets. Conversely, if the market price was substantially lower than the cost to build a new widget company, no one would build any new companies that produced widgets. The profitability—and the stock prices—of the existing businesses would rise. Eventually the profits would justify the construction of new widget businesses. Jeremy Grantham, one of the founders of GMO, a global asset management company with over $100 billion under management, refers to replacement value as the "bedrock of value."[18]

As with so much in economics, this idea was first stated by John Maynard Keynes. For instance, in 1936 in *The General Theory of Employment, Interest and Money* he wrote:

> [The] daily revaluations of the Stock Exchange, though they are primarily made to facilitate transfers of old investments between one individual and another, inevitably exert a decisive influence on the rate of current investment. For there is no sense in building up a new enterprise at a cost greater than that at which a similar existing enterprise can be purchased; whilst there is an inducement to spend on a new project what may seem an extravagant sum, if it can be floated off on the Stock Exchange at an immediate profit.[19]

The relationship between market value and replacement cost was formalized by the Nobel laureate James Tobin in 1969 with the introduction of the *q-ratio*. In the words of Tobin, q is:

> ... the ratio between two valuations of the same physical asset. One, the numerator, is the market valuation: the going price in the market for exchanging physical assets. The other, the denominator, is the replacement or reproduction cost: the price in the market for newly produced commodities.[20]

In the world of publicly traded companies, q is defined as the ratio of two valuations of the same business: The numerator is the market capitalization of the business and the denominator is the replacement cost. The theory is that market prices tend to move in such a way that the q-ratio will continually swing back to a long-term value of around 1.0. If it gets too far above 1.0, it will tend to fall back to 1.0 and even overshoot it. If the ratio falls too far below 1.0, it will tend to increase to 1.0 and, as before, may even overshoot it. In other words, the ratio hovers about 1.0 as if an elastic band had one end attached to the value of q and the other end to the number 1.0. In technical language this is referred to as *mean reversion*.

Despite the intuitive appeal of this idea, it is important to see whether it holds in practice. One hindrance to carrying this out is that it is impossible to analyze a company from the outside to determine what it would cost to replace it or build a similar company. This difficulty is circumvented by taking book value as a proxy for

replacement value. But now we are back with all the problems associated with book value as a measure of the fair value of a business.
The standard way around this involves three steps.

1. The first step is to consider only manufacturing companies
   since the way that debt is handled in financial companies can
   distort the results.
2. The second step is not to look at the q-ratio for individual
   companies since, as we have seen, the relationship between
   market price and book value can vary enormously between
   sectors and even between different businesses in the same
   sector. Rather, market capitalization is summed over all suitable companies. This is then compared with the total equity
   of the same companies. Since 1945 the U.S. Federal Reserve
   has provided tables in the *Flow of Funds Accounts* that allow this
   to be done for various classes of companies. Taking our lead
   from Andrew Smithers and Stephen Wright,[21] we use the table
   for nonfarm, nonfinancial corporate businesses.[22] Using this
   data, for each year from 1945, we calculate q as the ratio of
   the total market value of the companies divided by their total
   net worth or equity.
3. The third step is to calculate the long-term average of the
   q-ratio and to use it as a base line. The degree of over- or
   undervaluation is determined on a year-by-year basis by comparing the q-ratio for each year with the long-term average.
   Since 1945 the average is 0.72. There are various explanations
   why the observed average is not equal to, or at least closer
   to, 1.0. According to one explanation, various data sets suggest that the long-term return on corporate equity is less than
   long-term market return. To avoid arbitrage over the long
   term requires that q be less than 1.0 on average.

The results of these calculations are shown in Figure 6.2: The
horizontal line at 0.72 is the long-term average of the q-ratio. The
figure shows yearly data from 1945 to 2009. Clearly the level of q
does not have an upward or downward trend but oscillates about its
long-term average. Over this period the highest level for q is 1.76
in 1999, right at the time of the tech bubble in the stock market.
Rapid growth to this extreme level started in 1990 when q was at its

**Figure 6.2**   Plot of the q-Ratio from 1945 to 2009

This figure shows the levels of the q-ratio at the end of each year from 1945 to 2009. The data is compared to the long-term average of 0.72. The overvaluation grew rapidly from 1990 until 1999 and dropped almost as rapidly to just below the long-term average in 2008. By the end of 2009 it was again above the long-term level.

*Source:* U.S. Federal Reserve, Z1 *Flow of Funds Accounts,* March 11, 2010, Table B.102.

long-term average level, and continued for the next five years. After that it dropped almost as quickly to slightly below its long-term level. By the end of 2009 it had bounced back above this level. The lowest q-ratio since 1945 is 0.33 in 1974, the time when the Dow Jones Industrial Average dropped over 40 percent in the previous 18 months. On the figure, q dropped from 0.90 at the end of 1972 to 0.33 at the end of 1974.

The dizzying heights of q around the turn of the millennium make the financial crisis during 2008 seem almost inevitable. Its return at the end of 2009 to above the long-term average is partly due to the fact that the market has started to rise but also, to a lesser effect, because asset values have fallen. The question now is what is going to happen next. Are we headed for another bubble or will the market settle again relative to underlying values? What monetary actions are being planned by the Federal Reserve and other regularity bodies? And what effect will it have on overall market values and the q-ratio?

### Strengths and Weaknesses of Valuation Using q-Theory

As we have presented it here, q-theory is the hypothesis that the ratio of total market capitalization to total net value or equity is mean-reverting, which simply means that it continually comes back to, or near to, its long-term average. The following is a summary of the strengths and weaknesses of this method.

> *Strength 1: General guide.* Although q-theory does not apply to individual companies, it is a general guide to whether the market is undervalued or overvalued. So it may be helpful in deciding what proportion of a portfolio should be held in cash and what proportion should be invested in the stock market. If the level of the market q is high, then it may make sense to keep more of your money in cash. One of the themes of this book is that you don't invest in the stock market (unless you use index funds); rather, you invest in individual companies. Nevertheless, belief that the market is overvalued may cause you to be even more careful in making stock selections for an investment portfolio. Also, you would anticipate finding fewer quality investments. Conversely, if the market q was low, holding less cash may be the most profitable way to proceed.

The following is an outline of the main weaknesses:

> *Weakness 1: Does not apply to individual companies.* As previously explained, q-theory does not apply to individual companies. Even when it is applied to overall categories of companies, it is usual to leave out finance companies and farm companies with considerable land assets.
>
> *Weakness 2: Various definitions.* The q-ratio is not a standard valuation method and so information about it can be difficult to find. Furthermore, academics give various definitions of the ratio.

## The Bottom Line

1. Balance sheet methods such as book value, liquidation value, net current asset value, and replacement value use line items from the balance sheet to estimate value.
2. As absolute measures of value, balance sheet methods are of limited use because many important assets of a company are not included on the balance sheet or, if they are included, the value assigned to them is a poor indicator of their market value.
3. By looking at trends or at comparisons with other companies or groups of companies, balance sheet methods can be helpful in deciding whether a company is worth looking at in more detail.

# CHAPTER 7

# A Bird in the Hand

*A bird in the hand is worth two in the bush.*

—Aesop[1]

*The proper price of any security, whether a stock or a bond, is the sum of all future income payments discounted at the current rate of interest in order to arrive at the present value.*

—Robert Wiese[2]

In the nineteenth century, T. B. Sprague described a revolutionary idea for valuing stocks. Sprague, as the editor of the *Journal of Institute of Actuaries and Assurance Magazine*, published a footnote to an 1869 paper by W. M. Makeham. In this note he described a formula for the discounted present value of "successive annual payments" growing at a specified rate. Instead of using simple dividend yields and book value, the standard methods at the time, investors were invited to calculate a so-called "true" value of the equity using discounted estimates of future dividends. Comparison of this value with the actual market price determined the attractiveness of the investment.

It seems that little use was made of this approach until Robert Wiese popularized it in 1930 in an article he wrote for *Barron's* where he explained that both stocks and bonds could be valued as the discounted value of all future payments. The main point is that he was talking about future income payments and not just the dividend yield. A second point is that he indicated that even if we are talking about a stock, we should perform a present-value calculation just like the well-known method for bonds.

Building on the work of Wiese, John Burr Williams wrote a key book in 1938 called *The Theory of Investment Value*. (In 1940 he was awarded his doctorate by Harvard University for his work.) The book opens with the statement: "Separate and distinct things not to be confused, as every thoughtful investor knows, are real worth and market price." In other words, do not confuse real worth with the price in the market. Williams' book is all about valuing stocks as the sum of the dividends discounted back to present time. This is called the *dividend discount valuation method*.

Not all companies pay dividends, and a second discount method, the *discounted cash flow method*, does not involve them. Currently, this method has mostly replaced Williams' dividend discount valuation method. With the second method, the investor instead uses forecasts of its profits or *earning power* to value a business. Even though the dividend discount method was developed before the discounted cash flow method, because the latter is more commonly used we will describe it in this chapter as part of a general discussion on discount methods. The description of the dividend discount method, along with two variations, will be postponed to Chapter 8.

## Discounted Cash Flow

Discount methods involve three steps:

1. Estimating various future financial items such as earnings, free cash flow, or dividends.
2. Discounting them back to present time.
3. Taking the sum of these discounted values.

The methods can be understood by piecing together how they work on a year-by-year basis.

Suppose you know you will receive a payment of $5.00 in a year's time and $5.25 in two year's time. Suppose also that you believe that a reasonable discount rate is 10 percent, allowing for the risk of not receiving the payment and inflation. Then the equivalent of $5.00 in one year is $5/(1 + 10\%) = \$4.55$ now. In other words, you have discounted $5.00 back to present time at the rate of 10 percent. (With apologies to Aesop, we are saying that $4.55 in the hand is worth $5.00 in the bush, by which we mean one year into the future with all the uncertainties that come with this delay.) For the second payment, $5.25 in two years' time, discounting this back to present time gives the value $5.25/(1 + 10\%)^2 = \$4.34$. Now suppose you know the payments for all future years. If you discount them in the same way and add the results, then you arrive at the intrinsic value or real worth of the stock according to the discount method.

Instead of focusing on dividends as was the case with Williams, in this chapter we focus on cash that could be distributed to shareholders without affecting the viability or profitability of the business. This is done in the sense of the quote by Warren Buffett that the intrinsic value of a stock is the "discounted value of the cash that can be taken out of a business during its remaining life."[3]

## Discounted Cash Flow Calculation of Intrinsic Value

According to the discounted cash flow model, intrinsic value is the sum of the discounted values of the cash that can be taken out of a business during its remaining life.

When discount methods are put into practice, the idea of "remaining life" is implemented as an infinite number of years or "in perpetuity." We will see that this is a source of major problems with the method. But before worrying about that, we will set up the method in mathematical terms. The core formula for all discount methods is:

$$V = c_1/(1+r) + c_2/(1+r)^2 + c_3/(1+r)^3 + \cdots$$

where
  $V$ denotes the intrinsic value
  $r$ denotes the discount rate
  $c_1$ denotes the cash in year 1
  $c_2$ denotes the cash in year 2, and so on

We will call this the *discounted cash flow* (DCF) formula.

The first term is simply the cash $c_1$ discounted back one year by the rate $r$. For example, if the cash was $10.00 and the discount rate was 12 percent, then the first term would be $10/(1 + 12\%) = \$8.93$. Similarly, the second term is the cash $c_2$ discounted back two years by the rate $r$. This formula can be stated in terms of the total business, in which case $V$ is the intrinsic value of the entire enterprise. More usually, however, the terms $c_t$ represent cash per share in year $t$ so that $V$ is the intrinsic value per share. We won't keep talking about these cases separately; rather, we want to allow the reader to decide whether to interpret everything at the level of the company or the level of single shares.

*Note*: The symbol "$\cdots$" means that we are required to add an infinite number of terms.[4] The requirement to sum an infinite series has a number of consequences in terms of mathematics and finance. For example, from mathematics we need to ask what it means to sum an infinite series and from finance we need to ask what restrictions this places on the permissible values of the free cash flow. These and related questions are examined in Appendix B.

To be able to apply the discounted cash flow formula, we need to answer three questions:

1. What do we mean by the cash that can be taken out of a business?
2. How fast is this cash growing and for how long?
3. What discount rate should we use?

We will examine these questions and various answers in the next three subsections.

### Free Cash Flow

The first question asks the meaning of cash that can be taken out of the business, because it is this cash that is substituted in the formula for intrinsic value. At first we might think that it is the net profit of the company. However, net profit involves accrual accounting with noncash items such as receivables, payables, and depreciation, which are not always able to be "taken out of a business." What we are looking for is a measure of the cash a company has left over after investing in the growth of its business. This is called *free cash flow*.

The simplest approach builds on the fact that the cash flow statement already expresses everything in cash or reconciles the items

**Table 7.1** Free Cash Flow Calculations for Wal-Mart

| Entry | 2010 | 2009 | 2008 |
|---|---|---|---|
| Net cash provided by operating activities | $26,249 | $23,147 | $20,642 |
| Payments for property and equipment | $12,184 | $11,499 | $14,937 |
| Total free cash flow | $14,065 | $11,648 | $5,705 |
| Diluted shares outstanding | 3,877 | 3,951 | 4,072 |
| Total free cash flow per share | $3.63 | $2.95 | $1.40 |

Data is in millions of dollars except for the per-share calculations. Calculation of free cash flow for Wal-Mart for the financial years ending on January 31 for the years 2008, 2009, and 2010. The data is taken from the cash flow statement and the income statement given in Chapter 4.

back to cash. This means that we start with the cash flow statement and define free cash flow as the net cash provided by the operating activities of continuing operations in the financial year minus payments for property and equipment made in the same financial year. Table 7.1 shows the calculation of free cash flow for Wal-Mart over the past three years using the data in its cash flow statement (Table 4.4 of Chapter 4). We also calculate free cash flow per share and so need the number of shares outstanding (Table 4.3 of Chapter 4). Table 7.1 shows that free cash flow has risen strongly from $1.40 per share to $3.63 per share. Wal-Mart asserts that the increase is primarily the result of improved operating results and inventory management.

The company, however, makes an important disclaimer, which is a helpful reminder of the importance of not focusing too heavily on any particular method or measure. Wal-Mart explains:

> Free cash flow is considered a non-GAAP financial measure under the SEC's rules. Management believes, however, that free cash flow, which measures our ability to generate additional cash from our business operations, is an important financial measure for use in evaluating the company's financial performance. Free cash flow should be considered in addition to, rather than as a substitute for, income from continuing operations as a measure of our performance and net cash provided by operating activities as a measure of our liquidity.[5]

**Formal Definition of Free Cash Flow**  The preceding definition of free cash flow was based on the cash flow statement. In contrast, the formal definition of free cash flow is based on the income statement.

It requires three steps. Starting with net profit, since it contains various noncash items such as depreciation and amortization, the first step is to add these items back to the net profit. The second step is to remove the actual capital expenditure. As an example, suppose net profit for the year is $100,000. Suppose that during the year the only capital expenditure was the purchase of a car for $20,000 for which depreciation of $5,000 was claimed. After the first two steps we arrive at:

$$(\$100,000 + \$5,000) - \$20,000 = \$85,000$$

The third and final step is to consider changes in *working capital*, which represents the day-to-day operating liquidity available to a business. Working capital is calculated as current assets minus current liabilities. The general idea is that if a company needs to increase its working capital, then the amount of this increase is no longer available as part of the free cash flow. Along with fixed assets such as plant and equipment, working capital is considered a part of operating capital. It may also be necessary to make adjustments for other noncash items such as allowances for taxation.

Continuing with the previous example, suppose that the working capital in the current year is $5,500 and in the previous year it was $4,000. The interpretation is that the company has $1,500 less "in the kitty" to use for short-term needs and so this money must be removed from the calculations. This means that free cash flow is:

$$[(\$100,000 + \$5,000) - \$20,000] - \$1,500 = \$83,500.$$

Summarizing the three steps, free cash flow is defined as net profit plus depreciation and amortization less capital expenditures less changes in working capital. If this final figure is divided by the number of shares outstanding, we arrive at free cash flow per share.

As a slight variation, Warren Buffett likes to talk about *owner earnings*. The definition is the same as for free cash flow except that instead of subtracting increases in working capital, he subtracts "the average annual amount of capitalized expenditures for plant and equipment, etc. that the business requires to fully maintain its long-term competitive position and its unit volume."[6] The first difference is that Buffett requires an average to be used instead of the amount for each year. The second difference is that he appears to use capital expenditure associated only with maintenance and not capital expenditure associated with growth, although this may be drawing more from his definition than he really means.

This is a simple introduction to free cash flow. There are variations that take into account such things as interest payments and changes in debt levels.[7] Whatever definition you use, the process is the same to calculate intrinsic value via the discount method. The important idea is to think of the free cash flow as money due to the shareholders, the "owners" in Buffett's language. Some of this money may come directly as dividends and some may come as capital gains through management using it to grow the business.

---

 **Warning: Compare Free Cash Flow and Net Profit**

For large, stable companies it might be expected that free cash flow and net profit would be similar over the years. For example, capital items would be continuously replaced each year and so it might be expected that the outlay for their purchases would roughly match the depreciation. This means that if current and past free cash flow has been significantly less than net profit, it may be a cause for concern. It could be that the standard GAAP measures of the company present a rosier picture of its financial health than what is warranted by its actual business performance. Table 4.3 of Chapter 4 shows that Wal-Mart's net profit for its three most recent financial years was $14,335 million (January 31, 2010), $13,400 (January 31, 2009), and $12,731 (January 31, 2008). Table 7.1 shows that for each year the free cash flow was less than the net profit, with a particularly large gap for 2008.

---

**Experiment with Earnings in Place of Free Cash Flow**

We will shortly be looking at specific intrinsic value calculations. As well as substituting free cash flow into the formulas, you can also substitute earnings per share. If the values differ by large amounts, take it as a pointer to look more closely into the financials of the company and the related forecasts. In Chapter 8, we examine the results of substituting dividends into the formula.

## Growth Rates

The second question before applying the DCF formula is how to forecast the cash generated by the company over its life. The problem is that the formula for intrinsic value using discount methods involves an infinite number of terms. To apply the formula, values must be estimated for all the terms $c_1$, $c_2$, $c_3$, and so on. The standard way of doing this is to assume that the terms grow at a specified rate (or rates). This reduces the problem to forecasting growth rates rather than the actual terms. Typically, three different forecast models are used: the constant growth model, the two-stage model, and the three-stage model.

**Constant Growth Model**    When the free cash flow is assumed to grow at a constant rate in perpetuity, it is called the *stable* or *constant growth model*. In this case the formula for the intrinsic value $V$ is what mathematicians call a geometric sum. There is a standard formula for calculating the result for such a sum.

Suppose that the initial value for the free cash flow is $c$ and that it grows at the rate $g$. The values of the free cash flow in DCF formula become:

$$c_1 = c \times (1 + g)$$
$$c_2 = c \times (1 + g)^2$$
$$c_3 = c \times (1 + g)^3$$

and so on. In this case, a standard mathematical calculation[8] shows that intrinsic value $V$ from the formula is given by:

$$V = c \times (1 + g)/(r - g)$$

**Two-Stage Model**    The more usual assumption is that the free cash flow grows at a constant rate for a certain period, generally 10 years, then at a slower rate for the remainder of time. These are referred to as the *initial* or *growth period* and the *stable* or *terminal growth period*. When this is the assumption, it is possible to calculate the contribution from the two periods and add them to get the intrinsic value. This is called the *two-stage model*. An example is given in Table 7.2 later in the chapter.

**Three-Stage Model** On occasion it can make sense to divide the growth periods into three stages to get the three-stage model: Stage 1 is the *initial growth period*, stage 2 is a *transition period*, and stage 3 is the *terminal growth period*. The growth rates are specified for the first and third stages. In the second stage the growth rate varies between the initial rate at the start of the stage and the terminal rate at the end of the stage.

Whether we use growth rates, as in these models, or some other method for making forecasts of free cash flow, we are skating on very thin ice because we are being asked to make forecasts out to infinity. For now, we just state the formalities without looking at the consequences of such a requirement.

---

### Discounted Cash Flow Models

There are three discounted cash flow models distinguished by the assumptions about the growth rate of the free cash flow:

1. *Constant growth.* The free cash flow is assumed to grow at a constant rate over the entire life of the business.
2. *Two-stage model.* The growth is assumed to be constant for a fixed period, typically 10 years, and then a new rate is assumed for the remaining life of the business. This is the model most commonly used by analysts.
3. *Three-stage model.* The growth is assumed to be constant for stage 1 (the initial stage) and stage 3 (the terminal stage). For stage 2 (the transition stage) the growth rate moves between the rates of stage 1 and stage 3.

---

### Discount Rates

The third question we need to answer to apply the DCF method concerns the discount rate to use in the discount formula. The idea of the discount rate is to match payments today with payments in the future so that they are equivalent in terms of value. As stated earlier, the payments in the DCF methods are the free cash flow amounts.

In many areas of finance, a rate called the *risk-free rate* is used for various discount calculations. Although nothing can be completely free of risk, the rate used for this is the interest rate within a country representing agreements that have the lowest amount of risk. In the United States typically it would refer to the various rates associated with government Treasury bills, notes, and bonds. From these financial instruments the U.S. Treasury and other organizations calculate a rate of interest for different periods out to 30 years. In other countries it may be an interbank rate, which is the rate at which the largest banks in the country lend money to each other.[9]

For the stock market, free cash flow and dividend payments do not have this level of security. This means that we need to ask the question, what rate of return would I require to compensate me for the risk of investing in this business? Or, putting it more specifically, assuming that the risk-free 10-year rate is 3.5 percent, what extra premium would I require to invest in the business based on the forecasts of the free cash flow?

The formal approach to deciding on a discount rate is via the capital asset pricing model (CAPM), briefly described in Chapter 2. The discount rate is set at the expected annual return calculated using CAPM. However, this relies on a statistical analysis of historical price movements. There is no allowance for the merits of the actual business. For example, it is reasonable to require a rate of return that will vary between stocks depending on the perceived risks of the investment. If it is a very stable company with a secure and established income stream, then you may be satisfied with a return in the range of 10 to 11 percent. This could be the case for companies such as Wal-Mart or Johnson & Johnson. In contrast, if it is a business with higher risk such as a telecommunications company or a company with aggressive competitors, then you may want to use a higher rate of return in the calculations, perhaps 14 to 15 percent; for exploration and resource companies, higher still.

Once you have specified your required rate of return, calculate the intrinsic value $V$ of the stock using the DCF formula with the discount variable $r$ equal to your required return (say 12 percent per annum), and compare the resulting value with the current price. Whether the current price is greater or less than the intrinsic value indicates that you are overpaying or underpaying for the stream of cash in relationship to your required rate of return. If the intrinsic value is below the current price, then it may become a target price.

The strategy is to wait until "Mr. Market" makes it available to you at this price. If this does not happen, then you do nothing. In the opposite case, the intrinsic value above the current price indicates that it may be time to buy. Of course, in practice we probably would not act unless the price is significantly below the intrinsic value. This brings in the idea of a *margin of safety*, a topic we examine in detail in Chapter 13.

Alternatively, you can adjust the rate $r$ until the result of the DCF formula equals the current price. Under the theory of DCF methods, this price represents a fair price to pay to get a return at the rate $r$. Then it is up to you to decide whether this return is adequate to make a purchase allowing for the perceived riskiness of the actual investment.

Finally, some analyst reports using DCF methods talk about the *weighted average cost of capital* (WACC) as the discount rate. As the name suggests, it is the average interest rate that a company is expected to pay its shareholders and debt holders to finance its assets. To satisfy its shareholders and creditors, a company should be able to earn on its existing asset base at least the WACC. Otherwise they may withdraw their support by either selling their shares, in the case of shareholders, or cancelling or renegotiating their loans in the case of creditors. Providing estimates for the WACC can be difficult and is usually only attempted by professional analysts.[10] Because of the assumptions that go into the calculations of the WACC, despite it having such a formal name, it is open to all the usual behavioral biases discussed in Chapter 2.

## Assumptions Required for DCF Methods

Quite severe assumptions are required in the DCF methods to be able to calculate the sum of the infinite series. These assumptions are incorporated in the three main versions of the DCF model described earlier: constant growth, two-stage growth, and three-stage growth. The most common version, the two-stage model, is based on three assumptions:

1. The discount rate $r$ is constant in perpetuity.
2. The growth rate of the free cash flow is constant for an initial period, typically 10 years.
3. The growth rate for the remaining time is constant.

Of the financial analysis companies that use DCF methods, some publish partial details of the inputs they use. Standard & Poor's is one of these companies. For example, in its report on Microsoft Corporation dated March 13, 2010, Standard & Poor's writes: "Our DCF model assumes an 11.1 percent weighted average cost of capital and 3 percent terminal growth rate, yielding an intrinsic value of $36."[11] This means that the assumed discount rate is 11.1 percent for the (infinite) life of the company and that the company will grow by 3 percent per year after the initial growth period. In other words, the company is assumed to grow at 3 percent per year in perpetuity. Finally, the figure of $36 is the calculation of intrinsic value. At the time of the report the price of Microsoft was $27.84, so it was at a slight discount from the estimated intrinsic value.

### Example: Calculation of Intrinsic Value Using a Formula and a Table

Suppose an analysis of a company leads to a forecast that the current free cash flow of $1.00 will grow at 12 percent for 10 years and at 3 percent thereafter. Also suppose that the WACC is deemed to be 10 percent. The formula given in Appendix B shows that the intrinsic value $V$ is $28.68. However, to get a better understanding of just what goes into a two-stage calculation via a formula, preparing the year-by-year data in a table is useful. Carrying out this exercise a few times gives more appreciation of the roles of the different variables and how many years of data are required to get a satisfactory level of accuracy. For instance, in the current example, Table 7.2 shows that after 10 years the sum is still only $11.06, which means that it has to more than double to reach the actual value of $28.68. After 25 years, the table gives a value of $22.10, an error of over $5.00 from the true value. Even after 50 years, the table still has an error of over 4 percent.

Of course, it is not actually necessary to build up the final result by performing calculations for each year. As just explained, there are standard mathematical formulas for doing this, some of which are described in Appendix B. The main point is that, even if a formula is used to calculate the intrinsic value, the calculations require reliable forecasts of the growth rate and discount rate to be made for many decades, even centuries, into the future. In other words, there are two possibilities, neither of which is attractive: (1) Use formulas that have built into them the unrealistic assumption that accurate forecasts can

**Table 7.2**    Free Cash Flow Growth: Two-Stage Model

| (1) Year | (2) Free Cash Flow | (3) Discounted Free Cash Flow | (4) Running Total |
|---|---|---|---|
| 1 | $1.12 | $1.02 | $1.02 |
| 2 | $1.25 | $1.04 | $2.05 |
| 3 | $1.40 | $1.06 | $3.11 |
| 4 | $1.57 | $1.07 | $4.19 |
| 5 | $1.76 | $1.09 | $5.28 |
| 6 | $1.97 | $1.11 | $6.39 |
| 7 | $2.21 | $1.13 | $7.53 |
| 8 | $2.48 | $1.16 | $8.68 |
| 9 | $2.77 | $1.18 | $9.86 |
| 10 | $3.11 | $1.20 | $11.06 |
| 11 | $3.20 | $1.12 | $12.18 |
| 12 | $3.29 | $1.05 | $13.23 |
| … | … | … | … |
| 25 | $4.84 | $0.45 | $22.10 |
| … | … | … | … |
| 50 | $10.13 | $0.09 | $27.41 |

Free cash flow growth under the assumptions that the initial free cash flow is $1.00 and will grow at 12 percent for 10 years and at 3 percent thereafter. The weighted average cost of capital is assumed to be 10 percent. Column (1) shows the year and column (2) shows the free cash flow for the year. It grows at 12 percent per year for the first 10 years and 3 percent per year after that. Column (3) is the amount in column (2) discounted back to present time by the rate 10 percent. Column (4) is a running total of the discounted free cash flow in column (3). This running total will converge to the valuation of the stock. Years 25 and 50 are included to give an idea of the sizes of the values far in the future. If you continue the table far enough, the numbers begin to converge to a single outcome, which is the intrinsic value.

be made decades, even centuries, into the future; or (2) build up the result with tables based on forecasts over more practical time frames with the possibility of large approximation errors further down the road.

## DCF Methods and Value Ratios

Before looking at the strengths and weaknesses of the discounted cash flow methods, we will make a few remarks about the value ratio associated with the method. As stated in Chapter 3, the value ratio (VR) is the ratio of intrinsic value per share $V$ and price $P$. It is needed when deciding whether an investment represents real value. Starting with the discounted cash flow formula for intrinsic value, define the associated *cash yields* as the ratios $c_1/P$, $c_2/P$, and so on, where $c_t$ denotes the cash per share in year $t$. These are akin to the price yields described in Chapter 5 with earnings per share replaced by cash per share.

Taking the DCF formula on a per-share basis, divide all the terms in the formula by the price $P$. All the terms on the right-hand side now become cash yields, and the value ratio is the total of the discounted value of all the forward cash yields taken over the life of the company. This is quite a statement to digest. Basically it is saying that the drivers for real value are the cash yields of the business. People often choose stocks because of healthy dividend yields. Now we are saying that according to DCF methods, it makes sense to choose stocks because of a healthy combination of certain cash yields.

This means that there is the possibility of achieving the goal of calculating the VR without actually calculating (or estimating) the cash terms $c_1$, $c_2$, ... provided there is a way of calculating (or estimating) cash yields. The point is that the idea of choosing to use DCF methods to avoid using some type of cash yield is an illusion. Even if they are not expressed directly, they are an essential part of any final determination of whether to buy. Of course, the idea of actually estimating an infinite string of cash yields is rather daunting. In Chapter 11 on ratio methods we will simplify this and focus on a single ratio.

An advantage of the ratio approach to value is that it is possible to build tables of value ratios. This enables specific cases to be checked quickly by looking them up in a table. As explained in Chapter 3, the ultimate goal is to determine the value ratio and not a calculation of an isolated intrinsic value. Table 7.3 shows the value ratios for a range of free cash flow growth rates and initial ratios of price to free cash flow. To keep the analysis simple, it is assumed in the table that the initial period lasts 10 years and that after that the growth rate is 3 percent. It is also assumed that the discount rate is 11.0 percent.

As an example, consider a stock with an initial price-to-free-cash-flow ratio of 12. Assume that the free cash flow is expected to grow by 10.0 percent for the first 10 years and 3 percent per year thereafter. The table shows that the ratio of intrinsic value to price is 146 percent. In other words, the stock is trading at a discount to its intrinsic

**Table 7.3**   Value Ratios Depending on Free Cash Flow

| | | Price-to-Free-Cash-Flow Ratio | | | | | | |
|---|---|---|---|---|---|---|---|---|
| | | 6 | 8 | 10 | 12 | 14 | 16 | 18 | 20 |
| | 0.0% | 148% | 111% | 89% | 74% | 63% | 55% | 49% | 44% |
| Free | 2.5% | 175% | 131% | 105% | 87% | 75% | 66% | 58% | 52% |
| Cash | 5.0% | 207% | 155% | 124% | 103% | 89% | 78% | 69% | 62% |
| Flow | 7.5% | 246% | 184% | 147% | 123% | 105% | 92% | 82% | 74% |
| Growth | 10.0% | 292% | 219% | 175% | 146% | 125% | 109% | 97% | 88% |
| | 12.5% | 347% | 261% | 208% | 174% | 149% | 130% | 116% | 104% |
| | 15.0% | 414% | 310% | 248% | 207% | 177% | 155% | 138% | 124% |

This shows the value ratio consisting of intrinsic value calculated using the two-stage discounted cash flow model divided by share price based on the current ratio of price to free cash flow and the forecast growth rate of the free cash flow. In each case the growth rate is assumed to hold for 10 years; after that the growth is assumed to be 3 percent. The calculations assume a discount rate of 11.0 percent.

value of approximately one-third. Should it be necessary to get an actual amount for the intrinsic value, this can be achieved by multiplying the share price by the value ratio. If the price is $50, the intrinsic value is $73; if the price is $100, the intrinsic value is $146, and so on.

## Dividends . . . or Not

At various times we have talked about whether it is advantageous for a company to use its earnings to pay dividends. The same question applies to its free cash flows: Should they be used to pay dividends? In terms of DCF valuation, we also need to ask whether paying dividends will change the calculation of the intrinsic value. For example, if a company pays out all its free cash as dividends, there will be less retained money to use to grow the business; hence we would expect the growth rate to be less. However, estimates of growth rates are already part of the requirements of DCF calculations. This means that once estimates of the growth rates are made, provided there are no changes in the dividend policy, the DCF method does not have, and does not need, a specific mention of dividends.

As a simple example, suppose that the initial book value is $20 and the estimates of the free cash flows in the first two years are $5.00 and $10.00. Suppose also that retained free cash flows are the only contribution to changes in book value. Assuming the company pays no dividends, at the end of two years the book value will be $35.00. However, if the company pays all its free cash flows as dividends, at the end of two years book value will remain at $20.00 but the investor will have received $15.00 in dividends. Once again, the total is $35.00. The catch here is that in practice, if the company paid this level of dividends, there would likely be no growth in free cash flows. However, as stated earlier, the DCF method only requires a forecast of free cash flows after all assumptions on dividend levels have been made.

## Three Bears' Valuation

Up to this point we have looked at the theory of DCF methods. Now it is time to evaluate the method in a practical setting. The basic investment question is whether any given stock is undervalued, fairly valued, or overvalued under established conditions. Unfortunately, with discount methods it turns out that this is really like the temperature of the porridge in the three bears' house visited by Goldilocks. Some might calculate intrinsic value and conclude that the stock is undervalued; others might get a different intrinsic value and conclude that it is overvalued; while others might conclude that it is trading at its fair price.

Consider Wal-Mart. To apply the two-stage DCF method we need its current free cash flow and four estimates: the period of the initial growth rate, the growth rate over this period, the terminal growth rate, and the discount rate.

We calculated earlier in Table 7.1 that the free cash flow for Wal-Mart is $3.63. This leaves the four forecasts to be made. As a starting point, use 10 years as the period of the initial growth rate. (We will return to all these assumptions shortly.) From the financial year ending January 31, 2001, to the financial year ending January 31, 2010, earnings per share for Wal-Mart have grown from $1.40 to $3.70. This is an average annual growth of 11.40 percent. Similarly, sales per share have grown from $42.80 to $107.82, an average annual growth of 11.08 percent. Also, in March 2010, the consensus estimate for the average annual growth of earnings per share was 11.40 percent for five years. (This data is available on the MSN Money web site.) The three growth rates are close to each other, indicating that a reasonable starting point for our forecast is around 11 percent per year. However, the data is for earnings and sales and not for free cash flow. We also want a forecast for 10 years. Because of these difficulties, we will be a little more conservative and take 10 percent per year as our forecast of free cash flow for the first 10 years.

Turning to the long-term growth rate, let us start with 3 percent. As Pat Dorsey, the director of stock analysis at Morningstar, Inc., wrote, "Three percent is generally a good number to use as your long-run growth rate because it's roughly the average rate of U.S. gross domestic product [GDP] growth. If you're valuing a firm in a declining industry, you might use 2 percent."[12]

All that remains to estimate is the discount rate. Let us start with the assumption that we believe that 12 percent represents a fair return for investing in Wal-Mart, taking into account all that we know about the company. This does not mean that we would not like a higher return, simply that we would be interested in investing in Wal-Mart if we could be confident of a 12 percent return.

Using the two-stage DCF model gives a result of $67.61 for Wal-Mart. (It is shown in row 1 of Table 7.4.) In September 2008, the price touched $60.00. But by April 2010 it had dropped to around $55.00, so it appears to be undervalued.

But what if we are not happy with assuming a growth of 10 percent for the next 10 years? What if you think Wal-Mart has essentially reached a ceiling in the United States and can only rely on growth in same-store sales? Also, what if you think that its international growth is not sustainable? Perhaps you would then assume an initial growth period of only three years. This gives an intrinsic value of $49.86, showing that the stock is now overvalued. Alternatively, suppose that you are confident about the growth of Wal-Mart and use 20 years as the initial growth period. Now the intrinsic value jumps to $89.38. These variations are in the length of the initial growth period and

**Table 7.4** Variation of Intrinsic Value for Wal-Mart

| (1)<br>Free Cash Flow | (2)<br>Initial Growth Rate | (3)<br>Final Growth Rate | (4)<br>Discount Rate | (5)<br>Intrinsic Value |
|---|---|---|---|---|
| $3.63 | 10% | 3% | 12% | $67.61 |
| $3.63 | 11% | 4% | 9% | $130.73 |
| $3.63 | 9% | 2% | 14% | $48.30 |

Column (1) shows the initial free cash flow in each case to be $3.63. Column (2) shows the growth rate for the initial period (assumed to be 10 years), after which the growth is shown in column (3). The discount rate is shown in column (4). Column (5) shows the resulting intrinsic value using the discounted cash flow method.

not even on the rate of growth. Nevertheless, they can change the result from being highly overvalued to highly undervalued.

The intrinsic value becomes even more uncertain when the forecasts of the growth rates and discount rates are also considered. Changes in these inputs by only a few percentage points can easily lead to variations of 200 percent or more in the output. Suppose two analysts or investors meet and do a careful analysis of Wal-Mart. They agree on everything regarding Wal-Mart in general terms: its limited potential for domestic growth, the extent of its international opportunities, and so on. However, when it comes to particular estimates, they have slight differences. For example, one thinks that the initial growth rate will be 11 percent while the other prefers 9 percent. One thinks that the long-term growth rate will be 4 percent; the other thinks it will be 2 percent. Also, one prefers a discount rate of 9 percent while the other prefers 14 percent. Table 7.4 shows that the intrinsic value for one set of inputs is $130.73 (row 2) and for the other set of inputs it is $48.30 (row 3).

The point is, we are only talking about small differences in the inputs. Yet the outcome could be a range of intrinsic values from around $48 to over $130, a variation of 270 percent, from undervalued to highly overvalued. If we also allow different time periods for the initial growth, the variation can now go from around $36 to over $190. It is even worse than that: Because the estimates of the discount rates and the long-term growth rates are over infinite time periods, we can never decide whose estimates were the more accurate—we cannot wait for an infinite number of years to test the analysts' forecasts. This means that behavioral biases explored in Chapter 2, such as anchoring and herding, are highly likely to be present.

On the positive side, there is a chance that the price of a stock is so low that it is undervalued under a genuinely wide range of independently provided values of the input variables. In the case of Wal-Mart, this might mean a current price of $40 or less. However, if this were the case, there would be many other signs that the stock was trading at a highly undervalued level. For example, since the current earnings per share is $3.70, its price-to-earning (P/E) ratio would be around 10.81. Since the lowest P/E ratio over the past 10 years was 12.50 (including the difficult economic period over the past 18 months), a P/E of 10.81 would be an extreme result. In such a case, we would probably not need any sophisticated DCF methods to determine that it is undervalued.

## Examples of Discount Rates

A few financial institutions kindly provide the rates that they use for their long-term forecasts. As mentioned earlier, one of these institutions is Standard & Poor's. Consider the three diverse companies Microsoft (MSFT), Google (GOOG), and The Toro Company (TTC). Microsoft is a $200 billion company that builds software and related computer products, Google is a $135 billion company centered on a search engine for the Internet, while The Toro Company is a $1.2 billion company focused on lawn care products. In terms of debt, the debt-to-equity ratio of Microsoft is 9 percent, Google has no debt, and The Toro Company has a debt-to-equity ratio of 62 percent. Despite their diversity, in stock reports produced by Standard & Poor's at the time of writing (March 2010), the WACC for Microsoft was assumed to be 11.1 percent, for Google 11.0 percent, and for The Toro Company 10.6 percent.[13] According to the reports, these figures are used in their DCF calculations of intrinsic value. This means that for the infinite future, the authors believe that there is almost no difference between the discount rates required to calculate the intrinsic value of MSFT, GOOG, and TTC.

There is even less variation in the long-term growth forecasts. The Standard and Poor's reports mentioned earlier listed the perpetuity growth rates of all three companies at 3 percent. Presuming that 3 percent is the standard forecast of the growth of the GDP, perhaps it will turn out that the average growth of all listed U.S. companies will be 3 percent over, say, the next 20 years. But this is of little use for calculating the value of individual companies since the variation between companies could mean that the value could be wrong by orders of magnitude. It is like trying to decide what to wear in New York based on being told that the average daily maximum temperature over a whole year is 62 degrees. It is a true statement but of little practical use since typically the daily maximum ranges from 39 degrees to 85 degrees.

Another disconcerting consequence of this one-size-fits-all forecast of 3 percent for the long-term growth rate is that it is a very low opinion of the company. A growth rate of only 3 percent after 10 years doesn't say much about the attractiveness of the products and services of the business, or about management's ability to grow the company. At the right time, making conservative forecasts is admirable, and much of Chapter 13 is devoted to this topic. However, in the setting of discounted cash flow methods, 3 percent is portrayed as the actual forecast of the long-term growth rate. If this growth rate eventuates, all we can look forward to is long-term capital gains of around this level. It begins to make the idea of investing in the stock market for long-term security rather pointless.

Unfortunately, the whole structure of the DCF method makes it hard to use anything much different than 3 percent. A long-term forecast higher than 3 percent can suddenly double or triple the intrinsic value. For example, if the long-term rate in the first row of Table 7.4 is replaced by 6 percent, the intrinsic value increases to $86.48. If it replaced by 9 percent, it jumps to $143.06. The underlying problem is that the actual method is encumbered right at the start with the requirements of making forecasts out to infinity. So problems and inconsistencies are always going to occur.

## Strengths and Weaknesses of Discounted Cash Flow Methods

Prior to the work of Robert Wiese and the book by John Burr Williams mentioned at the start of this chapter, there was no systematic understanding of how to value a company. The advent of valuing a stock as the discounted value of a stream of payments was a major development in establishing a clear difference between investing and speculating. We start with the strengths of the discounted cash flow method:

*Strength 1: Clear definition.* The definition is quite specific in terms of the input variables and the calculations used to combine them. Under various assumptions the method is amenable to being programmed and, with care, can even be calculated using a calculator or spreadsheet.

*Strength 2: Rational definition.* A standard bond consists of a series of dividends plus the return of the face value at its expiration. Consequently, its value is calculated as the discounted value of the dividends plus the discounted value of the face value. The definition of value of a stock using the DCF approach is a rational extension of the calculation of value of a standard bond.

*Strength 3: Easy interpretation.* It is easy to interpret the outcome of a DCF calculation as the true value of a stock and to compare this value with its market price in order to facilitate buy/hold/sell decisions.

*Strength 4: Wide applicability.* The method is applicable to a wide variety of companies and not just to those that are publicly listed. For example, it is commonly used to value small private companies looking for new investors or as part of the prospectus for larger companies planning to list on a stock exchange.

*Strength 5: Easy conversion.* By dividing the terms in the basic DCF formula for intrinsic value $V$ by the price $P$, the value ratio associated with the discounted cash flow method can be converted easily to the discounted value of all the forward cash yields taken over the life of the company. Hence there is no direct need of the cash terms in absolute dollar values, only through their ratios with the price.

*Strength 6: Consistent basis.* The calculation of intrinsic value by the DCF method provides a consistent basis for comparing possible investments. For example, the value ratios (value divided by price) can be calculated for a range of companies, with the companies with the highest ratios singled out as more attractive investments compared to those with lower ratios.

*Strength 7: No dividends.* The DCF method uses any of the variants of free cash flow as its main input and does not require any assumptions on dividends, or even whether the company actually pays them.

*Strength 8: Wide acceptance.* Perhaps the greatest strength of DCF methods is that they are very widely accepted. The methods are taught in most finance and stock valuation courses as the standard way to calculate intrinsic value. In fact, in the literature and the finance industry, DCF methods are often synonymous with intrinsic value. This means that when a valuation is done using a DCF method, it is frequently accepted with little further discussion.

There are 10 main weaknesses of DCF methods, mostly hinging on the requirements to make forecasts for an infinite number of years. The first weakness, however, is common to all methods where intrinsic value is calculated as a dollar amount. Even if a company is highly undervalued, we still do not know when, or if, the price will start to move upward. Benjamin Graham talked about this as the "hazard of tardy adjustment of price to value."[14]

*Weakness 1: May not convert to profit.* The first weakness is that they are theoretical formulas. Just because a stock has a high intrinsic value calculated by one of the DCF formulas compared to its price does not mean that it will be a profitable investment in terms of return. For example, it may continue at its current price levels. The standard approach is to introduce, either formally or informally, the price ratio that we defined in Chapter 3 as $V/P$, where $V$ is the intrinsic value and $P$ is the price. But now the definition of $V$ via the discounted cash flow formula shows that the price ratio is an infinite sum of discounted ratios of free cash flow divided by price.

*Weakness 2: Many variations.* There are many variations of the discounted cash flow method, giving a range of different values. A stock could be undervalued according to one variation, but overvalued according to another.

*Weakness 3: Unstable results.* All the formulas are highly unstable, meaning that small changes in the input numbers lead to extremely large variation in the output. Table 7.4 gives examples of this instability.

*Weakness 4: Easily manipulated.* Another consequence of the instability just described is that the final result for intrinsic value is easy to manipulate by making small changes in the input variables. Because these changes are so small, they are easily defended. The outcome is that it is easy to get an intrinsic value result that supports any opinion about the stock, ranging from highly overvalued to greatly undervalued.

*Weakness 5: Untestable inputs.* It is impossible to test the accuracy of the key inputs in the formulas, such as the terminal growth rate and the discount rate, because they require forecasts out to infinity. For example, if I forecast the long-term growth rate of Wal-Mart as 4 percent and you forecast it as 3 percent, we can never decide who made the more accurate forecast. Even if we wait 100 years and compare the forecasts with the actual results, we still cannot test the forecasts since we still do not meet the requirement of waiting for an infinite number of years.[15] Moreover, as we saw earlier, the differences of a few percent can make an enormous difference in the outputs.

To avoid the problem of instability and making untestable inputs, some commentators suggest that we use a two-stage model with the first stage as 10 years, and only consider the contribution to the valuation from the first stage. Then all the inputs are over the testable period of 10 years. However, as the calculations in Table 7.2 show, this is not satisfactory since it is simple to find reasonable examples where the contribution of the second stage is far greater than the first stage. This is particularly true for newer companies where the initial growth is anticipated to be comparatively low. Hence, by omitting the second stage and only using the first stage, you could be losing 90 percent of the calculated value or more.

*Weakness 6: Anchoring vulnerability.* The potential bias of anchoring was introduced in Chapter 2 and consists of the tendency to focus on numbers that have already been presented to you or that are already known. All estimates and forecasts are vulnerable to this bias, which would express itself as new forecasts or estimates *anchoring* on those that are already known. However, in most cases the true results of any estimates or forecasts can be verified at a later date. If an earnings forecast is made for the next financial year, it can be verified at that time. Or if a 12-month forecast of a share price is made, again it can be verified after 12 months. Hence it is reasonable to suppose that there is some control over the forecasts that are made, due to the fact that their accuracy can eventually be tested. But this control disappears for the inputs of the discount rate and the long-term growth rate in the discount models since, as just explained, they cannot be tested.

Consider the discount rates used by Standard and Poor's for Microsoft (MSFT), Google, and The Toro Company, quoted earlier. Even though they are completely different companies, there was only a minor difference between the forecasts of their long-term discount rates. The forecast ranged from 10.6 percent to 11.1 percent. Even more surprising was the forecasts of the long-term growth rates of these three companies. In each case it was set at 3 percent.

We don't know the thinking behind the estimates given by Standard and Poor's and other financial institutions. But it is hard not to believe that anchoring plays a major role. Past forecasts have been shown to give reasonable values for the intrinsic value, so new forecasts are anchored on these with almost no regard for the individual companies. Finally, I know of no study that has gone back 20 years or more, looked at the long-term forecasts made back then for individual companies, and compared the forecasts with the actual results. However, if we assume that the long-term forecasts made 20 years ago for Microsoft and The Toro Company were the standard 3 percent, then up until now they are far from accurate. (We cannot include Google since it only listed in 2004.) Using the growth rate of earnings as a proxy for the growth rate of free cash flow, over the past 10 years Microsoft has grown by an average of 11 percent per year and The Toro Company by 15 percent per year.[16] Furthermore, the majority of analysts do not believe that 3 percent is reasonable for the next five years since the consensus forecasts over this period are much higher: 11.4 percent for Microsoft, 15.0 percent for The Toro Company, and 26.6 percent for Google.

*Weakness 7: Infinite sums.* As stated earlier, the DCF formula is an infinite series. As such, it requires an infinite number of inputs for the values, which cannot be done one at a time and must be specified through a rule. This is a limitation on the values that are possible for the inputs. A second limitation is that mathematics only allows the summation of certain types of infinite sums. There are no formulas to calculate most infinite sums. A third limitation is that in the terminal period, the growth rate of the free cash flow must be less than the discount rate, otherwise the series would have an infinite sum. This looks like it should be desirable since it is saying that the intrinsic value is so high it is infinite. However, it removes the ability to properly analyze companies with rates satisfying this condition since we can no longer calculate the value ratio. It also does not allow comparisons via intrinsic value of such companies since their value ratios will all be infinite.[17]

*Weakness 8: False objectivity.* The method gives the appearance of objectivity because of its terminology, such as *intrinsic value,* and its use of college-level mathematics, such as the requirement to sum infinite series, that would be unfamiliar to most people. Yet it is highly subjective because of the instability of the calculations and the impossibility of verifying key input variables.

*Weakness 9: Limited research.* Despite the widespread use and acceptance of DCF methods, the large number of books published on it, and its universal appearance in college courses on investing and finance, there is actually limited academic research on the method. This is probably because the calculation of value using DCF methods is highly variable depending on the input variables, and so it less amenable to rigorous research. In the private sector, some informal research is carried out by various analysis companies but little of it is made available to the public. To its credit, Morningstar is open about its results.

The core of Morningstar's approach is the calculation of the intrinsic value of stocks using "a detailed discounted cash-flow model that factors in projections [to get] an analyst-driven estimate of the stock's fair value."[18] These stocks are then ranked using a star system: The most undervalued companies are awarded five stars, the next level of companies are awarded four stars, and so on down to one star. Finally, the performance of various portfolios based on the star rankings is compared to key market indexes. As an example, one portfolio is formed by buying a stock when it is awarded five stars and held until it drops to its fair value according to their DCF calculations. The stocks in the portfolio are all equally weighted, meaning that the same dollar amount is spent when buying each stock.

Since the inception of the portfolio in August 2001 through to the end of July 2009, the portfolio had an average annual return of 4.07 percent, compared to 2.82 percent for a portfolio made of an equally weighted S&P 500 portfolio. This is good news. However, when the portfolio is compared to an equally weighted portfolio made up of all the stocks covered by Morningstar the results are not so good. The average annual return of this portfolio was 5.86 percent.[19]

*Weakness 10: Confused objectives.* There are two completely different objectives of DCF methods. The theoreticians and academics want an elegant, comprehensive theory while investors want a practical tool to profit in the stock market. Unfortunately, these objectives are mutually exclusive. For example, from the theoretical point of view it is acceptable to use forecasts to infinity and to not worry about the instability of the results. But this is not acceptable for investors; they want practical, stable results that rely on forecasts over reasonable time periods. Even requiring reliable forecasts over 10 years is a very large commitment. However, as we saw in Table 7.2, using forecasts and calculations out as far as 25 years still gives poor approximations of the intrinsic value, with wide variations in results.

## One Final Comment

Many writers and market commentators state that Warren Buffett uses DCF methods. However, there is consistent evidence that this is not the case. For example, Alice Schroeder, as the author of the biography *The Snowball: Warren Buffett and the Business of Life*, had unprecedented access to Buffett and his archives and papers. On November 6, 2008, at a "Value Investing Conference" at the Darden School of Business, University of Virginia, she said, "[Warren Buffett] doesn't do any kind of discounted cash flow models or anything like that." This is supported by Charlie Munger, Buffett's friend and partner for many decades, who I heard say at the annual meeting of Berkshire Hathaway in 1997 that he had never seen Buffett do any discounted cash flow calculations.

### The Bottom Line

1. Discounted cash flow methods are widely used to calculate the intrinsic value of a stock. The basic idea is that the intrinsic value is the discounted value of the free cash generated by the business over its life.
2. The main variations occur because of varying assumptions about the type of growth of the free cash flow.
3. Although they are the methods most used in the financial industry and taught in finance courses, discount methods need to be applied with extreme care, particularly because of problems related to the instability of the results and the requirement to make forecasts in perpetuity.

CHAPTER

8

# The Joy of Dividends

*A cow for her milk, a hen for her eggs,*
*And a stock, by heck, for her dividends.*
— John Burr Williams[1]

*Dividend payments can serve as a signal to shareholders about*
*managers' expectations of the firm's future prospects. Firms may also*
*pay dividends to attract a certain type of shareholder base.*
—Krishna Palepu, Paul Healy, and Victor Bernard[2]

There is something very attractive about receiving dividends. John D. Rockefeller is supposed to have said, "Do you know the only thing that gives me pleasure? It's to see my dividends coming in." Because they tend to be more certain and less volatile than stock prices, some investors and advisers base their whole strategy on seeking out stocks with consistent and growing dividends. There is, however, more to dividends since, among other benefits, they can be used to calculate the intrinsic value of a stock. The basic idea is similar to the discounted cash flow method of the previous chapter, except that dividends replace free cash flow. This means that the intrinsic value is the present value of all the dividends paid by the company over its entire life. The method is called the *dividend discount method*.

An advantage of the dividend discount method is that the size and growth of dividends can be approached indirectly via the dividend payout ratio, which is the proportion of earnings paid out as dividends. The earnings, in turn, can be approached via return on equity and the clean surplus relationship introduced in Chapter 4. The result is a useful variation of the standard dividend discount method. A second variation uses residual income which is, roughly speaking, earnings minus a charge for the use of the capital. The result is an expression for intrinsic value that starts with book value and either builds on it or subtracts from it, depending on the present value of the residual incomes over the life of the business. This is a useful means of evaluating the performance of management: Do its actions increase or decrease the book value of the business? These two variations of the basic dividend discount method are covered in this chapter. There is a third variation based on discounted values of abnormal earnings growth. Because it can be seen as an extension of formulas credited to Benjamin Graham, it will be looked at along with Graham's formulas later in Chapter 12.

## Dividends and Dividend Ratios

There are two ratios that are helpful in understanding dividends: the dividend yield and the payout ratio. *Dividend yield* is the total of dividends over a 12-month period divided by the stock price at the end of the period. It is a measure of the return on a stock purchase in terms of dividends without taking into account capital gains. The *payout ratio* is the dividends divided by the net profit or earnings. A payout ratio of 0 percent means that the company is not paying dividends, while a payout ratio of 100 percent means that it is paying all its earnings as dividends. Sometimes the payout ratio will exceed 100 percent. Usually this only occurs when the company has suffered a drop in earnings but still wishes to continue paying dividends at a similar level to what it has done in the past as a sign of confidence in the future success of the business.

Dividends are paid from the profits of a company. For most countries, including the United States, they are generally paid from after-tax profits and the recipient is taxed on them again. This is referred to as the *double taxation* of dividends. Other countries may do this differently. For example, in Australia investors are allowed a credit for the taxation paid by the company when their own tax bill is calculated. This is called *tax imputation*.

For this reason, Australian investors tend to favor companies with higher dividends in order to get an associated tax offset.

Australian companies recognize this and usually pay higher levels of dividends. For example, over 2008 the average dividend yield for all the companies in the S&P 500 index was 1.99 percent and the average payout ratio was 24.31 percent. In contrast, in Australia where there is no double taxation the figures are significantly higher, 5.14 percent and 42.24 percent for the group of companies in the S&P/ASX 200. Without further analysis, choosing companies merely because of a higher dividend yield is not rational. Frequently investors choose mediocre businesses with a high dividend yield while passing up companies that are likely to have a substantially higher capital growth. The result is that any extra reward from a higher dividend yield is often more than offset by poor or non-existent capital gains.

As just stated, dividends are paid from earnings. A company can take three actions with the earnings or net profits that it generates. It can use all or part of them to expand the business either organically or by purchasing other companies, it can buy back its shares, or it can pay the profits out as dividends. If a company has opportunities to use its earnings profitably as measured by a high return on equity, then it makes financial sense for it to keep the dividends low or nonexistent. Conversely, if it does not see such opportunities, then it may be better to pay them out as dividends. (The three options named here relate to the core business of the company. If the company wanted to step outside its core business it could, for example, start an investment portfolio. As explained in Chapter 6, this was what happened with Berkshire Hathaway. Buffett began to systematically invest money from Berkshire Hathaway in other ventures, eventually turning it from a textile business to an investment company.)

From the point of view of an investor looking for quality investments, there are three problems to watch out for. First, watch out for companies that keep their earnings and invest them in poor businesses. This is usually the outcome of management being overconfident about its abilities. It may be that the core business is successful so management believes it can purchase other businesses and bring them up to a similar level of success. Investing in poor businesses can also be a result of plain empire building by management, particularly the CEO. Look in the annual reports for statements announcing that management has divested itself of certain investments to bring the company back to its core business. If these statements appear regularly, invariably this means that hubris took control in the past, resulting in unwise purchases. Unless they make a frank admission that these past purchases were a mistake, there is a good chance that they will do it again.

Second, watch out for companies that continue to pay high dividends when they have clear opportunities to invest their net profits elsewhere for high returns. This could be judged by a high return on equity. Third, watch out for companies that maintain or increase their dividends every year no matter what the level of the earnings. If the earnings start to drop, this can result in higher and higher payout ratios, often over 100 percent. Even worse, it can result in the company increasing its borrowings in order to fund the dividends.

## Dividend Discount Methods

As discussed in Chapter 7, intrinsic value via the discounted cash flow method is the discounted sum of the free cash flow generated by the business over its life. Similarly, for the dividend discount method intrinsic value is calculated as the discounted sum of the dividends paid by the business over its life. This is called the *dividend discount* (DD) method. (In formal academic literature the method is often called *present value of expected dividends*, or PVED.)

In formal terms, suppose that $d_1$, $d_2$, $d_3$, ... represent the forecasts of dividends of a business for years 1, 2, 3, ... and so on. These dividends need to be discounted back to the present time to allow for risk and inflation. Let us denote the discount rate by $r$. This means that $d_1$ should be discounted by the rate $r$ for one year, $d_2$ should be discounted by the same rate for two years, and so on. Adding this infinite list of discounted values gives the present value or intrinsic value $V$ of the stock, namely

$$V = d_1/(1+r) + d_2/(1+r)^2 + d_3/(1+r)^3 + \cdots$$

This is the standard formula for the dividend discount method. John Burr Williams introduced the formula in his 1938 book *The Theory of Investment Value*, where he defined "the investment value of a stock as the present worth of all the dividends to be paid upon it."[3] He analyzed it in considerable detail and popularized the approach of valuing equities via their expected dividends.

## Dividend Discount Calculation of Intrinsic Value

According to the dividend discount method, intrinsic value is the sum of the discounted values of the expected dividends to be paid by a business during its remaining life.

### Companies Must Eventually Pay Dividends

The first question to consider regarding the dividend discount method is what to do with companies that have never paid dividends and look as if they will not pay any in the foreseeable future. An obvious example is Berkshire Hathaway. This company has not paid any dividends for the past 20 years. Furthermore, by everything written by Warren Buffett, the company's chairman and CEO, it looks like it will not pay any dividends, at least so long as Buffett is in charge. How can we apply the formula to companies such as this? When we make a simple application of the dividend discount formula, we get an intrinsic value of $0. At first this may appear contradictory. At times Berkshire Hathaway has traded at over $150,000, the furthest from $0 of any stock. However, when we analyze it using the greater fool theory, the contradiction disappears.

The *greater fool theory* in the stock market asserts that whenever you buy a stock, you can always find someone to buy it from you at a higher price, the so-called greater fool. (Implicit in the definition is the assumption that the sale can take place in a reasonable time after the purchase at a price high enough to be genuinely profitable.) Accepting the validity of such a theory means that we don't have to concern ourselves with stock analyses and value estimates. You can always make a profit. As you will recognize, it is the greater fool theory that is behind all the major stock market bubbles. Significant numbers of people continue to buy at inflated prices, believing that they can always find another person (the fool) who is willing to pay even more. Understandably, we reject the greater fool theory.

Returning to the issue of dividends, start with the assumption that everyone believes that a particular company will never pay dividends. When an investor buys stock in such a company, it must be with the plan to eventually sell to another investor at some time in the future since this is the only way to benefit from the purchase.[4] (In some cases the intention may be to pass the stock on to heirs. In this case we consider the family as the investor.) This second investor buys with the same intention, and so on.

Hence, without dividends now or in the future, any purchase is based on the assumption that all future purchasers will acquire the stock only for capital gains. In other words, there will always be the opportunity to sell at a higher price. But now we are in the grip of the greater fool theory. Each person buys expecting to sell for a profit to a greater fool since none of the purchasers believe that they will get any direct remuneration for holding the stock. Clearly this is untenable.

We conclude that every stock has a value based on the belief that it will eventually pay dividends even if it is only a single dividend from the liquidation or sale of the company. Of course, earnings are important. But John Burr Williams explains the importance of dividends over earnings as follows: "Earnings are only a means to an end, and the means should not be mistaken for the end. Therefore we must say that a stock derives its value from its dividends, not its earnings. In short, a stock is worth only *what you can get out of it.*"[5]

### Eventual Dividend Payment

Every stock has a value based on the belief that it will eventually pay dividends, even if it is only a single dividend from the liquidation or sale of the company.

This means that, in principle, the dividend discount method can be used to value a stock, even if it is currently not paying dividends. We have to include forecasts in the formula that after a specified time, either dividends will be paid or there will be a single dividend from the liquidation of the company.

Up to a point, private equity firms such as Kohlberg Kravis Roberts & Co. (KKR) evaluate companies on the basis of a single final dividend from their liquidation or sale. In broad terms, KKR and other private equity firms aim to purchase private or publicly listed companies with the prospect of quickly restructuring them, selling the divisions that are the lowest performers, and then selling or listing the remainder of the company. From the perspective of the private equity firm, the valuation is based on a single final payment (or a small number of closely spaced payments) that it believes it can receive.

## Free Cash Flow and Dividends

When everything is proceeding smoothly, a company's free cash flow (or earnings) is likely to have stable growth along with a consistent dividend payout ratio. However, in more difficult times, there can be a lot of variation in how management responds to the question of payment of dividends. For example, the earnings may drop but the company may still maintain its dividends in order to show support for the shareholders or to demonstrate confidence in the company. At the other extreme, in such a case the company may cut or stop its dividends in order to preserve its capital.

New companies can provide a different scenario. For example, as a matter of policy such a company may pay no dividends and show no indication of paying any in the foreseeable future. It prefers to keep the cash it generates to grow the business. Nevertheless, investors will invest in the company since they believe that ultimately the cash will flow through to higher dividends.

Despite this uncertainty about the levels of dividends, as we just saw in the setting of the dividend discount method, ultimately it is the distribution of dividends to the shareholders that determines the value of the company to its shareholders. This means that, no matter how much free cash flow is generated, it is the anticipated future reward to shareholders from dividends that will determine the value.

One issue, though, is that for most ongoing companies, dividends are less than free cash flow. For example, in broad terms, on a per-share basis free cash flow is equal to earnings per share and, as previously noted, on average only about a quarter of earnings is paid out as dividends. Hence, on average, intrinsic value calculated via free cash flow as described in the previous chapter would be around four times greater than intrinsic value calculated using dividends. Can we make sense of this?

The standard answer depends on the likelihood of a full takeover, since in this case the new owners have control of the dividend policy. This means that they can pay dividends in a way that is most beneficial to them. In this case valuation via the DCF method is the method of choice. However, if such a takeover is not possible or likely, then using the dividend discount method is more appropriate. Damodaran expressed it as follows:

> As for which of the two values is the more appropriate one to use in evaluating the market price, the answer lies in the openness of the market for corporate control. If there is a sizable probability that a firm can be taken over or its management changed, the market price will reflect that likelihood, and the appropriate benchmark to use is the value from the [DCF] model. As changes in corporate control become more difficult, either because of a firm's size and/or legal or market restrictions on takeovers, the value from the dividend discount model will provide the appropriate benchmark for comparison.[6]

### Special Case: Constant Dividends

Some companies pay dividends at a constant level, or close to it. In this case, a consequence of the dividend discount formula is that the intrinsic value is dividends divided by the discount rate. For example, if the dividends are $2.00 and the discount rate is 12 percent, then the intrinsic value is 2/0.12 or $16.67. The reason for this is that by the standard dividend discount formula, intrinsic value $V$ is described by

$$V = d/(1+r) + d/(1+r)^2 + d/(1+r)^3 + \cdots = d/r$$

where
  $d$  is dividends per share
  $r$  is the discount rate (see Appendix B for this last equality)

Many companies have constant dividends because they pay out all the earnings as dividends. When this happens, there are no retained earnings to grow the business and so generally the growth of both earnings and dividends is flat. In this case, the intrinsic value can also be written as $e/r$, since earnings per share and dividends per share are equal. What is interesting about this result is that the ratio $e/r$ is the first term in the abnormal earnings growth model described in Chapter 12.

A group of companies that often have dividends at a relatively constant level are master limited partnerships (MLPs). They are similar to real estate investment trusts in that they do not pay income taxes, and their shares trade on the major stock exchanges just like regular stocks. The general partner of an MLP is responsible for running the partnership, while the individual investors are limited partners called unit holders. The income of MLPs passes through to the unit holders, who are responsible for the tax. Expenses such as depreciation are also passed on to the unit holders.

As an example, Buckeye Partners is a master limited partnership engaged in the transportation and storage of petroleum products. The original Buckeye Pipe Line Company was founded in 1886 as part of the Standard Oil Company and became a publicly owned, independent company after the dissolution of Standard Oil in 1911. Here is how Buckeye describes its distribution policy:

> We generally make quarterly cash distributions of substantially all of our available cash, generally defined as consolidated cash receipts less consolidated cash expenditures and such retentions for working capital, anticipated cash expenditures, and contingencies as Buckeye GP deems appropriate. Distributions of cash paid by us to a Unitholder will not result in taxable gain or income except to the extent the aggregate amount distributed exceeds the tax basis of the LP Units owned by the Unitholder.[7]

Table 8.1 shows the annual earnings and dividends per unit holder of Buckeye Partners for the past six years. During 2009 the actual earnings were $1.84 per unit. However, this included a significant level of noncash and special items. Without these items the net profit per unit was $3.63, as shown.

 **Warning: Don't Rely on Dividends**

Even though this section makes clear the importance of dividends, buying stocks because they currently pay a high rate of dividends, without taking into consideration other factors including the likelihood of capital gains, may be costly for investors. This is because dividend yields are generally considerably lower than the capital gains that can be obtained in the stock market.

**Table 8.1**    Earnings and Dividends for Buckeye Partners

| Per Unit | Dec 04 | Dec 05 | Dec 06 | Dec 07 | Dec 08 | Dec 09 |
|----------|--------|--------|--------|--------|--------|--------|
| Earnings | $2.75 | $2.69 | $2.64 | $3.03 | $3.15 | $3.63 |
| Dividends | $2.64 | $2.83 | $3.03 | $3.23 | $3.43 | $3.63 |

Companies are aware that paying higher dividends is attractive to certain investors, particularly to retirees and those nearing retirement age. In some cases, management will exploit this tendency of the retired and near retired to seek out dividends and deliberately pay dividends at a rate that could be damaging to the company in later years. For example, taking on extra debt to maintain or increase dividends should be a concern for careful investors. Also, stocks with higher dividend yields may have lower capital appreciation so that, even when dividends are included, the net gain is relatively modest compared to the market.

## Dividend Discount Method via Return on Equity

As described in Chapter 6, book value as a method for valuing stocks fell from favor with most investors over 50 years ago. Yet starting with book value, correction terms can be applied to give a valuation that is based on the dividend discount method. As with the discounted cash flow methods in the previous chapter, there are severe criticisms of the dividend discount methods. However, there are welcome advantages in transforming the dividend discount method into one based on book value. One advantage is that it gives a criterion for whether the activities of the business are adding to or subtracting from its current book value. What is particularly interesting is that the criterion depends on return on equity. Another advantage is that the series for the calculation converges much faster so that a fewer number of terms is needed to get reasonable accuracy.

There are two ways of recasting the dividend discount method in terms of return on equity. In the first, the book value is multiplied by a *correction factor* based on return on equity and the payout ratio to get a valuation for the stock. In the second, the correction factor depends on residual income calculations and is added to the book value. These methods stem from the work of James Ohlson and Gerald Feltham.[8]

Both cases depend on the clean surplus relationship introduced in Chapter 4 which, on a per-share basis, states that:

$$B' = B - d + e$$

where

$B$ is the initial book value
$d$ is dividends per share
$e$ is earnings per share
$B'$ is the resulting book value

In other words, all the changes in equity are captured in the income statement less total dividends. This, however, is not the full story. As we know, apart from dividends and earnings there are other transactions that lead to changes in equity. However, we will assume that the clean surplus relationship is valid. (Alternatively, earnings can be redefined so that the clean surplus relationship is valid.)

Recall that return on equity (ROE) is the earnings of a business over a 12-month period, usually a financial year, divided by the equity at the end of the period. It is a historical measure of the performance of management over that period. The payout ratio (PR) is the proportion of earnings that are paid out as dividends. Suppose we know the book value at the start of a financial year and the ROE and the PR for that year. Assuming the clean surplus relationship, it is possible to calculate the earnings and dividends for the year and the book value at the end of the year.

We can repeat this for each successive year, building up information on dividends which can then be substituted into the standard dividend discount formula described earlier. There is another crucial assumption behind this version of the dividend discount method. It is that each year the company has the ability to reinvest its net earnings at the ROE rate for the previous year, where *net earnings* are defined as the earnings left over after paying the dividends.

The single-stage model provides a simple example. Suppose that the initial book value is $10 and that the forecasts of the ROE and PR are 15 percent and 50 percent. Also suppose the discount rate is 10 percent. Table 8.2 builds up the company data for the first 10 years. It also includes years 100 and 200 to give an idea of how the numbers grow.

## Dividends and Return on Equity

By assuming the clean surplus relationship, dividends can be expressed in terms of return on equity and the payout ratio. This means that the dividend discount method can be modified to express intrinsic value in terms of book value and forecasts of return on equity, the payout ratio, and the discount rate.

**Table 8.2**  Dividend Growth: Return on Equity Model

| (1)<br>Year | (2)<br>Book Value at<br>Start of Year | (3)<br>Earnings<br>per Share | (4)<br>Dividends<br>per Share | (5)<br>Book Value at<br>End of Year | (6)<br>Discounted<br>Dividends | (7)<br>Running<br>Total |
|---|---|---|---|---|---|---|
| 1 | $10.00 | $1.62 | $0.81 | $10.81 | $0.74 | $0.74 |
| 2 | $10.81 | $1.75 | $0.88 | $11.69 | $0.72 | $1.46 |
| 3 | $11.69 | $1.90 | $0.95 | $12.63 | $0.71 | $2.17 |
| 4 | $12.63 | $2.05 | $1.02 | $13.66 | $0.70 | $2.87 |
| 5 | $13.66 | $2.22 | $1.11 | $14.77 | $0.69 | $3.56 |
| 6 | $14.77 | $2.39 | $1.20 | $15.96 | $0.68 | $4.24 |
| 7 | $15.96 | $2.59 | $1.29 | $17.26 | $0.66 | $4.90 |
| 8 | $17.26 | $2.80 | $1.40 | $18.66 | $0.65 | $5.55 |
| 9 | $18.66 | $3.03 | $1.51 | $20.17 | $0.64 | $6.20 |
| 10 | $20.17 | $3.27 | $1.64 | $21.81 | $0.63 | $6.83 |
| ... | ... | ... | ... | ... | ... | ... |
| 100 | $22,488.91 | $3,646.85 | $1,823.43 | $24,312.34 | $0.13 | $35.30 |
| ... | ... | ... | ... | ... | ... | ... |
| 200 | $54,675,804 | $8,866,346 | $4,433,173 | $59,108,978 | $0.02 | $41.52 |

This shows how the data is built up year after year, starting with an initial book value of $10.00 and assuming return on equity 15 percent, payout ratio 50 percent, and discount rate 10 percent. Column (2) shows the book value at the start of each year, starting with $10 in year 1. Column (3) and column (4) are the earnings and dividends per share for each year, and column (5) is the book value at the end of each year. The entries in column (4) are 50 percent of the entries in column (3) since 50 percent is the payout ratio. The entries in column (3) are 15 percent of the entries in column (5) since 15 percent is the return on equity. Notice that column (2) plus column (3) less column (4) equals column (5), confirming that the entries satisfy the clean surplus relationship. The entries in column (6) are the dividends in column (4) discounted by 10 percent for the number of years in column (1). Column (7) is a running total of the discounted dividends in column (6). This running total will converge to the valuation of the stock. Years 100 and 200 are included to give an idea of the output far in the future. As the number of years increase, the running total converges on to the intrinsic value.

The calculations for years 100 and 200 are included to show how slow the convergence can be in this method. After 10 years the estimated value is $6.83, after 100 years it is $35.30, and after 200 years it $41.42. Even without knowing the correct answer, clearly the final outcome depends strongly on dividends hundreds of years in the future. Although in some cases convergence is faster, this example highlights once again the major problem with all these discount methods, namely that the outcome is highly sensitive to the input variables, particularly the long-term forecasts. As we will see in Chapter 13, it is hard enough to make reasonable forecasts over the next quarter, let alone for decades and even centuries. Yet this is required for these methods.

We can make this weakness more explicit. By using direct mathematics, as explained in Appendix B, the final result is $42.86. In Table 8.2 the value after 10 terms was $6.83, giving a huge error of 84 percent compared to the true value of $42.86. After 100 terms the table value was $35.30, giving a sizeable error of 18 percent. Even after 200 terms the table gave $41.52, so the error is still approximately 3 percent. This is a clear case of a very high number of terms needed to achieve workable levels of accuracy.

As explained with regard to the DCF method, the main point is that, even if a formula is used to calculate the intrinsic value, the calculations require reliable forecasts of the growth rate and discount rate to be made for decades, even centuries, into the future. If this is not done and the results are built up year by year, the consequences are large errors.

The example just given is a single-stage application of the dividend discount method using return on equity and the payout ratio. The more usual application divides the forward estimates into two parts, an initial growth period typically over 10 years and a stable growth period for the remainder of the time. However, the general idea is the same with the same difficulties related to long-term forecasts.

### Dividend Discount Method (ROE) Applied to Wal-Mart

We have already seen that at the end of January 31, 2010, Wal-Mart's return on equity was 20.26 percent (Table 5.2 in Chapter 5), its book value was $18.25 (Chapter 6) and its payout ratio was 29.4 percent (Chapter 4). As a starting point we could use these as estimates for

**Table 8.3**   Variations of Intrinsic Value for Wal-Mart

| (1) Book Value | (2) Initial ROE | (3) Initial Payout Ratio | (4) Final ROE | (5) Final Payout Ratio | (6) Discount Rate | (7) Intrinsic Value |
|---|---|---|---|---|---|---|
| $18.25 | 20.00% | 29.4% | 7.50% | 50% | 10% | $35.45 |
| $18.25 | 15.00% | 29.4% | 5.00% | 25% | 11% | $11.99 |
| $18.25 | 20.00% | 29.4% | 10.00% | 75% | 9% | $57.93 |
| $18.25 | 20.00% | 29.4% | 15.00% | 75% | 10% | $76.61 |

Column (1) shows the initial book value in each case to be $18.25. Columns (2) and (3) show the return on equity and dividend payout ratio over the initial period, which is assumed to be 10 years in each case. Columns (4) and (5) show the return on equity and dividend payout ratio over the remaining period. The discount rate is shown in column (6). Column (7) shows the resulting intrinsic value using the dividend discount method based on return on equity and dividend payout ratios. The values range from $11.99 to $76.61.

the first 10 years (rounding off return on equity to 20 percent). But now what? Most likely return on equity will get lower in future years as it becomes harder for Wal-Mart to find growth opportunities at the same level of profitability. This may also mean that its payout ratio will increase. As a start, assume that the long-term return on equity, the long-term payout ratio, and the discount rate are 7.5 percent, 50 percent, and 10 percent, respectively. In this case, the intrinsic value is $35.45. As soon as we start to make small changes in the forecasts, the intrinsic value changes markedly. Table 8.3 gives a range of inputs showing the extreme variations in the results for the intrinsic value. As for the DCF methods in the previous chapter, we are faced with the problem of making highly accurate forecasts out to infinity, or at least for decades. Otherwise the calculations provide widely varying outcomes.

## Dividend Discount Valuation via Residual Income Estimates

The second variation of the dividend discount method shows that the value of a stock can be described in terms of its book value plus contributions from the residual income generated by the company over its entire life. This gives extra insight into factors that generate the intrinsic value. It also makes the series converge at a faster rate to the final intrinsic value so that fewer terms (years) are needed to achieve reasonable accuracy.

On the surface the residual income valuation (RIV) method does not look like a dividend discount method since there is no direct mention of dividends or dividend payout ratios. However, the RIV formula proceeds directly from the basic formula for the DD method using the clean surplus relationship.

Residual earnings are defined[9] as

$$R = e - r \times B$$

where

   $e$ is the earnings per share over a financial year
   $B$ is the book value at the start of the year
   $r$ is the discount rate

Residual earnings is understood as earnings minus a charge for the use of the capital $B$. When it is positive, the forward return on equity $e/B$ exceeds the discount rate $r$, indicating a profitable year. (Return on equity was defined in Chapter 5 as earnings over a financial year divided by equity at the end of the year. Forward return on equity is similar except that the earnings are divided by book value at the start of the year.)

By carefully manipulating the terms in the original formula for the dividend discount formula and using the clean surplus relationship, it is possible to recast the expression for the intrinsic value $V$ as:

$$V = B + R_1/(1+r) + R_2/(1+r)^2 + R_3/(1+r)^3 + \cdots$$

where

   $B = B_0$ denotes the initial book value
   $R_t = e_t - r \times B_{t-1}$

(Here $e_t$ is the earnings per share for year $t$ and $B_{t-1}$ is the book value at the end of year $t - 1$.)

If the residual income is always positive, that is, if $R_t$ is always greater than zero, then it is anticipated that each year the company will be adding value to the initial book value $B$. If the residual income is always zero, there is no change in value and the intrinsic value remains at $B$. If the residual income is anticipated to be always negative, then the actions of the company are decreasing the initial book value.

As foreshadowed, this formula calculates intrinsic value starting with the book value and adding the discounted values of future residual income terms. To apply the formula in practice you need estimates of the residual income terms, which in turn depend on estimates of earnings and book value. However, we saw earlier in the ROE method that these can be calculated from estimates of return on equity and the payout ratio. Hence, although it looks like an entirely different method on the surface, underneath the two variations of the dividend discount method are essentially the same.

## Intrinsic Value, Book Value and Residual Income

The dividend discount method can be modified to express intrinsic value in terms of book value and the discounted values of residual income taken over the life of the company.

### Criteria for a Business to Add Value to Its Book Value

Often when we take a different perspective on something, key features that were hidden or obscure become clearer. This is true of the dividend discount method after it is recast in the residual income form. The variation provides insight into what business factors add to the book value of the company.

For a company to increase its valuation above a simple book value the residual income must be consistently positive. From the definition of residual income, this means that the forward return on equity $e_n/B_{n-1}$ has to consistently exceed the discount rate $r$. In symbols, the condition is:

$$fROE > r$$

The clean surplus relationship shows that the relationship between forward return on equity fROE and return on equity ROE is:

$$fROE = ROE/(1 + ROE \times PR - ROE)$$

where PR is the payout ratio. This means that we must have

$$ROE > r/[(1 + r) - (r \times PR)]$$

For example, if the company pays out all its earnings as dividends (meaning $PR = 1.0$), then the condition reduces to requiring:

$$ROE > r$$

At the other extreme, if the company pays no dividends, the condition becomes:

$$ROE > r/(1 + r)$$

Since the discount rate is generally quite small, the denominator $[(1 + r) - (r \times PR)]$ is approximately equal to 1, so the condition essentially asks that the return on equity should exceed the discount rate.

This criterion for ROE gives you an insight into why Warren Buffett places so much importance on this ratio. For example, for many years Buffett has written in Berkshire Hathaway's annual report that he is looking for companies that meet a list of criteria including "good returns on equity." Whether we are talking about forward return on equity or the usual return on equity makes little difference. Unless return on equity is consistently above the discount rate, the business is actually destroying value. Since the discount rate is really just the return that you require to compensate for the risks of investing in a particular company, we are actually saying that we need investments for which return on equity exceeds our required rate of return.

### Return on Equity Requirement

As a minimum, look for return on equity to be consistently above the rate of return required to compensate us for the risks of investing in a particular business.

Whether it is wise to use earnings to pay a dividend was discussed in Chapter 5 in the section on dividend policy. It was explained that if a company has opportunities to use its retained earnings to generate a high return on equity, it is generally better to have a low payout ratio. Otherwise, it is better to pay the money to its shareholders—that is, either to have a high payout ratio or to institute a share buyback.

## Strengths and Weaknesses of Dividend Discount Methods

In this chapter we looked at the basic dividend discount method, followed by a variation using return on equity and a variation using residual income. For simplicity we will look at their strengths and weaknesses in a single list, making specific comments when necessary to distinguish between the variations. All the methods are based on the basic dividend discount formula, really a variation of the discounted cash flow formula. Hence, most of the strengths and weaknesses are similar to those of the DCF methods. For this reason, in some cases we only give shorter descriptions because more details were given in the previous chapter on DCF methods. The list starts with 10 strengths.

*Strength 1: Clear definition.* The definition and the two variations are quite specific in terms of the input variables and the calculations used to combine them. Under various assumptions the method is amenable to being programmed and, with care, can even be calculated using a calculator or spreadsheet.

*Strength 2: Rational definition.* A standard bond consists of a series of dividends plus the return of the face value at its expiration. Consequently its value is calculated as the discounted value of the dividends plus the discounted value of the face value. The definition of value of a stock using the DD method or one of its two variations is a rational extension of the calculation of value of a standard bond.

*Strength 3: Easy interpretation.* It is easy to interpret the outcome of a DD method, including either of its two variations, as the true value of a stock and to compare this value with its market price in order to facilitate buy/hold/sell decisions.

*Strength 4: Accessible data.* The levels of dividends are readily accessible from the financial statements of a company so there is no dispute about them. In contrast, free cash flow usually takes an investigation of various entries in the accounts, which may be specified in different ways for different companies. Also, there may be disagreement about which entries should or should not be included in the final determination.

*Strength 5: Easy conversion.* By dividing the basic dividend discount formula through by the price $P$, the value ratio associated with the method can be converted easily to the discounted value of all the forward dividend yields taken over the life of the company. Hence there is no direct mention of the dividend terms, only their ratios with the price.

*Strength 6: Dividend security.* When a company pays a dividend of $1.00, you actually receive the payment and benefit from it. Alternatively, if the company invests the money back into the company, there is uncertainty about your receiving financial benefit from it. Hence there is more security in valuing a company via dividend discount methods rather than via those that use discounted cash flows.

*Strength 7: Intuitive variations.* As described earlier, instead of trying to make direct forecasts of dividends, they can be made via forecasts of return on equity and the payout ratio. These forecasts may be a more intuitive way of approaching the future estimates needed for the dividend discount method, giving more confidence in the final result for the intrinsic value.

*Strength 8: Value creation.* Another strength of the dividend discount method is that, as described earlier, it can be recast in what is called the residual income form. In this form the final valuation starts with the familiar notion of book value and then adds the discounted value of the residual income generated by the company. It may be positive or negative and so may add to or subtract from the book value. This gives insights into what types of business performance will add value.

*Strength 9: Faster convergence.* As explained already, if building up the result using a table on a year-by-year basis, generally a very large number of terms is needed for the dividend discount method to achieve reasonable accuracy. This means that in practice, formulas with an infinite number of terms are used, requiring forecasts to infinity. However, since the RIV summation is front-loaded by the value of the initial book value, convergence is often much faster. Hence it may be reasonable to use a truncated summation, which in turn only requires forecasts over a shorter (finite!) time horizon. Figure 8.1 gives two examples comparing the rate of convergence of the RIV method and the dividend discount method.

*Strength 10: Wide acceptance.* Although dividend discount methods do not have the same level of acceptance as discounted cash flow methods, they are still widely recognized.

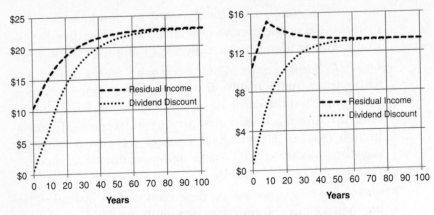

**Figure 8.1**    Convergence of Dividend Discount and Residual Income Methods

Two examples comparing the convergence of the dividend discount method and the residual income method of stock valuation. In both cases the book value is $10, the discount rate is 10 percent, the return on equity is 15 percent for the first 10 years, and the payout ratio is 50 percent for the first 10 years. After that, for the chart on the left the return on equity is 15 percent and the payout ratio is 75 percent. We can see from the chart that the long-term value is approximately $23. (The exact figure is $22.92.) Since the series for the RIV method starts with the book value of $10, it converges faster to the long-term value than the series for the dividend discount method. The inputs for the chart on the right are the same except that the terminal return on equity is 8 percent. Since this is less than the discount rate, it means that the company starts to lose value after 10 years: The residual income terms switch from positive to negative. In both methods the series converge to the long-term value of $13.29.

The following is a list of weaknesses of dividend discount methods. Since at their basis they are variations of general discount methods, the weaknesses will be similar to those of the DCF methods described in the previous chapter.

*Weakness 1: May not covert to profit.* The first weakness is that the dividend discount methods are theoretical formulas. Just because a stock has a high intrinsic value when calculated by one of the formulas compared to its price, does not mean that it will be a profitable investment in terms of return.

*Weakness 2: Many variations.* There are many variations of the basic dividend discount method plus the two extra variations described earlier. They give a range of values, such that a stock could be undervalued according to one formula but overvalued according to another.

*Weakness 3: Unstable results.* Just as for the DCF methods, all the formulas and variations for the dividend discount methods are unstable. This means that small changes in the input numbers lead to extremely large variation in the output. Using Wal-Mart as an example, Table 8.3 shows how large these variations can be.

*Weakness 4: Easily manipulated.* Another consequence of the instability just described is that the final result for intrinsic value calculated via the DD method or any of its variations is easy to manipulate by making small changes in certain input variables. Because these changes are so small, they are easily defended.

*Weakness 5: Untestable inputs.* It is impossible to test the accuracy of the key inputs in the formulas such as the terminal growth rate and the discount rate because they require forecasts out to infinity. Even to get reasonable accuracy may require making accurate forecasts for decades and even centuries.

*Weakness 6: Anchoring vulnerability.* The dividend discount method is vulnerable to similar anchoring problems for the long-term forecasts as described for the discounted cash flow methods. As explained in Chapter 7, these problems will always occur since forecasts are required to be made out to infinity.

*Weakness 7: Infinite sums.* All the dividend discount methods and their variations are infinite sums. As such they require an infinite number of inputs to calculate the values. This cannot be done one at a time and requires them to be specified through a rule, which is a limitation on the values that are possible for the inputs. A second limitation is that mathematics only allows the calculation of the sum of a limited number of infinite sums. There are no formulas to calculate the sums of most infinite series. A third limitation is that in the terminal period the growth rate of the dividends must be less than the discount rate, otherwise the series would have an infinite sum. This looks like it should be desirable since it is saying that the intrinsic value is so high it is infinite. However, it removes the ability to properly analyze companies with rates satisfying this condition since we can no longer calculate the value ratio. Also, it does not allow comparisons via intrinsic value of such companies since their value ratios will all be infinite.[10]

*Weakness 8: False objectivity.* The method gives the appearance of objectivity because of its terminology, such as the *intrinsic value,* and its use of college-level mathematics, such as the requirement to sum infinite series which would be unfamiliar to most people. Yet it is highly subjective because of the instability of the calculations and the impossibility of verifying key input variables.

*Weakness 9: Difficult forecasts.* Because dividends are directly under the discretion of the board and senior management of the company, they are harder to forecast. Two companies with similar business and economic characteristics could have completely different dividend policies ranging from no dividends to a 100 percent payout or more. This policy may change from year to year based on the business environment or changes in board or management policy. Consequently it is very difficult to make any forecast regarding dividends, particularly when the period is longer than the expected tenure of the board and senior management. In contrast, when making forecasts of, say, free cash flow, we start with the assumption that businesses are always trying to maximize their levels. This means that forecasts are more directly tied to the success of the business.

The difficulty is compounded when a company has not paid any dividends for many years. To apply any of the dividend discount methods in this case requires assumptions that (1) the company will start paying dividends in the future and you can specify the time when they start, and (2) you can specify the rate at which they will be paid.

At first it may seem that the ROE and RIV variations get around the problem of forecasting dividends. However, the ROE variation uses forecasts of the payout ratio and the RIV variation uses the clean surplus relationship and forecasts of earnings. Hence, they both indirectly rely on forecasts of dividends.

*Weakness 10: Limited research.* As noted in Chapter 7, there is limited research on DCF methods. Dividend discount methods are used less frequently and so there is even less research on them. The valuation of a stock using a DD method is highly variable depending on the input variables. Hence, it is difficult to come to buy/sell/hold conclusions in any formal study. With one set of input variables a stock may appear undervalued. With another set of equally plausible variables it may appear to be overvalued.

*Weakness 11: Confused objectives.* As for the DCF methods, there are two completely different objectives of dividend discount methods which are mutually exclusive. The theoreticians and academics want an elegant, comprehensive theory while investors want a practical tool to help them profit in the stock market. Table 8.2 points up this conflict. Long-term forecasts give accurate calculations of intrinsic value but such forecasts are not practical. In contrast, forecasts over shorter periods give poor approximations of intrinsic value.

*Weakness 12: Assumes validity of the clean surplus relationship.* The derivations of the ROE and RIV methods from the standard dividend discount method assume that the clean surplus relationship is valid. This relationship may be approximately valid but there are many cases when its inaccuracy is likely to be material. Change in the number of shares outstanding is one of these. The example of Wal-Mart in Table 4.7 of Chapter 4 shows the magnitude of the discrepancy when the clean surplus relationship is assumed. It is, however, possible to construct interesting variations of the dividend discount formula that avoid the clean surplus relationship. One of these variations involves abnormal earnings and is described in Chapter 12.

### Even More Variations

Some investment web sites and financial organizations have developed their own versions of discount methods and it is impossible to evaluate them all here. Hopefully the discussions in this and the previous chapter will allow you to determine whether they are suitable for your needs.

As an example, in Australia consensus forecasts are generally only available for earnings releases for the next two years. With this constraint, Aspect Huntley (now part of Morningstar) provides a modified version of the residual income valuation formula. Its inputs are the current book value per share, the current payout ratio, consensus earnings forecasts for the next two years, the long-term earnings growth, the long-term industry average return on equity, and the discount rate. The long-term earnings growth is based on the growth of an exponential curve fitted through both historical earnings (up to 10 years) and two years of consensus forecast earnings. The long-term industry ROE uses the average return on equity within a given sector. The rationale for using the average return on equity within a sector is that over time the return on equity for individual companies will revert to this long-term average. The discount rate is estimated using the capital asset pricing model (CAPM) as described in Chapter 2.

The method uses the input data and the clean surplus relationship to estimate return on equity and book value in four stages: years 1 and 2, years 3 to 8, years 9 to 15, and years 16 on. Since residual incomes are earnings minus the discount rate multiplied by book value, residual income can also be written as book value multiplied by the difference between the (forward) return on equity and the discount rate. This information is used to estimate residual income for each year. These estimates are discounted and combined in the usual way to calculate intrinsic value according to the Aspect Huntley version of the residual income valuation model.

### The Bottom Line

1. The basic idea of dividend discount methods is that the intrinsic value is the discounted value of the dividends paid by the business over its life.
2. Dividend discount methods can be modified using return on equity or residual income and so do not refer directly to dividends.
3. As with discounted cash flow methods, dividend discount methods need to be applied with extreme care, particularly with problems related to the instability of the results and the requirement to make long-term forecasts.

# CHAPTER

# 9

## Don't Get Mad, Get Even

*[The payback period] forms the foundation of every capital-spending decision by management. When developers purchase tracts of land and price the parcels for sale to builders, they calculate how quickly their investments in new streets, sewers, and utility hookups will pay off. The sooner their start-up investment is returned, the sooner they can deploy the proceeds into another development.*

—Timothy Vick[1]

*Anything with a conservative payback in three years is good business.*
—Bob Wolf[2]

"How long will it take to get our money back?" is a question commonly asked by managers when faced with capital allocation decisions for new projects. "If we spend $2 million on a new computer IT system, how many years will it take to pay for itself?" is a standard business question. In this chapter, we see ways of asking and answering similar questions, but this time in the setting of the stock market. The idea is to introduce the element of time into any stock valuation by estimating how long it will take to get your money back, where the money is measured in terms of elements generated by the business such as earnings or dividends. In general terms, the shorter the time period, the better. This means that the valuation is not in terms of how much the stock is undervalued or overvalued according to the ratio of intrinsic value in dollars divided by the share price. Rather, the valuation is in terms of the number of years required for

219

the earnings or dividends to match the initial price. We will also be able to build into the valuation an allowance for the risk associated with the company's capacity to continue to generate its earnings or dividends at the specified rate.

## Simple Calculation of the Payback Period

In the case of fixed-interest investments, everything is simple regarding the time taken to get your money back. If you invest $100 at 10 percent per year, after 10 years the interest payments you have received will have added to a total of $100. You could say that after 10 years, everything is pure profit. If the interest rate you receive is 5 percent, then it will take twice as long for total of these payments to have added to the original amount. We will refer to the number of years for the payments to add up to the original amount as the *payback period*. In general terms, the shorter the payback period the better. There is a proviso, however, which centers on the confidence that we have in receiving the interest payments. If there was any doubt about them arriving in our bank account, intuitively we would want more interest payments to compensate for this extra risk (assuming that the size of the payments is fixed).

As stated in the opening paragraph, the idea of using the length of the payback period is well known in private enterprise for assessing new ventures. The task before us now is to transfer this approach over to equities, using as a guideline the discussion of bonds in the preceding paragraph. In the case of bonds, the wealth being returned to the bondholders is the interest payments. With equities, as explained in earlier chapters, there are a number of possibilities regarding money being generated by the business, including earnings, free cash flow, and dividends. We will keep it simple and develop the method using earnings per share. But keep in mind that what is being said could also be expressed using other financial quantities such as those just mentioned. After looking at the payback period in terms of earnings, we will have a brief look at the method in terms of dividends.

For a start, the length of the required payback period due to earnings will depend on how much is initially paid for shares in the company. Furthermore, since we are talking about earnings per share, it is natural to suppose that the payback period will depend on the price-to-earnings (P/E) ratio. This is, in fact, the case. A simple explanation of the P/E ratio is that it is the number of years required for the earnings to add up to the share price, assuming that the earnings remain constant and there is no discounting. For example, assume that the share price is \$60 and the earnings per share (EPS) is \$5 so that the P/E ratio is 12. Now suppose that the earnings do not change. Then it will take 12 years at \$5 per year for the earnings to add up to the share price of \$60. It is important to notice that the payback period depended on the P/E ratio and not on the actual price. We will make use of this later.

### Payback Period and the P/E Ratio

If earnings remain constant and we do not take into account any risk, then the payback period is simply the P/E ratio since it is the number of years required for the earnings to add up to the share price.

In general, the earnings will grow over time so the payback period will be less than the P/E ratio. In the opposite direction, as previously stated, it seems reasonable that the payback period should be longer when we take into account the time value of money and the risk associated with the company being able to generate its forecasted earnings. We want to receive a higher number of payments to compensate for the risk. To explain further, suppose that it is possible to tap into a stream of payments that pay \$10 per year through an outlay of \$100. We want to answer the question: How many years would it take for these payments to be worth the original \$100? If the risk was low, we might be satisfied with an interest rate of 5 percent. This would mean that we keep adding terms:

$$10/(1 + 5\%) + 10/(1 + 5\%)^2 + 10/(1 + 5\%)^3 + \cdots$$

until the sum equals or exceeds \$100. The number of years to do this is the payback period. In this case the period is 15 years. Now suppose that there is more risk associated with the payments so that we require an interest rate of 8 percent. This time we keep adding terms in the sum:

$$10/(1 + 8\%) + 10/(1 + 8\%)^2 + 10/(1 + 8\%)^3 + \cdots$$

Calculations show that the payback period has grown to 18 years. In other words, now it will take an extra three years of $10 payments to match the initial outlay of $100.

Putting it another way, the process is like looking at a range of bonds in which the variation is in the number of years that payments are to be received instead of in the sizes of yearly payments. Normally we want *higher* payments when the risk is higher. In the payback scenario, we ask for *more* payments.

Coming back to equities, the definition of the *payback period* is the number of years it takes for the discounted earnings of a company to total the current share price. If we think of the earnings as money being returned to the investor through either dividends or capital gains, then stocks with shorter payback periods should be favored over those with longer periods. The issue of what discount rate to use was discussed at some length in Chapter 7 so there is no need to go through it again. Briefly, the discount rate can be thought of as the return that the investor would expect to receive to be compensated for the risks associated with the particular investment.

### Payback Period

The payback period for an equity is the number of years required for the discounted earnings of a company to total the current share price. Instead of earnings, other financial quantities such as free cash flow or dividends can be used.

As an example, suppose that an equity costs $60 and has a P/E ratio of 12 with earnings growth of 10 percent. Take 11 percent as the discount rate. Table 9.1 shows the sum of the discounted earnings on a year-by-year basis. Note that somewhere between 12 years and 13 years of earnings are required for the sum to reach the original share price. Working in whole years and rounding upward, we conclude that the payback period is 13 years.

When the P/E ratio is lower, fewer years are required to pay back the share price, showing that, assuming that the other parameters remain unchanged, low P/E stocks are preferable to high P/E stocks. Similarly, when the growth rate is higher or the discount rate is lower, fewer years are required. In contrast, when the P/E ratio is higher,

**Table 9.1**  Growth of Sum of Discounted Earnings

| (1) Year | (2) EPS | (3) Discounted EPS | (4) Total |
|---|---|---|---|
| 1 | $5.50 | $4.95 | $4.95 |
| 2 | $6.05 | $4.91 | $9.87 |
| 3 | $6.66 | $4.87 | $14.73 |
| 4 | $7.32 | $4.82 | $19.55 |
| 5 | $8.05 | $4.78 | $24.33 |
| 6 | $8.86 | $4.74 | $29.07 |
| 7 | $9.74 | $4.69 | $33.76 |
| 8 | $10.72 | $4.65 | $38.41 |
| 9 | $11.79 | $4.61 | $43.02 |
| 10 | $12.97 | $4.57 | $47.59 |
| 11 | $14.27 | $4.53 | $52.11 |
| 12 | $15.69 | $4.49 | $56.60 |
| 13 | $17.26 | $4.45 | $61.05 |
| 14 | $18.99 | $4.40 | $65.45 |
| 15 | $20.89 | $4.37 | $69.82 |
| 16 | $22.97 | $4.33 | $74.14 |
| 17 | $25.27 | $4.29 | $78.43 |
| 18 | $27.80 | $4.25 | $82.68 |
| 19 | $30.58 | $4.21 | $86.89 |
| 20 | $33.64 | $4.17 | $91.06 |

The original share price is $60 with P/E ratio 12. This means that the initial earnings per share is $5.00. Starting with $5.00, the earnings per share (EPS) in column (2) grows at 10 percent per year so that in year 1 it is $5.50. After being discounted back to present time by 11 percent per year, the results are shown in column (3). Column (4) is the running total of the discounted earnings at the end of each year. The goal is to determine how many years it will take to *pay back* the original outlay of $60. Column (4) shows that it is somewhere between 12 and 13 years.

or the growth rate is lower, or the discount rate is higher, more years are required. In some cases, no matter how many years we go out, the sum of the discounted earnings never reaches the original share price. For example, if the share price is $60, the EPS is $6, the discount rate is 15 percent, and the growth rate is 0 percent, then the sum of all discounted earnings is $40. Since this is less than $60, there is no payback period.[3] One more point: The payback period does not depend on the share price independently of earnings per share. It actually depends on their ratio—that is, the P/E ratio. This is the logic behind Table 9.2 only using the P/E ratio with no direct mention of price.

## Two-Stage Payback Calculations

We could call the preceding an example of the single-stage payback method since we assume that the earnings grow at the specified rate over the payback period. Just as for the discounted cash flow methods and the dividend discount methods, it makes sense to split the growth period into two or more parts. As usual, the first part is called the initial or growth period and the remaining part is called the stable or terminal growth period.

Table 9.2 shows the payback periods for a range of growth rates and P/E ratios using the two-stage payback method.[4] To keep the analysis simple, the calculations in the table assume that the initial period lasts 10 years and after that the growth rate is 3 percent. The calculations also assume that the discount rate is 11 percent. As an example, consider a stock with a P/E ratio that is expected to be 12. Assume that its earnings are expected to grow by 10 percent for the first 10 years and after that at 3 percent per year. Table 9.2 shows that it will take 14 years for the discounted earnings to reach the initial share price. (This result can be verified by setting up a year-by-year

**Table 9.2**    Payback Periods in Years Depending on P/E Ratios and Earnings Growth

|  |  | P/E Ratio | | | | | | | | |
|---|---|---|---|---|---|---|---|---|---|---|
|  |  | 4 | 6 | 8 | 10 | 12 | 14 | 16 | 18 | 20 |
|  | 0.0% | 6 | 11 | 19 | 42 | NR | NR | NR | NR | NR |
|  | 2.5% | 6 | 9 | 14 | 22 | 45 | NR | NR | NR | NR |
|  | 5.0% | 5 | 8 | 12 | 16 | 23 | 39 | NR | NR | NR |
| EPS | 7.5% | 5 | 7 | 10 | 13 | 17 | 23 | 33 | NR | NR |
| Growth | 10.0% | 5 | 7 | 9 | 11 | 14 | 17 | 21 | 28 | 40 |
|  | 12.5% | 4 | 6 | 8 | 10 | 12 | 14 | 16 | 20 | 24 |
|  | 15.0% | 4 | 6 | 7 | 9 | 10 | 12 | 14 | 16 | 18 |
|  | 17.5% | 4 | 6 | 7 | 8 | 9 | 11 | 12 | 13 | 15 |
|  | 20.0% | 4 | 5 | 7 | 8 | 9 | 10 | 11 | 12 | 13 |

This shows the number of years for a company to generate enough discounted earnings to match the original investment based on the stated P/E ratio and the forecast growth rate of earnings. In each case the growth rate is assumed to hold for 10 years; after that the growth is assumed to be 3 percent. The results are shown in whole years and rounded upward when necessary. The calculations assume a discount rate of 11.0 percent. NR signifies "no result."

table similar to Table 9.1 with these new input values.) The results in Table 9.2 are displayed in whole years by rounding upward. For some combinations of the expected P/E ratio and growth rate, the sum of the discounted earnings never reaches the original share price. In other words, even though extra earnings are being added each year, they are not growing fast enough to compensate for the rate at which they are discounted for the sum to reach the share price. These entries are marked as NR to signify "no result." Notice that everything is done using ratios; at no stage did we need the actual share price in constructing the table. Also, notice that lower P/E ratios and higher growth estimates result in shorter payback periods.

## Payback Calculations Using Dividends and Return on Equity

The previous calculations use earnings but could just as easily apply to dividends. Everywhere that earnings are used, simply replace them by dividends. For example, instead of a P/E ratio the ratio of price to dividends, the inverse of the dividend yield, is used. However, once the switch is made to thinking of the payback period in terms of dividends, it is useful to use the ideas in Chapter 8 to modify the method and look at dividends in terms of return on equity and the payout ratio. Instead of starting with the P/E ratio, the price-to-book (P/B) ratio is used.

Examples of these types of payback results for a two-stage model are given in Table 9.3. Just as for Table 9.2, the results are displayed in whole years by rounding upward. For some combinations of the expected return on equity and dividend payout ratio, the sum of the discounted dividends never reaches the original share price. As before, these entries are marked as NR to signify "no result." In this table, the payout ratio is assumed to be 50 percent for the first 10 years (the growth period) and 100 percent after that (the terminal period). The return on equity is assumed to remain fixed over both periods. The calculations use a discount rate of 11 percent. As an example, suppose the initial P/B ratio is 2.0. If the ROE is 15 percent, then the sum of discounted dividends will never reach the share price. If the ROE is 17.5 percent, it will take 28 years, dropping to 18 years if the ROE is 20 percent. Of course, achieving an ROE of 20 percent or higher is a significant achievement even for a single year.

At least using payback methods we can see that the forecasts used in the method are only required for a finite number of years, the

**Table 9.3**    Payback Period in Years Depending on ROE and Payout Ratios

| | | Price-to-Book Ratio | | | | | | | | | |
|---|---|---|---|---|---|---|---|---|---|---|---|
| | | 0.8 | 1 | 1.2 | 1.4 | 1.6 | 1.8 | 2 | 2.2 | 2.4 | 2.6 |
| | 10.0% | 25 | NR | NR | NR | NR | NR | NR | NR | NR | NR |
| | 12.5% | 15 | 21 | 34 | NR | NR | NR | NR | NR | NR | NR |
| Return | 15.0% | 12 | 14 | 18 | 23 | 33 | NR | NR | NR | NR | NR |
| on | 17.5% | 10 | 12 | 14 | 16 | 18 | 22 | 28 | 53 | NR | NR |
| Equity | 20.0% | 8 | 10 | 12 | 13 | 14 | 16 | 18 | 21 | 24 | 30 |
| | 22.5% | 7 | 9 | 10 | 11 | 12 | 13 | 14 | 16 | 17 | 19 |
| | 25.0% | 6 | 8 | 9 | 10 | 11 | 12 | 12 | 13 | 14 | 15 |

This shows the number of years for a company to generate enough discounted earnings to match the original investment based on the P/B ratio and the forecast of the initial ROE. In each case the ROE is assumed to remain fixed. The payout ratio is assumed to be 50 percent for the first 10 years and 100 percent after that. The results are shown in whole years and rounded upward when necessary. The calculations assume a discount rate of 11 percent. NR signifies "no result."

payback period. Otherwise there is no length of time that will allow for a complete payback. Furthermore, this method only asks that the share price be met by dividends. It does not include any capital gains coming from the growth in the share price. However, this applies to all the dividend valuation methods described in Chapter 8.

## Strengths and Weaknesses of the Payback Period Method

The main strength of the payback period method is that it brings a new perspective to discount methods while at the same time overcoming many of their weaknesses. The following is a summary of its strengths, followed by a summary of its weaknesses.

*Strength 1: Coherent basis.* The foundation of the method is that it is desirable to choose stocks with lower P/E ratios, higher growth rates, and lower discount rates. These inputs are combined in a coherent way to give the number of years it would take for the sum of the discounted earnings to equal the original share price.

*Strength 2: Adaptable method.* Even though the preceding description is in terms of earnings, the same method applies with earnings replaced by free cash flow, dividends, or other financial quantities. It can also be set up using any of the dividend discount methods based on return on equity described in Chapter 8.

*Strength 3: Easy interpretation.* It is easy to compare two companies as potential investments: Simply choose the one with the shortest payback period. In addition, since it easy to calculate the payback period of a fixed-interest investment, it is simple to compare investments in equities with fixed-interest instruments.

*Strength 4: Based on DCF method.* The method is based on the discounted cash flow method; the key difference is that the discounting is over a finite time frame instead of an infinite period. This means that the payback method inherits many of the advantages of the discounted cash flow methods, such as a widely accepted conceptual framework.

*Strength 5: Finite forecast period.* The major weaknesses of the discounted cash flow method are that forecasts of growth rates and discount rates have to be made over an infinite period, leading to the impossibility of testing their accuracy and the instability of the intrinsic value that is calculated. The payback method does not have these weaknesses.

The main weakness of the payback period method is that it is not a standard measure of value. The following is a summary of this and its other weaknesses.

*Weakness 1: Nonstandard measure.* The first weakness is that the result of the payback calculation is neither a dollar intrinsic value nor an estimate of percentage return. Even though it is expressed in years, it is not a standard measure of value that is expressed in dollars (for intrinsic value) or a percentage (for expected shareholder return).

*Weakness 2: May not convert to profit.* Just because one stock has a shorter payback period than another does not mean that it will be more profitable. For example, the price of the stock with the shorter payback period may stay flat or even decrease over its payback period while the price of the other stock may rise.

*Weakness 3: Longer-term forecasts.* Forecasts of growth rates and discount rates need to be made for the entire payback period. Even though the method avoids the infinite periods required for the discounted cash flow methods, the period may still be lengthy.

*Weakness 4: Comparative analysis.* If the payback period is calculated for a single company, it is difficult to know whether the length of the period is a sign of an attractive investment. Effective implementation requires the payback periods to be calculated for two or more companies as a means to choose between them. Alternatively, the payback period can be calculated for large numbers of companies and then these companies can be ranked according to their payback periods. A portfolio could be formed based on companies with payback periods in, say, the lowest 10 percent.

## The Bottom Line

1. A fundamental method used by businesses to analyze and compare competing projects is the length of time required for the project to pay for itself. This is called the payback period.

2. The payback methods in this chapter use this idea to measure the time needed for money generated by publicly listed companies to repay investors for their original outlay.

3. The payback methods can be used with free cash flow, earnings, or dividends, and can be set up in two growth periods, initial and terminal, along with a discount rate to compensate for future uncertainty. The methods can also be set up using single-stage, two-stage, or three-stage variations.

# CHAPTER 10

# PEG and Friends

*The P/E ratio of any company that is fairly priced will equal its growth rate. But if the P/E ratio is less than the growth rate, you may have found yourself a bargain.*

—Peter Lynch[1]

*In general, the P/E should equal the long-term growth rate in percent. A ratio of one is considered to represent fair value and a ratio greater than one indicates a more "expensive" stock.*

—Aspect Equity Review[2]

In earlier chapters, valuation was done via ratios of the share price and dollar amounts (such as the book value or discounted cash flow methods). In the previous chapter the valuation was expressed in terms of the number of years it would take for amounts such as earnings or dividends to pay back the original outlay. In this chapter we open the analysis up further by looking at valuations in terms of less concrete measures, or indexes. In their calculation there seems to be only one rule: All else being equal, if the share price goes up the index should indicate less value, and if it goes down it should indicate more value. The core measure in this chapter is the *PEG ratio*, which is the P/E ratio divided by the growth rate of earnings. In general terms, the lower the ratio the better. This is followed by the *PEGY ratio*, a modification of the PEG ratio that includes dividends. Finally, a more involved method called the *expectations risk index* is described.

## PEG Ratio

The PEG ratio, sometimes called the P/E growth ratio, is very simple. It is the ratio of the P/E ratio of an equity divided by the forecast of the percentage growth rate of its earnings. Many web sites display it as a simple rule of thumb to test whether an equity is worth looking at in more detail. For example, if the P/E ratio is 15 and the forecast of earnings per share is 10 percent, the PEG ratio is $15/10 = 1.5$; if the P/E ratio is 10 and the forecast of earnings per share is 15 percent, the PEG ratio is $10/15 = 0.67$. The PEG ratio differs from the methods in the previous chapters in that it calculates neither intrinsic value nor a payback period. Rather, it gives a ratio that indicates value when it is as low as possible. The PEG ratio incorporates two ideas: (1) The higher the growth rate of the earnings of a company, the more attractive it is as an investment; and (2) the higher the company's P/E ratio, the less attractive it is as an investment.

Stocks with a PEG ratio of 1.0 are considered fair value. The goal is to find stocks with a PEG ratio as low as possible and certainly less than 1. It is not known who was the first person to use the PEG ratio but Peter Lynch popularized it in *One Up on Wall Street* when he wrote, "In general, a P/E ratio that's half the growth rate is very positive, and one that's twice the growth rate is very negative."[3] In other words, look for stocks with a PEG ratio of 0.5 and avoid those with a PEG ratio of 2.0. Lynch continued, "We use this measure all the time in analyzing stocks for the mutual funds."

### PEG Ratio

The PEG ratio is the ratio of the P/E ratio and the forecast of the percentage growth rate of earnings. As a simple rule of thumb, the goal is to find stocks with a PEG ratio as low as possible and preferably below 1.0.

If we assume that the clean surplus relationship is valid, that there are no dividends, and that the return on equity is constant, then the growth in earnings is (approximately) equal to the return on equity (ROE). Hence, another way of viewing the PEG ratio is as the P/E ratio divided by ROE.

Finally, it is possible to use the PEG ratio to make a simple formula for the fair value of a company. Peter Lynch asserts that a PEG ratio of 1.0 represents fair value. In this case the P/E ratio equals the growth rate, so that we can use the definition of the P/E ratio to write

$$V = \text{EPS} \times g$$

where
   $V$ is the fair value of the company
   EPS is earnings per share
   $g$ is the expected growth

The reason we rewrote it in this form is that it leads into value formulas developed by Benjamin Graham and explained later in Chapter 12.

In terms of research, an unpublished study by David Lipshutz concluded that a portfolio of stocks with low PEG ratios outperformed a portfolio with high PEG ratios.[4] From January 1986 to July 1997, Lipshutz examined the top 1,000 stocks by market capitalization. Each month stocks with data such as negative earnings projections or no growth rates were placed in a portfolio called "No Data." The PEG ratio was calculated for the remaining stocks using a P/E ratio based on the next 12 months' estimated EPS (so it was a forward P/E) and the five-year Institutional Brokers' Estimate System (commonly referred to as I/B/E/S) forecast as the growth rate. These stocks were divided into 10 deciles from lowest PEG ratios to the highest. In this way, 11 portfolios were formed each month.

Over the period of the study, stocks in the decile with the lowest PEG ratio (decile 1) provided an average annual return of 21.7 percent compared to a return of 14.9 percent for the benchmark universe. Stocks in the decile with the highest PEG ratio returned only 4.3 percent per year. The author acknowledged several weaknesses of the study but concluded that the "PEG effect was so pronounced" that they would not make an appreciable difference to the main conclusion. One surprise was that the No Data portfolio marginally outperformed the benchmark with a return of 15.2 percent.

### Strengths and Weaknesses of the PEG Ratio Valuation Method

The main strength of the PEG ratio is that it combines important financial parameters to provide quickly a simple estimate of value.

As such, a low PEG ratio could be a signal to look at the company in more detail and a high PEG ratio could be a signal to move on to other companies. The following is a summary of its strengths, followed by a summary of its weaknesses.

*Strength 1: Rational basis.* The financial parameters used in the PEG ratio are the P/E ratio and the forecast growth rate of earnings. Intuitively we want to select stocks with the lowest P/E ratio compared to the forecast of earnings growth. The PEG ratio is set up to do this.

*Strength 2: Easy calculation.* The most obvious strength of the method is that it is very easy to calculate. All it needs is the current P/E ratio and a forecast of the growth rate of earnings, items that are readily available on most stock market web sites and in stock reports.

*Strength 3: Quick evaluation.* If the PEG ratio of a company is around 0.5 or lower, then according to this method it is highly undervalued. An alternative explanation is that there has been some recent news that has caused the market to lower the price and hence the P/E ratio. In either case, it may make sense to investigate such companies in more detail.

*Strength 4: Growth forecast.* Peter Lynch wrote, "The P/E ratio of any company that's fairly priced will equal its growth rate." If we accept the validity of this statement, then we have an implicit forecast of the growth rate of a stock by the market. The market sets the price of a stock and hence sets the P/E ratio. Suppose that the P/E ratio is 10. Accepting that the PEG ratio of a fairly priced stock is 1.0 is really the same as saying that the consensus of the market is that the growth rate of the stock is 10 percent.

The main weakness of the PEG ratio is that it is an oversimplified approach to measuring value. The following is a summary of its weaknesses.

*Weakness 1: Too simple.* The first weakness is that it is an oversimplified approach to value since it combines just two financial parameters in a simple ratio.

*Weakness 2: Artificial ratio.* The second weakness is that the result of the PEG calculation is not intrinsic value, a payback period, or an estimate of percentage return (as explained in the next chapter). Rather, it is a ratio that has no rational conceptual framework and is instead a simple ad hoc combination of two financial quantities, one a ratio and the other a growth rate. It is artificial in that there is no rational reason why only these parameters are used and why they should be combined as a ratio in favor of many other possibilities. In addition, there is no reason why the particular level of 1.0 should represent fair value.

*Weakness 3: No dividends.* The third weakness is that dividends are not included in the ratio. For example, if a company has a low growth compared to its P/E ratio, it will have a high PEG ratio. Nevertheless, it still might be an attractive investment because it has a dividend yield that is high and stable. Even better, it might have a growing dividend yield.

*Weakness 4: Cannot handle low growth rates.* The conclusions of the method can be absurd when the growth rate is very low. Suppose that a company has a growth rate of 2 percent. The method would require a P/E of 2 or less for it be considered good value. The results are even more unsatisfactory when the growth forecast is 0 percent since the PEG ratio would now be undefined (division by zero). Continuing along this line, if a negative growth was forecast, the method would require a negative P/E ratio. Still, with very low or negative growth rates, perhaps the companies are rarely going to be the type of companies sought after by investors looking for value.

## PEGY Ratio

After introducing the PEG ratio in *One Up on Wall Street,* Peter Lynch recognized that dividends should also be considered. This led to the *PEGY ratio,* a modification of the PEG ratio that includes the dividend yield. The definition of the PEGY ratio is the P/E ratio divided by the sum of the forecast of the growth rate of earnings as a percentage and the dividend yield.[5] For example, a company with a 15 percent growth rate, a 3 percent dividend yield, and a P/E of 12 would have a

PEGY ratio of $12/(15 + 3) = 0.67$. Lynch describes the same example except with a P/E ratio of 6, giving a PEGY ratio of 0.33, a result he describes as "fabulous."

### PEGY Ratio

The PEGY ratio extends the PEG ratio by incorporating dividends. It is the ratio of the P/E ratio and the sum of forecast of the percentage growth rate of earnings and the dividend yield. Just as for the PEG ratio, the goal is to find stocks with a PEGY ratio as low as possible.

The logic behind summing the growth forecast and dividend yield is that together they give an estimate of the total shareholder return for the next year. This can be seen by building on the previous example and assuming that the stock pays dividends. Assume that the current share price is $60. Also assume that the P/E ratio of 12 remains constant for the next year. Since the P/E ratio is 12 and the growth rate is 15 percent, the current EPS is $5 and in 12 months it will be $5.75. Since the P/E remains at 12, the share price is now $69. The dividend yield is 3 percent, showing that the dividend is $1.80. This means that an outlay of $60 for a single unit of stock would generate wealth of $69.00 + $1.80 = $70.80 after 12 months. Comparing this number with the original outlay of $60 shows a total return of 18 percent. However, this is also the sum of the percentage growth rate (15 percent) and the dividend yield (3 percent).

The conclusion is that the sum of the growth forecast and dividend yield gives the total shareholder return for the next year in the case when the P/E ratio remains constant. This provides motivation for using the PEGY ratio as a means of measuring value, since a low PEGY ratio means that the P/E ratio is low compared to an estimate of the total shareholder return for the next 12 months.

David Lipshutz, who carried out the study on the PEG ratio described earlier, did a follow-up study on the PEGY ratio. Just as for the PEG ratio, he found that portfolios with low PEGY ratios had higher performance than portfolios with high PEGY ratios. They also had less volatility.[6] The turnover required to maintain the portfolio of around 100 stocks with low PEGY ratios was approximately 70 percent per year. From the point of view of an individual investor, this is an example of the standard weakness of academic studies: To get the higher returns described in the studies, large portfolios are required with a high turnover rate.

Theoretically, the PEGY ratio is an improvement on the PEG ratio as an indicator of value since it includes dividends in the calculations. Apart from that, its strengths and weaknesses are similar to those of the PEG ratio just described.

## Expectations Risk Index

The expectations risk index (ERI) is similar to the PEG and PEGY ratio methods since it also is an index rather than a calculation of a dollar intrinsic value or percentage return. As with the PEG ratio, ERI includes the P/E ratio and forecasts of the growth rate of earnings. However, it goes further and includes the past growth rate of earnings and a discount rate. The method focuses on two questions:

1. What proportion of the price of a stock depends on future growth of the company?
2. How difficult will it be for the company to achieve that growth?

Alfred Rappaport[7] introduced and investigated a specific valuation method based on answering these questions. In general, a stock is more undervalued if less of the price depends on future growth (question 1) and this growth is easily achieved relative to past performance (question 2).

### Expectations Risk Index

The expectations risk index (ERI) measures the proportion of the price of a stock that depends on future growth of the business and how easy is it to achieve that growth.

The ERI is easiest to understand using an example. Start with a stock with a current price of $80. The method begins by calculating the intrinsic value using the standard single-stage discounted cash flow model described in Chapter 7, assuming that there is no growth in free cash flow. The rationale for doing this is to calculate the proportion of the stock price that does not depend on any growth of the company. Assume that the discount rate is 11 percent and the initial free cash flow is $5.00. If we assume that free cash flow remains at this level, from the standard summation formula described in Appendix B, the intrinsic value is $45.45. This means that $34.55 or 43.18 percent of the stock price comes from investors' expectations about the future growth. Call it the *future growth proportion*. It gives an answer to the first question by providing a measure of the proportion of the stock price that depends on future growth—the lower the better.

The second stage of the process adjusts this percentage according to how much the forecast of the growth of free cash flow is above or below historical growth. Suppose that the forecast of future growth is 10 percent and the historical growth was 15 percent. The *acceleration factor* is defined as $(1 + 10\%)/(1 + 15\%) = 0.956$. The factor answers the second question by measuring how difficult it will be to achieve future growth. If the forecast equals the historical growth rate, the acceleration factor is 1. Otherwise it is above or below 1, depending on whether the forecast of future growth is above or below the past growth rate. The *expectations risk index* is the product of the future growth proportion and the acceleration factor. In this case it is $0.4318 \times 0.956 = 0.41$. The goal is to find companies where the ERI is as low as possible since they have the greatest likelihood of meeting expectations of their growth. As a consequence, the investment is likely to be more profitable when the ERI is lower.

A closer analysis of this method shows four important facts.

1. The ERI method incorporates a simple application of the discounted cash flow method. In particular, it uses the single-stage model and assumes that there is no growth of free cash flow.
2. Instead of free cash flow, the entire process can be repeated with any of the usual financial parameters measuring performance per share, such as normalized earnings, earnings, or even dividends. (For simplicity, the remaining discussion of this method will use earnings per share instead of free cash flow per share.)
3. We do not actually need both the share price and earnings (or free cash flow) per share. All that is needed is the P/E ratio

(or the ratio of the price to the free cash flow). This makes it easier to form tables containing the ERI over wide ranges of input data. Table 10.1 is an example of this.

4. In the calculations for the first stage, sometimes the intrinsic value (calculated assuming that there is no growth in earnings) will exceed the share price. In this case, the future growth proportion will be negative, giving a negative ERI. For instance, in the previous example the proportion will be zero when the P/E ratio equals 9.09 and it will be negative when the P/E ratio is less than 9.09. This can be checked using the calculations in Appendix B. Basically the reason is when the P/E ratio is 9.09, the intrinsic value (assuming a discount rate of 11 percent and no growth) is $80, the initial share price. Since the goal is for the ERI to be lower when the earnings forecast is less than the historical growth rate, we need to replace the acceleration factor as previously defined with its inverse when the future growth proportion is negative.

It is not difficult to calculate ERI. To give an idea of the relative sizes and ranges of ERI, Table 10.1 displays the index for a range of P/E ratios and acceleration factors assuming that the discount rate

**Table 10.1**   ERI Depending on P/E Ratios and Acceleration Factors

| Acceleration Factor | P/E Ratio | | | | | | | |
|---|---|---|---|---|---|---|---|---|
| | 6 | 8 | 10 | 12 | 14 | 16 | 18 | 20 |
| 70% | −0.74 | −0.19 | 0.06 | 0.17 | 0.25 | 0.30 | 0.35 | 0.38 |
| 80% | −0.64 | −0.17 | 0.07 | 0.19 | 0.28 | 0.35 | 0.40 | 0.44 |
| 90% | −0.57 | −0.15 | 0.08 | 0.22 | 0.32 | 0.39 | 0.45 | 0.49 |
| 100% | −0.52 | −0.14 | 0.09 | 0.24 | 0.35 | 0.43 | 0.49 | 0.55 |
| 110% | −0.47 | −0.12 | 0.10 | 0.27 | 0.39 | 0.48 | 0.54 | 0.60 |
| 120% | −0.43 | −0.11 | 0.11 | 0.29 | 0.42 | 0.52 | 0.59 | 0.65 |
| 130% | −0.40 | −0.10 | 0.12 | 0.32 | 0.46 | 0.56 | 0.64 | 0.71 |

This shows the ERI for a range of P/E ratios and acceleration factors. The calculations assume a discount rate of 11 percent. To apply to particular cases, calculate the acceleration factor as $1 + g$ divided by $1 + h$, where $g$ is the forecast of the free cash flow and $h$ is the historical rate of growth. Stocks with lower levels of ERI are favored over those with higher levels.

is 11 percent. (The columns cover different P/E ratios but, as just explained, they could be other ratios such as the price to free cash flow ratio.)

To understand how to use the table, consider the previous example. The ratio of price to free cash flow was 16, so we need to look in the sixth column of the table. The acceleration factor was approximately 95 percent, which is between the third and fourth rows of the table. This means that we expect the ERI to be roughly 0.41, which is what we saw earlier. In general, the lower the P/E ratio, the more attractive the investment. The table shows this with the ERI dropping in value as we move to the left. For the columns, as the forecast growth becomes lower with respect to the historical growth, once again the investment becomes more attractive. Again, the table shows this, with lower values of the ERI corresponding to lower values of the acceleration factor.

Since the ERI involves both the P/E ratio and the forecast of the growth rate, it is natural to compare it with the PEG ratio. The following are three areas where the two methods agree and disagree with each other.

1. Equities with low PEG ratios or low ERIs are more attractive than those with higher levels.
2. Both the PEG ratio and the ERI involve the P/E ratio and are lower when the P/E ratio is lower.
3. Both the PEG ratio and the ERI involve forecasts of earnings. However, while the PEG ratio is lower when the growth is higher, the ERI is higher when the growth rate is higher. The reason for this difference is that for the PEG ratio we are looking for high-growth stocks relative to the P/E ratio. In contrast, in the ERI we have already calculated and incorporated a simplified version of the intrinsic value of the stock, assuming no growth. The method asks for this value to be as achievable as possible by looking for companies with growth forecasts as low as possible compared to historical growth.

Rappaport mentioned some initial studies using the ERI approach in the areas of communication technology stocks and food stocks over the years 1994–1996. In both cases, stocks in the lowest ERI quartiles outperformed their sectors.[8]

## Strengths and Weaknesses of the ERI Valuation Method

The main strength of the ERI method is that it combines a broad range of important financial parameters to provide a simple estimate of value. The following is a summary of its strengths, followed by a summary of its weaknesses.

> *Strength 1: Rational basis.* The twin goals of the method are to choose stocks with (1) a lower proportion of the current price depending on future growth, and (2) future growth that is easy to achieve compared to past growth. The method incorporates financial parameters in a rational way to achieve these goals.
>
> *Strength 2: Easy interpretation.* It is easy to compare two companies as potential investments: simply choose the one with the lower ERI.
>
> *Strength 3: Financial parameters.* The financial parameters used in the ERI method are the P/E ratio, the historical growth rate, the forecast growth rate, and the discount rate of the company. This is a reasonably broad range (particularly compared to the PEG ratio) and so the method captures more information about the company.

The main weakness of the ERI is that it is an artificial index without a coherent framework to support the particular combination of financial parameters. The following is a summary of its weaknesses.

> *Weakness 1: Artificial index.* The first weakness is that the result of the ERI calculation is not intrinsic value, or a payback period, or an estimate of percentage return. Rather, it is an index made up of a particular combination of financial data and forecasts. It is artificial in that there is no coherent framework to explain why it should be this combination and not some other.
>
> *Weakness 2: Related to the discounted cash flow method.* As noted earlier, calculation of the ERI starts with a simplified version of the discounted cash flow valuation method. This means that it takes on many of the weaknesses of the method, such

as requiring lifetime forecast of the discount rate and being unstable. In addition, the fact that the ERI only uses the single-stage model accentuates these weaknesses.

## The Bottom Line

1. Instead of expressing valuations in concrete terms such as dollars or years, valuations are carried out using other indexes or ratios.
2. Simple examples are the PEG and PEGY ratios. The PEG ratio is the ratio of the P/E ratio and the forecast of the percentage growth rate of earnings. PEGY is similar but includes dividends. Another example is the expectations risk index or ERI.
3. These methods are best used as a means of comparing the attractiveness of different companies by comparing their indexes.

# CHAPTER 11

## What Rate of Return Can I Expect?

*Your goal as an investor should simply be to purchase, at a rational price, a part interest in an easily understandable business whose earnings are virtually certain to be materially higher five, ten, and twenty years from now. Over time, you will find only a few companies that meet these standards—so when you see one that qualifies, you should buy a meaningful amount of stock. You must also resist the temptation to stray from your guidelines: If you aren't willing to own a stock for ten years, don't even think about owning it for ten minutes. Put together a portfolio of companies whose aggregate earnings march upward over the years, and so also will the portfolio's market value.*

—Warren Buffett[1]

*Earnings, earnings, earnings... ultimately the earnings will decide the fate of a stock.*

—Peter Lynch[2]

Up to this point, the underlying question has been: What is the true worth of a stock? There has also been a secondary question. If the stock is undervalued, we need to ask: Is the market price substantially below the true worth? The importance of this second question comes from the assumption that stocks that are more undervalued will initially rise in price more quickly than those that are less undervalued. In other words, they will have a higher rate of return. There is, however, an even more fundamental question for investors, namely: What rate of return can I confidently expect? Or, putting it more simply, how much money can I expect to make over the period of my choice for every dollar that I outlay? Everything else is secondary to this question. All the other questions and analyses of financial statements are measured by their contributions to this question.

If we still lack confidence in achieving an appropriate return, it does not matter whether a stock is undervalued by any particular method, or by a range of methods. For example, even being under-valued by 50 percent or more still does not tell us when, or if, it will move upward. It may stay at its current price for years.

This means that behind all of our calculations is the desire to know what sort of return can be expected. In this chapter we address the primary question of return right from the start without introducing or calculating intrinsic value in the sense of a monetary expression of true worth. The answer is given in terms of price-to-earnings (P/E) ratios, earnings growth, and dividend yield. In answering this question, we also need to measure the degree of confidence we can have in the expected return. We touch upon this second requirement in this chapter, but most of the discussion about this is reserved for Chapter 13 as part of the topic of margins of safety.

## Expected Return or Price Ratio Methods

Chapter 3 introduced the notion of the value ratio (VR), defined as the ratio of intrinsic value $V$ and price $P$. It was emphasized that this ratio determines whether a stock represents value. There is no need to perform a separate calculation of intrinsic value without price. In fact, it may be more useful and intuitive to include price right from the outset. Since it has to be included at some stage, why not do it right at the start? With this in mind, consider the definition of the P/E ratio as price divided by earnings per share (EPS). This can be rewritten as:

$$\text{Price} = \text{EPS} \times \text{P/E ratio}$$

In other words, the price of an equity has been broken or decomposed into two components.

At first this formula may seem a misleading breakdown of the price since the P/E ratio is actually defined in terms of price and EPS. However, the P/E ratio is given a more independent existence by thinking of it as the amount that the market is willing to pay for each dollar of EPS. A P/E ratio of 10 means that the market is willing to pay $10 for each dollar of earnings per share. There is no specific mention of either the actual price or the actual earnings per share. If the financial statements show the EPS as $1.00, the price is calculated as $10.00; if the EPS is $2.00, the price is $20.00, and so on.[3] An immediate consequence of this breakdown of price is that for the price to increase, either the EPS or the P/E ratio must increase (or both). Similarly, for the price to decrease, either the EPS or the P/E ratio must decrease (or both).

One way to think of this decomposition of price into earnings and P/E ratio is in terms of objective and subjective factors. The EPS of a company is objective, since it is a direct calculation from the financial statement of the business. (To be more accurate, we should say that it is *essentially* objective, since the financial statements produced by two accountants for the same business may be different. As well, two data companies may decide to treat certain line items in the financial statements in different ways, resulting in different outcomes for the earnings per share.) In contrast, the P/E ratio is subjective since it encapsulates the overall market opinion of the value of a single dollar of earnings per share of the company. In Chapter 3 we described value (or, more accurately, real value) as a combination of the price (as the objective perspective) and intrinsic value (as the subjective perspective). Now we continue this analysis in terms of objective and subjective by viewing price as a combination of the objective EPS and the subjective P/E ratio. By keeping this in mind, we can make sure we use tools appropriate for the objective component of price and different tools appropriate for the subjective component of price.

In broad terms, when dealing with earnings we employ linear rational arguments based on approved and audited financial data. In contrast, when dealing with the P/E ratio we need to be more flexible and make allowances for changes in the moods of the market. Figure 11.1 illustrates the relationship between the forecast of the growth rate of EPS, the anticipated P/E ratio, and the expected rate of return.

In Chapter 3, value was identified with the value ratio, which came from combining intrinsic value and price. Now the emphasis is on identifying value with return, which comes from combining

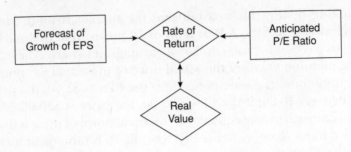

**Figure 11.1**    The Components of Value

growth and the P/E ratio. If it is necessary to place emphasis on this meaning of value, I will again use the term *real value*. It will be clear from the context whether we mean it in terms of the value ratio (as described in Chapter 3) or in terms of the anticipated rate of return (as just described).

The difference between how we used the term *value* in Chapter 3 and how we use it here is that in Chapter 3 there was no inclusion of time in the notion of value. If a stock was undervalued, there was no way of calculating when, or if, its price would start to move upward. In other words, there was no way of estimating its return. In contrast, the goal of calculating the return is included right at the outset in the notion of value expressed using price ratio methods.[4]

With this in mind, Figure 11.1 also links the expected rate of return and real value. There are, however, no hard and fast rules about this relationship. Table 11.1 gives an indication of an association between the two. For example, allowing for uncertainties in the inputs and calculations, we could say that a stock with an expected return above 18 percent represents excellent value. Other circumstances

**Table 11.1**    Value in Terms of the Expected Return

| Expected Return | Value |
| --- | --- |
| Above 18%. | Excellent |
| Between 12% and 18% | Good |
| Between 10% and 12% | Above average |
| Between 8% and 10% | Below average |
| Below 8% | Poor |

that may affect the required levels of the expected return are the risks of the company in areas such as its market capitalization, debt levels, track record of sales and earnings, and product strength and differentiation.

We don't only want increasing profit for the company as described by increasing earnings; we also want this profit to be converted into profit for the investor. This is done via the P/E ratio, which converts company earnings into share price. In view of the decomposition of price into EPS and the P/E ratio, clearly an investment will be highly attractive if its EPS continues to grow over time and its P/E ratio also grows. I like to refer to these companies as *double-dip* investments.[5] Of course, we don't have the same control over choosing companies that will have growth in the P/E ratio as we do for companies with a reliable growth in earnings. But later in the chapter we will see rules for helping to know when a P/E ratio is likely to be at or near a low point.

### Look for Double-Dip Investments

The growth of EPS measures the increasing profits of the business, and the P/E ratio describes how these profits are converted into the share price, which represents the profits for the investor. Double-dip investments have growth in both EPS and the P/E ratio.

The discussion up to this point only looked at profit in terms of the growth of the share price—in other words, capital gains. To get the complete picture, dividend income needs to be included. Once this is done, we define *expected return* or *price ratio methods* as calculations of the return of an investment in terms of price and dividends based on changes in the P/E ratio, growth rate of earnings, and dividend levels. Instead of the standard earnings, these methods can be carried out using a range of financial parameters such as normalized earnings, free cash flow, and even dividends. For example, instead of the P/E ratio, use the price-to-free-cash-flow ratio, and instead of the growth rate of earnings use the growth rate of free cash flow. To keep the discussion focused on the essential ideas, everything further is presented in terms of earnings.

When incorporating dividends into the analysis, there are three possibilities.

1. We can assume that the dividends are to be used to buy more shares at the prevailing price to give the total return or total shareholder return.
2. We can assume that the dividends are to be reinvested in a different security, particularly a fixed-interest bond.
3. We can remove the dividends from the calculation to focus on capital gains.

We can also look at these possibilities allowing for taxes on dividends and capital gains taxes. However, instead of looking at all the variations, we will focus on the results when dividends are used to buy more shares, since total shareholder return is a standardized benchmark for measuring performance and comparing different investments. It does not mean that you are required to reinvest your dividends, just that the calculations allow the comparison of apples to apples by incorporating both capital gains and dividend payments. Instead of developing the general theory, we give a series of examples of increasing complexity to highlight the key ideas.

*Example 1:* Start by assuming that the P/E ratio remains fixed and the earnings grow, but there are no dividends. Suppose that earnings per share grow by 15 percent per year over the next five years. It follows that the stock price will grow by an average of 15 percent per year over the next five years.

*Example 2:* Now suppose that the P/E ratio increases by a total of 20 percent over five years but there is no change in earnings. This time the stock price will grow by a total of 20 percent over five years. Because of compounding this is an average growth of 3.71 percent per year over this period.

*Example 3:* For the next example, continue with no dividends, but assume that both EPS and the P/E ratio change. Combining the previous two examples, suppose that the earnings grow by 15 percent per year over the next five years along with a total increase of 20 percent for the P/E ratio. We saw that if the growth and P/E ratio assumptions were applied

**Table 11.2**    Growth of the Share Price

| Year | Price at Start of Year | Earnings per Share | Price at End of Year |
|---|---|---|---|
| 1 | $100.00 | $11.50 | $138.00 |
| 2 | $138.00 | $13.23 | $158.70 |
| 3 | $158.70 | $15.21 | $182.51 |
| 4 | $182.51 | $17.49 | $209.88 |
| 5 | $209.88 | $20.11 | $241.36 |
|  | Average annual return | | 19.27% |

This shows the growth of the share price starting with $100 as the initial price. EPS is initially $10. Assume that the earnings grow by 15 percent per year and the P/E ratio increases by a total of 20 percent. Data is built up year by year. For example, in the first year earnings, growing by 15 percent per year, increase from $10 to $11.50. Using a P/E ratio of 12 gives a price of $138.00 at the end of the year. The price after five years is $241.36, representing an average annual return of 19.27 percent.

separately, then the two average annual growths of the share price would be 15 percent and 3.71 percent. Adding these gives 18.71 percent. However, each year the EPS and P/E ratio combine with each other so that the average growth in the stock price is actually 19.27 percent. To see why this is true, assume that the initial share price is $100 and earnings per share is $10. Table 11.2 shows how the share price grows from $100 at the start of the first year to $241.36 at the end of the fifth year. This amounts to an average annual return of 19.27 percent. In the other direction, suppose that the P/E ratio is anticipated to drop by 20 percent. Using a similar table would show that the stock price will now only grow by an average of 9.98 percent per year over the next five years, despite the EPS growing at an average of 15 percent per year.

For this simple case the actual formula for the average growth in share price is:

$$\text{Average return per year over five years} = [(1 + R)^{1/5} \times (1 + g)] - 1$$

where

$R$  is the increase in the P/E ratio over five years
$g$  is the average annual growth rate of earnings

*Example 4:* For the fourth example, assume that the company also pays dividends, and that the dividends are to be used to buy more shares. As a specific example, assume that the company has a policy of paying out 20 percent of its earnings as dividends. Also assume that EPS is growing at 15 percent per year over the next five years. For simplicity we assume that the P/E ratio remains constant. Finally, assume that the initial stock price was $50 and EPS was $5.00. Our goal is to track what happens over the next five years with the dividends being reinvested.

Over the first year, EPS grows by 15 percent to $5.75. Since the P/E is constant, this means that the share price becomes $57.50. In addition, the dividend is $1.15 which is 20 percent of $5.75. Given that the share price is now $57.50 it is possible to buy 1.15/57.50 = 0.02 new shares. This means the holding is now 1.02 shares at $57.50, a total wealth of 1.02 × $57.50 = $58.65. Table 11.3 shows the results of doing this for five years, resulting in total value of $111.04 at the end of this time. Since the original outlay was $50, this represents an average return per year of 17.30 percent.

**Table 11.3**  Growth of Portfolio Value Assuming Dividend Reinvestment

| (1) Year | (2) Price | (3) EPS | (4) Dividends | (5) New Shares | (6) Total Number | (7) Value |
|---|---|---|---|---|---|---|
| 0 | $50.00 | $5.00 | | | 1.0000 | $50.00 |
| 1 | $57.50 | $5.75 | $1.15 | 0.0200 | 1.0200 | $58.65 |
| 2 | $66.13 | $6.61 | $1.32 | 0.0204 | 1.0404 | $68.80 |
| 3 | $76.04 | $7.60 | $1.52 | 0.0208 | 1.0612 | $80.70 |
| 4 | $87.45 | $8.75 | $1.75 | 0.0212 | 1.0824 | $94.66 |
| 5 | $100.57 | $10.06 | $2.01 | 0.0216 | 1.1041 | $111.04 |
| | | | | | Average annual return | 17.30% |

The initial portfolio consists of a single share purchased for $50. At the end of each year the dividends are used to purchase further shares. The growth rate of EPS and the dividend payout ratio are assumed to remain constant with values of 15 percent and 20 percent. The P/E ratio is assumed to be constant with a value of 10. The share price at the end of each year (1) is shown in column (2). The EPS in column (3) grows at 15 percent per year. Each year, column (2) divided by column (3) gives the P/E ratio as a constant 10. The dividends shown in column (4) are obtained from column (3) using the dividend payout ratio of 20 percent. These dividends multiplied by the number of shares in the previous year are used to buy new shares, the number purchased being shown in column (5). The total number of shares in column (6) is multiplied by the share price in column (2) to give the value of the investment, shown in column (7). Growth of $50 to $111.04 over five years means an average return of 17.30 percent per year.

**Table 11.4**   Average Total Annual Returns Assuming Dividend Reinvestment

| | | | | Dividend Payout Ratios | | | | |
|---|---|---|---|---|---|---|---|---|
| | | 0% | 10% | 20% | 30% | 40% | 50% | 100% |
| | -5.0% | -5.00% | -4.05% | -3.10% | -2.15% | -1.20% | -0.25% | 4.50% |
| | -2.5% | -2.50% | -1.53% | -0.55% | 0.43% | 1.40% | 2.38% | 7.25% |
| | 0.0% | 0.00% | 1.00% | 2.00% | 3.00% | 4.00% | 5.00% | 10.00% |
| | 2.5% | 2.50% | 3.52% | 4.55% | 5.57% | 6.60% | 7.62% | 12.75% |
| Earnings | 5.0% | 5.00% | 6.05% | 7.10% | 8.15% | 9.20% | 10.25% | 15.50% |
| Growth | 7.5% | 7.50% | 8.58% | 9.65% | 10.73% | 11.80% | 12.88% | 18.25% |
| Rate | 10.0% | 10.00% | 11.10% | 12.20% | 13.30% | 14.40% | 15.50% | 21.00% |
| | 12.5% | 12.50% | 13.63% | 14.75% | 15.88% | 17.00% | 18.13% | 23.75% |
| | 15.0% | 15.00% | 16.15% | 17.30% | 18.45% | 19.60% | 20.75% | 26.50% |
| | 17.5% | 17.50% | 18.68% | 19.85% | 21.03% | 22.20% | 23.38% | 29.25% |
| | 20.0% | 20.00% | 21.20% | 22.40% | 23.60% | 24.80% | 26.00% | 32.00% |

Over five years the P/E ratio is assumed to be constant with value 10. The columns display different rates of the dividend yield and the rows display different rates of EPS growth. Dividends are assumed to be reinvested. The calculations display the average annual total return over five years.

Instead of calculating the return by constructing a table with year-by-year results as was done in Tables 11.2 and 11.3, it is possible to construct tables showing total return for different ranges of values. This is done in Table 11.4 under the assumption that the P/E ratio remains constant. It shows average annual total returns calculated over five years for various values of the payout ratio and the growth rate of earnings. The return calculation of 17.30 percent derived in the previous example is seen in the column with dividend payout ratio of 20 percent and the row with EPS growth of 15 percent.[6]

### Relationship Between ROE and Share Price

There are two important outcomes of the fundamental relationship of price as the product of earnings per share and the P/E ratio. The first is that it completes the two-step argument stated in Chapter 5 that high ROE leads, over time, to high growth in price. In Chapter 5 it was stated that a high and consistent ROE leads directly to high growth in earnings. The specific relationship was that, to a reasonable level of approximation, growth in earnings equals ROE times the earnings retention rate. (Details are given in Appendix A. It also assumes that the company retains most of its earnings.) This was the first step. Now we have the second step: Assuming that the P/E ratio is reasonably constant, high growth in earnings leads to high growth in the price of the stock. This relationship between ROE and price is the reason for the repeated statements by Buffett and others about the importance of high return on equity and return on capital. In broad terms, over time, whatever returns a company makes on its equity and capital will be the return made by investing in the company's stock. Putting it simply, money cannot come from nowhere. (In fact, depending on the dividend policy of the company, the return on equity is more like an upper limit to the return made from investing in the stock.)

### From Return on Equity to Growth in Share Price

Over time, whatever returns a company makes on its equity and capital will be approximately an upper limit on the return made by investing in the company's stock. In particular, high and consistent return on equity with a low payout ratio means a high growth in price.

The second outcome of the fundamental relationship is based on the fact that, over time, EPS can grow indefinitely, but the P/E ratio will stay roughly in a band. Moreover, the P/E ratio has certain mean-reverting properties: If the P/E ratio gets too high, rational investors will no longer buy the stock and it will tend to decrease, and if it is too low, actions by rational investors will tend to buy the stock, thereby pushing up the P/E ratio. This means that, although we are looking for double-dip stocks, over time the earnings part of the requirement is more important than the P/E ratio part. If earnings multiply by four to six times or more over 10 years, provided you paid a reasonable P/E ratio, it is going to be a healthy investment. It is like buying prime real estate with ocean views 20 years ago. You may have thought you paid too much at the time, but now it has grown so much in value that the original price is a distant memory.

Charles ("Charlie") Munger, the vice chairman of Berkshire Hathaway and longtime friend of Warren Buffett, explained it as follows:

> Over the long term, it's hard for a stock to earn a much better return than the business which underlies it earns. If the business earns 6 percent on capital over 40 years and you hold it for that 40 years, you're not going to make much different than a 6 percent return—even if you originally buy it at a huge discount. Conversely, if a business earns 18 percent on capital over 20 years or 30 years, even if you pay an expensive looking price, you'll end up with a fine result.[7]

### Calculation of Target Prices

It is possible to flip the previous calculations to calculate the maximum price to pay in order to get a desired return or better. For example, suppose that to compensate for the risk of investing in a particular company you desire a total shareholder return of 15 percent per year over the next five years. It is a question of modifying the price until the return that would be generated is the required 15 percent. This price becomes the target price for any planned purchases. This puts you in the strong position of being able to specify the maximum price that you are willing to pay to achieve your desired return. Market volatility expressed by Benjamin Graham's Mr. Market now becomes your friend.

## Making Forecasts

There are three forecasts that need to be made to apply the price ratio methods: the growth rate of earnings, the P/E ratio, and the dividend payout ratio. Of these three forecasts, the most important is earnings. Because of this, the subject of forecasts of earnings is reserved for a later chapter, Chapter 13, where it can be explored in more detail as part of a general discussion on margins of safety. In the remainder of this chapter we look at making forecasts of P/E ratios and the payout ratio. Even though we are talking about making forecasts, in Chapter 13 we will see that the key to successful investing is not the accuracy of the forecasts, but rather the ability to make forecasts that are robust enough to withstand downturns in the business or the market.

## Forecasting P/E ratios

Since the price ratio methods described thus far depend on P/E ratios, it makes sense to analyze P/E ratios and their forecasts. For a start, as mentioned earlier, P/E ratios are mean-reverting in the sense that, provided the movement of earnings per share is reasonably consistent over time and that there are no years when the company suffers a loss, very low P/E ratios will tend to swing upward and very high P/E ratios will tend to swing downward. (The last time mean-reversion series were discussed was the q-ratio in Chapter 6.)

Consider Wal-Mart. Figure 11.2 displays the low, the high, and the average P/E ratios for the past 11 financial years ending January 2000 through January 2010. Figure 11.3 shows the earnings per share for Wal-Mart over the same years. There are a number of features to notice. First, both charts have consistent growth, but in opposite directions. The P/E ratios have trended downward while the earnings have trended upward. Given the decomposition of price in terms of EPS and P/E ratio, the likely outcome would be that these two trends would cancel each other out with little overall change in price.

This is precisely what happened. At the start of 1999 the share price was $35.53. Eleven years later at the start of 2010 it was $53.93. This is a modest average capital gain of 4.26 percent per year, not much more than the rate of inflation. There is nothing wrong with the company. Figure 11.3 shows how successful it was in growing its earnings over that time. The problem is that people got excited about the stock market 10 years ago and were willing to pay almost any level in terms of P/E ratios. But at multiples of anything from 25 to 55, it was going to be almost impossible to make money over the next 5 to 10 years, and perhaps longer.

Second, there is a large range between the low and the high P/E ratios on a year-by-year basis. On average, over the 11 years of the chart, the difference between the high and low P/E ratios was almost 40 percent. This is despite the consistency of the growth of earnings and the business strength of Wal-Mart. For companies without this stability and strength, the range is usually much higher. Third, there are periods when there is little change from year to year in the low, high, and average P/E ratios. For example, over the most recent four

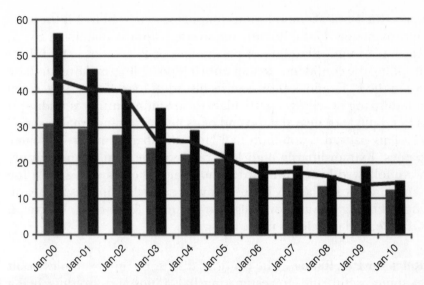

**Figure 11.2**    Low, High, and Average P/E Ratios for Wal-Mart

The bars show the lowest and highest P/E ratios for the 11 financial years ending January 31, 2000, through January 31, 2010. The line shows the average P/E ratio for these years.

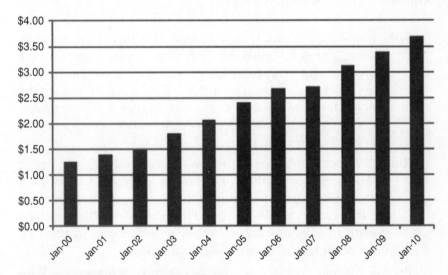

**Figure 11.3**    Earnings per Share for Wal-Mart

The bars show the earnings per share for the 11 financial years ending January 31, 2000, through January 31, 2010. The average growth per year is approximately 11.5 percent.

years, the low P/E ratio has been approximately 13 to 14, the high approximately 17 to 19, and the average approximately 15 to 17. Having an understanding of past ranges of P/E ratios is useful for instilling the confidence to wait until it is possible to make a purchase when the P/E ratio is at or near its historical lows. Conversely, if you are thinking of selling a particular stock, waiting until it is trading at a P/E ratio at or near the top end of its historical range makes sense.

This pattern is common to a large number of major U.S. companies. Extraordinarily high P/E ratios at the turn of the century were followed by a downward trend over the ensuing years. At the same time, it has largely been business as usual with sales and earnings trending upward for Walgreen, Johnson & Johnson, Procter & Gamble, and Oracle, to name a few.

**Rules for P/E Ratios**    The previous discussion and examples point to some useful rules for estimating P/E ratios and avoiding being drawn into high forecasts. Rules 1 and 2 compare the P/E ratio with its own historical levels; rules 3 and 4 compare the P/E ratio with the P/E ratios of other companies; and rules 5 and 6 suggest absolute requirements about the P/E ratio.

Rule 1. *Know the history of the P/E ratio.* It is important to have, at least, a general understanding of the levels of the low, the high, and the average P/E ratios over at least the past 10 years or a full economic cycle. Questions to ask: What are the average levels of the low, high, and average P/E ratios? Are there any trends? Are there any differences between recent years and earlier years?

Rule 2. *Do not buy unless the P/E ratio is toward the lower end of its historical range.* If the P/E ratio has tended to stay within a certain range in the past, then it makes sense to buy only when the P/E ratio is at the lower end of the range. Otherwise, any growth in earnings may be offset by a decrease in the P/E ratio, resulting in a stagnating share price.

Rule 3. *Compare the P/E ratio with the P/E ratios of competitors.* Who are the company's main competitors? How do the current and past P/E ratios of these competitors compare with the P/E ratios of the company being considered? Business is very competitive, with similar companies watching each other closely. Any innovation or change of procedure that brings increased profits to one will be studied by the others, with an aim either to adopt it or to institute changes to lessen its impact. Hence, there is always a tendency for the profit ratios and growth of high-profit companies to settle over time. This will be reflected by the market becoming less willing to pay prices representing high P/E ratios compared to ratios of its competitors.

Rule 4. *Compare the P/E ratio with the average P/E ratio for the same sector or the overall market.* This is similar to rule 3 except that the P/E ratio of the company is compared to the average P/E ratio of the sector or broad market indexes.

Rule 5. *Be wary about buying when the P/E ratio is high.* It is not reasonable to say never invest in a company that has a high P/E ratio, say above 15 or so. It may be a wonderful company and you have complete confidence that earnings will continue to grow at an exceptional rate. Just the same, the slightest interruption in the growth of earnings, hint of bad news, or disturbance in the economy may lead to a significant drop in the share price. Benjamin Graham was well-known for being very conservative regarding estimates of growth of businesses and hence of P/E ratios. For him, a P/E ratio of around 16 formed an upper limit for defensive investors. As he explained over 70 years ago, "People who habitually purchase common stocks at more than about sixteen times their average earnings are likely to lose considerable money in the long run."[8] As part of the discussion, Graham also says that it is not a mistake to pay more than this, but such a purchase should be regarded as speculative. Figure 11.2 of historical P/E ratios for Wal-Mart shows that avoiding high P/E ratios would have ruled out investing in the company until around 2006 or 2007.[9]

Rule 6. *Look at the earnings yield.* As discussed in Chapter 5, the earnings yield is the earnings per share divided by price, the inverse of the P/E ratio. As explained by Benjamin Graham, you can think of the earnings yield as "what the company might be expected to earn year after year if the business conditions prevailing during the period were to continue unchanged."[10] By looking at earnings yield in this way we can get an idea of the minimum return that can be anticipated, and anything above this level is due to the growth of earnings.

Since a P/E ratio of 15 to 16 corresponds to an earnings yield of around 6 to 7 percent, asking for a P/E lower than this level is the same as asking for an earnings yield above 6 to 7 percent.

As a final comment on P/E ratios, some financial institutions make it clear that they estimate "fair" P/E ratios by comparing them to broad market indexes (rule 4) and with historical levels (rule 1). As an example, a March 2010 report by Standard & Poor's on Wal-Mart (WMT) stated: "Applying a multiple of 15.6X, a 3.7 percent discount to WMT's five-year median P/E but in line with the forward 12-month P/E for the S&P 500, to our FY 11 EPS estimate of $3.95 implies a value of $62."[11] In other words, the report uses a P/E ratio of 15.6, arguing that it is reasonable by comparing it to a P/E ratio related to the S&P 500 index and that it is at a discount to historical levels. The report also includes a forecast of $3.95 for the earnings per share for the financial year ending January 31, 2011. The conclusion is that the fair value in January 2011 is 15.6 times $3.95, which is $61.62 or approximately $62.

### Forecasting Payout Rates

By and large, companies tend to maintain fairly constant dividend payout ratios. Just the same, when making a forecast it is helpful to examine the payout ratio over the past 5 to 10 years to see if there have been any trends or sudden changes. For example, Table 11.5 shows that the payout ratio of the medical company Johnson & Johnson was in the tight band of 36 percent to 45 percent over the past 10 years. The band for the payout ratios of Genuine Parts Company, a multibillion-dollar company mainly in the area of automotive replacement parts, was not quite as tight. Over the past 4 years it has risen from 48 to 64 percent.

Next, look in the annual report or the 10-K report to see if the company gives any indication of what it intends to do in the future. In its 2009 10-K report, Johnson & Johnson declared, "The Company increased its dividend in 2009 for the 47th consecutive year . . . expects to continue the practice of paying regular cash dividends." Similarly, after describing the increase in dividends over the past few years in its 2009 10-K report, Genuine Parts Company stated, "The Company expects this trend of increasing dividends to continue in the foreseeable future." Nothing is guaranteed. Nevertheless, consistent data

**Table 11.5**  Payout Ratios

| Year | Johnson & Johnson | Genuine Parts |
|------|-------------------|---------------|
| 2000 | 36% | 50% |
| 2001 | 38% | 66% |
| 2002 | 37% | 55% |
| 2003 | 39% | 58% |
| 2004 | 39% | 53% |
| 2005 | 37% | 50% |
| 2006 | 39% | 48% |
| 2007 | 45% | 48% |
| 2008 | 39% | 53% |
| 2009 | 44% | 64% |

and statements such as we have just seen help us make more reliable forecasts of future payout ratios.

## Strengths and Weaknesses of Expected Return or Price Ratio Methods

A major component of most of the methods discussed in the previous chapters is that they all started with a stand-alone calculation of the intrinsic value. This is particularly true of the discount methods. When the words *intrinsic value* are used for equities, most people immediately think of discount methods. In contrast, price ratio methods involve the use of price right from the start. However, as described in Chapter 3, even with the discount methods, the final value decisions must take account of the price of the securities being valued. Hence, in the end it makes no difference if the calculations proceed via intrinsic value or go straight to the goal of determining whether or not the asset represents value.

The main strength of price ratio methods is that they answer the fundamental question regarding what rate of return can be expected over a specified number of years. In addition, all the forecasts are over the same specified time frame.

*Strength 1: Fundamental question.* Ratio methods answer the most fundamental question of investing: What rate of return can I confidently expect with this investment over a specified period? All other activities in investing should aim, directly or indirectly, to help answer this question.

*Strength 2: Match between forecast and investment period.* If the anticipated holding period is five years, the forecasts are made for
five years. If the anticipated holding period is 10 years, then
the forecasts are/made for 10 years. In other words, there is
a match between specified return or holding period and the
forecast period.

*Strength 3: Reasonable forecast period.* Even though the method can
be applied to any period, working with five years seems a
reasonable middle ground. It is far enough for the market
to meet any sound forecasts of the P/E ratio using the rules
described earlier. But it is not so far that it is impossible to
make sensible forecasts of growth, the P/E ratio, or the dividend payout ratio. This is particularly true when margins of
safety are employed, as described in Chapter 13. In addition,
five years means that use can be made of consensus five-year
forecasts available on most major financial web sites.

*Strength 4: Testable parameters.* In contrast to the discount methods, because the financial parameters such as the growth
rate of earnings are made over reasonable periods, they are
testable.[12]

*Strength 5: Parameter analysis.* If the rate of return that is forecast
from an application of the ratio method is not achieved, then
one can check which of the input parameters did not meet
the forecasts.

*Strength 6: Flexible procedure.* The method is flexible in terms of the
parameters used. For example, instead of P/E ratios, other
ratios such as price to free cash flow can be used. In addition,
it is possible to use the method to calculate the return after
taxes on dividends and capital gains.

*Strength 7: Dividend management.* The method can be modified to
calculate the return assuming that dividends are reinvested
or are invested elsewhere.

Turning to the weaknesses of the price ratio methods, their main
weakness hinges on the need to forecast or estimate P/E ratios.

*Weakness 1: P/E ratio is used.* P/E ratios are, in a sense, a con-
densation of the opinion of the market regarding the worth
of the earnings per share of the stock. Hence it may seem

inappropriate that these ratios are included in a valuation method. However, since any final decision involves price, it makes no logical difference if price is incorporated at the end of any series of calculations, or right at the beginning. Price ratio methods choose to include price right at the beginning in combination with earnings via the P/E ratio.

*Weakness 2: P/E ratios need to be estimated.* Because P/E ratios are partly driven by market opinion, compared to other financial parameters there is less of a secure basis to use when estimating reasonable levels for any future P/E ratios. For example, if the P/E ratio of the company being considered has been high for a number of years, despite the best of intentions, it may be hard not to make forecasts that are also high. This is the behavioral problem of anchoring. The same difficulty applies if the P/E ratios for the sector or the overall market have been high for an extended period. This is why the rules for P/E ratios described earlier are important to help increase the objectivity in any forecasts. Of course, there is a similar problem with DCF methods described in Chapter 7, except that there it is more hidden. To get to the level of making a decision you need the value ratio, which in turn relies on estimates of forward cash yields. Cash yields are simply the inverse of the price-to-cash ratios. So instead of estimating a single P/E ratio, DCF methods require estimates for an infinite sequence of price-to-cash ratios.

*Weakness 3: Dividend payout.* The dividend payout ratio depends on decisions of the board and not directly on the performance of the company. This means that the board could cut or change the payout ratio for reasons that may not be in the best interests of the shareholders.

*Weakness 4: Reliance on earnings.* The approach to the price ratio methods described earlier relies on earnings and earnings forecasts. Even though they are subject to GAAP standards, verified by auditors, and thoroughly examined by analysts, they are vulnerable to manipulation by management. Of course, as explained, everything could be done with normalized earnings or free cash flow, which are less affected by this vulnerability. Chapter 13 on margins of safety tackles the problem of making more reliable forecasts of earnings.

*Weakness 5: No stand-alone calculation of intrinsic value.* It has been explained that from the point of view of making a value-based decision on whether to buy, to sell, or to do nothing, it is not necessary to make a stand-alone calculation of intrinsic value. Nevertheless, there may be times when such a calculation is advantageous, such as when using the equity in a portfolio to guarantee a loan. However, as explained in Chapter 1, a target price can always be backed out of the calculation that will state the price necessary to achieve a specified return. The final result is similar to the intrinsic value calculated using the discounted cash flow and dividend discount methods, where the discount rate is the required rate of return.

### The Bottom Line

1. The primary investing question is, what rate of return can I confidently expect to get?
2. The price of an equity can be decomposed into a product of earnings per share and the P/E ratio. This means that for the price to rise, either EPS must rise or the P/E ratio must rise (or both).
3. Expected return or price ratio methods estimate total shareholder return over any prescribed period using forecasts of earnings per share, the P/E ratio, and the dividend payout ratio.

# CHAPTER 12

# Please, Sir, I Want Some More

*Our study of the various [valuation] methods has led us to suggest a foreshortened and quite simple formula for the evaluation of growth stocks, which is intended to produce figures fairly close to those resulting from the more refined mathematical calculations.*

—Benjamin Graham[1]

*A variety of valuation methods are employed in practice.... Since each technique involves different advantages and disadvantages, there are gains to considering several approaches simultaneously.*

—Krishna Palepu, Paul Healy, and Victor Bernard[2]

**C**harles Dickens' character Oliver Twist was not satisfied with what he was given for breakfast and asked for more. It is the same with valuation methods. Not satisfied with existing methods, many people have applied their minds to developing their own valuation methods. In some cases, their names are still attached to the method they developed. In most cases, however, the methods have become just another tool used by investors in their search for value, without any clear record of who developed them. Of course, it is likely that many other methods never gathered a following and have now disappeared from the arena without any evidence of their existence.

The only universal rule to such methods seems to be that—all else being equal—price and value are inversely related: the higher the price the less the value, and the lower the price the more the value. After that, it seems that anything and everything has been drawn into at least one of the formulas. In this chapter we look at a range of valuation methods, including two of Benjamin Graham's lesser-known methods. Then we look at the abnormal earnings growth method by James Ohlson and Beate Juettner-Nauroth; assets, earnings power, and profitable growth methods by Bruce Greenwald and his co-authors; the benchmark method by Kenneth Lee; the magic formula method by Joel Greenblatt; and the factor method by Robert Haugen. We also briefly introduce a valuation method that uses options.

## Graham's Intrinsic Value Formulas

Benjamin Graham was so multitalented that after he graduated from Columbia in New York, the departments of English, mathematics, and philosophy all offered him teaching positions.[3] However, he chose to work on Wall Street for a company called Newburger, Henderson & Loeb, but it wasn't long before he started his own company. He was a prolific writer and also seemed to enjoy deriving different mathematical formulas for determining value. For example, in Chapter 6 we saw various examples of his methods related to the balance sheets of businesses. In this chapter we look at some of his intrinsic value methods that use current earnings and earnings forecasts.

In *The Intelligent Investor*, Graham introduced the formula:

$$V = \text{EPS} \times (8.5 + 2g)$$

where $V$ is intrinsic value, EPS is the current earnings per share, 8.5 is a constant (presumably selected by Graham after trial and error as a figure that seemed to work well), and $g$ is the average annual growth of earnings per share "expected over the next seven to ten years" expressed as a percentage.[4] Graham referred to $(8.5 + 2g)$ as the *multiplier* since, according to the formula, multiplying by this number converted earnings per share into the fair price of the stock. In this sense, the fair value of the P/E ratio of a company is 8.5 plus twice the expected growth rate. This is now easily compared to the PEG ratio described in Chapter 10. Since Lynch asserted that the PEG ratio for fairly priced companies was 1.0, it follows that the fair value of the P/E ratio is the expected growth rate. Stating this in the same form as Graham's formula,

$$V = \text{EPS} \times g$$

Hence, the intrinsic value from the PEG ratio is always considerably less than the intrinsic value from Graham's method, provided the expected growth is positive. Of course, the PEG ratio formula is meaningless when the growth rate is zero; in that case, we cannot even calculate the PEG ratio. In contrast to the PEG ratio, from Graham's formula the fair P/E ratio is 8.5 when companies have no expected growth. In this sense, Graham's method is an extension and a modification of the PEG ratio.

As an example, consider Johnson & Johnson (JNJ). At the time of this writing (March 2010), its EPS over the past 12 months was $4.40 and the consensus five-year forecast was 7.60 percent per year. Hence the intrinsic value according to Graham's formula is

$$4.40 \times [8.5 + (2 \times 7.60)] = \$104.28$$

Since the current price of JNJ is $64.57, it is heavily undervalued according to Graham's formula. Putting it another way, since the multiplier is 23.7 (that is, $[8.5 + (2 \times 7.6)]$), the formula implies that the fair value for the P/E ratio is 23.7. It does seem rather high but it is not out of the question. It was over 35.0 eight or nine years ago but for the past five years it has been below 20. It may be that the consensus forecast of 7.6 percent is the main factor distorting the result. As remarked in an earlier chapter, Graham was well-known for making very conservative growth forecasts for businesses. Quite likely he would never have made a forecast of 7.6 percent for Johnson & Johnson, particularly since this is only marginally lower than its average growth over the previous five years of 8.3 percent. There is no allowance for any slowing of growth.

Graham described how the formula could be inverted and used to determine the rate of growth implied by the current market price. For example, returning to JNJ, the rate of growth implied by the price of $64.57 is 3.09 percent.

A weakness of the formula was that it did not allow for changes in the basic rate of interest. Graham recognized this and modified his formula to incorporate interest rates. He explained that when he published his first formula the yield on AAA corporate bonds was around 4.4 percent. After that it grew to 7.5 percent, and then to 9.5 percent. What he wanted to do was to modify the formula so that the stock valuation varied inversely with the interest rates and reflected the original formula when the AAA rate was 4.4 percent. This led to a new formula, which stated that the value $V$ was given by

$$V = [\text{EPS} \times (8.5 + 2g) \times 4.4]/Y$$

where the new variable $Y$ is the yield on corporate AAA bonds.[5]

What this formula does is modify the earnings multiplier by an amount that varies with the ratio of 4.4 percent divided by the AAA bond yield. This means that when rates rise, value goes down and when rates decrease, value goes up. It is interesting to note that this is similar to a general assumption in the marketplace called the *Fed model*. In general terms, the model says that the yield on 10-year U.S. Treasury bonds should be approximately equal to the average dividend yield on stocks in the S&P 500 index. Consequently, if the bond rate rises, yields must also rise and so the fair prices of stocks must be lower. Conversely, if the bond rate falls, yields must also fall and so the fair prices of stocks must be higher. Currently the 10-year AAA bond yield in the United States is 3.92 percent.[6] Using this for the rate in Graham's second formula gives a value of

$$[4.40 \times (8.5 + 2 \times 7.60) \times 4.4]/3.92 = \$117.05$$

for Johnson & Johnson. According to this new formula, JNJ is even more undervalued than it was using the first formula.

It is not clear how much use Graham made of these formulas. In *Value Investing Made Easy* by Janet Lowe, the author quotes Warren Buffett as saying, "I never use formulas like that. I never thought Ben was at his best when he worked with formulas either." Despite Buffett being critical of Graham's involvement in developing formulas to measure intrinsic value, Buffett's comment does suggest that Graham used these methods in his investment management business.

In discussing the second formula, Graham explained that the intrinsic value calculation used a multiplier that only depended on expected growth and interest rates without any dependence on a company's financial structure and debt position. He did not see a way of extending the formula to allow for companies with a "below par debt position."[7] Hence, to have confidence in the formulas, they need to be restricted to businesses that "meet criteria of financial soundness." Finally, he mentioned that he requires a margin of safety when using this approach. These are all ideas that we return to in Chapter 13.

### Strengths and Weaknesses of Graham's Valuation Formulas

The main strength of Graham's valuation formulas is that they give a quick estimate of intrinsic value, which can then be compared to the share price. The other side of this benefit is that the formulas are very basic. The following is a summary of their strengths followed by a summary of their weaknesses.

>    *Strength 1: Rational use of financial parameters.* The financial parameters used in Graham's valuation formulas are the current earnings per share and their estimated growth rate. The formulas increase the estimate of the intrinsic value when these parameters increase. The second formula includes the AAA bond rate, and the intrinsic value drops when the rate increases.

>    *Strength 2: Easy application.* As for the PEG ratio, Graham's formulas are easy to apply. All they need are the current earnings per share and a forecast of the growth rate of earnings, plus the AAA bond rate for the second formula. These items are readily available via the Internet.

>    *Strength 3: Implicit forecast of growth rate.* By substituting the actual share price of a company into either of the formulas as the intrinsic value, it is possible to invert the calculation to determine a forecast of growth rate.

Turning to the weaknesses of the methods, the main one is that they oversimplify calculations of intrinsic value.

>    *Weakness 1: Too simple.* The first weakness is that Graham's formulas are an oversimplified approach to value. They involve only two or three parameters along with several constants. To be fair, Graham writes that you should only use the formulas with companies that have conservative debt structures, and only with a sufficient margin of safety.

*Weakness 2: No justification for the constants.* The formulas involve the constants 4.4 and 8.5 but there is no justification for them. Presumably Graham tried other numbers but settled on these as giving the best results. He does say that he tried to lower the multiplier to allow for companies with a poor debt position but could not find a satisfactory way of doing it.

## Abnormal Earnings Growth Method

The next method in this chapter is the *abnormal earnings growth method* developed by James Ohlson and Beate Juettner-Nauroth.[8] It is a variation of the dividend discount method, where intrinsic value is the sum of the discounted values of the dividends expected to be paid by a business during its remaining life. Chapter 8 explained that it is more usual to transform the dividend discount formula in different ways so that the new formula does not require any direct forecasts of dividends. One approach was via estimates of the return on equity (ROE) and payout ratio, and a second approach was via estimates of residual income. Apart from the usual problems associated with discount methods such as requiring forecasts to infinity, both methods rely on the validity of the clean surplus relationship. In addition, the ROE approach relies on the forecasts of the payout ratio, which is dangerous since its size is a decision of the board and not a direct outcome of the strength of the business.

The abnormal earnings growth (AEG) method avoids both these problems. It is based on estimates of the growth of later-year abnormal earnings over and above the expected earnings of the business in its first year. The reason I include it in this chapter and not in the chapter on dividend discount methods is that the method can be viewed as a generalization of Graham's formulas. Instead of calculating intrinsic value as a multiple of earnings per share (EPS), in this method intrinsic value is a multiple of EPS plus a correction factor. The other difference is that the earnings used are the expected EPS over the first year, instead of the current EPS.

Let $e_1$ denote the expected EPS in the first year, and suppose that the discount rate is $r$. Assume that the yearly earnings remain constant at the level $e_1$. Then the intrinsic value in terms of the discount value of earnings is

$$V = e_1/(1 + r) + e_1/(1 + r)^2 + e_1/(1 + r)^3 + \cdots = e_1/r$$

where the final equality is an application of the sum on an infinite geometric sum that we have used before. The quantity $e_1/r$ is the capitalization of receiving the earnings $e_1$ each year and is the starting point for the AEG method. With care, the terms in the standard dividend discount formula can be reorganized to give the result:

$$V = e_1/r + z_1/(1 + r)^1 + z_2/(1 + r)^2 + \cdots$$

where each term $z_t$ has the form $z_t = [e_{t+1} + r \times d_t - (1 + r)\, e_t]/r$.

At first the $z_t$ terms may look strange but on closer examination they make sense from the point of view of analyzing the "abnormal" profitability and growth of a business. To see this, rewrite $rz_t$ as

$$rz_t = [e_{t+1} + (r \times d_t)] - [(1 + r) \times e_t]$$
$$= e_{t+1} - [e_t + r \times (e_t - d_t)]$$

The component $e_t + r \times (e_t - d_t)$ is referred to as the benchmark for the earnings in the year $t + 1$ since $e_t$ is the earnings per share in year $t$ and $r \times (e_t - d_t)$ is the profit from the retained earnings $(e_t - d_t)$ invested at rate $r$. Hence $rz_t$ measures the excess of the year $t + 1$ earnings over this benchmark and $z_t$ measures the capitalized value from investing these excess earnings. In keeping with this analysis, the terms $z_t$ are called *abnormal earnings*. (A technical requirement for the validity of the preceding transformation is that $e_t/r^t$ converges to 0 over time.)

## Intrinsic Value and Abnormal Earnings Growth

The dividend discount method can be modified to express intrinsic value in terms of the capitalized value of expected earnings in the first year plus the discounted value of the expected abnormal earnings over the life of the business.

It is always important to understand when particular actions of a business add value. We did this for the residual income valuation (RIV) method and concluded that a business added value to its initial book value whenever earnings always exceeded the profit on the book value at the start of each year invested at the discount rate. In the case of the abnormal earnings growth method, a business adds value to the initial term $e_1/r$ when the $z_t$ terms are positive—in other words when the abnormal earnings are positive. This is the case when the earnings $e_{t+1}$ in year $t + 1$ exceed the benchmark $e_t + [r \times (e_t - d_t)]$ for the earnings. A rearrangement of this requirement shows that a business continues to add value when the growth rate of earnings exceeds the product of the discount rate and the earnings retention rate.

To illustrate this, suppose that the business pays out all its earnings as a dividend. Then the benchmark is $e_t$, so the condition for adding value is simply that earnings grow each year. At the other extreme, suppose that the company pays no dividends. Then $rz_t = e_{t+1} - [(1 + r) \times e_t]$ and so the condition for adding value is that the growth rate of earnings exceeds the discount rate.

As an example, suppose we require a return of 12 percent to invest in the company and suppose the payout ratio is 30 percent. Then the growth rate of earnings must exceed 12 percent times 70 percent, or 8.4 percent for operations of the business to be adding value. If growth is less than this, then value is being destroyed.

### Minimum Earnings Growth

Analysis of the abnormal growth method shows that the operations of the business will add value to the original capitalized earnings term, provided the growth rate of earnings exceeds the product of the discount rate and the earnings retention rate.

If all the earnings are paid out as dividends and there is no growth in the earnings, as just stated, all the abnormal earnings terms are zero. Hence, the intrinsic value is simply the initial term $e/r$, where $e$ is the (constant) earnings term.

### Special Case: Constant Growth of Earnings

In the 1981 annual report of Berkshire Hathaway, Warren Buffett gave a specific example of the valuation of a perpetual bond. Suppose that we have a 7 percent perpetual bond. This means that every year the bondholder receives the same dividend, 7 percent of the face value of the bond. Also suppose that the required rate of return before tax is 14 percent to compensate for the riskiness of the investment. Buffett asserts that such a bond "might be worth fifty cents on the dollar."[9] With a bit of imagination, Buffett's assertion can be seen to be a special case of a formula for intrinsic value for equities that pay out all their earnings as dividends since in this case generally there is no growth in dividends. (This is because there are no residual earnings to use for the growth of the company.) The formula is:

$$V = R/r \times b$$

where

> $R$ is return on equity
> $r$ is the required rate of return
> $b$ is book value[10]

Using Buffett's example, return on equity $R$ is 7 percent and required return $r$ is 14 percent. The book value $b$ corresponds to the face value of the bond, so the formula shows that the value is 50 percent of the book value.

To see why this formula is true, write ROE as earnings per share $e$ divided by book value $b$. Hence, the right-hand side of the preceding formula can be rewritten as $e/r$. This means that we need to show that $V = e/r$. But we saw earlier that this is the no-growth version of the dividend discount method.

The ratio $e/r$ is also the first term in the abnormal earnings growth method, and the remaining abnormal earnings terms are all zero. Hence, the preceding formula is really a restatement of the no-growth version of the standard dividend discount method, as well as a simple version of the abnormal earnings growth method. Simple as it is, it can still provide a quick rule-of-thumb evaluation of a restricted class of equities consisting of companies that have no growth and pay out all their earnings as dividends.

### Strengths and Weaknesses of the Abnormal Earnings Growth Method

Apart from the usual strengths and weaknesses associated with discount methods, the abnormal earnings growth method has some unique strengths. To understand these we start with the observation that the method begins with the intrinsic value calculated as the discount value of expected dividends. There is no mention of earnings. Next, the leading term $e_1/r$ is introduced as the primary estimate of the intrinsic value. However, since this term includes earnings and there are no earnings in the dividend discount formula, the initial term needs to be counterbalanced. This is done by amortizing it piece by piece over the abnormal earnings terms. The final result is precisely the same as the dividend discount calculation as if earnings were never involved. At first, this may look like a roundabout approach. However, there are sound benefits in this approach.

*Strength 1: Quick estimate.* The first term $e_1/r$ of the abnormal earnings growth calculation provides a quick estimate of intrinsic value. All that is required is an estimate of earnings $e_1$ for the next financial year and the required rate of return $r$.

*Strength 2: Value creation.* Looking at what is required for the abnormal earnings terms to be positive shows management what they must do to add value and shows investors what to look out for in deciding whether actions of management are likely to create value or not. Briefly, what is required is that the growth rate of earnings exceeds the product of the discount rate and the earnings retention rate.

*Strength 3: Faster convergence.* Since the series used in the AEG method begins with an estimate of intrinsic value, it has a head start in converging to the final value. This means that generally the same number of terms in the AEG series will be far closer to the final result than the same number of terms in the dividend discount method. Consequently, estimates of earnings and dividends need to be made over fewer years to achieve the same level of accuracy.[11] This is similar to the residual income valuation method described in Chapter 8.

*Strength 4: Clean surplus relationship not required.* Even though the AEG method involves both earnings and dividends estimates, it does not require the clean surplus relationship.

*Strength 5: Forecasts of the dividend payout ratio not required.* Usually when a method involves both earnings and dividends, it is assumed that the dividend payout ratio is fixed and can be estimated. These assumptions are not required for the AEG method.

*Strength 6: Extension of Graham's valuation formulas.* Suppose that the estimated growth rate of EPS for the first year is $g$. This means that the AEG formula can be rewritten as:

$$V = \text{EPS} \times (1 + g)/r + S$$

where $S$ is the sum:

$$S = z_1/(1 + r)^1 + z_2/(1 + r)^2 + \cdots$$

This is similar to Graham's valuation formulas except that instead of the intrinsic value being a multiple of earnings per share, it is a multiple plus a correction term.

The main weaknesses of the AEG method are the standard weaknesses of all the discount methods, namely instability and forecasts over unreasonably long time periods. We will not present all the details again.

*Weakness 1: Modification of the dividend discount method.* The series in the AEG method is just a modified version of the series for the dividend discount method, with both series converging to the same value. This means we still face the same issues discussed in Chapter 8 as to whether it is a reasonable way to calculate intrinsic value. If you would like a reminder of the weaknesses arising from these issues, check the list in Chapter 8.

*Weakness 2: Unstable results.* Even though the series may closely approximate the final value with fewer terms than required for the standard dividend discount method, the final result is still sensitive to small changes in the input variables relating to the expected growth rate of dividends and the discount rate.

## Assets, Earnings Power, and Profitable Growth Methods

In the preceding chapters, we have seen different aspects of measuring the value of stocks. Bruce Greenwald and his co-authors recognize the advantages of using a range of valuation methods in their book

*Value Investing: From Graham to Buffett and Beyond* by describing three methods which they refer to as the asset method, the earnings power method, and the profitable growth method.[12] We briefly outline the methods, putting emphasis on their position in the framework of valuation methods that we have already developed.

The asset method is actually a collection of three valuation methods based on the balance sheet. The first method is the straight book value. The second method is what we referred to as the Graham liquidation value strategy in Chapter 6. The third method is called *reproduction value* and is based on guidelines for modifying the elements in the balance sheet, starting at the top and working down line by line, to reflect the amount "a competitor would have to pay to replace them today, at the currently most efficient way of producing them."[13] There is a major difference between the book value methods described in Chapter 6 and the reproduction cost method. The methods described earlier start with the book value and lower it in different ways. In contrast, the reproduction cost method may actually increase the allowance for certain items and even include items that are not normally in the balance sheet. For example, a proportion of the amount spent on research and development may be included, arguing that a potential competitor would have to spend this amount to "reproduce" an equivalent business.

The second method, *earnings power value*, is single-stage discounted cash flow with care taken to "adjust the reported earnings in order to arrive at a figure that represents the cash the investors can extract from the firm and still leave it functioning as before."[14] It also requires the "selection of a discount rate that reflects both interest rates and the riskiness of the firm relative to other investment alternatives."[15] One of the adjustments suggested is taking an average of special charges for the current and previous four years and deducting them from operating income. Another is to add back a percentage of research and development costs. (The figure of 25 percent is suggested.) A third adjustment is to add back 25 percent of depreciation and amortization costs (rather than the full 100 percent in the usual free cash flow calculations).

Denote these modified earnings by $e$. For reasons that we will see shortly, it is useful to think of $e$ as $C \times R$, where $C$ is the capital in the business and $R$ is return on capital (ROC). (We are using the simple definition of return on capital that only has earnings in the numerator.) If we assume that $e$ does not grow over the years and is discounted by the cost of capital rate $r$, then the earnings power valuation (EPV) is

$$\text{EPV} = e/(1+r) + e/(1+r)^2 + \cdots = e/r = C \times R/r$$

The third method, *growth valuation*, builds on earnings power value in two ways. First, it assumes that there is a fixed rate of growth $g$ for the business. Second, it modifies the earnings term $e$ by removing an estimate of the investment needed by the company to provide for this growth. Under the second assumption, if the cash $C$ grows by the rate $g$, then this removes the amount of $C \times g$ available to existing shareholders. In other words, $e$ needs to be replaced by $e - C \times g$. But this can be rewritten as:

$$e - (C \times g) = C \times (R - g)$$

This means that the present value (PV) allowing for the modified earnings and with a growth rate of $g$ is

$$\text{PV} = [C \times (R-g)]/(1+r) + [C \times (R-g)(1+g)]/(1+r)^2 + \cdots$$

Adding the terms in the series gives the result for PV:

$$\text{PV} = [C \times (R-g)]/(r-g)$$

The expression for PV is the same as that for earnings power value (EPV) except that the growth rate is zero in the expression for EPV.

The idea is to use EPV as the benchmark for the valuation since it does not involve any growth assumptions for the business. Then the greater the amount by which PV exceeds EPV, the greater the margin of safety provided by the growth of the company as compared to the no-growth valuation.

This leads to the primary question: When does growth add value and when does it remove value? In other words, when does PV exceed EPV and when is PV below EPV? The answer is simple: From the perspective of PV and EPV, growth adds value when return on capital $R$ exceeds the discount rate $r$; otherwise, value is destroyed. This makes sense. If we are going to invest in a company, we would want management to be earning a higher rate on their capital than we require from the investment.

## Condition for Growth to Add Value

From the perspective of PV and EPV, growth adds value to a company when return on capital exceeds the discount rate; otherwise, value is destroyed.

Table 12.1 gives examples of the ratio of PV and EPV. It is expressed in terms of two ratios. The first ratio is return on capital $R$ divided by the discount rate $r$. Call it the *capital ratio*. Moving from left to right in the table shows that the growth of the business adds value whenever the ratio $R/r$ exceeds 1.0. The second ratio is the growth rate $g$ divided by the discount rate $r$. Call it the *growth ratio*. When return on equity $R$ exceeds the discount rate $r$, as this second ratio $g/r$ grows, increasing the growth of the business adds more value. In other words, more growth is desirable. In contrast, if $R$ is less than $r$, then any increase in growth of the business relative to the discount rate accelerates its loss of value. In other words, we only want extra growth when the return on capital exceeds the discount rate. This is similar to the conclusion reached in Chapter 8 that required return on equity to exceed the discount rate for a company to add value to its book value.

The strengths and weaknesses of the asset valuation method are similar to the strengths and weaknesses of the balance sheet methods described in Chapter 6, so there is no need to describe them again. However, the asset method does not just rely on the balance sheet (for example, some of the expenditure related to research and development may be included as an asset), so it overcomes some of the stated weaknesses. The strengths and weaknesses of the earnings power and growth method are similar to those of the discounted cash flow methods described in Chapter 7. As explained, the two methods

**Table 12.1** Ratio of PV and EPV

|  |  | Capital Ratio (R/r) |  |  |  |  |  |
|---|---|---|---|---|---|---|---|
|  |  | 0.75 | 1.00 | 1.50 | 2.00 | 2.50 | 3.00 |
| Growth | 0.25 | 0.89 | 1.00 | 1.11 | 1.17 | 1.20 | 1.22 |
| Ratio | 0.50 | 0.67 | 1.00 | 1.33 | 1.50 | 1.60 | 1.67 |
| (g/r) | 0.75 | 0.00 | 1.00 | 2.00 | 2.50 | 2.80 | 3.00 |

are based on a single-stage description of the growth rate. This is the way it is done by Greenwald, et al. However, the authors acknowledge the limitations of assuming a constant growth rate and indicate that the methods would be improved by splitting the analysis into two parts, a period of initial growth and a period of terminal growth. This would be what we referred to as the two-stage model.[16] A special feature of the growth method is that it modifies the earnings of the business by removing the component of the earnings needed to fund the growth of the business.

## Benchmark Valuation Method

As explained in Chapter 6, the price-to-book (P/B) ratio is the price of the equity divided by the book value. Even for well-known companies, examples show that the P/B ratio ranges from under 1.0 to over 40. Kenneth Lee proposed a valuation method, which he called *benchmark valuation*, loosely based on the assumption that over time the P/B ratio for each individual company is mean-reverting.[17] In other words, if the P/B ratio is low compared to previous years, then the price is likely to rise, causing the P/B ratio to rise. In the opposite direction, if the P/B ratio is high compared to previous years, then the price is likely to fall, causing the P/B ratio to fall. The benchmark method also contains an adjustment based on whether the return on equity is high or low compared to the average of previous years. The general idea of the method is to calculate two prices, called the downside target price and the upside target price. If the current price is below the downside target price, it is time to buy. The stock is held until the price moves above the upside target price.

Instead of explaining the method in a general setting, it will be clearer to present it using actual data. As we have often done, we will use Wal-Mart as the example. Table 12.2 shows the data that is necessary to apply the method. The table consists of the return on equity, book value, and the lowest and highest market prices for each of the past 10 financial years. It also includes the average ROE, low price, and high price for each year.

The next step is to calculate three ratios: The *ROE factor* is the current ROE divided by the average ROE; the *low P/B factor* is the average low price divided by the average book value; and the *high P/B factor* is the average high price divided by the average book value. These ratios are displayed in Table 12.3.

**Table 12.2**   Data for the Benchmark Method for Wal-Mart

| Year | ROE | Book Value | Low Price | High Price |
|------|-----|-----------|-----------|------------|
| 2001 | 20.1% | $7.01 | $41.44 | $64.94 |
| 2002 | 19.0% | $7.88 | $41.50 | $59.98 |
| 2003 | 20.4% | $8.95 | $43.72 | $63.94 |
| 2004 | 20.8% | $10.12 | $46.27 | $60.20 |
| 2005 | 20.8% | $11.67 | $51.08 | $61.31 |
| 2006 | 21.1% | $12.77 | $42.31 | $53.74 |
| 2007 | 18.3% | $14.91 | $42.31 | $52.15 |
| 2008 | 19.7% | $16.26 | $42.09 | $51.44 |
| 2009 | 20.5% | $16.52 | $46.25 | $59.23 |
| 2010 | 21.0% | $18.69 | $47.35 | $56.27 |
| Average | 20.17% | $11.79 | $44.43 | $58.32 |

The final step is to calculate what Lee calls the *downside target price* (which is the product of the ROE factor, the low P/B factor, and the book value) and the *upside target price* (which is the product of the ROE factor, the high P/B factor, and the book value). This means that:

$$\text{Downside target price} = 1.04 \times 3.77 \times \$18.69 = \$73.28$$
$$\text{Upside target price} = 1.04 \times 4.95 \times \$18.69 = \$96.22$$

Since the current price of Wal-Mart is around $55, according to this method the stock is highly undervalued. The obvious question is whether this is a reasonable conclusion or whether it is an artifact of the method. The main drivers of the result from this method are

**Table 12.3**   Ratios for the Benchmark Method

| | |
|---|---|
| ROE Factor | 1.04 |
| Low P/B factor | 3.77 |
| High P/B factor | 4.95 |

The first row is the current ROE (21.0%) divided by the average ROE for the past 10 years (20.17%); the second row is the average low price for the past 10 years ($44.43) divided by average book value ($11.79); and the third row is the average high price for the past 10 years ($58.32) divided by average book value ($11.79).

the low and high P/B factors. We would like them to be reasonable estimates of the actual low and high P/B ratios of the company over the past 10 years. In the case of Wal-Mart the current P/B ratio is around 3.0 (assuming the price is $55). Hence, the low and high P/B factors are substantially higher than the current P/B ratio. The reason this happened with Wal-Mart was that the P/B ratios were very high going back from 5 to 10 years. For example, from Table 12.2 the P/B ratios 10 years ago using the low price and the high price were 5.9 and 9.3. If you think that Wal-Mart is going to return to these levels in the future, you would conclude that it is currently undervalued. However, this argument is similar to saying that 10 years ago the P/E ratio of Wal-Mart was over 40 (it reached 46) and so it should reach this again.

This is the difficulty with most ad hoc methods. The methods are developed and refined using historical data, often with exceptional results for theoretical portfolios. However, because their foundations are usually quite weak, after a time the results drop away. As explained in Chapter 2, this phenomenon is typical of data mining methods in technical analysis. In the case of the benchmark method, one way to view it is as a type of data mining method using return on equity and book values instead of the usual price and volume patterns.

## Magic Formula, CAN SLIM, and other Filtering Methods

A number of investment methods in the financial literature require the calculation of different fundamental ratios as a filtering method. They are not valuation methods in the sense that we use the term in this book, since they do not produce a final number that we could refer to as intrinsic value or some other type of valuation index. Nevertheless, it makes sense to couple most of the valuation methods in this book with judicious use of the key ratios in Chapter 5 indicating solid management performance (as measured by ratios such as return on equity and return on capital), not too much debt (as measured by the debt-to-equity ratio), and reasonable short-term viability (as measured by the current ratio and quick ratio). In this section we look briefly at five filtering methods, starting with magic formula investing and a method called CAN SLIM. They can be used on their own or as part of any of the specific valuation methods that we have described.

### Magic Formula Investing

In the book *The Little Book That Beats the Market*, author Joel Greenblatt describes what he calls *magic formula investing*.[18] It consists of putting together a portfolio of stocks that are selected using only two ratios. Greenblatt calls these ratios *return on capital* and *earnings yield*, although their definitions differ from the definitions of these terms given earlier in this book. The definitions used by Greenblatt are more complicated but they still have the same general form. For simplicity, in this section we will follow Greenblatt and refer to them as return on capital and earnings yield even though they differ from our earlier, more standard definitions.

The first ratio, return on capital, measures the performance of management and so we want it to be as high as possible. It was explained in Chapter 5 that return on capital was a key measure of the effectiveness of management in establishing a profitable business. The second ratio, earnings yield, measures the level of earnings compared to the market price, so we want this one to be as high as possible as well. Earnings yield is the inverse of the P/E ratio. As described in Chapter 11, it is a useful tool for making sure that you do not get drawn into buying stocks with excessively high P/E ratios. Looking at the earnings yield was rule 6 for P/E selection. Based on what we have established in earlier chapters, if we were going to base our whole stock selection process on only two ratios, return on capital and earnings yield are natural choices.

Greenblatt outlines how these ratios are used to select stocks. Starting with the largest 2,500 companies, the first step is to rank them from 1 to 2,500 from the highest earnings yield to the lowest. This is akin to favoring stocks with the lowest P/E ratios. Next, the companies are ranked from the highest to the lowest using earnings yield. This is akin to favoring stocks with the most effective management. Finally, the two rankings are added to form a final ranking. The stocks with the smallest ranking number are the ones likely to be the most profitable. Greenblatt declares that back-testing over the past 17 years using a theoretical portfolio chosen using these ratios substantially outperformed the market.

**Return on Capital**    For the magic formula approach, *return on capital* is earnings before interest and taxes (EBIT) divided by tangible capital employed.[19] We have already seen EBIT as part of the calculation of the interest coverage ratio in Chapter 5. *Tangible*

Table 12.4    Return on Capital for Wal-Mart

| Entry | Amount |
|---|---|
| Earnings from continuing operations before interest and taxes (EBIT) (1) | $23,618 |
| Current assets (2) | $48,331 |
| Current liabilities (3) | $55,561 |
| Working capital (4) | ($7,230) |
| Property and equipment, net (5) | $99,544 |
| Property under capital lease, net (6) | $2,763 |
| Net fixed assets (7) | $102,307 |
| Tangible capital employed (8) | $95,077 |
| Return on capital (9) | 24.84% |

Data is in millions of dollars. Working capital (4) is the difference between current assets (2) and current liabilities (3). Net fixed assets (7) is the sum of net property and equipment (5) and net property under capital lease (6). Tangible capital employed (8) is the sum of working capital (4) and net fixed assets (7). The return on capital (9) is the ratio of EBIT (1) and tangible capital employed (8).

*capital employed* is working capital plus net fixed assets. *Working capital*, introduced in Chapter 6, is the difference between current assets and current liabilities. *Net fixed assets* is the value of the fixed assets on the balance sheet less depreciation. Table 12.4 shows the calculation of this variation of return on capital for Wal-Mart for the financial year ending January 31, 2010. The data are taken from the balance sheet and income statement in Chapter 4. The return on capital calculated using this method is 24.84 percent. This is substantially higher than the return on capital in Chapter 5, which was 13.38 percent. However, most of this can be explained in the case of Wal-Mart by the use of EBIT ($23,618 million) instead of net profit ($14,335 million). If EBIT is used in Table 5.2, return on capital jumps to 22.04 percent.

**Earnings Yield**    In the setting of the magic formula approach, *earnings yield* is EBIT divided by *enterprise value*, the market capitalization of the company plus net interest-bearing debt. In a sense, enterprise value is the final amount of money that you would have to pay to buy the entire company. You would need to start by buying the entire company (this is the market capitalization part). Next, you could use the cash in the business to pay off any of the loans. If there are still loans remaining, their net amount is added to the market capitalization. If there is enough cash to pay off the loans, the remaining

**Table 12.5**    Earnings Yield for Wal-Mart

| Entry | Amount |
|---|---|
| Earnings from continuing operations before interest and taxes (EBIT) (1) | $23,618 |
| Share price (2) | $53.131 |
| Shares outstanding (3) | 3,877 |
| Market cap (4) | $205,985 |
| Long-term debt (5) | $33,231 |
| Long-term obligations (6) | $3,170 |
| Long-term debt due within one year (7) | $4,050 |
| Total debt (8) | $42,249 |
| Cash and cash equivalents (9) | $7,907 |
| Enterprise value (10) | $238,107 |
| Earnings yield (11) | 9.88% |

Amounts in millions. Market cap (4) is the product of the current share price (2) and the number of shares outstanding (3). Lines (5), (6) and (7) describe the total debt (8). The enterprise value (10) is market cap (4) plus the total debt (8) less cash and cash equivalents (9). Finally, earnings yield (11) is the ratio of EBIT (1) and enterprise value (10).

cash is subtracted from the market capitalization. Table 12.5 shows the calculation of this variation of earnings yield for Wal-Mart for the financial year ending January 31, 2010. The result is 9.88 percent.

The current P/E ratio for Wal-Mart is around 14 so, as for the previous ratio, the result using Greenblatt's method is significantly higher. Once again, for this company most of the difference can be explained by the use of EBIT instead of net profit.

**Can We Use the Standard Ratios?**    We could look at the definitions of the ratios given by Joel Greenblatt and compare them with the standard definitions. After that, we could argue each line in the definitions to see whether the changes are likely to make the ratios more effective or not. For example, Greenblatt chooses to use EBIT instead of net profit to avoid "distortions arising from differences in tax rates and debt levels."[20] However, interest and taxes are genuine expenses just as much as the wages bill, so it would seem to make more sense to keep them in. Instead of debating these points one by one, if you are attracted to Greenblatt's approach, or are simply curious, a more practical approach would be to mimic what he does using the standard definitions. If the results are successful, you have a much simpler investment strategy since the values of the standard ratios are either readily available or easily calculated from available data. It may be that the complications introduced by Greenblatt are not really necessary and that the standard versions of return on capital and earnings yield perform just as well.

## CAN SLIM Investing

What if we analyzed over many years stocks that had performed exceptionally well? What if we managed to isolate seven characteristics of these stocks? Would it mean that if we could find companies today that have these characteristics they would perform exceptionally well in the future? William O'Neil thought so and set himself the task of finding such characteristics, looking at companies going back to 1953. He first wrote about his findings in his book *How to Make Money in Stocks*, published in 1988.[21] He called the method CAN SLIM since each letter in the words stands for a rule based on one of these characteristics. Since 1988, O'Neil's book has been republished a number of times with updates of the descriptions of the seven rules.

The method is a combination of fundamental analysis and technical analysis. In fact, a substantial portion of O'Neil's book is on technical analysis with headings such as "How to Spot a Saucer-with-Handle Price Pattern" and "Recognizing a Double-Bottom Price Pattern." In the 1995 edition, at one point there is a series of over 100 price charts with a recommendation to "study them carefully, and refer to them often."[22] The 2009 addition has added a new first chapter consisting of an extra 100 pages of charts. Overall, the CAN SLIM method is outside the theme of this book. Nevertheless, I have included it for two reasons: (1) The method is often referred to in discussions of the stock market, and (2) more importantly, the first two rules concern the importance of the growth and stability of earnings, reinforcing what we talked about in Chapter 11. In addition, although not part of the original description, the 2009 edition includes a requirement of a "big return on equity" for the second rule.[23]

The following is a brief description of the rules described in the 2009 edition of the book.

$C =$ *Current quarterly earnings.* The first rule is to choose stocks that have earnings over the current quarter at least 25 percent to 50 percent higher than the quarterly earnings one year ago.

$A =$ *Annual earnings increases.* The second rule puts emphasis on the growth and stability of earnings. O'Neil says that we should "select stocks with 25 to 50 percent and higher annual earnings growth rates."[24] In the 1995 edition he explains why: "Owning common stock is just the same as being a part owner in a business. And who wants to own part of an establishment showing no growth?"[25] Also, as mentioned earlier, this rule now has a requirement of a high return on equity. Finally, O'Neil has a method for measuring stability of the growth of earnings, emphasizing the importance of "the stability and consistency of annual earnings growth over the past three years."[26]

$N =$ *New products and management.* O'Neil explains that "it takes something new to produce a startling advance in the price of a stock."[27] It could be new products and services or it could be new management. It could even be a major development within the company's industry.

$S =$ *Supply and demand.* The general idea of this rule is to look for stocks that have a small capitalization and a relatively small number of shares outstanding. It is admitted, however, that sometimes large-cap stocks outperform small-cap stocks. It is also suggested that low debt to equity is usually better, something that we said in Chapter 5 on ratios.

$L=$ *Leader or laggard.* When deciding to invest in a particular sector, the idea with this rule is to invest in the top two or three stocks, those that have shown the strongest price movement.

$I =$ *Institutional sponsorship.* The method requires that the stock be owned by "at least a few institutional investors with better-than-average performance records and that have added institutional owners in recent quarters."[28]

$M =$ *Market indexes or market direction.* The basic idea of this rule is to invest when the major market indexes such as the Dow Jones Industrial Average and the S&P 500 are heading upward. This is where technical analysis enters in a dominant way, with the stated requirement that daily charts of the main indexes must watched carefully every day.

### Haugen Factor Model

CAN SLIM is based on the opinions of William O'Neil of the best characteristics of successful stocks, with the assumption that stocks with these characteristics will be successful in the future. Robert Haugen, working with Nardin Baker, took a more rigorous approach to isolating the most profitable characteristics. He meticulously analyzed the impact of 71 factors on the returns of stocks on a month-by-month basis.[29] The factors were in the areas of risk, liquidity, stock price relative to several measures of corporate income and cash flow, profitability, stock return history, analyst estimates, and macroeconomic and sector influences. The goal was to find which of the factors at the end of a month had the most effect on stock performance over the following month.[30]

At the end of each month, the weights of the factors were recalculated and used to rank the stocks from those that are likely to be the highest performers for the next month down to those likely to be the lowest performers. These were divided into 10 deciles, with decile 1 containing the stocks with the lowest expected performance and decile 10 containing the stocks with the highest expected performance.

Some of the factors that were the most important in the positive direction were the earnings-to-price ratio, return on equity, and the book-to-price ratio. According to the study, this means that stocks with higher earnings-to-price ratios (or lower P/E ratios), higher return on equity, and higher book-to-price ratio (or lower P/B ratios) in one month were likely to have higher performance in the next month compared to the market. In the opposite direction, some of the factors that were the most important were the one-month and two-month excess return. This means that the more a stock outperformed the market over the previous one and two months, the less likely it was to perform well over the next month.

According to Haugen and Baker, over the period 1979 to 1993 the stocks in decile 10 had an average annual return of 30.9 percent compared to an average annual return of –4.5 percent for stocks in decile 1. The average annual return for the market at the time was 16.7 percent. From the perspective of individual investors, criticisms of this study, as for many academic studies, are the effect of transaction costs on performance and the requirement of holding a very large portfolio. When restricting the strategy to the 1,000 largest U.S. stocks, limiting the number of transactions and factoring in transaction costs, Haugen and Baker reported that the annualized return of the maximum return portfolio above the market index was more modest, approximately 4 percent.[31]

## Earnings Power Charts

In Chapter 6 we saw a number of valuation methods developed by Benjamin Graham based on different modifications of the balance sheet. Hewitt Heiserman Jr. provides a filtering method based on modifying the income statement.[32] The result is two variations of earnings per share called *defensive profit* and *enterprising profit*.

Heiserman starts by renaming as *accrual profit* the earnings per share found in the income statement. Next, he introduces defensive profit as a variation of free cash flow per share. The main steps in its calculation are subtracting the investment in fixed capital and increases in working capital from the revenue of the company.

Enterprising profit is a variation of economic value added (EVA). The first main step is to remove outlays for research and development and advertising from the list of expenses in the income statement and treat them as assets. More generally, the idea is to estimate the intangible growth-producing initiatives of the company and treat them as assets instead of expenses. This will generally increase the revenue. The second main step is to estimate the cost of the company's capital (equity plus debt) using the weighted average cost of capital introduced in Chapter 7 and treat this cost as an expense.

The requirement is that both the defensive earnings and the enterprising earnings should be positive and increasing over time. When the yearly results are placed as points on a two-dimensional chart called an *earnings power chart*, the idea is to look for companies that have an upward-trending sequence of points. Heiserman explains that "this two-dimensional approach will guide you toward companies with authentic earnings power and away from those that have poor fundamentals—even if the accrual income statement looks impressive."[33]

## Clean Surplus Return on Equity

At various times we have used the clean surplus relationship to derive and modify various valuation methods. Joseph Belmonte makes the relationship the center of a filtering method.[34] The idea is to start with the book value of any company that you are interested in at a specified year in the past, say 1987, and to build up the book value on a year-by-year basis using the clean surplus relationship. In other words, for each year after 1987 the book value is the book value of the previous year plus earnings less dividends. This modified book value is used as the denominator in the calculation of return on equity. The overall method is to calculate this modified return on equity for a range of stocks and to choose those with the highest ratio.

## Option-Pricing Methods of Valuation

Suppose a company has assets of $500 million and debts of $250 million payable in 10 years at the rate of 8 percent. What would be a fair price to pay now to have the right, but not the obligation, to buy the company in 10 years? With only this data it is impossible to answer the question. Surprisingly, however, with only a few more facts it is possible to use option-pricing theory to get an answer.

First, note that to buy the company the purchaser will have to pay at least $250 million in 10 years since to get control of the assets the bondholders will have to be paid first. Hence, if the assets of the company were less than $250 million in 10 years, the purchaser would not proceed with the transaction. The potential buyer would lose the entire payment. Alternatively, if the assets of the firm are above $250 million, say $700 million, then the potential purchaser obtains a company with a value of $450 million. This is because on taking control of the company, the debt of $250 million could be paid, leaving a profit of $450 million.

Phrased like this it sounds like a European option, and in fact, this is precisely what it is. It is a European call option with price $500 million and strike $250 million. Assume that the interest rate is 8 percent, the time period is 10 years, and the volatility is 15 percent. This means that the yearly standard deviation of the assets is 15 percent of $500 million, which is $75 million. The standard Black-Scholes formula shows that the fair price of this option is $387.7 million.[35]

This is a simple application of what is referred to as *real option analysis*. These methods assist in making budgeting and capital allocation decisions while allowing for real-world uncertainty. Instead of using DCF methods or net present value methods to make decisions regarding, for example, investing in a new project, many believe that the approach of real option theory provides a more realistic valuation and analysis. This approach is not really appropriate for businesses that are already publicly traded but is more relevant when valuing risky projects, particularly in the mining and petroleum areas.

## The Bottom Line

1. Benjamin Graham was active in deriving new valuation methods. Two variations of an intrinsic value formula are a simple combination of current earnings per share, a growth estimate, and the bond rate (for the second variation). Their extreme simplicity means that they are probably of limited use.

2. The abnormal growth model is a variation of the dividend discount method for stock valuation. It can provide a guide to what actions of a company are needed in order to create value. Other methods are the benchmark method of Kenneth Lee, magic formula investing by Joel Greenblatt, CAN SLIM by William O'Neil, factor analysis by Robert Haugen, earnings power charts by Hewitt Heiserman, and clean surplus return on equity by J. B. Farwell.

3. Real option theory is a specialized area for assisting in decision making by valuing competing projects under more realistic conditions involving uncertainty.

# CHAPTER 13

## Forecasting and the Three Most Important Words in Investing

*The three most important words in investing are margin of safety.*
—Benjamin Graham[1]

*We insist on a margin of safety in our purchase price. If we calculate the value of a common stock to be only slightly higher than its price, we're not interested in buying. We believe this margin-of-safety principle, so strongly emphasized by Ben Graham, to be the cornerstone of investment success.*

—Warren Buffett[2]

Benjamin Graham continually used the phrase "margin of safety" throughout his book *Security Analysis*, but it was not until *The Intelligent Investor* that he talked about it as the "central concept of investment."[3] He made it the sole focus of the final chapter of the book, declaring that if he had to "distill the secret of sound investment into three words," then those words would be "margin of safety."[4] In broad terms, a margin of safety is a buffer against forecasts that end up not being met by the performance of the company. It is also a buffer against the market not responding to performance levels of a business to the degree that you anticipated.

Margins of safety are usually applied in an informal way. In contrast, in this chapter, in keeping with our use of quantitative valuation methods, we emphasize the use of carefully constructed and measured margins of safety. Careful use of margins of safety is like stress testing an investment before actually making a purchase. We can now be more confident of a favorable outcome because we have allowed for a type of worst-case scenario. As Nassim Nicholas Taleb said, "It is not the estimate or the forecast that matters so much as the degree of confidence with the opinion."[5] The main discussion centers on earnings forecasts in valuation models and how a systematic use of a margin of safety can assist in removing substantial risk. We also touch on margins of safety for P/E ratios and dividend payout ratios. Overall, the goal of this chapter is to show practical steps to finding the double-dip stocks described in Chapter 11, stocks that have reliable growth in both earnings per share and the P/E ratio. This means increasing profits for the business, translating into increasing profits for the investor.

## Analysis of Growth Rates

As explained in Chapter 11, forecasting earnings and earnings per share (EPS) is a major part of the role of professional market analysts employed by financial institutions, brokerage houses, and mutual funds. For example, almost every company listed on the New York Stock Exchange, the NASDAQ, or the American Stock Exchange has at least one analyst following the company and making forecasts about its earnings. For the major companies there are sizable groups of 20 or more following them. The forecasts may be for the earnings per share to be announced at the next earnings release, or they may be forecasts for the next full financial year or the one after. Other forecasts are for the average growth rate over the next five years. The forecasts of the analysts in the leading financial firms are averaged and reported on the major investment web sites. This average is referred to as a *consensus estimate*. As examples, consensus estimates for Microsoft use forecasts from about 25 analysts while consensus estimates for Wal-Mart use forecasts from about 17 analysts.

Even though the forecasts are made by professionals and published by large financial institutions, they are still of questionable accuracy. Everything would be simple if we could just plug these estimates into a price ratio method or other methods for calculating intrinsic value. There is just one problem: Careful large-scale academic studies show that these forecasts are highly unreliable. We look at some of these studies not simply for curiosity, but to help set benchmarks to measure the success of the margin of safety methods later in this chapter.

## Accuracy of Analyst Forecasts

One person who has looked at analyst forecasts in detail is David Dreman. In his book *Contrarian Investment Strategies* he describes the results of studies with Michael Berry that looked at 94,251 quarterly earnings estimates over the years 1973 to 1996.[6] The estimates were made for earnings to be reported at the end of the current quarter, and analysts could revise their estimates up to two weeks before the reporting date. Before a stock could be included in the study, it had to have estimates by at least four separate analysts. The study measured errors as the difference between the actual earnings and the forecast earnings divided by the absolute value of the actual earnings. For instance, if the actual EPS was $2.50 and the forecast EPS was $2.00, the error would be calculated as $(2.50 - 2.00)/250$, which is 20 percent. The average absolute error for the entire 94,251 estimates was 44 percent.[7]

Dreman and Berry also analyzed the data by measuring how often forecasts were within a reasonable range of the actual value. They found that only about one in four forecasts were accurate to a level of plus or minus 5 percent. When the required accuracy was relaxed to plus or minus 10 percent, only 46.8 percent forecasts fell within the interval. Finally, only 58.3 percent of forecasts were within the error band of plus or minus 15 percent. In other words, nearly half of the current-quarter forecasts were wrong by 15 percent or more.

Another part of the results showed that the forecasts were heavily weighted toward optimism. In other words, the average negative earnings surprise was significantly larger (in absolute terms) than the average positive earnings surprise. Over the period from 1973 to 1996, the average positive earnings surprise was 23.7 percent compared to −76.5 percent for the average negative earnings surprise. Furthermore, these percentages hardly varied whether the years were periods of business expansion or business recession.

Dreman and Berry's results applied to forecasts for the next quarterly earnings release, so they were for periods of three months or less. The shortness of this period means that, even if accurate, they are really of little use for the valuation methods we discussed in

Chapter 11, which generally required a period of five years or more. We could hope that for longer periods the accuracy does not get any worse. Unfortunately, we will see that this is not the case.

Consider five-year forecasts. Many web sites and financial institutions make them readily available. Instead of forecasting the actual earnings, as was the case for the study just described, the usual way is to forecast the average annual growth. George Bulkley and Richard Harris carried out a study looking at the accuracy of 4,201 five-year forecasts on the earnings growth of U.S. companies over the period 1982 to 1989.[8] They could not show that there was any correlation between the forecasts of the analysts and the actual growth of earnings. Putting it another way, there was no statistically significant evidence that the five-year forecast of an individual analyst for a particular company was any better than simply taking the average forecast over all years and all analysts.

There are a number of attempts at explaining these results. I think that three stand out. The first is that much of the error in forecasting can be attributed to the tendency of analysts to follow the lead of others—the behavioral problem of herding.[9] The second is that on average, analysts are too optimistic with their forecasts. The third is that they are particularly optimistic when the earnings of the company are hard to predict; in other words, analysts are more optimistic when they get poor results in the past.[10] Since these are behavioral biases, it is clear that we need to look elsewhere to achieve the goal of reliable forecasts. The remainder of this section is devoted to developing and analyzing objective forecasting methods that can be easily implemented on large databases of companies.

### Unstable Growth of Earnings

One of the problems is that many companies are in a volatile industry, in a precarious financial state, or particularly vulnerable to changes in the general economy. This means that any forecasts that turn out to be accurate are more likely to be the result of good fortune rather than careful analysis. One example is Ford Motor Company, shown in Figure 13.1. Evidently, at any stage in the past 11 years it would have been extremely difficult to make any reliable earnings forecasts, no matter how much analysis was carried out.

Another example is Crown Holdings, the world's leading producer of steel and aluminum cans for food, beverage, household,

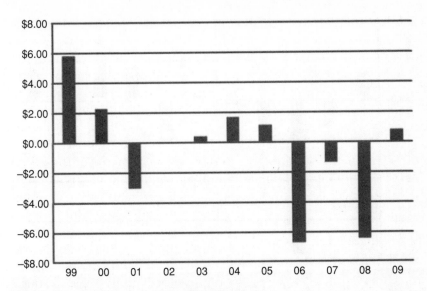

**Figure 13.1**    Earnings per Share for Ford Motor Company

The bars show the earnings per share for each year for the 11 financial years ending December 1999 through December 2009.

and other consumer products. Formerly called the Crown Cork & Seal Company, the company started with the invention of the crown cap for bottled carbonated beverages in 1891. As of December 31, 2009, the company operated 136 plants located in 41 countries, employing over 21,000 people. If you first heard about a business with such basic, indispensable products, you might think that its growth in earnings would be completely stable year after year. Yet, for a variety of reasons, some out of its control (such as world prices for steel and aluminum) and some under its control (such as past very high debt levels and paying too much for various related companies before being forced to sell at a loss), its growth has been unstable, as seen in Figure 13.2. As for Ford, clearly it would be very hard to make reliable forecasts about its growth over, say, the next financial year, let alone for five years or more.

This problem is even more serious for discounted cash flow methods since the forecasts have to be made for an indefinite period. We could feel sorry for analysts instructed by their firms to provide forecasts for companies such as Ford Motor Company or Crown Holdings. Fortunately, there is a way out of this problem for investors. There are many thousands of companies on the major exchanges

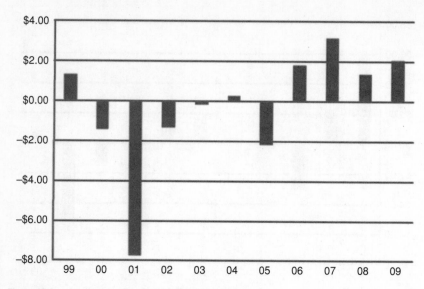

**Figure 13.2**    Earnings per Share for Crown Holdings

The bars show the earnings per share for each year for the 11 financial years ending December 1999 through December 2009.

in the United States and around the world. As investors, we can keep moving from company to company until we meet those that are more amenable to growth forecasts. We are not assigned any particular companies. If it looks like it is going to be difficult to make reliable forecasts for a company we simply move on. Admittedly, this opens up a different problem: How do we recognize those companies about which we can make reliable forecasts, and how do we make those forecasts?

We next examine three characteristics of such companies. The first two, stable growth in earnings and stable return on equity, are based on histories of financial data taken from the financial statements. The third one, strong economic moat, is based on the ability of the company to protect itself from competitors.

### Stability of Growth in Earnings

Figures 13.1 and 13.2 showed companies with highly unstable historical earnings. As explained, it is clear that making reliable forecasts about their future would be extremely difficult. This does not mean that it would not be profitable to buy shares in the companies, just that such a purchase would be speculative. In contrast, Figures 13.3

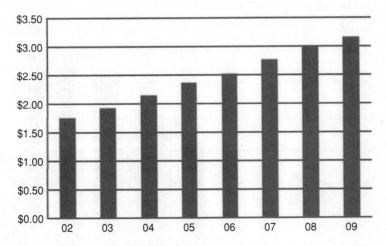

**Figure 13.3**   Earnings per Share for Kellogg Company

The bars show the earnings per share for each year for the eight financial years ending December 2002 through December 2009.

and 13.4 tell a completely different story. Figure 13.3 shows the earnings per share for Kellogg Company, the well-known manufacturer and marketer of ready-to-eat cereal and other convenience foods. Its products are manufactured in 18 countries and marketed in more than 180 countries around the world. Some of its brands are Kellogg's, Keebler, Cheez-It, Murray, Austin, and Famous Amos.

Figure 13.4 shows a similar pattern of growth and stability for the earnings of FactSet Research Systems Inc., a provider of financial data, information, and analytics for the global investment community.

Evidently the growth in both cases is highly stable. It is reasonable to investigate whether the growth of stable companies in the future tends to be similar to the growth they achieved in the past. The good news is that this is the case: For these companies, generally the past growth rate is a good indicator of the future growth rate. There are two ways to examine this. The first would be to look at the earnings histories of companies one by one and pick out those that had stable growth up to few years ago. Then check whether this growth rate of earnings was a reliable guide to recent growth. The problem is that it would be very time consuming and hard to come up with rigorous findings either for or against the continuation of stable growth. The second way is to automatically scan databases of thousands of companies, looking for stable growth in earnings

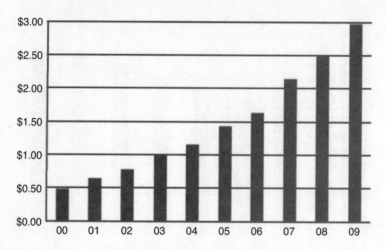

**Figure 13.4**    Earnings per Share for FactSet Research Systems

The bars show the earnings per share for each year for the 10 financial years ending August 2000 through August 2009.

over different periods. Then systematically compare the relationship between forecasts of earnings (using past growth rates of earnings) and the actual earnings.

To implement and test this second method, I developed a function called STAEGR® (pronounced *stay-ger*).[11] It measures the stability or consistency of the growth of historical earnings per share from year to year, expressed as a percentage in the range 0 to 100 percent. When applied to data over any number of years, high STAEGR corresponds to high stability and low STAEGR corresponds to low stability. STAEGR of 100 percent signifies complete stability, meaning that the data is changing by exactly the same percentage each year.[12] The function has the feature of adjusting for data that could overly distort the result, such as one-off extreme data points, negative data, and data near zero. It also puts more emphasis on recent data.

While STAEGR measures the stability or consistency of the growth of earnings, it is independent of the actual growth. This means that whether a company has high or low stability of earnings is independent of whether the earnings are growing or contracting. In this way the two measures, stability and growth, complement each other in describing qualities of historical earnings. Table 13.1 shows the stability of the earnings per share of a selection of companies over

**Table 13.1**   Stability and Growth for Selected Companies

| Company | Ticker | STAEGR | Growth |
|---|---|---|---|
| Ford Motor | F | 20.21% | –35.84% |
| Crown Holdings | CCK | 18.95% | 24.55% |
| United Technologies | UTX | 97.45% | 13.74% |
| FactSet Research | FDS | 97.37% | 21.75% |
| Walgreen | WAG | 95.10% | 13.26% |
| Microsoft | MSFT | 85.46% | 11.23% |
| Wal-Mart | WMT | 97.79% | 9.79% |

Stability as measured by STAEGR and average annual earnings growth for a selection of companies over their most recent 10 financial years.

the past 10 years as measured by STAEGR. It also shows the average annual growth over the same period.[13]

### Analysis of Forecasting Using STAEGR

Over the years, I have carried out many studies using STAEGR as a basis for making more accurate forecasts of earnings. The following is a description of a study that I carried out using annual data of companies listed on the NYSE, AMEX, or NASDAQ ranging from 1999 to 2009.

The first step was to select companies for which earnings per share and sales per share annual data was available for the seven financial years ending in 1999 through to 2005. This dropped the number of companies to approximately 2,800 from about 5,000. (When we talk about, for example, the financial year 2005, we mean the financial year ending in 2005. For example, depending on the company, it could be the financial year starting July 1, 2004, and ending June 30, 2005, or it could be the financial year starting January 1, 2005 and ending December 31, 2005.)

The second step was to measure the stability and the historical growth rates of earnings and sales over the six data points 1999 to 2004 (which is actually a five-year period). The companies were then ranked from the highest stability of earnings to the lowest. Those companies with STAEGR above 85 percent were selected, and the earnings growth rate over the years 1999 to 2004 was used to forecast the earnings for the following financial year.

The third step was to calculate the percentage error between the forecast and the actual earnings, and to analyze these errors.

Let EST(EPS) and ACT(EPS) denote the estimated earnings per share and the actual earnings per share for 2005. When the actual earnings are very small, then proportional errors can be very large and distort the results. For example, if the estimated earnings were $2.10 and the company actually reported $2.00, the percentage error would be 5 percent. However, if the estimated earnings were $0.20 and the company reported only $0.01, the error would be 1,900 percent. David Dreman recalculated the numbers in the studies mentioned earlier by removing companies that reported quarterly earnings in the plus or minus 10 cents range. The average forecast error for the next quarter was 23 percent, which Dreman described as "more than quadruple the size that market pros believe could set off a major price reaction."[14]

Another approach is to add a small amount to the divisor. This will only have a marginal effect for most of the data and will lessen the effect of extreme percentage errors when the actual earnings are very small. Lex Hulberts and Russell Fuller use this approach and add 50 cents to the divisor.[15] Since they are using annual data and Dreman is using quarterly data, these adjustments are similar in size. With this in mind, we define the forecast error (FE) as:

$$FE = \frac{[ACT(EPS) - EST(EPS)]}{[|ACT(EPS)| + 0.50]}$$

Notice that FE is positive when there is a positive earnings surprise, and negative when there is a negative earnings surprise.

Finally, the preceding three steps were repeated for the financial years ending in 2006 through to 2009. This meant that the study involved separate forecasts for the years 2005 through 2009. Each year the original database consisted of approximately 5,000 companies. Of these, about 480 had the required number of years of data and STAEGR above 85 percent, while about 275 had STAEGR above 90 percent.

The result is that over the five years, the companies with stability over 90 percent had a median absolute error of 13.72 percent, and those with stability over 95 percent had a median absolute error of 16.17 percent. In contrast, looking at the entire range of companies, the error was 41.13 percent. In other words, even forecasting over a full 12 months instead of just the next quarter (which would mean that the average length of the forecast period would be even less than three months), the accuracy achieved by first filtering for high stability using STAEGR is considerably better than consensus estimates described earlier by Dreman.

Closer analysis shows that this is not a complete comparison between the stability approach to earnings forecasts and forecasts provided by analysts. For instance, the study cited by Dreman used a different database. Also Dreman used means whereas my study used medians. The reason for this was that results with means can be distorted by a small number of outliers. Another difference is that Dreman's study looked at forecasts for the remainder of each quarter over 14 years, whereas the latter study covered only five years but looked at forecasts over a full 12 months. It did, however, include forecasts over 2008 and 2009, a time when many companies had very large unexpected drops in earnings. In addition, if analysts were asked to make forecasts only for high-stability companies, then it is likely that they would be more accurate than shown by existing studies that covered all companies.

Despite these differences, the study indicated that STAEGR provides an automated method for obtaining forecasts that have practical reliability, do not require any outside opinions, and are free from herding and other behavioral biases. Later in this chapter we build on this method using margins of safety to improve the reliability and usefulness of the forecasts obtained using this approach.

### Stability of Return on Equity

It was stated in Chapter 5 that, assuming the clean surplus relationship, whenever return on equity is constant, then the growth rate of earnings each year is approximately equal to return on equity times the dividend retention rate. For example, if a company pays no dividends, the growth rate of earnings and return on equity will match very closely. This gives us another way of approaching growth forecasts: Look for those companies with fairly constant return on equity and dividend retention ratio (or payout ratio), and use this to assist in forecasting the growth rate of earnings. Of course, return on equity is defined in terms of earnings (and equity), and so it is not that return on equity actually implies information about the growth of earnings. Rather, understanding the relationship between return on

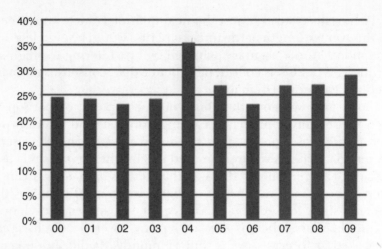

**Figure 13.5**    Return on Equity for FactSet

Over 10 years the return on equity has been very stable. Apart from 2004, it ranges from a low of 23.1 percent to a high of 28.9 percent.

equity and earnings growth is another example of how the measures of business performance fit together.

With this in mind, it is often possible to get more evidence for any forecast of earnings by analyzing return on equity. If both the return on equity and the payout ratio are stable, then (assuming that the clean surplus relationship is valid) we will have a stable growth in earnings which we can closely estimate. For example, Figure 13.5 shows the return on equity for FactSet Research Systems for the past 10 years. Just as Figure 13.4 showed stable growth in earnings, Figure 13.5 shows a consistent level in its return on equity. The next step is to see how they fit together.

Table 13.2 shows the return on equity, the payout ratio, and the earnings per share for FactSet for the past 10 financial years. The average return on equity for FactSet was 26.4 percent and the average payout ratio was 16.9 percent. This suggests that the growth rate of earnings should be around 26.4% × (1 − 16.9%), or 21.93 percent. The actual average annual growth rate for FactSet was 21.75 percent, almost a perfect match between the estimated growth rate and the actual growth rate.

Agreement between the direct measurement of the growth rate of earnings per share and calculations via the return on equity and retention ratio is generally not as high as we saw for FactSet. In

**Table 13.2**   Data for FactSet Research Systems

| Year | ROE | Payout | EPS |
|------|-----|--------|-----|
| Aug. 2000 | 24.5% | 22% | $0.49 |
| Aug. 2001 | 24.2% | 14% | $0.64 |
| Aug. 2002 | 23.1% | 15% | $0.78 |
| Aug. 2003 | 24.2% | 14% | $0.99 |
| Aug. 2004 | 35.3% | 15% | $1.15 |
| Aug. 2005 | 26.8% | 14% | $1.43 |
| Aug. 2006 | 23.1% | 13% | $1.64 |
| Aug. 2007 | 26.8% | 14% | $2.14 |
| Aug. 2008 | 26.9% | 22% | $2.50 |
| Aug. 2009 | 28.9% | 26% | $2.97 |
| Average or growth | 26.4% | 16.9% | 21.75% |

some cases, the actual growth rate of earnings is less than anticipated using the clean surplus relationship. This happens because there is *leakage* in the relationship, meaning that there are entries in the equity statement that have a negative effect on the equity. Examples are pension liability adjustments and share buybacks. Such items are not permitted to be called expenses since then they would be in the income statement. Just the same, they have a similar effect on equity. In Chapter 4, I referred to them as off-income-statement transactions. Because of items such these, the equity at the end of each financial year is not as high as expected from the clean surplus relationship in terms of equity at the start of the year and earnings and dividends over the year. This, in turn, makes the ROE higher. Hence, even if the return on equity stays at the same level over the years, the earnings do not grow as fast as expected from a simple analysis of the ROE and retention rate.

Consider Wal-Mart. The data in Table 4.7 in Chapter 4 shows that for the past three financial years, the equity at the end of the year was less than expected from the clean surplus relationship. So it is likely that growth in earnings will be less than anticipated from ROE and the retention rate. Over the past five years, Wal-Mart had an average ROE of 20.1 percent and an average retention ratio of 75.0 percent. This would indicate that the growth in earnings over the past five years should be around 15.0 percent. In fact, as foreshadowed, the average growth was significantly lower at 10.4 percent. However, on the positive side, when there is consistent return on equity and a consistent retention ratio, then the growth rate of earnings is usually stable, making it easier to forecast growth with more confidence.

**Changes in Return on Equity**   When the return on equity is not constant, then the way this change shows up in the growth of earnings per share is more complicated. Roughly speaking, small increases in return on equity are exaggerated by large increases in earnings. Similarly, small drops in return on equity are exaggerated by large decreases in earnings. (The actual formula is given in Appendix A.)

Table 13.3 shows the expected growth of earnings per share from one year to the next assuming the clean surplus relationship. The rows show the return on equity for the first year and the columns show the return on equity for the second year. It is assumed that the dividend payout ratio is 10 percent. For example, suppose that return on equity is 10 percent for both years. By the original formula, the growth in earnings per share would be approximately 10 percent times 90 percent which is 9 percent. The exact growth rate is actually 9.9 percent, as shown in the table. If the return on equity jumps to 15 percent in the second year, the earnings would be expected to increase by 73.4 percent. In the opposite direction, if the return on equity drops to 7.5 percent, the earnings would be expected to drop by −19.6 percent.

**Table 13.3**   Growth in Earnings per Share Related to Return on Equity

|  |  | Return on Equity Year 2 | | | | | |
|---|---|---|---|---|---|---|---|
|  |  | 7.5% | 10.0% | 12.5% | 15.0% | 17.5% | 20.0% |
|  | 7.5% | 7.2% | 46.5% | 87.8% | 131.2% | 177.0% | 225.2% |
|  | 10.0% | −19.6% | 9.9% | 40.8% | 73.4% | 107.7% | 143.9% |
| Return | 12.5% | −35.7% | −12.1% | 12.7% | 38.7% | 66.2% | 95.1% |
| on | 15.0% | −46.4% | −26.7% | −6.1% | 15.6% | 38.5% | 62.6% |
| Equity | 17.5% | −54.0% | −37.2% | −19.5% | −0.9% | 18.7% | 39.4% |
| Year 1 | 20.0% | −59.8% | −45.1% | −29.6% | −13.3% | 3.9% | 22.0% |
|  | 22.5% | −64.3% | −51.2% | −37.4% | −22.9% | −7.7% | 8.4% |
|  | 25.0% | −67.8% | −56.0% | −43.7% | −30.6% | −16.9% | −2.4% |

Suppose a company has a dividend payout ratio of 10 percent. The table shows the growth in earnings per share that could be anticipated using the clean surplus relationship, assuming that there is a change in the return on equity. The rows show the return on equity for the first year and the columns show the return on equity for the second year.

**Warning: Watch for Increases in ROE**

Watch out when growth in earnings is accompanied by growth in return on equity. Even though growth in ROE is desirable, increase in ROE can give a one-off boost to the growth rate of earnings, which may mean that the growth is not sustainable. Start with the assumption that return on equity is not going to increase any further and see what this implies about future earnings growth.

## Economic Moats

Repeatedly Warren Buffett talks about the importance of economic moats. For example, recently he described how he does not judge the performance of his investments by what their prices do during the year. Rather he applies two tests:

> The first test is improvement in earnings, with our making due allowance for industry conditions. The second test, more subjective, is whether their "moats"—a metaphor for the superiorities they possess that make life difficult for their competitors—have widened during the year.[16]

An *economic moat* is a sustainable competitive advantage that ensures that customers keep coming back for the products or services provided by the company. A strong economic moat means protection against changes in such areas as the buying habits of consumers, existing and new competitors, government legislation, and the general economy. Other benefits of a strong economic moat are that it allows the company to increase prices at least as fast as the rate of inflation without decreasing sales, and it is a buffer against poor management decisions.

### Economic Moat

An economic moat is a sustainable competitive advantage that ensures that customers keep coming back for the products or services provided by the company. A strong economic moat helps to give extra confidence in continued growth and profit levels.

The great advantage of a strong economic moat is that we can have more confidence about earnings forecasts. This is particularly true when coupled with the stability approach described earlier. With a history of stable growth in earnings and a strong economic moat, we have extra assurance that the growth will continue into the future. Types of economic moats include:

- *Geographical.* Quarries and shopping malls control large areas around them, making it expensive for any competitors to get started.
- *Location.* Walgreens will spend extra millions of dollars to get the right location.
- *Brand name.* Large numbers of people will choose by name instead of generic products. Coca-Cola is a prime example.
- *Licenses or patents.* Drug companies spend billions of dollars to get patentable drugs.
- *Cost of entry.* Some industries are exorbitantly expensive for a company to enter as a competitor. Computer chip manufacturing is an example. There are only two major companies, Intel and AMD.
- *Trapdoor.* This is an attribute of a company that makes it easy to start using its products and services, but difficult to transfer away to those of its competitors. Banks, telecommunication, and software manufacturers companies try to establish these features.
- *Network effect.* The bigger the network or the larger the number of users, the stronger it becomes. Google is a leading example: Since more people use it as their primary search engine than any other, naturally it attracts the most advertisers who pay for the service.

An indication of the strength of an economic moat of a company is its position on the continuum from price taker to price maker. A company is a *price taker* if, as either a buyer or a seller, it has to accept the prices set by the general market. As a seller, generally this means that the products are generic and indistinguishable from those of its competitors. It also means that there are no significant barriers for new companies to be formed that produce similar products. If the company is a buyer, it means that it has to accept the prices offered to it with little or no opportunity to negotiate. This means that price takers have no or very weak economic moats.

At the other end of the continuum are *price makers*, companies that have products that are so unique and in such strong demand that they can raise their selling prices with little or no drop in sales. Alternatively, if they are buyers, they can insist that the suppliers lower their prices. These correspond to companies with strong economic moats.

As an example, most commodity producers are price takers. The world prices for oil, iron ore, and coal are set by global demand with little room for individual producers to increase prices. This is why most mining companies are high-risk investments; it could take many years, even decades, and billions of dollars of infrastructure to reach the production stage, only to find that in the meantime prices have dropped. (To help protect against such drops, typically they make substantial use of forward contacts and other types of derivatives.) However, just because a company is in the mining sector does not mean that it is necessarily a price taker. For example, mining companies that produce certain rare earth metals have a lot of power in setting prices. There are two reasons for this. First, increasingly large amounts of rare earth metals are required in green industries such as hybrid cars, wind turbines, and low-energy light bulbs. Second, although there are major areas outside China with large deposits of rare earth metals, about 95 percent of world production comes from China.

For many years, Microsoft was viewed as a price maker with a monopolistic position. This resulted in legal actions against the company under the Sherman Antitrust Act. There is a parallel situation for sellers. As a monopoly is to producers, so a *monopsony* is to buyers. The word describes the situation where a dominant buyer can choose from many suppliers. This enables the buyer to control terms with its suppliers—in other words, to be a price maker. Because of its huge buying power, in some product areas Wal-Mart is thought to be a monopsony.[17]

One of the quantitative signs of a strong economic moat is a high and consistent return on equity without excessive leverage. I like to think of it from the perspective that the world of business is difficult and highly competitive. If a company has a high and consistent return on equity, its competitors and potential competitors will have noticed this. Being willing to work at a lower level of profitability, it would be thought that they could win some of the customers or contracts away from the company by offering lower prices. Yet, in spite of the best efforts of its business competitors, there is something special about the original company, allowing it to maintain its sales and profits.

## Warren Buffett Talking about Economic Moats

Every day, in countless ways, the competitive position of each of our businesses grows either weaker or stronger. If we are delighting customers, eliminating unnecessary costs, and improving our products and services, we gain strength. But if we treat customers with indifference or tolerate bloat, our businesses will wither. On a daily basis, the effects of our actions are imperceptible; cumulatively, though, their consequences are enormous.

When our long-term competitive position improves as a result of these almost unnoticeable actions, we describe the phenomenon as "widening the moat."

—Berkshire Hathaway Annual Report, 2005

A truly great business must have an enduring "moat" that protects excellent returns on invested capital. The dynamics of capitalism guarantee that competitors will repeatedly assault any business "castle" that is earning high returns. Therefore a formidable barrier such as a company's being the low-cost producer (GEICO, Costco) or possessing a powerful worldwide brand (Coca-Cola, Gillette, American Express) is essential for sustained success.

Business history is filled with "Roman Candles," companies whose moats proved illusory and were soon crossed. Our criterion of "enduring" causes us to rule out companies in industries prone to rapid and continuous change. Though capitalism's "creative destruction" is highly beneficial for society, it precludes investment certainty. A moat that must be continuously rebuilt will eventually be no moat at all. Additionally, this criterion eliminates the business whose success depends on having a great manager.... [I]f a business requires a superstar to produce great results, the business itself cannot be deemed great.

—Berkshire Hathaway Annual Report, 2007

## Examine High ROE Companies

To refine your ability to analyze the business side of companies, find companies with high and consistent return on equity and not too much debt. Try to determine what is special about them—what economic moats do they have? Look at any moats in terms of type, strength, and durability. In terms of strength, a minimal level is that the moat enables the company to increase its prices at least as fast as inflation.

## Engineering and Margins of Safety

So far, this chapter has been devoted to examining means to get reliable earnings forecasts. This misses an important point. Not all gaps between forecasts and actual results are the same. It depends whether the actual earnings are above or below the forecast, whether it is a positive earnings surprise or a negative earnings surprise. When buying stocks, we want to do all that we can to make forecasts that lead to a positive earnings surprise and to minimize the likelihood of a negative earnings surprise. To achieve this we need the idea of a margin of safety.

Referred to as load testing, stress testing, or applying safety factors, the use of margins of safety is common throughout architecture and engineering. By spending a little time to understand the basic ideas and principles in this setting, we will be in a better position to apply the concept of a margin of safety to investments in the stock market. Before doing this, it is interesting to note that this is another example in investing where Benjamin Graham appears to be the first to understand and use the idea. Not only was he the first to explain the need to make systematic use of a margin of safety, but he also recognized that when it is introduced into calculations, it is "somewhat as an engineer does in his specifications for a structure."[18]

In architecture and engineering, margins of safety are generally applied in a multilayered fashion. For example, in the construction of a bridge, the application of safety factors could start with determining the anticipated loads on the various girders and beams and insisting that they withstand static loads of four or five times that amount and cyclical loads to even higher levels. Models may be constructed to test for the ability to withstand winds, to be resistant to swaying and buckling, and to support anticipated loads. Overall, there are two types of testing in an engineering environment: testing to destruction and stability testing. Testing to destruction means applying a heavier and heavier static load to the structure until it collapses. Alternatively, it could mean repeated application of a load or action until collapse. In contrast, stability testing means applying a load or stressing the structure and observing whether it returns to normal levels. The level of the load will generally be a suitable multiple of what is expected under a normal range of operating conditions. Another factor in the design of the stress or load tests is the proposed use of the structure. If large numbers of lives are at risk, such as in airplane construction, the safety factors will be much higher than, for example, when the construction is a bridge to carry water pipes.[19]

Warren Buffett used the language of engineering in an article called "The Superinvestors of Graham-and-Doddsville," an edited version of a famous talk given at Columbia University in 1984 commemorating the fiftieth anniversary of *Security Analysis*, written by Benjamin Graham and David Dodd. "You don't try and buy businesses worth $83 million for $80 million." Buffett wrote. "You leave yourself an enormous margin [of safety]. When you build a bridge, you insist it can carry 30,000 pounds, but you only drive 10,000-pound trucks across it. And that same principle works in investing."[20]

Interestingly, the area of banking and finance has adopted the terminology of engineering where the financial positions of major financial institutions are required to pass various *stress tests*. The idea is that computer-modeled shocks and extreme scenarios are applied to the financial positions of institutions to see if there is a sufficiently large buffer to absorb them and maintain stability.[21] For example, the Bank for International Settlements regularly produces documents setting out banking requirements. The most recent one is the Basel II Framework, with the term *stress testing* used throughout the document. It is worth giving a specific example, since it helps point out areas of concern for us as investors in the stock market. We use paragraph 434 for this purpose:

> An [internal ratings–based] bank must have in place sound stress testing processes for use in the assessment of capital adequacy. Stress testing must involve identifying possible events or future changes in economic conditions that could have unfavorable effects on a bank's credit exposures and assessment of the bank's ability to withstand such changes. Examples of scenarios that could be used are (i) economic or industry downturns; (ii) market-risk events; and (iii) liquidity conditions.[22]

In terms of investing in publicly traded companies, economic or industry downturns could affect the ability of the company to meet forecasts of its growth rates; market-risk events could apply to the market (that is, the share price), not reflecting the performance of the business; and liquidity conditions could refer to the business carrying excess debt.

The conventional idea of a margin of safety is often expressed as buying $1 bills for 50 cents, or words to that effect. The idea is to calculate the intrinsic value of stocks and favor those where the current price undercuts it by a substantial amount, perhaps by 50 percent or more. In this context, intrinsic value typically refers to the value calculated by one of the discount methods that we have discussed in earlier chapters. The first problem with this approach is that there is a tendency to give the calculation of the dollar value an exactness that it does not warrant. I use the word *tendency* here and do not want to overstate the acceptance of this viewpoint. However, even the statement "$1 bills for 50 cents" contains the implication that we really know the true worth of the stocks, the "$1 bills" that we are buying. A problem, though, is that there is a large range of valuations from discount methods due to the range of methods and their extreme sensitivity to the input parameters.

Another problem with this approach is that it fails to recognize the different effects of the individual input variables. For example, suppose the intrinsic value is 25 percent above the share price. Some input variables (such as payout ratios) generally do not vary much over the years, while others are more volatile (such as earnings growth). Hence a 25 percent buffer may be adequate if it was based on an estimate of the dividend payout ratio, but not if it was based on an estimate of the growth rate of earnings.

To overcome the vagueness of this approach, instead of performing the calculation and applying the margin of safety to the outcome by making comparisons with the actual price, the second approach is to apply margins of safety to the input parameters themselves. Once again, we see that Graham actually had already taken steps in this direction. With book value, the conventional approach would be to calculate the book value of a stock and look for companies with low prices compared to their book values. This would give a margin of safety based on the final calculation, the idea of getting $1 bills for 50 cents. Instead, as we saw in Chapter 6, Graham applies different safety factors to the different input variables such as reducing receivables to 75 to 90 percent of their face value, inventory to 50 to 75 percent of its face value, and fixed assets to 1 to 50 percent of their face value. Then he recalculates the book value and compares it with the current price of the stock.

## Stress-Testing Investments

Use the ideas of engineering and architecture to stress test potential investments by applying the margins of safety to the input parameters themselves.

In the remainder of this chapter, we focus on methods for calculating automatic margins of safety for the price ratio methods of Chapter 11. This means looking at margins of safety for forecasts of earnings, P/E ratios, and dividend payout ratios. Some of the ideas can, however, be carried over to the input variables of the other methods we have discussed in the earlier chapters.

## Margins of Safety for Earnings Growth Rates

Suppose we are considering buying shares in a company and we want to evaluate the investment using the price ratio method by estimating the return over the next five years. We need to make forecasts for earnings, the P/E ratio, and the payout ratio. Start with the earnings. Suppose you make a forecast of 15 percent growth over the next five years. If you buy shares in the company and the actual growth over the next five years turns out to be 20 percent, then you will be a satisfied investor. But if the average growth drops to 10 percent, then you may be wishing you had not made the purchase. This means that limiting negative earnings surprises is more important than worrying about outcomes with positive earnings surprises. This is where the idea of a margin of safety enters.

With this in mind, I developed a function called ESAFETY (pronounced "e-safety") that calculates an automatic margin of safety for growth rates of earnings based on historical financial data for the company. The idea is that if the data shows features that would make it more likely that future growth could not be maintained, then the forecast of earnings would be made lower.

One of its steps involves a comparison of sales and earnings growth. For instance, if sales per share growth is lower than earnings per share growth, then this can act as a curb for earnings to continue growing at the historical rate. This is because for the historical growth rate to be maintained, either the net profit margin would need to increase or the growth rate of sales would need to increase, both of which are difficult to achieve. In this case the historical growth rate of sales would be used as a guide to lower the estimate of the growth rate of earnings. Another of its features uses the stability of earnings: if the stability is low as measured by STAEGR, then the margin of safety for the forecast of earnings will be lowered.

I tested tens of thousands of cases to ensure that forecasts using ESAFETY satisfied two practical goals. First, they provided a margin of safety that reduced the severity and proportion of negative earnings surprises. Second, they provided forecasts high enough to use as a basis for profitable investments. The remainder of the chapter looks at the results of one of these studies followed by an application to Wal-Mart.

## Putting It into Practice

Using the database previously described in the stability study, focus was placed on the effect of the margin of safety function ESAFETY in reducing the frequency and size of negative earnings surprises. Only companies with STAEGR above 90 percent over the five years prior to the time of making the forecast were considered. Each forecast was for 12 months over the five calendar years 2005 to 2009. Since only companies with high stability for the growth of historical earnings are considered, we started by following the earlier method, which used the historical growth as the forecast for future growth. The results for these companies are shown in the first row of Table 13.4. The median forecast error for the negative earnings surprises was −17.4 percent with 69.0 percent of errors in the negative direction.

The next step was to make earnings forecasts using the margin of safety function. The median error of negative earnings surprises

**Table 13.4**  Errors for Negative Earnings Surprises for High-stability Companies

| Forecast Method | Median Negative Error | Percentage Negative Surprises |
| --- | --- | --- |
| Historical data | −17.4% | 69.0% |
| Margin of safety | −12.3% | 55.8% |

dropped to –12.3 percent. Just as importantly, the actual proportion of negative earnings surprises dropped to 55.8 percent. In other words, both the median error for the negative earnings surprises and the proportion of these surprises dropped significantly.

The effect of the steps on improving forecasts can be seen in Figures 13.6, 13.7, and 13.8. In each figure the forecast of EPS is shown on the horizontal axis and the actual EPS is on the vertical axis. The diagonal line signifies companies for which the actual EPS equals the estimate using historical data. This means that the closer the points are to this line, the more accurate the forecasts. Data points below the line indicate negative earnings surprises, and data points above the line indicate positive earnings surprises.

The companies were ranked from the highest stability measured by STAEGR to the lowest stability. In each case, the stability was measured over the previous five years (six data points). These companies were then divided into five quintiles, the first quintile containing stocks with the highest stability down to the fifth quintile containing stocks with the lowest stability. Figure 13.6 shows the data for the low-stability quintile where the forecasts are made using the historical growth rate. The figure shows that the data points are highly random

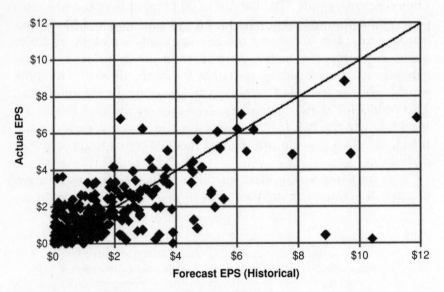

**Figure 13.6**    Accuracy of Forecasts for Low-stability Stocks

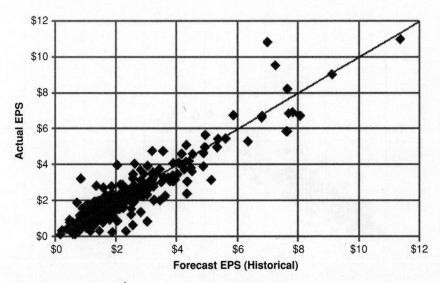

**Figure 13.7**    Accuracy of Safety Forecasts for High-stability Stocks

with minimal correlation between the forecast results and the actual results.

The next step repeats the previous step with the stocks in the high-stabilty quintile. The data points are now much closer to the diagonal line, indicating a higher correlation between the EPS that was forecast using past growth rates and the actual EPS. This is shown in Figure 13.7.

The final step is to see if we can decrease the proportion of negative earnings surprises and at the same time decrease their average size. This is done by modifying the forecasts for the high-stability stocks using the margin of safety function previously described. Figure 13.8 shows the results for these modified forecasts. At first Figures 13.7 and 13.8 may appear to be the same. However, on closer examination it becomes clear that some of the data points have moved to the left, which means that the forecasts have been lowered. For example, in Figure 13.7 there is a point in the top right-hand corner. It represents a forecast of $11.33 and an actual result of $10.99, a small negative surprise. In Figure 13.8 this point has moved to the left with a forecast of $10.33. Since the actual result was $10.99, it now represents a positive earnings surprise.

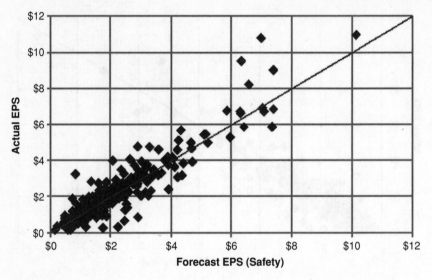

**Figure 13.8**    Accuracy of Forecasts for High-stability Stocks after Applying a Margin of Safety

## Margins of Safety for P/E Ratios and Payout Ratios

Chapter 11 included a discussion of what to be aware of regarding P/E ratios. It listed six rules for estimating P/E ratios and avoiding being drawn into making higher forecasts than can be properly substantiated. These rules can be used to set up an automatic procedure for calculating a margin of safety for P/E ratios. For example, making sure that any forecasts of P/E ratios are at the lower end of the ranges of historical P/E ratios is a good start. The example of Wal-Mart in Figure 11.2 in Chapter 11 shows just how large the range of P/E ratios can be on a year-by-year basis. Additionally, if a P/E ratio is high, make sure that the margin of safety is larger than if the P/E ratio is low. Suppose you are trying to make a margin-of-safety forecast for five years in the future. The idea is to set a level that is likely to be reached at some point in around five years. It is not required to be above the level all the time or to be precisely this level in five years.

For the payout ratio, a good first step is to set any forecast at the lower end of its levels over the preceding four or five years. For example, Figure 13.9 shows Wal-Mart's dividend payout ratio for the past 11 financial years. Eleven years ago it was 16 percent, and has been trending upward ever since until last year it was 29 percent. Extra security for assuming that the payout ratio will continue at

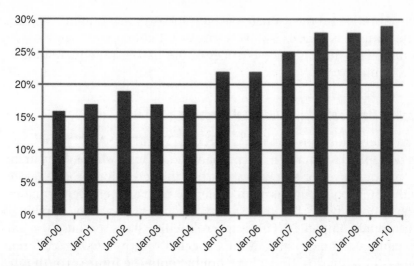

**Figure 13.9**    Payout Ratios for Wal-Mart
The bars show the dividend payout ratios for Wal-Mart for the 11 financial years ending January 31, 2000, through January 31, 2010.

approximately this level is provided by a statement in the company's 2010 10-K report: "We have increased our dividend every year since the first dividend was declared in March 1974." This suggests that the company will try to maintain or improve its payout ratio for otherwise it may have to lower its dividends.

Even though it is possible to incorporate margins of safety for the P/E ratio and payout ratio in a case-by-case analysis, as for the growth rate I wanted an automatic procedure to rule out behavioral biases and to be able to handle large databases. The margin of safety function I created for P/E ratios is called PESAFETY (pronounced "p-e-safety"). It examines the current P/E ratio and the average P/E ratio over any specified number of years to construct a conservative estimate using these data. We cannot have the same degree of confidence about the future behavior of P/E ratios that we can have about the growth of earnings per share. Nevertheless, by applying the safety function for P/E ratios, it is unlikely that the P/E ratio will drop by any significant amount below the safety level while it is likely that it will be higher. Hence, we are well on our way to finding the desired double-dip stocks.

Similarly, the margin-of-safety function for the payout ratio, called PRSAFETY (pronounced "p-r-safety"), examines the current payout ratio and the average payout ratio over any number of years. The output is a conservative estimate of the payout ratio in the future. This increases the chances of the payout ratio increasing in the coming years.

### Applying Margins of Safety to Individual Companies

The safety functions ESAFETY, PESAFETY, and PRSAFETY are set up to be applied to databases of company data. This is what is done in the Conscious Investor software as part of the screening process, along with other requirements in areas such as management performance, debt, and stability. The three safety functions can also be applied to individual companies. This is where the fun starts, because you can instantly see the changes in the expected return based on different inputs or scenarios. If you have doubt about the future growth rate, lower the forecast even further and see the effect on the future total shareholder return. Or if you think the safety forecast is too conservative, increase it and notice what happens. The same applies to the P/E ratio and the payout ratio: Modify them and track the effect. The goal is to look at the future performance under a range of scenarios. In particular, we want to find companies that will give us a return that compensates us for the risks associated with the business even under worst-case scenarios. What is more, we want this to be done in an automated way so that we can immediately know the answer.

There are two steps when applying these automated margins of safety to individual companies, with an optional third step. The first step is calculating the expected return using the methods described in Chapter 11 with the estimates of growth rate, P/E ratio, and payout ratio, based on historical data. The second step is finding new estimates of the input variables via the safety functions and using these inputs to recalculate the expected return. This return is what could be expected under a fairly stringent worst-case scenario. The optional third step is for those investors who like to add their own insights, knowledge, and opinions. This is done by overriding the automatic historical and safety estimates of growth rate, P/E ratio and payout ratio with your own inputs. To make these steps more concrete, we will follow them through with Wal-Mart. Assume that the current price is $55.07 and the earnings per share over the past 12 months is $3.70. This means that the current P/E ratio is 14.88.

Starting with the first step, based on historical data the default estimates in Conscious Investor for Wal-Mart over the next five years are a P/E ratio of 15.53, growth of 8.92 percent, and a payout ratio of 29 percent, as shown in Figure 13.10. Of course, when using historical data as a basis for any forecasts, we are assuming that all the standard requirements have been applied concerning historical consistency and stability. The price ratio method in Chapter 11 shows that the expected average total shareholder return over the next five years is 11.9 percent. Regarding the estimate of the growth rate, as a point of comparison, in April 2010 the consensus estimate on MSN Money for the growth of Wal-Mart was 11.5 percent for the next five years. What is surprising is that the consensus forecast is considerably higher than the five-year historical growth of Wal-Mart. Perhaps this is another example of the bias of analysts towards optimistic forecasts.

The second step, shown in Figure 13.11, applies the safety functions to the default estimates of the growth rate, P/E ratio, and payout ratio described in the first step. Using ESAFETY, a margin of safety forecast for the earnings of Wal-Mart is an average of 7.59 percent per year over the next five years compared to the historical rate of 8.92 percent. For the P/E ratio, the margin of safety forecast using PESAFETY is 12.88 compared to the current P/E ratio of 14.88 or the estimate of 15.53 based on historical levels used in Figure 13.10.

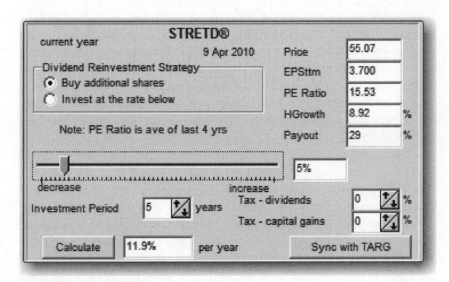

**Figure 13.10**     Estimated Return for Wal-Mart

A screenshot from Conscious Investor showing the estimated return for Wal-Mart based on historical levels of earnings growth, P/E ratio, and payout ratio. The STRETD calculations shows an average return of 11.9 percent per year over the next five years, before taxes.

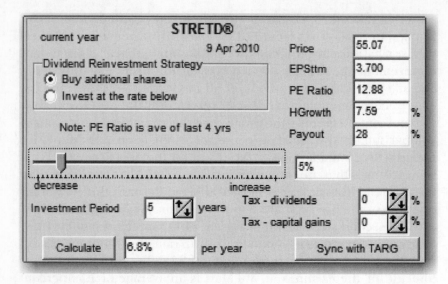

**Figure 13.11**   Estimated Safety Return for Wal-Mart

A screenshot from Conscious Investor showing the estimated return for Wal-Mart based on automatic margins of safety applied to levels of earnings growth, P/E ratio, and payout ratio. The STRETD calculations shows an average return of 6.8 percent per year over the next five years before taxes.

Finally, the margin of safety for the payout ratio using PRSAFETY is 28 percent instead of the current level of 29 percent. Each one on its own is not a large drop. For many companies the decrease in an individual input can be 50 percent or more. Nevertheless, even in this case, when the individual safety margins are combined, the estimated average total shareholder return over the next five years is 6.8 percent, a drop of over 5 percent from the result based on historical data.

The interpretation is that if everything continues more or less as it has in the past, you could expect an average total shareholder return of approximately 11.9 percent per year over the next five years. However, if we want to make allowances for market volatility or the deterioration of business performance, then it would be sensible not to anticipate an average total shareholder return of more than approximately 6.8 percent per year.

Finally, as an optional third step, it is easy to change the level of stress on the input values of the earnings growth, P/E ratio, and payout ratio and recalculate the expected return. This would be done if you have further information about the company that leads you to believe that the safety estimates are too lenient or too severe. It is even possible to change the initial value of earnings per share. For example, if there has been a spike in the earnings over the past year, you might want to use a lower value that is more indicative of the long-term trend. It also makes sense to look at returns under ranges of values to have a better idea of the impact of any changes in the values of the input parameters. Even if the safety estimates seem reasonable, since we do not know what the actual values will be over the next five years, it makes sense to vary the input values and examine the output.

What action should be taken regarding Wal-Mart? In 2003, Warren Buffett wrote that unless "we see a very high probability of at least 10 percent pretax returns (which translate to $6^{1}/_{2}$–7 percent after corporate tax), we will sit on the sidelines."[23] Applying the methods just described shows that one way to get a return of 10 percent for an investment in Wal-Mart would be to have earnings growth of 10 percent and P/E ratio of 14 over the next five years. This is a possibility. However, if we want to maintain the growth forecast of earnings at the safe level of 7.59 percent, the P/E ratio at the safe level of 12.88, and the payout ratio at 28 percent, another way would be for the price to drop to $47.50. This is a possibility since it traded below this price in July 2009. Volatility now becomes your friend since you know what price you are willing to pay to achieve your desired return under clear assumptions. Putting it altogether, based on the available information, at the moment I am not giving up my seat on the sidelines for Wal-Mart. The good news is that there are thousands of other companies to choose from. Among these companies we are after stocks that, even under margins of safety applied to the input values, still show a return high enough to more than compensate for the associated risks.

## The Final Goal

The final goal is to find stocks that, even under margins of safety applied to the input values, still show a return high enough to compensate for the associated risks. This is like a worst-case scenario describing a minimum return. In practice, the actual return is likely to be much higher. Putting it another way, our aim in using the steps just described is to find investments with a very low possibility of poor returns and a high possibility of excellent returns.

One last point: If the company has excessive debt, struggling margins, or a weak economic moat, it is always going to be risky no matter how large the margin of safety you use in your valuation calculations. It is better to move on to companies with better characteristics and not waste time trying to work out a safe price to pay. Benjamin Graham made this clear in 1934 when he wrote:

> Observation over many years has taught us that the chief losses to investors come from the purchase of *low-quality* securities at times of favorable business conditions.... These securities do not offer an adequate margin of safety in any admissible sense of the term.[24]

## The Bottom Line

1. More reliable forecasts of earnings can be made by choosing companies with stable growth in earnings, stable return on equity, and a strong economic moat.
2. Although reliable earnings forecasts are important, more important is avoiding negative earnings surprises. By automating margin of safety forecasts of earnings per share, it is possible to decrease the size and frequency of negative earnings surprises in a consistent manner for large databases of companies.
3. Applying the three safety functions for earnings growth, P/E ratios, and payout ratios is a clear, systematic method for finding successful investments. The functions apply practical margins of safety to the respective areas of business performance, market opinion, and board dividend policy.

# CHAPTER

# 14

## Where Do We Go from Here?

*I hear and I forget. I see and I remember. I do and I understand.*
—Xun Zi[1]

*What's needed is a sound intellectual framework for making decisions and the ability to keep emotions from corroding that framework.*
—Warren Buffett[2]

**V**aluation methods do not spring up in isolation. They start with individuals trying to distinguish which markers are the best indicators of value for publicly traded companies. At first these markers may be quite general, such as high return on equity (ROE) is better than low return on equity, or high growth compared to the price-to-earnings (P/E) ratio is better than the converse. This is followed by attempts to quantify these indicators and meld them into a final numerical result.

We saw that there was actually a wide range of methods, all of which have been applied with good effect in different areas by investors with different needs and viewpoints. We also saw that to make a final decision on what and when to buy, when to hold, and when to sell, price needs to be included in the calculations. This means, for example, that real value can be described in terms of intrinsic value and price. It can also be described in terms of the percentage return that can safely be expected.

To apply valuation methods to get the best results with maximum confidence, it is important to think through what is important for your needs, and then to look for the method or methods that best meet them. Part of this process should also include whether you want to look at companies one at a time, or use databases to scan sectors or even the whole market; whether you want a method that you can do in your head, on a piece of paper, or via a computer program; and what type of data you have access to.

For example, if you think that all you need is the P/E ratio and growth, then the PEG ratio may be sufficient, or perhaps the PEGY ratio if you want to include dividends. Data for these methods is easily found and the calculations are simple. If you think that the balance sheet is important because it is simple and easy to understand the assumptions that go into it, then you might move toward one of the balance sheet methods developed by Benjamin Graham. You could implement them using calculations on paper or in a spreadsheet.

Because they are so widely used, you might like to try discount methods with the discounted cash flow approach. If dividends are important to you, then one of the dividend discount methods might be best. Or you could use the payback approach with dividends if you also think that the time it takes to get your money back is a critical measure. If you like working with companies with stable growth and want to go straight to the expected return, then price ratio methods coupled with automatic safety margins would be the best choice.

## Free Access to Key Functions

As a free bonus, you can try functions for some of the main valuation methods in this book by visiting www.theconsciousinvestor.org. They include a discounted cash flow function, a price ratio function, and the stability function STAEGR®. The functions work within Excel for Windows and are easy to set up. For example, there are Excel templates that show you how to use the functions with market data to value companies. There is also a checklist using some of the ratios in Chapter 5 to help you find companies with strong financials and consistent growth as a basis for the valuation methods. Using this list will help you avoid companies with weaknesses such as too much debt and poor return on equity, signs that they are never likely to be safe investments, no matter how undervalued they may seem to be.

The functions and other material on the web site are provided so that you can see the strengths and weaknesses of the methods in a practical setting. In mathematical research we talk about this as getting your hands dirty. In the context of the valuation methods, it means experimenting with the different valuation functions by trying different sets of data, looking at how changes in the data affect the outcomes, and comparing the results using different functions.

## Being a Conscious Investor

We have covered the theory and practice of being a conscious investor in how we find the real value of stocks. The theory means looking at the rational basis of the methods along with their strengths and weaknesses. Practice means looking at back-testing results as well as trying the methods for yourself.

As stated in the Introduction, another dimension to being a conscious investor concerns the types of companies to invest in. When we invest in a company, we want the revenue and earnings to increase. This generally means an increase in the sales of the actual products and services provided by the company. Being aware of the consequences of such an increase for yourself, your family, and the wider community is also part of being a conscious investor. How would you feel if the amount that the products or services are used in your neighborhood increased significantly? What would be your reaction if they were more easily available to people in general? What do you think would be the social consequences if the company increased its sales by 10 to 15 percent each year? These are personal questions with no definitive answers since individuals have different values. Yet addressing questions such as these ties together the two roles of conscious investing: the role of making money and gaining financial security, and the role of providing capital and supporting those companies that you believe play a positive role in society with minimum harm.

# APPENDIX A

# Relationship between Return on Equity and Growth of Earnings

In Chapter 5 we made the important statement that within a few percentage points, assuming that the return on equity remains constant, the growth rate of earnings equals return on equity times the earnings retention rate. The following calculations show how to derive this and the other statements given at that time and used in later chapters. Of course, these relationships depend on the accuracy of the clean surplus relationship.

For notation, let $B_i$ denote the book value at the end of year $i$ for $i = 1, 2$. Denote the earnings and dividends during the year as $e_i$ and $d_i$. Denote the payout ratio by $p_i = d_i/e_i$ and return on equity by $R_i = e_i/B_i$.

Writing the clean surplus relationship as

$$B_2 - e_2 + d_2 = B_1$$

and substituting for $B_1$ and $B_2$ we get

$$e_2/R_2 - e_2 + p_2 e_2 = e_1/R_1$$

Dividing by $e_1$ and reorganizing gives:

$$e_2/e_1 = (R_2/R_1) \times 1/[1 - R_2(1 - p_2)]$$

323

This is the formula used in Table 13.3. By a standard approximation:

$$e_2/e_1 \approx (R_2/R_1)[1 + R_2(1 - p_2)]$$

Hence, as asserted, if return on equity is constant (so that $R_2 = R_1$), the growth rate of earnings is approximately return on equity multiplied by $1 - p_2$, the retention ratio.

We can also get similar expressions for the growth of dividends. Since $d_i = p_i \times e_i$, it follows that

$$d_2/d_1 = (p_2 R_2/p_2 R_1) \times 1/[1 - R_2(1 - p_2)]$$

and hence

$$d_2/d_1 \approx (p_2 R_2/p_2 R_1) \times (1 + R_2(1 - p_2))$$

verifying the assertion that if the payout ratio and the return on equity are constant, the growth rate of dividends is approximately return on equity multiplied by $1 - p_2$, the retention ratio.

Finally, suppose that $R_1$ and $R_2$ denote forward return on equity, meaning that they are the earnings for each year divided by the book value at the start of the year instead of at the end of the year. The growth of earnings formula becomes:

$$e_2/e_1 = (R_2/R_1) + R_2(1 - p_2)$$

Hence, if forward return on equity remains constant,

$$e_2/e_1 = 1 + R_2(1 - p_2)$$

showing that, instead of an approximation, the growth rate of earnings is equal to the forward return on equity multiplied by $1 - p_2$, the retention ratio.

# APPENDIX B

# Calculations for Discount Methods

This appendix briefly introduces some of the formulas for calculating intrinsic value using the discount methods in Chapters 7 and 8. It is included as a guide for those who want to try their hand at calculating the results for themselves.

Behind all the discount methods is a single basic formula with variations depending on the specific method. The basic formula is that the intrinsic value $V$ is given by

$$V = a + a_1/(1+r) + a_2/(1+r)^2 + a_3/(1+r)^3 + \cdots$$

where

$r$ is the discount rate

The other inputs, $a$ and $a_1, a_2, a_3, \ldots$ for years 1, 2, 3, and so on, vary according to the specific methods.

We start with three examples:

*Example 1: Discounted cash flow method.* When $a = 0$ and $a_1, a_2, a_3, \ldots$ are the forecasts of annual free cash flows, the result is the basic discounted cash flow method. The variations of the method arise from the assumptions on the rate of growth of the free cash flow.

*Example 2: Dividend discount method.* When $a = 0$ and $a_1, a_2, a_3, \ldots$ are the forecasts of the dividends of the company, the result is the dividend discount method. The dividends can be substituted directly, or they can be calculated using return on equity and the dividend payout ratio. In this second case, the clean surplus relationship is required.

*Example 3: Residual income method.* This is another variation of the dividend discount method, where $a$ is the initial book value of the company and $a_1$, $a_2$, $a_3$, ... are estimates of the yearly residual incomes of the company.

What this means is that from a mathematical perspective, the problem of calculating intrinsic value using a discount method reduces to summing the basic infinite series displayed here. This produces two problems. First, since there are an infinite number of terms, these terms cannot be listed in a table and they require a formula to describe them, at least after a finite number of terms. Second, only a limited number of infinite series actually have formulas describing their sums. Mathematical theory may tell us that certain infinite series actually have sums. However, this does not help in calculating intrinsic value if we cannot calculate what the sum is.

In finance both these problems are overcome by limiting the types of series to those that are either geometric series or combinations of them. A geometric series is a series of numbers, where each successive term is a fixed multiple of the previous term. The general geometric series has the form:

$$b + bt + bt^2 + bt^3 + \cdots$$

For this series the value $t$ is called the growth rate of the series. When $-1 < t < 1$, this series has the sum $b/(1 - t)$.

In practice, what this means is that the basic infinite series given at the start of the appendix is one of three different types called a single-stage model, a two-stage model, or a three-stage model. It also means that the series themselves are all geometric series.

## Single-Stage Model

The single-stage model assumes that the values $a_1$, $a_2$, $a_3$, ... grow at a constant rate. Denote this rate of growth by $g$. Then the intrinsic value formula for $V$ can be written as

$$V = a + b/(1 + r) + b(1 + g)/(1 + r)^2 + b(1 + g)^2/(1 + r)^3 \cdots$$

Summing this expression as an infinite geometric series gives the value as the compact expression:

$$V = a + b/(r - g)$$

provided $0 < g < r$.

> *Example 1: Discounted cash flow method.* Suppose that the free cash flow per share over the previous year is $1.00 and that it grows at 10 percent annually. Also suppose that the discount rate is 12 percent. Then $a = 0$, $b = 1.1$, $g = 0.10$, and $r = 0.12$, so that the intrinsic value $V$ is $1.1/(0.12 - 0.1) = \$55.00$.

> *Example 2: Dividend discount method using return on equity.* Suppose we want to obtain a general formula for intrinsic value using the single-stage dividend discount method based on return on equity. Denote return on equity by $R$, the payout ratio by $p$, and the initial book value by $B$. We can apply the previous formula with $a = 0$, $b = pRB/m$, and $g = (1/m) - 1$, where $m = 1 - R(1 - p)$. This means that

$$V = pRB/[m(1 + r) - 1]$$

Consider the example in Chapter 8 shown in Table 8.2. In this case, the initial book value is $10 and the forecasts of the return on equity and payout ratio are 15 percent and 50 percent, while the discount rate is 10 percent. Substituting in the preceding formula gives $V = \$42.86$. Table 8.2 gave the result $41.52 after 200 years, showing that the line-by-line method can take 200 years or more to yield a reasonable approximation.

## Two-Stage Model

The basic assumption of the two-stage model is that the terms $a_1$, $a_2$, $a_3$, ... are described in two parts, each with its own growth rate. Typically the first part is assumed to last for 10 years and is called the *initial* or *growth* period. The remaining time is called the *stable* or *terminal growth* period.

Suppose that the growth rate over the first 10 years is $g$ and the growth rate over the remaining time is $h$. Then the basic intrinsic value formula for $V$ can be written as $V = V_1 + V_2$, where

$$V_1 = a + b/(1+r) + \cdots + b(1+g)^9/(1+r)^{10}$$

and

$$V_2 = b(1+g)^9(1+h)/(1+r)^{11} + b(1+g)^9(1+h)^2/(1+r)^{12} + \cdots$$

Standard calculations for finite and infinite geometric series show that

$$V_1 = a + b/(1+r)^{10}[(1+r)^{10} - (1+g)^{10}]/(r-g)$$

and

$$V_2 = b(1+g)^9(1+h)/[(1+r)^{10}(r-h)]$$

In both cases we require $r \neq -1$. In the first case we also require $g \neq r$ and in the second case we also assume $h \neq r$ and $0 < h < r$.

> *Example 1: Discount cash flow method.* Suppose that the initial free cash flow is \$1.00 and that it grows at 12 percent for the first 10 years and 3 percent after that. Also suppose that the discount rate is 10 percent. Then $a = 0$, $b = 1.2$, $g = 0.12$, $h = 0.03$, and $r = 0.10$, giving $V_1 = \$11.06$ and $V_2 = \$17.62$ with the result that the intrinsic value is \$28.68. This example is studied in detail in Chapter 7. Table 7.2 shows the result is \$27.41 after 50 years.

> *Example 2: Dividend discount method using return on equity—initial stage.* In this example we calculate the result for the initial stage of a two-stage dividend discount model based on return on equity. Suppose that the initial book value is \$10. Suppose also that the return on equity is estimated to be 10 percent over the next 10 years with a payout ratio of 50 percent. Finally, suppose that the discount rate is 15 percent. In this example we want to figure out the actual dividends over the first 10 years and calculate their contribution to the intrinsic value.

The first step is to calculate the growth rate of the book value. The clean surplus relationship described in Chapter 4 states that

$$B' = B - d + e$$

where
  $B$ is the initial book value
  $d$ is dividends per share
  $e$ is earnings per share
  $B'$ is the resulting book value

Let $R$ denote return on equity and $p$ denote the payout ratio. This means that $p = d/e$ and $R = e/B'$ Substituting in the clean surplus relationship followed by a little algebra gives:

$$B' = B/(1 - R + R \times p)$$

This is a key relation showing the growth rate of the book value in terms of the payout ratio and return on equity.

Using the values for this example, we find that the book value at the end of the first year is:

$$B' = 10/(1 - 0.1 + 0.1 \times 0.5) = \$10.53$$

Proceeding in this way, year upon year, shows that each year the book value grows by about 5.3 percent. (More precisely, book value grows by 5.263 percent each year.) Since return on equity is 10 percent, earnings in the first year are \$1.05 and since the payout ratio is 50 percent, dividends in the first year are \$0.53. Proceeding in this way, it is possible to build up a table showing book value, earnings and dividends each year. (See Table B.1.)

Allowing for rounding errors, notice in Table B.1 that (1) the earnings for each year divided by the book value at the end of the year is 10 percent; (2) the earnings for each year divided by the dividends is 50 percent; (3) the discounted dividends in the final column are at a 15 percent discount to the actual dividends; and (4) the initial book value is \$10.00. This means that the values in the table satisfy the original requirements for return on equity and payout ratio. The final column gives the value of dividends discounted back to current time. These discounted dividends add to \$3.17, which means that

**Table B.1**  Growth of Book Value, Earnings and Dividends

| Year | Book Value at Start of Year | Earnings per Share | Dividends per Share | Book Value at End of Year | Discounted Dividends |
|------|------|------|------|------|------|
| 1 | $10.00 | $1.05 | $0.53 | $10.53 | $0.46 |
| 2 | $10.53 | $1.11 | $0.55 | $11.08 | $0.42 |
| 3 | $11.08 | $1.17 | $0.58 | $11.66 | $0.38 |
| 4 | $11.66 | $1.23 | $0.61 | $12.28 | $0.35 |
| 5 | $12.28 | $1.29 | $0.65 | $12.92 | $0.32 |
| 6 | $12.92 | $1.36 | $0.68 | $13.60 | $0.29 |
| 7 | $13.60 | $1.43 | $0.72 | $14.32 | $0.27 |
| 8 | $14.32 | $1.51 | $0.75 | $15.07 | $0.25 |
| 9 | $15.07 | $1.59 | $0.79 | $15.87 | $0.23 |
| 10 | $15.87 | $1.67 | $0.84 | $16.70 | $0.21 |
| | | | | Total | $3.17 |

the present value of the discounted dividends over the first 10 years is $3.17.

Instead of using a table, this result can be obtained from the summation formula given earlier. Since we are using 10 terms, it suffices to use the formula for $V_1$. From the table, we see that the initial dividend is $0.53 and that the dividends grow by 5.26 percent per year. (More precisely, the initial dividend is 0.5263 and their growth is 5.2632 percent per year.) Substituting these results into the formula for $V_1$ gives $a = 0$, $b = 0.5263$, $g = 0.05263$, and $r = 0.15$, so that $V_1 = \$3.17$. Hence the results from the table and from the formula agree.

*Example 3: Dividend discount method using return on equity—terminal stage.* Continuing with the previous example, suppose that after 10 years the return on equity drops to 5 percent. Also suppose that the company does not see any opportunities for expansion and decides to pay out all the earnings as dividends. At the end of the tenth year, Table B.1 shows that the book value of the company will be $16.70. Since the company is intending to pay out all its earnings as dividends, according to the clean surplus relationship there will be no further growth in book value. This means that from this point on, earnings per share and dividends per share will be 5 percent

**Table B.2**    Growth of Second Stage

| (1) Year | (2) Book Value at Start of Year | (3) Dividends | (4) Discounted Dividends | (5) Running Total |
|---|---|---|---|---|
| 11 | $16.70 | $0.84 | $0.18 | $0.18 |
| 12 | $16.70 | $0.84 | $0.16 | $0.34 |
| 13 | $16.70 | $0.84 | $0.14 | $0.47 |
| 14 | $16.70 | $0.84 | $0.12 | $0.59 |
| 15 | $16.70 | $0.84 | $0.10 | $0.69 |
| 16 | $16.70 | $0.84 | $0.09 | $0.78 |
| 17 | $16.70 | $0.84 | $0.08 | $0.86 |
| 18 | $16.70 | $0.84 | $0.07 | $0.93 |
| 19 | $16.70 | $0.84 | $0.06 | $0.98 |
| 20 | $16.70 | $0.84 | $0.05 | $1.04 |
| ... | ... | ... | ... | ... |
| 30 | $16.70 | $0.84 | $0.01 | $1.29 |
| ... | ... | ... | ... | ... |
| 65 | $16.70 | $0.84 | $0.00 | $1.38 |

This shows the main data for years 11 to 20 plus years 30 and 65. Table B.1 shows that the book value at the end of year 10 is $16.70 and so this is the book value at the start of year 11 in this table. Each year ROE is 5 percent and the payout ratio is 100 percent. This means that the book value in column (2) stays at $16.70 and the dividends remain at $0.84 in column (3). Column (4) displays the dividends discounted back to the current time. Column (5) is a running total of the discounted dividends. After 10 years the running total is $1.04 and after another 10 years it is $1.29. If the table is continued, the running total converges to $1.38, seen in year 65.

of $16.70, which is $0.835. Table B.2 shows the growth of the sum of the discounted dividends for the next 10 years. After 10 years the sum is $1.04. After another 10 years the sum of the discounted dividends is $1.29. By approximately 65 years, the sum of the discounted dividends has settled to around $1.38.

As for the first stage, we don't need to rely on a table and instead we can use the formula for $V_2$. In this case, $a = 0$, $b = 0.5263$, $g = 0.5263$, $h = 0$, and $r = 0.15$. The result is $V_2 = \$1.38$, which agrees with the result obtained from the year-by-year table B.2 However, once again we see that a large number of terms are needed to obtain accurate results. The conclusion is that the intrinsic value is $4.55, the sum of the two components $3.17 and $1.38.

# Notes

## Chapter 1　What Is Intrinsic Value?

1. Benjamin Graham and David Dodd, *Security Analysis* (New York: McGraw-Hill, 1934), 17.
2. Warren Buffett, *An Owner's Manual* (first issued in 1996 with updated versions printed each year in the annual report of Berkshire Hathaway).
3. Graham and Dodd, *Security Analysis*, 17.
4. John Burr Williams, *The Theory of Investment Value* (Harvard University Press 1938; reprint, Fraser Publishing, 1997).
5. Burton Malkiel, *A Random Walk Down Wall Street* (New York: Norton & Company, 1990), 28.
6. U.S. Senate Committee on Banking and Currency, "Factors Affecting the Buying and Selling of Equity Securities," statement of Benjamin Graham, March 11, 1955.
7. See, for example, Toni Rønnow-Rasmussen and Michael J. Zimmerman, eds., *Recent Work on Intrinsic Value* (Heidelberg: Springer Verlag, 2006).
8. Buffett, *Owner's Manual*.

## Chapter 2　Price Is What You Pay . . .

1. Benjamin Graham, *The Intelligent Investor* (New York: Harper Business Essentials, 2003) 206. (First published in 1949, this is reprint of the 4th edition published in 1973 with a commentary by Jason Zweig.)
2. Warren Buffett, letter to partners in the Buffett Partnership, January 20, 1966.
3. A search on the term *technical analysis* on the web site of the bookseller Amazon.com listed 27,546 entries. On the search engine Google the term *technical analysis software* resulted in 99,300 entries.
4. In Ian Fleming's book *You Only Live Twice*, after James Bond defeats Tiger Tanaka, head of the Japanese Secret Service, in a game of Rock Paper Scissors, he says, "You are a man of rock and steel, Tiger. I guessed that the paper symbol would be the one you would use the least. I played accordingly."
5. In 1983 when my son, Matthew, got his first Apple II computer he wrote a program that implemented these two strategies. If you played against the computer, the program would look for biases toward one of rock, paper, or scissors along with a search for short-term patterns. If a bias or pattern was detected, it would adopt an appropriate countering strategy. It was surprisingly hard to

beat. Even when you tried to make random throws, there was still a tendency to fall into a bias or pattern.

6. David Aronson, *Evidence-Based Technical Analysis: Applying the Scientific Method and Statistical Inference to Trading Signals* (Hoboken, NJ: John Wiley & Sons, 2007).

7. One of these authors is Douglas Adams. In *The Hitchhikers' Guide to the Galaxy*, he writes, "Ford!" he [Arthur Dent] said, "there's an infinite number of monkeys outside who want to talk to us about this script for *Hamlet* they've worked out" (London: Pan, 1979; New York: Pocket Books, 1981, Chapter 9).

8. The methods used by Aronson are based on Halbert White's reality check and Timothy Masters' Monte-Carlo permutation method. More details are given in Aronson's book. See note 6.

9. Cheol-Ho Park and Scott Irwin, "What Do We Know About the Profitability of Technical Analysis?" *Journal of Economic Surveys* 21, no. 4 (2007), 786–826.

10. H. Kent Baker, Aaron Phillips, and Gray Powell, "The Stock Distribution Puzzle: A Synthesis of the Literature on Stock Splits and Stock Dividends," *Financial Practice and Education* 5 (Spring/Summer 1995), 24–37.

11. Jia Ye, "Excess Returns, Stock Splits, and Analyst Earnings Forecasts," *Journal of Portfolio Management* 25 (Winter 1999), 70–76.

12. Robert Conroy and Robert Harris, "Stock Splits and Information: The Role of the Share Price," Darden Business School paper 98-01 (1998).

13. Seoyoung Kim, April Klein, and James Rosenfeld, "Return Performance Surrounding Reverse Stock Splits: Can Investors Profit?" *Financial Management* 37 (Summer 2008), 173–192.

14. Academics talk about three different levels or strengths of the efficient market hypothesis. Since we are only talking in general terms, we will simply talk about the efficient market hypothesis without getting into finer details.

15. Michael Jensen, "Some Anomalous Evidence Regarding Market Efficiency," *Journal of Financial Economics* 6 (1978), 95–101.

16. Warren Buffett, Annual Report of Berkshire Hathaway, 1988.

17. Quoted in *Warren Buffett Speaks: Wit and Wisdom from the World's Greatest Investor*, by Janet Lowe (Hoboken, NJ: John Wiley & Sons, 2007), 125.

18. There are various critiques of CAPM. One example is *The New Finance: The Case Against Efficient Markets* by Robert Haugen (Upper Saddle River, NJ: Prentice-Hall, 2010).

19. For a light-hearted introduction to option pricing, see my article "Sherlock Holmes and the Case of the Missing Ten Pounds," *Derivatives Strategy* (September 1997); also reprinted in *Derivatives and Financial Mathematics* (New York: Nova Science, 1997). An introduction to the mathematics of option pricing is given in Price, "Optional Mathematics Is Not Optional," *Notices of the American Mathematical Society* 43 (September 1996), 964–971; reprinted in *Derivatives and Financial Mathematics*.

20. SFAS No. 123(R) is a Statement of Financial Accounting Standards dealing with the reporting of share-based payments.

21. The technical name for the random path that prices are assumed to follow is a *lognormal distribution* or a *geometric Brownian motion*. Instead of the upward and downward movements of prices following a normal distribution, the actual random path is generated by the returns or ratios of prices following such a distribution.

22. Technically, *volatility* is defined as the annualized standard deviation of price returns.

23. Statisticians refer to probability distributions with these properties as leptokurtic: *leptos*, meaning "narrow," plus *kurtōsis*, meaning "bulging."

24. Nassim Nicholas Taleb, *Fooled by Randomness: The Hidden Role of Chance in Life and the Markets* (New York: Random House, 2004), and *The Black Swan: The Impact of the Highly Improbable* (New York: Random House, 2007).

25. William Kinney, David Burgstahler, and Roger Martin, "The Materiality of Earnings Surprise," working paper, University of Texas at Austin, 2000.

## Chapter 3  . . . Value Is What You Get

1. Oscar Wilde, *Lady Windermere's Fan* (1892).

2. Warren Buffett, Berkshire Hathaway Annual Report, 1983.

3. Warren Buffett, Berkshire Hathaway Annual Report, 1991.

4. Quoted in an interview with Warren Buffett in *Forbes*, November 1, 1974.

5. Andrew Smithers and Stephen Wright, *Valuing Wall Street: Protecting Wealth in Turbulent Markets* (New York: McGraw-Hill, 2000).

6. Amos Tversky and Daniel Kahneman, "Judgment under Uncertainty: Heuristics and Biases," *Science* 185 (1974), 1124–1131.

7. Werner De Bondt, "Betting on Trends: Intuitive Forecasts of Financial Risk and Return," *International Journal of Forecasting* 9 (1993), 355–371.

8. Robert Olsen, "Implications of Herding Behavior," *Financial Analysts Journal* 52, no. 4 (July/August 1996), 37–41.

9. Brad M. Barber and Terrance Odean, "The Courage of Misguided Convictions," *Financial Analysts Journal* 55, no. 6 (November/December 1999), 41–55.

10. Chris Hill, "Interview with Alice Schroeder: One Big Misconception about Buffett," November 6, 2009, www.aliceschroeder.com.

11. Note that this statement about not selling applies to companies fully owned by Berkshire Hathaway. It does not apply to equities held by the company.

## Chapter 4    Follow the Money

1. Response given by Warren Buffett at the 1997 annual meeting of Berkshire Hathaway when asked what is the best way to prepare to be a successful investor.

2. Martin Fridson and Fernando Alvarez, *Financial Statement Analysis: A Practitioner's Guide* (New York: John Wiley & Sons, 2002), 5.

3. Howard Schilit, *Financial Shenanigans: How to Detect Accounting Gimmicks and Fraud in Financial Reports* (New York: McGraw-Hill, 2002), 284.

4. Fridson and Alvarez, *Financial Statement Analysis*, 13.

5. Arthur Levitt, "The Numbers Game," speech to the NYU Centre for Law and Business, New York, September 28, 1998.

6. Some of the books that I have found useful are *Understanding Financial Statements* by L. M. Fraser and A. Ormiston (Upper Saddle River, NJ: Prentice Hall, 2001), *Financial Shenanigans* (see note 3) and *Financial Statement Analysis* (see note 2).

7. Bradley Keoun, "Citigroup's $1.1 Trillion of Mysterious Assets Shadows Earnings," Bloomberg, July 13, 2008, www.bloomberg.com.

8. Elisa Martinuzzi, "Goldman Sachs, Greece Didn't Disclose Swap Contract," *Bloomberg*, February 17, 2010, www.bloomberg.com.
9. Russell Lundholm, "A Tutorial on the Ohlson and Feltham/Ohlson Models: Answers to Some Frequently Asked Questions," *Contemporary Accounting Research* 11 no. 2 (1995), 749–761.

## Chapter 5    Everything Is Number and Ratio

1. Warren Buffett, Berkshire Hathaway Annual Report, 2008.
2. Martin Fridson and Fernando Alvarez, *Financial Statement Analysis: A Practitioner's Guide* (New York: John Wiley & Sons, 2002), 287.
3. To see this, for simplicity assume that the current price is $100 and the current P/E ratio is 20. This means that the current EPS is $5. If the EPS grows by 20 percent per year it will be $30.96 in 10 years. If the P/E ratio remains constant, the share price in 10 years will be $619.17, giving a return of 20 percent per year, as expected. If the P/E ratio halves, the share price in 10 years will be $309.59, giving an average annual return of 11.96 percent.
4. Warren Buffett, Berkshire Hathaway Annual Report, 2007.
5. Charles Mizrahi, *Getting Started in Value Investing* (Hoboken, NJ: John Wiley & Sons, 2007), 117.
6. Pat Dorsey, *The Little Book That Builds Wealth* (Hoboken, NJ: John Wiley & Sons, 2008), 3.
7. Warren Buffett, Berkshire Hathaway Annual Report, 1977.
8. Robert Lenzer, "The Secrets of Salomon," *Forbes*, November 23, 1992, 123.
9. Warren Buffett, Berkshire Hathaway Annual Report, 1984.
10. Warren Buffett, Berkshire Hathaway Annual Report, 1986.

## Chapter 6    Measuring Value by Taking Snapshots

1. Benjamin Graham and David Dodd, *Security Analysis* (New York: McGraw-Hill, 1934), 493.
2. Martin Fridson and Fernando Alvarez, *Financial Statement Analysis: A Practitioner's Guide* (New York: John Wiley & Sons, 2002), 29.
3. Berkshire Hathaway has two classes of shares, A shares and B shares. Until recently, in calculations involving per-share ratios, a Class B share counted as one-thirtieth of a Class A share and the results determined on an equivalent Class A share basis. In early 2010, Class B shares underwent a 50-for-1 split.
4. Annual report of Berkshire Hathaway 2009; these performance figures are displayed each year in the annual report of the company.
5. *Best Global Brands 2009: The Definitive Guide to the World's Most Valuable Brands* (Interbrand, 2009).
6. Graham and Dodd, *Security Analysis*, 491.
7. More details of the sale of the textile portion of Berkshire Hathaway can be found in the 1980 annual report of Berkshire Hathaway.
8. Graham and Dodd, *Security Analysis*, 495–496.
9. First published in 1949, various editions and revisions of *The Intelligent Investor* by Benjamin Graham have since been published. In this book I refer to the

revised 1973 edition republished in 2003 by HarperBusiness Essentials, New York, with additional material by Jason Zweig.

10. Warren Buffett, Preface to the fourth edition of *The Intelligent Investor*.
11. Graham, *Intelligent Investor*, 391.
12. Henry Oppenheimer, "Ben Graham's Net Current Asset Values: A Performance Update," *Financial Analysts Journal* 42, no. 6 (1986), 40–47.
13. Joseph Vu, "An Empirical Analysis of Ben Graham's Net Current Asset Value Rule," *Financial Review* 23 (May 1988), 215–225.
14. I recall scanning the Value Line database in 1993 looking for companies that satisfy the NCAV criterion. At the time I could only find a single company, Intertan. Although it was listed in the United States, it was the holding company for Tandy electronics stores in Canada, Australia, and the United Kingdom.
15. Graham, *Intelligent Investor*, 392–393.
16. Ibid., 348.
17. Ibid.
18. Jeremy Grantham, *GMO Quarterly Letter* (January 2005).
19. John Maynard Keynes, *The General Theory of Employment, Interest and Money* (Cambridge, UK: Cambridge University Press, 1936), Chapter 12, section 3.
20. James Tobin and William Brainard, *Asset Markets and the Cost of Capital* (Cowles Foundation, 1976).
21. Andrew Smithers and Stephen Wright, *Valuing Wall Street: Protecting Wealth in Turbulent Markets* (New York: McGraw-Hill, 2000).
22. Data is taken from the Federal Reserve, Table B.102 of the Z1 *Flow of Funds Accounts of the United States*, March 11, 2010.

## Chapter 7    A Bird in the Hand

1. Around 600 B.C. Aesop wrote many fables, including one called *The Hawk and the Nightingale*. In this tale the Hawk preferred to keep the Nightingale as a meal, even though it was small, rather than let it go to get something bigger but with the risk of not getting anything at all. The fable is commonly paraphrased by the line "A bird in the hand is worth two in the bush."
2. Robert Wiese, "Investing for True Values," *Barron's* (September 8, 1930), 5.
3. This definition is regularly given in the annual report of Berkshire Hathaway in the section entitled "Owner-Related Business Principles," which in turn is based on an earlier booklet entitled *An Owner's Manual*.
4. Believe it or not, this is what the standard discounted cash flow method requires: summing an infinite number of terms. Often it is disguised by talking about "the life of the business" or "over the long term." However, when the analysts and authors turn to the mathematics, suddenly they are summing infinite series. If you find this a bit daunting you are in good company. There is evidence that even Sir Isaac Newton had difficulties in this area. How to actually add an infinite number of terms has a rich mathematical history with many centuries of effort by eminent mathematicians. To be able to give tractable formulas, most examples in finance are restricted to variations of the basic result for geometric series. More details are given in Appendix B. The practical and philosophical issues of being required to calculate intrinsic value in terms of infinite sums is

briefly touched upon in the lists of weaknesses of discount valuation methods later in this chapter.

5. Wal-Mart, 10-K report, 2010.

6. Warren Buffett, Berkshire Hathaway Annual Report, 1986.

7. Aswath Damodaran gives a thorough discussion and comparison of variations of free cash flow in *Investment Valuation: Tools and Techniques for Valuing Any Asset* (New York: Wiley, 1996).

8. There are various assumptions about $r$ and $g$ for this result to be valid. For example, if $r,g > -100\%$ (in particular if $r,g > 0$), then it is valid only when $g < r$. However, we won't keep stopping to discuss the requirements for these formulas to be valid. Except in exceptional circumstances, they are valid using the levels of the input variables that most commonly occur.

9. The most common of these is the London Interbank Offered Rate (LIBOR), based on the interest rates at which certain banks can borrow from each other.

10. There is a discussion of WACC and methods of estimating it in Chapter 4 of Damodaran's *Investment Valuation: Tools and Techniques for Valuing Any Asset* (see note 7). There are theoretical reasons why WACC should be used in some cases and why the required rate of return should be used in other cases. However, they are outside what we need to cover in this book.

11. Standard & Poor's Stock Report, Microsoft Corp (March 13, 2010; analysis prepared on February 5, 2010).

12. Pat Dorsey, *The Five Rules for Successful Stock Investing: Morningstar's Guide to Wealth and Building Wealth in the Market* (Hoboken, NJ: John Wiley & Sons, 2004), 147.

13. Standard & Poor's Stock Reports: Microsoft Corp, Google Inc., and The Toro Company (March 13, 2010).

14. Benjamin Graham and David Dodd, *Security Analysis* (New York: McGraw-Hill, 1934), 22.

15. In his masterpiece *The Logic of Scientific Discovery* (London: Hutchinson, 1959), Karl Popper explained that for a statement to be called scientific, it must be possible for it to be refuted. Since forecasts over infinite time periods cannot be refuted or falsified, they are unscientific. This means that DCF methods are not scientific since they rely upon forecasts of discount rates and growth rates over infinite time periods.

16. Perhaps one way to incorporate more reasonable forecasts for the long-term growth rates that provides more differentiation between companies is to use a three-stage DCF approach. The usual forecast is used for the first 10 years, the standard forecast is used after 20 years, and in the intervening period the growth rate moves between the initial and final rates.

17. Allowance for the possibility of series that have infinite sums has to be made in multistep calculations such as in a computer program or a complex spreadsheet. Otherwise the calculations may produce spurious results.

18. Pat Dorsey, "FAQ: The Morningstar Rating for Stocks," *Morningstar*, August 15, 2008.

19. Warren Miller, "Stock Star Rating Performance Update," *Morningstar*, August 19, 2009. Some of the data was updated in an article titled "How Our Stock Calls Have Performed," by Pat Dorsey (*Morningstar*, January 25, 2010). Since its inception, the average annual return of the Morningstar portfolio described

here was 6.0 percent compared to 4.8 percent for the equally weighted S&P 500 portfolio. Hence, the gap between the Morningstar portfolio and the benchmark portfolio remained at around 1.2 percent per year. No figures were given for the equally weighted total coverage portfolio.

## Chapter 8    The Joy of Dividends

1. John Burr Williams, *The Theory of Investment Value* (Flint River, VA: Fraser Publishing Company, 1997; originally published by Harvard University Press, 1938), 58.
2. Krishna Palepu, Paul Healy, and Victor Bernard, *Business Analysis and Valuation Using Financial Statements* (Cincinnati: Thomson Learning, 2000), 9–20.
3. Williams, *Theory of Investment Value*, 55.
4. This does not necessarily apply to purchases in other areas. For example, art collectors might purchase works of art for their visual beauty and the pleasure they gain from looking at them, and not because they want to make a profit.
5. Williams, *Theory of Investment Value*, 57 (italics in the original).
6. Aswath Damodaran, *Investment Valuation: Tools and Techniques for Determining the Value of Any Asset* (New York: John Wiley & Sons, 1996), 234.
7. Buckeye Partners, LP, 10-K report, 2009, 39.
8. Two seminal papers are James Ohlson, "Earnings, Book Value and Dividends in Security Valuation," *Contemporary Accounting Research* 11 (Spring 1995), 661–687; and Gerald Feltham and James Ohlson, "Valuation and Clean Surplus Accounting for Operating and Financial Activities," *Contemporary Accounting Research* 11 (Spring 1995), 689–731.
9. There are a number of variations of residual earnings, although the definition given here seems to be the most common. More details are given in C.T. Horngren, G. Foster, and S.M. Datar, *Cost Accounting: A Managerial Emphasis*, 10th ed., (Upper Saddle River, NJ: Prentice Hall, 1999). Also, residual earnings is a variation of economic value added (EVA®), a financial measure introduced by the consulting firm Stern Stewart & Company. EVA® is a registered trademark of Stern Stewart & Company
10. As mentioned in the context of DCF methods, allowance for the possibility of series that have infinite sums has to be made in multistep calculations such as in a computer program or a complex spreadsheet. Otherwise the calculations may produce spurious results.

## Chapter 9    Don't Get Mad, Get Even

1. Timothy Vick, *Wall Street on Sale: How to Beat the Market as a Value Investor* (New York: McGraw-Hill, 1999), 105.
2. Quote attributed to Robert ("Bob") Wolf, chairman and CEO, UBS Group Americas.
3. Summation methods show that there is a finite payback period when the P/E ratio multiplied by the difference between the discount rate and the growth rate is less than 1.0 plus the growth rate. Otherwise there is no payback period. Appendix B contains more details of requirements for summations to work.

4. Timothy Vick has a table similar to Table 9.2 in *Wall Street on Sale* (see note 1) except that it is single-stage and does not contain a discount rate. Our development of the concept of payback (including multistage and adjustments for the discount rate) was carried out and included in Valuesoft prior to the publication of Vick's book.

## Chapter 10    PEG and Friends

1. Peter Lynch, *One Up on Wall Street* (New York: Penguin Books, 1989), 198.
2. *Aspect Equity Review* (Sydney: Aspect Financial, 2001), 24.
3. Lynch, *One Up on Wall Street*, 198.
4. David Lipshutz, "Low P/E Ratio to Growth Rate as a Stock Selection Strategy: When Analysts Love 'Em But Investors Don't Trust 'Em," Morgan Stanley Dean Witter (August 13, 1997).
5. Lynch, *One Up on Wall Street*, 198; Lynch actually flips the definition of the PEG ratio when he includes dividends and uses the inverse of the PEGY ratio in his book.
6. David Lipshutz, "If You Like PEG, You'll Love PEGY," Morgan Stanley Dean Witter (October 20, 1997).
7. Alfred Rappaport, *Creating Shareholder Value* (New York: The Free Press, 1998), 187.
8. Ibid., 188.

## Chapter 11    What Rate of Return Can I Expect?

1. Warren Buffett, Berkshire Hathaway Annual Report, 1996.
2. Peter Lynch and John Rothchild, *One Up on Wall Street: How to Use What You Already Know to Make Money in the Market* (New York: Simon & Schuster, 2000), Chapter 10.
3. Sale prices of private companies are often determined using ratios. By looking at the price-to-earnings or price-to-sales ratios of comparable companies, the negotiating parties will arrive at an acceptable price for the business.
4. The idea that there are two complementary viewpoints, one static and the other dynamic, in many areas of knowledge and science, starting with the foundations of mathematics, is explored in my article "Sets or Arrows: A Foundational Duality?" *Epistemologia* 2 (1979), 269–296.
5. In the 1984 annual report of Berkshire Hathaway, Warren Buffett talked about Washington Post being a triple-dip investment where the additional dip came from the company actively buying back its shares.
6. The calculations in the table are carried out using STRETD, a function in Valuesoft and Conscious Investor. The function is used to calculate total shareholder return over different periods with inputs of price, EPS, EPS growth, P/E ratio, and payout ratio. Calculations can also be done before or after capital gains tax and tax on dividends.
7. Lecture by Charles Munger to the students at the University of Southern California School of Business on April 14, 1994, *Outstanding Investor Digest* (May 5, 1991), 61.

8. Benjamin Graham and David Dodd, *Security Analysis* (New York: McGraw-Hill, 1934), 453.
9. In a later interview, Benjamin Graham stated that he preferred a criterion of not paying above "seven times the reported earnings for the past 12 months"; from "A Conversation with Benjamin Graham," *Financial Analysts Journal* (Sept–Oct 1976), 20–23. This seems a rather extreme requirement that may restrict the portfolio to low-tech companies in a distressed state.
10. Graham and Dodd, *Security Analysis*, 354.
11. Standard & Poor's Stock Report, Wal-Mart Stores Inc., March 13, 2010.
12. Hence the method is scientific as explained by Karl Popper (see note 15 of Chapter 7).

## Chapter 12    Please, Sir, I Want Some More

1. Benjamin Graham, *The Intelligent Investor—Revised Edition* (New York: Harper Collins, 2003), 295.
2. Krishna Palepu, Paul Healy, and Victor Bernard, *Business Analysis and Valuation Using Financial Statements* (Cincinnati: Thomson Learning, 2000), 11–19.
3. Janet Lowe, *Benjamin Graham on Value Investing: Lessons from the Dean of Wall Street* (Chicago: Dearborn Financial Publishing, 1994), 15.
4. Graham, *Intelligent Investor*, 295.
5. The second formula is described in "The Decade 1965–1974: Its Significance for Financial Analysts" (New York Research Library, Microfilm, 1974). This is a copy of a talk Graham gave to a conference called "The Renaissance of Value," organized by the Financial Analysts Research Foundation. The second half of the talk (without the formula) was printed in *Barron's* (September 1974) with the title "Renaissance of Value: Rare Investment Opportunities Are Emerging." It is also reprinted in *The Rediscovered Benjamin Graham: Selected Writings of the Wall Street Legend* by Janet Lowe (New York: John Wiley & Sons, 1999). Janet Lowe presents the formula in her book *Value Investing Made Easy* (New York: McGraw-Hill, 1996), on page 56.
6. http://finance.yahoo.com/bonds/composite_bond_rates.
7. Benjamin Graham, "The Decade 1965–1974: Its Significance for Financial Analysts" (New York Research Library, Microfilm, 1974).
8. James Ohlson and Beate Juettner-Nauroth, "Expected EPS and EPS Growth as Determinants of Value," *Review of Accounting Studies* 10 (2005), 349–365.
9. Warren Buffett, *Letter to Shareholders*, 1981 annual report of Berkshire Hathaway.
10. This was pointed out to me by Roger Montgomery.
11. In their paper, "Valuation Errors Caused by Conservative Accounting in Residual Income and Abnormal Earnings Growth Valuation Models" (Stockholm School of Economics working paper series in Business Administration, no. 2009:11, April 2009), James Ohlson and Beate Juettner-Nauroth consider differences between the RIV method and the AEG method in how well they withstand accounting and forecast biases. The results depend on the specific settings but the AEG approach may be slightly superior.

12. Bruce Greenwald, Judd Kahn, Paul Sonkin, and Michael van Biema, *Value Investing: From Graham to Buffett and Beyond* (Hoboken, NJ: John Wiley & Sons, 2001).
13. Ibid., 37.
14. Ibid., 123.
15. Ibid.
16. Valuesoft contains a two-stage version of the calculation of PV.
17. Kenneth Lee, *Trouncing the Dow: A Value-Based Method for Making Huge Profits* (New York: McGraw-Hill, 1998).
18. Joel Greenblatt, *The Little Book That Beats the Market* (Hoboken, NJ: John Wiley & Sons, 2006).
19. Because there are various definitions and uses of the terms used to calculate return on capital and earnings yield, it may be that the ratios calculated by Greenblatt differ slightly from my calculations.
20. Greenblatt, *The Little Book*, 139.
21. William O'Neil, *How to Make Money in Stocks: A Winning System in Good Times or Bad*, 4th ed. (New York: McGraw-Hill, 2009).
22. Ibid., 314.
23. Ibid., 162.
24. Ibid., 161.
25. Ibid. (1995 edition), 14.
26. Ibid. (2009 edition), 162.
27. Ibid., 171.
28. Ibid., 198.
29. Robert Haugen and Nardin L. Baker, "Commonality in the Determinants of Expected Stock Returns," *Journal of Financial Economics* 41 (1996), 401–439.
30. The study used *regression analysis*, a standard statistical method for evaluating the impact of various factors on a particular outcome. Regression analysis has two important benefits: (1) No assumption is made about which of the factors will have the biggest effect on performance, and (2) the analysis automatically ranks the factors from the most significant to the least significant.
31. Robert Haugen and Nardin Baker, "Case Closed." *The Handbook of Portfolio Construction: Contemporary Applications of Markowitz Techniques*, ed. John Guerard Jr. (New York: Springer, 2010), 601–619.
32. Hewitt Heiserman Jr., *It's Earnings That Count: Finding Stocks with Earnings Power for Long-Term Profits* (New York: McGraw-Hill, 2004).
33. Ibid., 105.
34. J. B. Farwell, *Buffett and Beyond* (Indiana: AuthorHouse, 2004).
35. There are many web sites with online option calculators. One example is www.option-price.com/. Function for calculating prices of options are also included in Valuesoft.

## Chapter 13    Forecasting and the Three Most Important Words in Investing

1. Benjamin Graham, *The Intelligent Investor—Revised Edition* (New York: Harper Business Essentials, 2003; first published in 1949), Chapter 20.
2. Warren Buffett, Berkshire Hathaway Annual Report, 1992.

3. Graham, *The Intelligent Investor*, 512.
4. Ibid., 512.
5. Nassim Nicholas Taleb, *Fooled by Randomness: The Hidden Role of Chance in Life and in the Markets* (New York: Random House, 2005, paperback ed.), 216.
6. David Dreman, *Contrarian Investment Strategies: The Next Generation* (New York: Simon & Schuster, 1998).
7. *Absolute error* means that we treat all errors as positive. For example, errors of −20 percent and +20 percent are the same as absolutes errors, namely 20 percent. In terms of averages, this means that the average absolute error of −10 percent and +20 percent is 15 percent.
8. George Bulkley and Richard Harris, "Irrational analysts' expectations as a cause of excess volatility in stock prices," *Economic Journal* 107 (1997), 359–371.
9. See, for example, Robert Olsen, "Implications of Herding Behavior," *Financial Analysts Journal* 52, no. 4 (July/August 1996), 37–41.
10. Lex Huberts and Russell Fuller, "Predictability Bias in the U.S. Equity Market," *Financial Analysts Journal* 51, no. 2 (March/April 1995), 12–28.
11. Chapter 14 explains how to get access to STAEGR in a form that can be applied to the earnings and sales of all stocks. Value Line and Investor's Business Daily have their own measure of stability which they publish for certain stocks.
12. For the technically minded, this means that the data lies on an exponential curve. It does not mean that it lies on a straight line.
13. Average annual earnings growth in this chapter is calculated using a function called HGROWTH. This modifies the usual method by making allowances for all the data (not just the data at the end points) and negative data. The two methods give the same result when the data has stable growth.
14. Dreman, *Contrarian Investment Strategies*, 93.
15. Lex Huberts and Russell Fuller, "Predictability Bias in the U.S. Equity Market," *Financial Analysts Journal* 51, no. 2 (March/April 1995), 12–28.
16. Warren Buffett, Berkshire Hathaway Annual Report, 2007.
17. Barry Lynn, "Breaking the Chain: The Antitrust Case against Wal-Mart," *Harper's Magazine* (July 2006), 29–36.
18. Graham, *Intelligent Investor*, 297.
19. Engineers sometimes don't get their stress-testing models right. The Millennium Bridge in London closed after only being open for a day because allowance was not made for the effect of large numbers of people walking in step across the bridge. The result was that the bridge started to sway from side to side. In another case, the giant Southern Star Ferris wheel in Melbourne, Australia, was forced to close because three days of high temperatures caused buckling and cracks in support structures. The good news is that the problem with the bridge has been corrected and it is now open to the public. Also the Ferris wheel is being rebuilt. The moral of the story for investors is that you can rarely be too severe in your stress-testing of potential investments.
20. Warren Buffett, "The Superinvestors of Graham-and-Doddsville," *Hermes* (Columbia Business School magazine), Fall 1984; based on a speech given on May 17, 1984, at the Columbia University School of Business in honor of the fiftieth anniversary of the publication of Benjamin Graham and David Dodd's book *Security Analysis*.

21. Despite the theory, with the huge volume of collateralized debt obligations flying around the world leading to the recent subprime mortgage crisis in the United States, it is clear that appropriate stress tests were not applied or, when they were applied, they were not sufficiently rigorous.
22. *Basel II: International Convergence of Capital Measurement and Capital Standards: A Revised Framework* (Basel, Switzerland: Bank for International Settlements, 2006).
23. Warren Buffett, Berkshire Hathaway Annual Report, 2003.
24. Graham, *Intelligent Investor*, 516.

## Chapter 14    Where Do We Go from Here?

1. Xun Zi (ca. 312–230 B.C.E.) was a follower of Confucianism. The quote is from his work called *Xunzi*.
2. Warren Buffett, writing in the Introduction to *The Intelligent Investor* by Benjamin Graham.

# Glossary

Definitions and terminology frequently vary between sources. From our point of view of looking for long-term value, if a company meets your criteria using one definition, but fails using another, it may be better to move on to another company.

**amortization**   A systematic, gradual reduction of the value of intangible assets over a given period of time. It is also used to describe the periodic repayment of debt, particularly when it is long-term.

**asset**   Something of value that is owned by or owed to the company.

**balance sheet**   A financial statement containing the three basic elements of a company: assets, liabilities, and stockholders' (or shareholders') equity. These three elements must balance according to the formula: Equity = Assets − Liabilities.

**basic earnings per share**   The earnings of a company (quarterly, semi-annually, or annually) divided by the number of shares outstanding, not taking into account options or warrants issued by the company.

**beta**   A statistical measure of the riskiness of a stock in terms of the variability of a stock price with respect to the variability of the market as a whole. Using this measure of risk, assets with a beta exceeding 1.0 are riskier than average. Assets with a beta below 1.0 are considered safer than average. See *capital asset pricing model*.

**book value**   This term usually refers to the stockholders' equity of a company on a per-share basis. This is an accounting measure of value and the actual value may be quite different. See also *price-to-book ratio*.

**capital**   The sum of the equity and long-term debt of a company. It is sometimes referred to as invested capital or capital employed. Capital can also include current debt.

**capital asset pricing model (CAPM)**   The CAPM is a general model describing the relationship between risk and return in equity markets.

The simple definition of risk using beta, a statistical analysis of stock prices, is at variance with the goals of long-term investing.

**capital spending**    Total outlay on plant and equipment. It does not include funds spent on acquisitions. It could be expressed on a per-share basis.

**cash**    This is the most liquid of the assets of a company and appears as the first line in the current assets in a company's balance sheet. It consists of money on hand and on deposit in banks.

**cash equivalents**    Security investments that can be readily converted to cash. Also referred to as marketable securities.

**cash flow**    The net earnings of a company plus depreciation, depletion, and amortization, less preferred dividends (if any). It may be stated for the entire company or on a per-common-share basis.

**clean surplus relationship**    The assumption that the book value at the end of a period (generally a financial year) equals the book value at the start of the period plus the earnings less the dividends over the period.

**Conscious Investor**®    Software and database to implement key valuation functions. See www.theconsciousinvestor.org for details.

**cost of sales**    The cost of producing a company's inventory, such as the cost of raw materials, labor, and production overhead.

**current assets**    Assets of a company that are cash, or are reasonably likely to be turned into cash within the next 12 months.

**current liability**    A liability of a company that is due within the next 12 months.

**current ratio**    The ratio of current assets to current liability.

**debt ratio**    The ratio of total liabilities to total assets. Also called debt-to-assets ratio.

**debt-to-equity ratio**    The ratio between the funds supplied by creditors, which is debt, and the funds supplied by investors, which is equity. In the event of bankruptcy, creditors must be paid before owners, so the debt-to-equity ratio is a measure of risk associated with the business. Usually the debt-to-equity ratio only includes long-term debt.

**depletion**    The equivalent of depreciation applied to the use of natural resources such as oil and gas, minerals, and forests.

**depreciation**    The accounting procedure that allocates the cost of a fixed asset such as plant and equipment (land is not depreciated) over its estimated useful life. It is generally included in the cost of sales item in the income statement.

**diluted earnings per share**    The earnings of a company (quarterly, semi-annually, or annually) divided by the number of shares outstanding plus the number of unexercised options and warrants issued by the company. See *basic earnings per share.*

**discontinued operations**    These are operations that have been or will be discontinued. They are reported separately from continuing operations in the income statement to improve the comparability of earnings from year to year.

**discount rate**    The rate at which entries in the discount valuation are discounted to compensate for their level of risk or the cost.

**dividend**    A payment in the form of cash or stock by a company to its shareholders.

**dividend payout ratio**    See *payout ratio.*

**dividend yield**    The percentage formed by dividing the annual dividend by the market price of the stock.

**DuPont analysis**    A decomposition of return on equity (ROE) into three components describing markup (net profit margin), turnover (total asset turnover), and debt (financial leverage multiplier).

**earnings**    A term used interchangeably with income and profit; also often referred to as net earnings, net income, or net profit. It is all the revenue of a company (operating and nonoperating) less all the expenses (direct, indirect, taxes, etc). It may or may not include income from discontinued operations. For investment purposes it is usually stated as earnings per share.

**earnings per share (EPS)**    The net earnings (after preferred dividends, if any) per share of common stock for a financial year or a particular quarter. Earnings per share can be quoted as basic or diluted.

**earnings per share trailing twelve months (EPSttm)**    The sum of the quarterly earnings per share for the previous four quarters. In Australia, the sum of the two most recent semiannual earnings per share.

**EBIT, EBITDA**    Acronyms standing for earnings before interest and taxes, and earnings before interest, taxes, depreciation, and amortization.

**efficient markets**    A theory or hypothesis that the prices of assets accurately reflect the information in the market place.

**equity**    The general term used to describe the theoretical value of the investment that the shareholders have in a company. Also referred to as net worth and stockholders' equity. It is the difference between total assets and total liabilities. See also *book value.*

**extraordinary item**    An entry in the income statement relating to transactions or events of a type that are outside the ordinary operations of the business, and are not of a recurring nature. Reporting them separately improves the comparability of earnings from year to year.

**Financial Accounting Standards Board (FASB)**    The FASB is the primary organization for the development of generally accepted accounting principles.

**financial leverage multiplier**    The ratio of total assets divided by total equity.

**first in, first out (FIFO)**    A common method of valuing inventory as the cost of the goods purchased or produced earliest and still in inventory. In an inflationary environment it tends to maximize earnings since it understates current production costs. See *LIFO*.

**fixed assets**    See *property, plant and equipment*.

**Form 10-K**    Each public company in the United States is required to submit annually a 10-K form to the Securities and Exchange Commission. Much of it is similar to the financial portion of the annual report sent to shareholders, but with more detail.

**Form 10-Q**    This is the quarterly report that each public company is required to submit to the Securities and Exchange Commission.

**free cash flow**    The net earnings of a company plus depreciation, depletion, and amortization, less the amount of capital expenditures. Other noncash charges also need to be added back. These could arise from deferred tax assets and deferred tax liabilities. Increments in working capital should be removed. Free cash flow may be stated for the entire company or on a per-common-share basis.

**generally accepted accounting principles (GAAP)**    These are principles that have evolved and been developed over the years which are now agreed upon by the accounting profession in the United States.

**goodwill**    Goodwill is an intangible asset that arises when the cost of acquisition of a company exceeds the equity value of the company.

**HGrowth**    HGrowth is a companion function to STAEGR that measures the average annual growth rate of earnings using all the data points and not just the first and last point.

**income**    See *earnings*.

**income coverage**    See *interest coverage*.

**intangible assets**    Assets in a balance sheet for nonphysical items such as patents, financing costs, and purchased goodwill. The value of these assets is reduced by amortization over a given period of time. Intangible assets are often by-products of acquisitions.

**interest coverage**   Earnings from continuing operations before interest and taxes over a financial year (commonly called EBIT) divided by the interest expense over the same period. It measures how many times EBIT covers the interest expense. Some sources replace EBIT by net earnings before interest and after taxes.

**inventory**   A company's merchandise, raw materials, and finished and unfinished products which have not yet been sold.

**last in, first out (LIFO)**   A common method of valuing inventory as the cost of the item most recently purchased or produced. In an inflationary environment it tends to minimize earnings since it overstates average production costs. See *FIFO*.

**liability**   A debt or obligation of the company. See *current liability* and *long-term liability*.

**long-term debt**   Borrowed funds that are due for payment after one year, usually over several years. It usually forms the main component of the long-term liabilities on the balance sheet.

**net profit margin**   Net profit divided by net sales; a measure of the profit after allowing for taxes and expenses.

**net sales**   This is the value from a company's sales of goods and services. It is the gross funds from the sale of goods and services less such items as allowances, discounts, and returns. Sales and net sales are usually interchangeable.

**net worth**   Same as equity. In some cases net worth is defined as the value of common equity plus the value of the preferred shares.

**nonrecurring**   An expression used to describe earnings that are unusual or one-time events.

**operating earnings**   A company's net sales less the cost of sales and operating expenses. Depreciation may also be subtracted. In this case, operating earnings equals EBIT.

**operating expenses**   See *selling, general and administration (SG&A) expenses*.

**operating margin**   Operating earnings as a percentage of sales or revenues.

**opportunity cost**   A measure of the sacrifice investors must make if they are to forgo the liquidity and relative safety of cash government securities in favor of common-stock investments.

**owner earnings**   A term introduced by Warren Buffett, defined as the "reported earnings plus depreciation, depletion, amortization, and certain other noncash charges less the average amount of capitalized expenditures for plant and equipment that the business requires to fully maintain its long-term position and its unit volume." If the business requires additional working capital, the increment should also be subtracted. Apart from asking for the average amount of capitalized expenditures instead of the actual amount, this definition is the same as free cash flow.

**payout ratio or dividend payout ratio**    The portion of the income of a company paid out as dividends rather than retained in the company.

**preferred stock**    A security similar to stock except that it gives the owner a prior claim over stockholders with regard to dividend payments and distribution of assets should the company be liquidated. Preferred stock is normally entitled to specified dividend payments.

**price-to-book ratio, P/B ratio**    The ratio of the market price of the stock and its book value.

**price-to-earnings ratio, P/E ratio**    The ratio of the market price of the stock and its earnings per share. The earnings are generally stated for the previous year.

**profit**    See *earnings*.

**property, plant and equipment**    The collection of assets of a permanent nature required to operate the business. They are also referred to as fixed assets. Land, buildings, plant facilities, machinery equipment, furniture, and capital lease equipment are considered to be fixed assets.

**quick ratio or quick test**    A ratio similar to the current ratio except that the numerator is restricted to the current assets that are cash or cash equivalents and trade receivables. As for the current ratio, the denominator is current liabilities. It is a more rigorous test of short-term liquidity than the current ratio since it eliminates inventory, usually the least liquid of the current assets.

**retained earnings**    The earnings of a company that are not paid out as dividends but are retained within the company as working capital or to finance fixed investment and acquisitions. They are also referred to as undistributed earnings or profits, accumulated profits, or retained income.

**return on _____**    There are four major ratios used to describe the return of a company: earnings divided by assets, equity, capital, or sales. These would be referred to as return on assets, return on equity, and so on. There are another four ratios formed by replacing earnings by operating profit.

**revenues**    Generally this term refers to the gross or total inflow of funds to the company, usually sales plus nonoperating income sources such as interest income.

**sales**    See *net sales.*

**selling, general and administration (SG&A) expenses**    A grouping of expenses in an income statement representing a company's operating expenses. They generally consist of salaries, advertising, sales commissions, marketing costs, office expenses, rents, insurance, travel, and entertainment.

**STAEGR**®    A proprietary function that measures the stability of the growth of historical data from year to year expressed as a percentage.

**stockholders' equity**    The equity in a company. May also need to subtract value of preferred stock. Also called shareholders' equity.

**total asset turnover**    Net sales divided by total assets; a measure of the efficiency of a company in using its assets to generate sales or revenue.

**total return**    The average annual return, capital gains plus dividends, that an investor would have received from holding an asset assuming that each dividend is reinvested in the asset at the time of its payment. The calculation is done before tax. Also called total shareholder return.

**Valuesoft**    A collection of valuation functions that can be used within Excel for Windows. See www.theconsciousinvestor.org for details.

**weighted average cost of capital (WACC)**    The average cost of the different components of financing a company, including debt, equity, and other securities used by it to fund its financial requirements. The costs are weighted according to the amounts required. It is used as the discount rate in some versions of the discounted cash flow methods

**working capital**    The capital required to run the daily affairs of the company, which is a measure of its liquidity. It is defined as the difference between a company's current assets and current liabilities.

# About the Author

John Price started his career as a research mathematician with positions in major universities around the world. After publishing two books and over 60 papers in peer-reviewed journals in mathematics, physics, and finance, Dr. Price set a research objective to understand the best investment methods of Benjamin Graham, Warren Buffett, John Burr Williams, Peter Lynch, and others. He personally programmed, tested, and compared over 30 different stock valuation methods in his search for the best of the best. This led to the development of investment software called Conscious Investor®, which his company has sold around the world for the past nine years. It also provided the background and research for *The Conscious Investor*. Dr. Price divides his time between the United States and Australia. For more details on the methods in this book, visit www.theconsciousinvestor.org.

# Disclaimer

Except where stated, all the financial data is from original company filings and stock market data. The data in Chapter 13 used in the forecast analysis is from Morningstar as supplied for the Conscious Investor software. Because of the possibility of human or mechanical error, no warranty is given for the accuracy, adequacy, timeliness, or availability of any data.

# Index